History of Sport and Physical Activity in the United States

History of Sport and Physical Activity in the United States

Betty Spears
University of Massachusetts

Richard A. Swanson
San Francisco State University

Edited by Elaine T. Smith

WM. C. BROWN
COMPANY PUBLISHERS
2460 Kerper Boulevard, Dubuque, Iowa 52001

GV
583
. S66

Contents

Preface

This is an introductory text in the history of sport and physical activity. Why sport? Why physical activity? In the early days of this country, sport as such existed only in a nebulous form, as amusements and pastimes; but since the beginning decades of this century sport has been the dominant component in physical education and at times is considered identical with school physical education. Sport in the school is greatly influenced by sport outside the school, and it is important for the student to understand the relationship between these two spheres. Dance and exercise, together with sport, are frequently included in school physical education, and therefore it seems appropriate to include them in this account. The history of physical education as it relates to sport is also appropriate to this text. For these reasons, we selected the title *The History of Sport and Physical Activity in the United States.*

Historians are necessarily selective in their choice of material. It is impossible to include every educator, every score, every player. It is impossible to show the development of every sport and form of physical activity. Rather, we have selected important information which helps explain the changes from yesterday's pastimes to today's complex, institutionalized sport. We have tried to tell how this development included all Americans— men, women, whites, blacks, and native Americans. The United States is made up of many different groups with different cultures, and we have worked to select data which relate a comprehensive history of sport and physical activity in the United States. Thousands of sources were studied, consulted, and evaluated, and in some of the handwritten original documents we found new and sometimes contradictory data. Wherever possible we have used primary sources rather than secondary material. Information available from several sources has not been footnoted, but where we have relied heavily on one researcher, we have acknowledged the source. Throughout the writing we have attempted to construct a reasonably accurate and consistent account of sport and physical activity in the United States.

The material is arranged chronologically because we believe that the student profits from an overall orderly presentation. However, the Olympic

Games are treated separately, in the last chapter, which may thus be used in several ways: as the final unit, similar to its placement in the text; the first half on the ancient Games after Chapter 2, as an additional section on peoples that influenced American sport and physical activity; or as an adjunct to Chapter 5 at the time of the founding of the modern Games, and the material on the modern Games at appropriate places thereafter.

Also, several features should facilitate learning for the student: a comparative time-line of relevant historical events and sport history events begins each chapter; a Summary at the end of the chapter emphasizes the development of sport theory; the Questions for Discussion which follow the Summary are designed for use in class and out of class, in order to stimulate the student's thinking, and to suggest possible topics for papers or projects. The Suggestions for Further Reading may be the basis for discussions, additional assigned readings, more in-depth study of one topic, or the beginning of a bibliography for a paper or project. We have chosen to compile many of the sources consulted into one bibliography at the end of the book. We hope that such a bibliography will be valuable to the teacher and to the student who desires further study. Any study of the history of American sport will, of course, be enhanced by a working knowledge of United States history. It is suggested that a standard American history text be available for review and consultation.

An enterprise of this nature is not the work of two people. We are indebted to many who have aided us in gathering material and preparing the manuscript. Librarians and archivists in universities, colleges, museums, cities, and towns have patiently helped us dig out facts and track down leads to new information. We are especially grateful to Georgia Reid for providing the information on dance throughout the book. Mrs. Jean K. Marsh assisted in the selection and procurement of the illustrations. We greatly appreciate the time and efforts of friends, colleagues, and students who reviewed portions of the manuscript and made many worthwhile comments. Our secretaries, Eleanor Fox and Marsha Borowski, have been invaluable, and Jules Garth-Graves cheerfully and efficiently helped us meet deadlines with his copy service. Finally, we are deeply indebted to Elaine T. Smith, who carefully and skillfully synthesized our individual writing styles, made valuable suggestions, and poked in archives to produce still more evidence of the history of sport and physical activity in the United States.

Betty Spears
Richard A. Swanson

1 History and the Study of Sport and Physical Activity

Two hundred years after the United States of America declared itself a nation, sport, dance, and physical activity had become essential elements of society. The twenty-first Olympiad captured front page headlines in 1976, arguments raged over the implementation of federal guidelines for equal opportunities for girls and boys in physical education classes and athletic programs, and the President of the United States appointed a commission to investigate amateur sport. Prime time on national television was devoted to a variety of sport programs, from the Roller Derby to the Super Bowl. Chris Evert, an outstanding woman professional tennis player, again captured the crown at Wimbledon, and the Rozelle rule in American professional football was declared unconstitutional. Many forms of dance, from ballet to jazz, attracted thousands to the theaters and dance halls across the United States. Sport, dance, and physical activity were accepted as a part of everyday life, as much by the average American and the local school board members as by the sport entrepreneur and the professional performer.

If several hundred years from now archaeologists were to investigate our civilization, they would find masses of artifacts documenting our involvement with sport—stadiums, swimming pools, running shoes, hockey sticks, skis, baseball gloves, tennis rackets, turnstiles, rolls of tickets, and pictures of sport stars. In sharp contrast, there were only vague indications of sport found by the early European explorers on this continent. Later, as the early settlers struggled for existence there was little time for games and amusements, but as life became easier the citizens of the new country did engage in such pastimes. The story of the development of these pastimes into modern sport and into an integral component of our society is the history of sport and physical activity in the United States of America.

History means different things to different people. To many, it is predominantly the study of political and economic events—the conquests of Alexander the Great, the English naval supremacy under Queen Elizabeth I, the expansion of American railroads, and the Bay of Pigs. For some, history is a study of the men and women, good and bad, who have shaped the events of their times. For others, history is something more than the story of leaders, wars, and political campaigns. Especially in the twentieth

1

century, history has also come to mean social history, or the study of persons as social beings, living, working and playing together. Historians now study the social groups in which people live, and for example, what being rich or being poor meant in any era in history, or being old, or female, or the member of a minority group. Social historians ask many questions about the everyday lives of people. What did the men, women, girls and boys do from day to day? How did social forces affect their manners and customs? How were marriage partners chosen? What ceremonies were celebrated in their lives? Did they have leisure time? Did they play games? What, for example, did ancient Greek athletes do when they were not competing or training? Did they, like most other Greek citizens, attend the theater to watch the great dramas of Euripides and Aristophanes? Why did the medieval tournaments persist long after gun powder was invented? When a little leisure time existed in colonial America, how did the settlers spend this time? What effect did the native Americans have on the lives of the frontiersmen? Did college students one hundred years ago have time for recreation? What did they do? What games, sports, and amusements have the people of the United States participated in for over three hundred years? What dances have they danced? How have they exercised? This aspect of history seems relatively new in its emphasis, yet in 1531 Sir Thomas Elyot wrote:

> Finally so large is the compase of that which is named historie, that it comprehendeth all thynge that is necessary to be put in memorie.[1]

Many of the memories people have, relate to their physical activities—their games, sports, amusements, pastimes, and dance. Sport-like activities and dance are age-old endeavors in which people participate for a variety of reasons. It may be for their own benefit and enjoyment as well as the enjoyment of others. Sometimes games and sports provide a sense of community: as spectators rooting for a team, as members of a team, as a group with a central interest, or as part of ceremonial activities. In this sense sport becomes a means of "joining" people rather than "dividing" them. Other physical activities, such as exercise, are undertaken to improve the participants either in a specific sense or to benefit their general health. While dance has not changed much in definition over the centuries, sport has had a variety of meanings. Samuel Johnson's 1775 *Dictionary of the English Language* defined it as "play, diversion, game, frolick and tumultuous merriment,"[2] but by 1968 it had become useful to examine sport as ". . . a

---

1. Sir Thomas Elyot, *The Boke Named the Governour,* Vol. II, ed. H.H.S. Croft (London: C. Kegan Paul & Co., 1880), p. 387.
2. Samuel Johnson, *A Dictionary of the English Language* (Dublin: Thomas Ewing, 1775), n.p.

highly ambiguous term . . . ." and to ". . . discuss sport as a game occurrence, as a social institution, and as a social situation or social system."[3]

The history of men and women, boys and girls competing in sport, testing themselves against nature and each other, dancing in joy or sorrow, and engaging in vigorous physical activities as a unique mode of human expression is part of the story of people seeking personal fulfillment. Readers of histories are also historians. As you study the unfolding drama of sport, dance, and physical activities in the United States, there are several concepts related to the study of history which it would be helpful to understand. These deal with people, time, and curiosity. If you habitually organize ideas into *who, what, when, where, how,* and *why,* think of the concepts related to people as *who* and *what;* the concepts related to time as *when* and *where;* and the concepts related to curiosity as *how* and *why.*

The first and most important concept to remember is that history is about people—real women and men, real girls and boys. The historian, Carl Becker, has reduced history to its simplest terms with the statement, "History is the memory of things said and done."[4] Human beings are unique in their sustained ability to remember and interpret past and present actions, making it possible to know and understand events and their influence on people. Being human means having desires, hopes, and ideas, and knowing fear, elation, and disappointment. Humans also know respect, love, contempt, and hate. For example, many athletes have the perseverance to undergo years of grueling practice in hopes of making the Olympic team. If the athlete makes the team, fear is undoubtedly present before the trials, and she or he will experience disappointment if the event is lost and elation if it is won. Many of us have had coaches and teachers whom we have respected and perhaps some for whom we have had contempt or hate.

Men and women, their deeds, both bad and good, and the effect of these deeds on their lives and the lives of others, are the players in the drama of sport and physical activities. In sport history, over 2700 years ago, Nestor gave his son advice on how to win a chariot race; in physical education history, over 2500 years ago, Lycurgus decreed exercise for girls so they would bear strong babies; and the Roman emperors entertained the masses with gladiatorial combats over 2000 years ago. In more modern times, Pierre de Coubertin, barely thirty years of age when he revived the ancient Olympic Games, designed them for men and stubbornly refused to consider women in the modern Games. Jack Johnson, an early black heavy weight champion, shocked middle-class Americans with his three white wives, and

---

3. John W. Loy, Jr. "The Nature of Sport: A Definitional Effort," *Quest* 10 (May, 1968): 1.
4. Carl Becker, *Everyman His Own Historian* (Chicago: Quadrangle Books, 1966), p. 235.

the debates among Charles McCloy, Jesse Feiring Williams, Jay B. Nash, and Delbert Oberteuffer over physical education theories dominated professional physical education meetings in the forties. The "battle of the sexes" was waged through tennis in 1973 when feminist Billie Jean King defeated self-avowed chauvinist Bobby Riggs. Throughout the history of sport and physical activity, real men and real women with human strengths and weaknesses have created significant events which have influenced that history.

The second concept, related to *time,* includes three important ideas. First, in history there is *only* the past. Although we speak of present-day problems and seek solutions to present issues, it is important to realize that, in fact, there is no present. Rowse reminds us that history is a continuum.

> History shows there is no break between the past and the future. While I write this sentence, what was the future has already become the past. . . . All is continuous.[5]

History, then, derives meanings from a continuum of events. For example, the founding of the modern Olympic Games in 1896 may seem to us to have happened a long time ago, but the modern Games were fashioned after the ancient Games, 776 B.C. to 393 A.D. To determine the background of today's Olympic problems and to make suggestions for the future, we must study the Olympic Games as a continuum from 776 B.C. to the present.

Thus, history relates and analyzes events of the past to help explain the changes that have occurred and to aid us in understanding both the past and the present. Although it is impossible to view an event exactly as it happened, it is important to know and comprehend the period in which an event took place. For example, the invention of gunpowder and the ensuing adaptations in warfare tactics changed the original purpose of the medieval tournament from preparation for war to a "sport spectacular" for the aristocracy. Late nineteenth-century industrial technology prompted many young men to move to the cities and, in an effort to occupy their time, basketball was promoted as an indoor sport. Today, with a television set in almost every home in the United States, the television industry controls a large segment of collegiate and professional sport.

Second, not only is it important to know the major influences of each period, but it is also essential *not* to superimpose today's ideas or standards on those of a former period. We must be aware of a few of the difficulties for those who ponder the past. We are all creatures locked into our own time, into our own place. We are the products of our own past—our family,

---

5. A.L. Rowse, *The Use of History* (New York: Collier Books, 1963), p. 24.

our town, our country, our decade, and our century—its education, food, songs, flag, expectations, sports, and language. The unstated beliefs and assumptions which we all share—unstated because these are "perfectly obvious"—which would be unthinkable to argue about, are particularly strong. Ordinarily, this condition is not one to struggle against; but when studying other ages, other countries, and other civilizations, it poses a problem. As historians, we should try, with our imagination and our feelings, to understand other persons and the "unstated beliefs and assumptions" of their society, although they may be quite alien and remote from ours. For example, to understand athletics in ancient Greece, it is useful to know that the Greeks accepted slavery as part of their society. They assumed that it was necessary to have slaves and that being a slave was a normal way of life for some people. Another example from sport history is the view of the native American Indians on dance and games. They did not separate work, play, dance, and games as we do, but made these activities part of their rituals and ceremonies. As for the Puritans, many believed literally in an everlasting hellfire which awaited sinners; therefore they attempted to keep themselves and their neighbors on the narrow path to righteousness, which did not include games or sport on Sunday. It would be improper to condemn the New England Puritan's ideas on sport and pastimes on Sundays without understanding their "narrow path to righteousness." Today women enter colleges and universities freely, but just one hundred years ago they were excluded from the major universities and colleges, partly because they were thought too delicate for the rigors of college life. It would be incorrect to "blame" the men's colleges and universities for excluding them without studying the views of women's health that were prevalent at that time. For each period of history of sport and physical activity, it is essential to understand the major events of the time, the scientific and general knowledge that was available then, and the ways in which the various social groups viewed contemporary problems. Historical events must be studied and understood as a part of the period in which they occurred.

The final idea related to *time* is to realize that the farther away a historical period is from the present, the more years the period tends to embrace and the easier it is to make generalizations about it. We speak of the period of the ancient Olympics and we talk about the early Games in general terms. Actually, the ancient Olympics covered approximately 1200 years, from 776 B.C. to 393 A.D. Imagine how a historian would be ridiculed for speaking of "recent sport" from 776 A.D. to 1976 A.D. As historians of sport and physical activity, we should be careful not to develop false generalizations about a period of time just because it occurred thousands of years before. The closer we come to contemporary times, the shorter is the time period which we consider to be significant. As we look back at the series of events of the past, it becomes perilously easy to make generalizations. We often feel that

> . . . we can only establish contact by imposing upon people, art, and events a retrospective order that is quite another thing than the rich disorder of involvement. History for us has whitened actuality into abstraction. . . . It can be repaid only by an effort of historical imagination, and then only in small part.[6]

At the same time, it is easy to become so sensitive to differences and so chary of generalizations that we become tongue-tied historians, incapable of the brilliant generalizations which clarify. We know ". . . the card index is not knowledge. It is only the beginning of knowledge, and the accumulation of facts is useless until they are related to each other and seen in proportion."[7]

The third concept to remember is that historians are curious. They seek answers to significant questions, those which add to our knowledge in sport, physical education, and dance. Earlier, history was defined as the memory of things said and done; however, not *everything* that has been said and done can be included in history. Many historians believe that an event is not history until it has been studied and written down: that is, investigated, placed in an accurate context, its significance explained, and the event interpreted.

In seeking answers to significant questions it is essential to discover as much evidence as is possible to support these answers. In fact, one historian, Winks, suggests that the historian uses many techniques of the detective in mystery stories. If you enjoy detective stories, you may have a head start in becoming a sport historian. The best evidence for solving a mystery or answering a historical question is called *primary* evidence. Primary evidence consists of indisputable first-hand evidence that the event occurred. For example, we have little primary evidence for the ancient Olympics other than the actual stadium at Olympia, the ruins of the wrestling grounds, the practice tracks, and the gymnasium; however, we have numerous examples of secondary evidence in references to the Games in contemporary writings. Primary evidence of a modern dance event might be a film of the first performance of the work and a program in which the dancers' names are listed. Frequently it is difficult or impossible to locate primary evidence about an event, and then *secondary* evidence must be used. Secondary evidence consists of references derived from a first-hand or some other account of the event.

---

6. Joseph Kerman, *The Beethoven Quartets* (New York: Alfred A. Knopf, 1967), p. 4.

7. C.V. Wedgwood, *The Sense of the Past* (New York: Collier Books, 1960), p. 91.

Regardless of whether the evidence is primary or secondary, it must meet certain criteria to be acceptable. It must be relevant, authoritative, consistent with other sources, and fit logically with the other evidence. Furthermore, the historian should understand the period from which the evidence was procured and know the source of the evidence. Sometimes historical questions seem to defy answers. Historians search and search to find the one piece of unquestionable evidence to answer a particular question. In such instances, curiosity, imagination, a guess, or a hunch may provide the key to the mystery. Under these circumstances, the application of the detective's approach works well. A logical but unexpected lead to an answer can help direct the historian to a much sought after answer. History, thus, is a continuous search for information about significant events that happened in the past.

In the United States today sport is organized in a variety of ways, one being in the public school system. However, sport instruction in the schools is sometimes equated with *physical education,* while athletics is usually considered as organized inter-institutional sport. Many times physical education also includes exercise and dance activities as well as sport. To further complicate the picture, nineteenth-century exercise programs were known as gymnastics programs; thus, nineteenth century *gymnastics* does not mean today's Olympic gymnastic events but rather, *exercise* systems. Also, in the late nineteenth century *physical training* was sometimes used to mean either gymnastics or physical education. This complex situation, resulting from the interaction of forces within and without education and sport, is also part of the history of sport and physical activity in this country. For the purposes of this book there are several terms which should be defined for the sake of clarity.

Sport

Sport will be considered to be activities involving physical prowess, competition, strategy and/or chance and engaged in for the enjoyment and satisfaction of the participant and/or others. This definition includes both organized sport and sport engaged in for recreational purposes. It clearly includes the component of sport as entertainment, which encompasses professional sport.

Dance

Dance is one of the earliest human rhythmic aesthetic activities and is woven into many aspects of our daily lives. Dance ranges from country dance to ballet and jazz dance, and it exists both within and without the public schools.

Exercise

Exercise (or an *exercise system*) is defined as a prescribed, formalized pattern of bodily movements of one or more parts of the body engaged in for particular reasons, with expected specific outcomes. These reasons could range from cardiovascular fitness to post-operative physical therapy.

Physical Education

Physical education is referred to as a program of physical activities, usually in educational institutions, including dance, exercise, bodily development activities, and sport.

To summarize this brief introduction to the study of history or historiography, there are three essential concepts to remember, as preliminary to the study of the special history of sport and physical activity.

1. History is about real men and women, who have both desirable and undesirable characteristics, and their deeds, both good and bad.
2. In history there is only the past. The present is only a "fleeting moment of reality," but because we have records of events and memories of them, we can study the past. The historian should understand as thoroughly as possible the period in which an historical event occurred; however, the historian should not impose contemporary ideas, values, and judgments on those of earlier periods and must be careful not to alter the essential truths of the past.
3. History is asking significant questions, locating evidence, and seeking answers.

Throughout this discussion of the history of sport and physical activity you may have been asking the questions, "Why study the history of sport and physical activity at all?" "How can the knowledge of history help solve contemporary issues?" In this chapter there have been a number of hints toward answering this question, but let us focus on four major reasons for studying the history of sport and physical activity. First, the roots of sport, dance, and physical activity in the United States lie in other cultures, the oldest of which is over 2500 years old. If you purport to be knowledgeable about your field of study, you should know and appreciate the evolution of the major developments and trends in that field. To understand such a modern phenomenon as the Olympic Games, the student of sport and physical activity should be familiar with the ancient Games as well as the modern ones. Second, in order to cope with today's problems it is necessary to understand their background. For example, in determining policies to comply with the 1975 federal regulations of Title IX, of the Educational Amendments of 1972, both women and men should understand the vastly different philosophies on which men's and women's sport and physical education were established. While other academic areas have rarely been divided by sex, the physical educator comes to his or her field with a history of sharply divided philosophies and programs—one for men, and one for women. Another example is the changing purposes of sport. Until about five hundred years ago many sports were conducted primarily to prepare men for war. Today, sport is conducted for the benefit and pleasure of the performer and/or spectator. To explain the reasons for participating in sport and physical activity from preparation for war to pleasure of the performer it is necessary to know and understand the events of the past.

The third reason to study the history of sport and physical activity is to help in molding the future of these fields. While most historians no longer adhere to the theory that history repeats itself, they do point out that factors which influenced decisions in the past can be studied and applied to the future. Thus, we can choose to embark on a course of action which we know will lead to certain results. If these results were not desirable in the past, and we believe would not be desirable in the future, we can select another route to pursue.

Finally, we study the history of sport and physical activity to enrich our understanding of our civilization, our nation, and our world. For many people, this is the most important reason for undertaking any study. The more we know about every aspect of our lives, the better we are able to foster humanistic values in our social institutions and to enhance the worth of each individual in our society.

The History of Sport and Physical Activity in the United States focuses on those aspects of history which have been the most influential on sport and physical activity in this country. Because our culture is the product of other cultures, we will examine those civilizations which have made a significant contribution to this part of our culture.

The second chapter analyzes the beginnings of sport and physical activity in the United States by examining the activities of the native Americans, the sports and pastimes of the Europeans whose descendants settled the American colonies, and the background of the Africans who were brought here as slaves. American sport began with the changes created in each culture as people came into contact with one another on a day-to-day basis and adapted their customs and pastimes to the new life and environment. Chapters 3, 4, and 5 trace the evolution of sport and physical activity from the relatively unorganized, spontaneous play of the eighteenth century through the first two decades of the twentieth, highlighting the establishment of formalized, structured programs in professional and amateur sport, public recreation, and school physical education. Particular emphasis is placed on the societal developments which influenced these changes in the sport, recreational, and educational life of the people in the United States during this period.

Chapters 6 and 7 deal with sport and physical activity in the United States after World War I in order to look at the influence of the Depression, affluence, technology, and the beginnings of a post-industrial society on sport, physical education, and dance in the middle of this century. The final chapter examines the ancient Olympic Games and the basis for the establishment of the modern Games, concluding with a review of the development of the Olympic Games from 1896 to 1976.

The history of sport and physical activity in the United States is a fascinating story of the American people pursuing vigorous physical activities for their own benefit and/or pleasure as well as for the entertainment of others. It is hoped that this book will encourage a life-long interest in comprehending human behavior through sport, dance, and physical activity.

Questions for Discussion

1. Define social history. Give three examples from sport that provide a rationale for the study of sport as social history.
2. Contrast Johnson's 1775 definition of sport with Loy's 1968 definition. Write down the differences between the two definitions. How can you account for the differences?
3. What aspects of today's society affect sport? When did these aspects of society first make their appearance in United States history?
4. Into what periods would you divide the history of the United States? Explain the reasons for the periods you have chosen.
5. Give three examples of primary evidence and three examples of secondary evidence that would help explain a particular incident in your own sport history.
6. Do you agree with the authors' definitions of sport, dance, exercise, and physical education? Select one definition and prepare a carefully thought-out paragraph supporting your position.

Suggestions for Further Reading

1. Eyler, Marvin H. "Some Reflections on Objectivity and Selectivity in Historical Inquiry." *Journal of Sport History* 1 (1974): 63-76.
2. Loy, John W., Jr. "The Nature of Sport: A Definitional Effort." *Quest* 10 (May, 1968): 1-15.

3. Michener, James A. *Sports in America.* New York: Random House, 1976.
4. Morison, Samuel Eliot. *The Oxford History of the American People.* New York: Oxford University Press, 1965.
5. Rowse, A.L. *The Use of History.* New York: Collier Books, 1963.
6. Winks, Robin W. *The Historian as Detective.* New York: Harper & Row, 1968.

Time Line

HISTORY

1400-1519
Aztec empire
1438-1538
Inca empire
1492
Columbus discovered America
1517
Beginning of Reformation: Luther posted 95 theses on church door in Germany
1607
First Virginia colony
1619
African immigrants
1620
First Massachusetts colony
1633
Laws requiring work
1636
Harvard College opened
1688
Triumph of Protestant Parliament in England
1730-60
Great Awakening, religious revival
1769
James Watt patented the steam engine
1776
Declaration of Independence

SPORT

1424
Margot, French woman, hand tennis champion
1564
LeMoyne painted Indian life
1618
King James' *Book of Sport*
1643
Account of Indian football
1732
Schuykill Fishing Company, Philadelphia
1762
Little Pretty Pocket Book
1768
Horse racing, Long Island

2 Peoples That Influenced American Sport and Physical Activity, 1492-1776

The history of sport, dance, and physical activity in the United States of America begins with the first accounts of Columbus and other early explorers of the fifteenth and sixteenth centuries. These accounts were only the beginning of information about America, for ". . . the New World was revealed: not suddenly with the news of Christopher Columbus's landfall, but very gradually over the course of more than half a century."[1] The early explorers described exotic plants and extraordinary birds and animals in the new land that conjured up for many Europeans a mystical, mythical land filled with marvels. "We found the people most gentle, loving, and faithfull, voide of all guile and treason, and such as live after the maner of the golden age."[2] Everything was strange and, perhaps, the strangest to them were the inhabitants. The natives differed in many ways from themselves—their color, language, dwellings, religious beliefs, and also their dances, games, and pastimes.

Cortes, in 1528, demonstrated these differences when he took back with him to Europe Mexican jugglers and ball players to exhibit at the Spanish court. LeMoyne, an artist who accompanied the explorer Laudonnière on an early voyage, depicted Indians playing a type of basketball game, and John White, another seventeenth-century artist, painted the natives of Virginia fishing and dancing. Later Torquemada described a ball, made of a "strange, resilient material" which *bounced,* and, much later, a traveler in the south recounted a game in which each player carried ". . . in their hands two wooden spoons, curiously carved, not unlike our large iron spoons."[3] These reports of a *rubber* ball, unknown at that time in Europe, and of *lacrosse,* also unknown in Europe, provide evidence of sport and

1. Hugh Honour, *The European Vision of America* (Kent, Ohio: The Kent State University Press, 1975), p. 2.

2. A. Barlowe, "Captain Arthur Barlowe's Narrative of the First Voyage to Virginia: 1584," in *Virginia Reader,* ed. F.C. Rosenberger (New York: E.P. Dutton & Company, 1948), p. 33.

3. Stewart Culin, *Games of the North American Indians* (New York: Dover, 1975), p. 587.

sport-like activities among the people living on the newly discovered continent.

These native Americans, or Indians as they were called, were one of three very different groups of people, each of which has had a special influence on sport, dance, and physical activity in the United States. In addition to the native Americans, there were Europeans and Africans. The European settlers, mostly from England, but also from France, the Netherlands, Spain, and a few other countries, brought with them the sports, games, and pastimes of late medieval Europe. There was little time for these amusements and pastimes during the arduous struggle to establish homes; furthermore, in New England the Puritans disapproved of all but "innocent" pleasures. However, later, when there was some leisure, the settlers played the games they had known in Europe, but adapted to the new environment and way of life.

Whereas most Europeans came to America for religious reasons or to improve their condition in life, most Africans came to this country as slaves, brought here from parts of Africa known today as Guinea, Ghana, Mali, Angola, and other West African countries. While C.E. Lincoln says that "Africans were prohibited from practicing and developing their art, their language, their religion, their family life—and for want of appreciation and practice, whatever was distinctively African soon died out in America,"[4] others, such as Haley, suggest that ". . . the memories and the mouths of ancient elders was the only way that early histories of mankind got passed along . . . for all of us today to know who we are."[5] African rhythms and dances soon became absorbed into the lives of the Afro-Americans in the colonies. Thus, the black heritage of American sport began in a somewhat different fashion from that of the Europeans or native Americans.

This chapter will consider four major themes in the beginnings of sport in the United States. First, we will examine the culture, sports, and games of the native Americans whom the explorers found living on the new continent. Next, we will investigate the games and pastimes of England and western Europe in the sixteenth and seventeenth centuries which the settlers might have brought with them to the new country. Then we will review the background of the Africans, most of whom were brought here as slaves. Finally, we will look at the development of the first settlements into colonies and the place of pastimes and sport-like activities in the life of the American colonies.

---

4. C. Eric Lincoln, *The Negro Pilgrimage in America* (New York: Bantam Pathfinder, 1967), p. 2.

5. Alex Haley, *Roots* (Garden City, N.Y.: Doubleday, 1976), p. viii.

The Native Americans

Authorities estimate that when Columbus reached the New World, about one million people, speaking some 600 dialects, inhabited the area of what is now the United States of America. Scholars theorize that the native Americans or Indians wandered east across the Bering Strait to Alaska and traveled southeast fanning out over the continent. Hundreds of cultures developed and lived side by side, each with its own language, customs, and means of livelihood. These cultures can be grouped according to geographical areas—northeast, southeast, plains and prairies, southwest, basin and plateau, California, and northwest.

The northeast Indians occupied the land north of Tennessee and east of the Mississippi River. They lived in tribes, five of which, including the Iroquois and Algonquian, banded together in the Iroquois League of Five Nations. Usually the tribes, in which strong family ties existed, lived in villages where the women farmed and managed the households while the men hunted and, at times, engaged in warfare with neighboring tribes. By the time the explorers arrived, weaving, braiding, carving, and pottery had been developed.

In the southeast the Indians honored warriors who engaged in war for the thrill and the prestige of the kill. They lived in small villages or settlements, fought with nearby tribes, farmed, and hunted. LeMoyne, the artist accompanying a sixteenth-century French expedition to Florida, described how the Indians hunted:

> The Indians have a way of hunting deer which we never saw before. They manage to put on skins of the largest which have previously been taken, in such a manner, with the heads on their own heads, that they can see out of the eyes as through a mask. Thus accoutred, they can approach close to the deer without frightening them. They take advantage of the time when the animals come to drink at the stream, and having their bows and arrows all ready, easily shoot them, as they are plentiful in those regions.[6]

With the invasion of the white man along the eastern seaboard, many Indian groups were pushed westward until the prairies west of the Mississippi River accommodated a number of different Indian cultures. Many established villages, raised crops, and lived a settled life, as did a number of the prairie Indians. Others, using the horse recently introduced by the Spaniards and the guns brought by the explorers, formed nomadic tribes

---

6. J. LeMoyne, cited in Herbert Manchester, *Four Centuries of Sport in America, 1490-1890* (New York: The Derrydale Press, 1931), p. 9.

FIG. 2.1 Florida Indians stalking deer. J. LeMoyne. Courtesy of the AMERICAN MUSEUM OF NATURAL HISTORY.

and thus created the "typical" plains Indian, galloping in eagle-feathered headdress and leather leggings, shooting buffalo.

Among the southwest Indians were pueblo dwellers and nomads, both of whom traded with the permanent settlers for their food and other needs. Many of the southwest tribes were peaceful and fought only to protect their property or themselves. From the southern part of Colorado north to Canada, the Indians hunted and roamed in bands rather than in permanent tribes.

The plateau and basin Indians were seminomadic, moving about their loosely defined territories, fishing, hunting, and gathering their food. Their tribal life lacked some of the complex organization of other Indians, but, generally, they were peaceful and industrious. One of the more simple social sub-cultures was that of the Indians who lived in California's ideal climate. Their government was informal, their homes modest, and their crafts limited.

Perhaps the wealthiest of the native Americans were the experienced sailors and fishermen who fished along the northwest coast. Fish was plentiful and wealth, in the form of food, baskets, and blankets, easy to acquire. Slaves from captured tribes helped in the everyday work. For these northwest Indians, life centered around the villages and the "potlatch," a feast during which the host Indian gave his guests many gifts, thus distributing the wealth among the group.

In spite of their cultural diversity, the Indians had certain common beliefs and practices regarding religion, myths, and rituals. Most tribes worshipped a great spirit and ascribed supernatural powers to objects such as animals and trees. Usually a medicine man or a specially designated person treated the sick and presided at special tribal ceremonies. Ritualistic rhythmic movement or dancing was central to the Indian cultures. Captain John Smith in 1607 recounts:

Their religion and Ceremonie I observed was thus: Three or foure dayes after my taking, seven of them in the house where I lay, each with a rattle, began at ten a clocke in the morning to sing about the fire, which they invironed with a Circle of meale, and after a foote or two from that, at the end of each song, layde downe two or three graines of wheate: continuing this order till they have included six or seven hundred in a halfe Circle; and after that two or three more Circles in like maner, a hand bredth from the other. That done, at each song, they put betwixt everie three, two, or five graines, a little sticke; so counting as an old woman her *Pater noster.*

One disguised with a great Skinne, his head hung round with little Skinnes of Weasels and other vermine, with a Crownet of feathers on his head, painted as ugly as the divell, at the end of each song will make many signes and demonstrations, with strange and vehement actions, great cakes of Deere suet, Deare, and Tobacco he casteth in the fire: till sixe a clocke in the Evening, their howling would continue ere they would depart.[7]

Nicholas Cresswell actually took part in an Indian dance:

Painted by my Squaw in the most elegant manner. Divested of all my clothes, except my Calico short breechclout, leggings, and Mockesons. A fire was made which we danced round with little order, whooping and hallooing in a most frightful manner. I was but a novice at the diversion and by endeavouring to act as they did made them a great deal of sport and ingratiated me much in their esteem. This is the most violent exercise to the adepts in the art I ever saw. No regular figure, but violent distortion of features, writhing and twisting the body in the most uncouth and antic postures imaginable. Their music is an old Keg with one head knocked out and covered with a skin and beat with sticks which regulates their times. The men have strings of Deer's hoofs tied round their

---

7. John Smith, "Captain John Smith's True Relation of Virginia," in *Virginia Reader,* ed. F.C. Rosenberger (New York: E.P. Dutton & Company, 1948), pp. 83-84.

ankles and knees, and gourds with shot or pebblestones in them in their hands which they continually rattle. The women have Morris bells or Thimbles with holes in the bottom and strung upon a leather thong tied round their ankles, knees and waists. The jingling of these Bells and Thimbles, the rattling of the Deer's hoofs and gourds, beating of the drum and kettle, with the horrid yells of the Indians, render it the most unharmonious concert, that human idea can possibly conceive. It is a favourite diversion, in which I am informed they spend a great part of their time in Winter.[8]

The early explorers observed many activities which resembled European games and hence identified them as games. However, the "games" of the native Americans, like their dances, may have been ceremonial in nature rather than for entertainment or pleasure.

Both men and women participated in these sport-like activities or games, which often ranged over the countryside from village to village. The teams were large, sometimes consisting of an entire village or a segment of a tribe, generating a mass excitement as the teams fought for the glory of the tribe or village. In other activities Indians competed for individual honors. Betting was heavy and generally accompanied all sport or game activities. Men and women sometimes played the same games, but, also, each had separate games. Men played lacrosse, other ball games, target games, and held foot races while women engaged in shinny and double-ball.

Men's Games

While many different games have been discovered, four ball games are of special interest in the history of sport.

Lacrosse

When a French Jesuit missonary saw a game played by Indians with objects resembling a bishop's crosier, he called the game "lacrosse," but other early explorers and travelers referred to the game as rackets. It was played throughout the country—the Algonquians and Iroquoians in the east, the Dakotas in the west, the Muskhogeans in the south, the Chinook and Salish in the northwest, and, occasionally, the Californians in the far west. The game is thought to have had deep religious and ceremonial significance, but, over the years, it became secular in nature. Many myths evolved around the game, such as the one reported by Culin:

Some old people say the moon is a ball which was thrown up against the sky in a game a long time ago. They say that two towns were playing against each other,

---

8. *The Journal of Nicholas Cresswell, 1774-1777* (New York: Lincoln MacVeagh, 1924), p. 109.

but one of them had the best runners and had almost won the game when the leader of the other side picked up the ball with his hand—a thing that is not allowed in the game—and tried to throw to the goal, but it struck against the solid sky vault and was fastened there, to remind players never to cheat. When the moon is small and pale, it is because some one has handled the ball unfairly, and for this reason they formerly played only at the time of a full moon.[9]

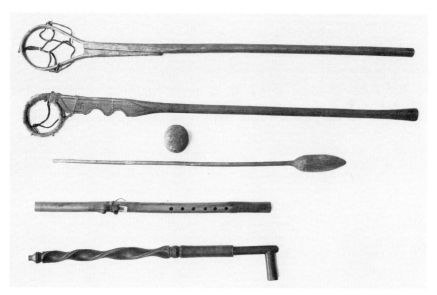

FIG. 2.2 Lacrosse sticks and ball. Courtesy of the AMERICAN MUSEUM OF NATURAL HISTORY.

Sometimes the game was played with one "cross" or stick and sometimes with two. The sticks varied in size and shape. When two sticks were used, they were usually small, as in a game described by an early traveler.

It is played with a ball, and with two staffs recurved and terminated by a sort of racket. Two posts are set up, which serve as bounds, and which are distant from each other in proportion to the number of players. For instance, if there are eighty of these, there will be a half league between the posts. The players are divided into two bands, each having its own post; and it is a question of driving the ball as far as the post of the opposing party without falling upon the ground or being touched with the hand. If either of these happens the game is lost, unless he who has committed the mistake repairs it by driving the ball with one stroke to

9. Stewart Culin, *Games of the North American Indians* (New York: Dover, 1975), pp. 586-87.

the bound, which is often impossible. These savages are so adroit in catching the ball with their crosses that these games sometimes last several days in succession.[10]

Not only did the size of the cross vary, but also the playing area and the number of people on each team. While the above account refers to a "field" of a half league, other reports speak of fairly short distances and still others of battling from village to village.

Basketball-type Games

Two games without names have been discovered which bear some resemblance to basketball. One is the rubber ball game similar to the Meso-American ball game. Courts similar to those in Mexico have been found in southwestern United States at the Hohokam site in Snaketown, Arizona. While it is possible that the game stems from the Meso-American game of about 1500 B.C., the Hohokam courts are dated about 800 A.D. Assuming the game is similar to the Meso-American ball game, it can be described as follows:

> It is . . . a combination of our modern games of basketball, volleyball, soccer, and *jai-alai*. It was played in a high-walled, paved court (usually 100 to 125 feet long and 20 to 50 feet wide) . . . the floor plans of which were in the shape of a "capital I" . . . the game had as its key the knocking of a solid, five-pound rubber ball, five to eight inches in diameter, through stone "hoops" set vertically in the center of each of the two long walls. The main objective of the play does not seem to have been to gain ground, . . . but to score. Since the inner diameter of the stone hoop varied from six to twelve inches, making a "goal" was no easy task.[11]

As was true for many Indian games there was heavy betting. Some scholars ascribe ritualistic meaning to the game and suggest that the losing captain was sacrificed. Other scholars suggest that the Hohokam courts might be dance areas rather than ball courts.

Another basketball-like activity was reported by Laudonnière, on a sixteenth-century visit to Florida, but it does not appear to have been played elsewhere:

> They exercise their young men to become excellent runners, and they give prizes to those who have the greatest endurance. They often practice at archery. They play ball in the following fashion: They use a tree standing in an open place, a

---

10. Charlevoix, *Journal d'un Voyage dans l'Amerique Septentrionnale,* v. 3, p. 319, Paris, 1744, cited in Stewart Culin, *Games of the North American Indians* (New York: Dover, 1975), p. 569.

11. Stephan F. de Borhegyi, "America's Ballgame," *Natural History* 69 (1960): 53.

tree eight or nine armlengths in height. At the top of the tree there is a square made from wood strips, and the scorer is the one who hits the square.[12]

FIG. 2.3 Basketball-type game of Florida Indians. J. LeMoyne. Courtesy of the AMERICAN MUSEUM OF NATURAL HISTORY.

Hockey-type Game

Shinny was a hockey-like team game played by both men and women with an unlimited number on each side. Each player used a long-handled wooden stick about two to four feet in length and curved at the bottom. The game began with an umpire, often a medicine man, who placed the ball in the middle of the field, either covering it over with dirt, leaving it in a hole in the ground, or tossing it up in the air. At a signal, the players rushed toward the center of the field and tried to bat or kick the ball toward their opponents' goal. Ordinarily, the first team to score four goals won the game.

---

12. Charles E. Bennett, *Three Voyages of René Laudonnière* (Gainesville: The University Presses of Florida, 1975), p. 11.

Other Games

Hoop-and-pole, played by men, consisted of throwing or attempting to throw a spear or shooting an arrow at a rolling hoop or ring. The rings varied in size and design, some of them being filled with woven patterns. The manner of rolling the hoops and attempting to shoot the hoop appears to have differed from tribe to tribe. Other ball games included a "football" game in which the hands could not be used to advance the ball toward the opponent's goal. The object of the game was to get the ball across the opposing team's goal posts, which were about a mile from the defenders' goal.

Women's Games

Women played shinny and a game which has been labeled "double-ball." It was played by most of the cultural groups in North America, usually in the spring or summer. It utilized two balls or two blocks—of wood or other materials—connected by a rawhide thong about six to twelve inches long. Sticks from two to six feet in length were employed to catch the cord between the two balls and to pass the double balls forward over an opponent's goal line, a "line" between posts or piles of dirt. The goals might be anywhere from 600 feet to a mile apart. While the usual number of players varied from five to ten, any number of women could play. The game was started by tossing the double ball up in the air, after which each team attempted to pass and throw the double ball between the goal posts. As was true in many games, the double ball could not be touched with the hands.

Explorers and early settlers reported that the Indians were strong swimmers and capable of rescuing canoeists who had capsized. They held contests with bows and arrows and also used them for practice for war. Some Indian tribes held public games each spring and fall.

The European Settlers

Although European explorers had probed the North American continent as early as the beginning of the eleventh century, it was not until the early seventeenth century that permanent settlements were established in the present-day United States. The people who established those settlements, and their memories of familiar lands and activities, are a part of this country's history. Sport and dance in sixteenth and seventeenth century Europe, where many of the early settlers originated, reflected the social groups which had emerged from medieval times. The nobles and higher clergy were the new aristocracy, and the peasants comprised the lowest social group. In the middle were the growing numbers of villagers and townspeople—

tradesmen, shopkeepers, professional men and, of course, their families. Pastimes and sport in sixteenth and seventeenth century Europe differed according to social class. The sport of the nobility set the pattern for the wealthier town dwellers to emulate. The townspeople also engaged in ball games and other activities sometimes associated with the lower classes. Because the early settlers in the American colonies came largely from towns, an account of the middle-class sport of these European town dwellers is important to the history of sport, dance, and physical activity in our country. Such an account must include the evolution of middle-class sport from the sport and dance of the nobility, on the one hand, and the sport and dance of the peasants, on the other.

Sport and Pastimes of the Nobility

The nobles were part of the feudal system, which can be thought of as a pyramid. "The king was at the top of the feudal pyramid: . . . A few dukes and counts were his direct vassals. They in turn had their vassals, rear vassals, and rear rear vassals. At the bottom of the pyramid was the simple knight with just enough land and peasant labor to support him, his family, and his horses."[13] Below this pyramid of nobles were the peasants, both freemen and serfs, who provided food, goods, and services in return for the protection of their family and land. Originally, the castle or manor house awarded a vassal was for use only during his lifetime, but over a long period of time, it came to be an inherited right for the vassal's family. From this system of inherited authority, titles, and land, the aristocracy of northwest Europe evolved. This new aristocracy saw themselves as a social group with a distinctive way of life, strict rules of etiquette, and chivalric codes of honor.

The nobleman was the head of his family and his main responsibilities consisted of looking after his estate, his family, and his vassals. However, much of his time was spent either in fighting real battles or mock battles in tournaments. The nobleman's wife, the noblewoman, had a paradoxical position in the early Middle Ages. Although legally under the complete control of her husband, she was often in sole command of the castle and lands during his frequent absences. Because privacy was almost unknown in castle life, the woman was well acquainted with the concerns of her husband as well as with all others of the household. In the early medieval period she was a vigorous woman who wore simple, loose garments which permitted her freedom of movement as she rode, hunted, and took part in other outdoor pursuits. The life of a lady in a remote medieval castle might be likened to the life of a woman upon an isolated Western ranch in the early 1900's.

---

13. Sidney Painter, *Mediaeval Society* (Ithaca: Cornell University Press, 1951), p. 16.

As chivalry and knightly codes of honor became more elaborate, the concepts of courtly love changed the ideal woman from that of a vigorous, skilled huntress to a delicate, inactive woman revered by an adoring knight. By the end of the medieval period the corset restricted her waist, and the shape of her dress bore little resemblance to the human figure. When she rode out for pleasure or for hunting, she sat primly on her side saddle.

The noble children were under the care of the mother and the servants during their early years. Later, both girls and boys were sent to the castle or manor of a respected relative or friend to be educated and trained. The boys and young men spent much of their time practicing precombat sports to prepare them for tournaments.

The Tournament

Almost any occasion called for a tournament—a wedding, a victory, settling a grudge, or simply the desire to test a knight's strength. The purpose of the tournament changed from its inception to its decline. The early tourneys served to develop and maintain the military, economic, and social aspects of chivalry. It was an accepted fact that tourneys provided the only true preparation for real battles and were considered "little wars themselves, and apprenticeship for great ones."[14] Economically, the early tourneys provided ransom money for the victors. The aim of the struggle was not to kill the opposing knight, but to capture him, his horse, and his equipment in order to collect a ransom. The tourney was a spectacle of pomp and pageantry, usually lasting several days. Socially, among the "new aristocracy," it provided a unique arena for the young men to prove themselves and bring fame and glory to themselves and their families.

Perhaps the best exhibitions of skill were performed by those knights who made their living by entering tournaments, either to collect the ransom money from their captives or the prizes which had been announced. The professional knight was typified by William Marshall, a well-known twelfth-century champion in northern France and England, who made his living for over twenty years by winning at tournaments. These professionals were usually sons of noblemen who would not inherit the families' titles and lands and, faced with penury, chose "touring the tournaments" as a way to make their living.

The increasing use of gunpowder, with its effect upon fighting style in warfare, eventually changed the major purpose of the tournament to maintaining and reaffirming the traditional codes of chivalry and membership in the aristocracy. Noble families continued to hold tournaments, which, by

14. William S. Davis, *Life on a Mediaeval Barony* (New York: Harper & Brothers, 1923), p. 208.

FIG. 2.4   Early sixteenth-century tournament in Europe. By Permission of the British Library Board.

this time, had developed into a program of formally arranged jousts. The tournaments excluded those not of aristocratic birth and furnished a playing field on which the young knights could seek the pageantry and thrill of former times. The legacy of the tournament, which had died out by the seventeenth century, was the identification of sport as a status symbol which helped set the aristocracy apart from the other classes. Further, the pomp and pageantry of the medieval "sport spectacular" were satisfying in the same way as the panoply surrounding today's sport events, such as the Tournament of Roses.

Tennis

Although the exact origin of tennis is not known, the well-developed game of court tennis was played by the nobility in the thirteenth century. While the action of tennis, or *tenetz* or *tenes,* hitting a ball back and forth between two persons, was the basic component of medieval tennis, there were many differences between the early court tennis and today's lawn tennis. The court is said to have developed from the rectangular shape of monastery courtyards where a form of tennis or handball was played by the clerics, from the student-priests to the bishops. No rackets were used and the game was called *jeu de paume,* the game of the palm of the hand. *Jeu de paume* could be likened to handball played in a court with the ball hit over a

FIG. 2.5   Medieval tennis court. By Permission of the British Library Board.

net, but also bounced against the walls and roof of the court. Over the years the game passed from the monastery into secular life where it became a favorite with the nobility and upper-class townspeople. Castles sometimes had courts built within the castle walls for the enjoyment of the nobles and their guests. Both men and women played *jeu de paume.* Although a type of racket was in use by the sixteenth century, today's modern game of tennis did not develop until the nineteenth century.

Hunting and Hawking

Both hunting and hawking were favorite sports of the nobility. Everyone hunted and hawked—the nobles, the knights, the clergy, the ladies, and the young people. Highly bred dogs and carefully cared for, ornately hooded falcons or hawks, were the constant companions of both noble men and noble women. Queen Elizabeth I, always fond of outdoor pursuits, was reported by a courtier to still enjoy hunting when she was seventy-seven years of age.

A hawking party was an all-day affair and a time of sport and merriment:

> Assuredly it is an exhilarating sight to see the castle folk go hawking on a fine morning. The baron, baroness, and all their older relatives and guests, each with bird on gauntlet, are on tall horses; the squires and younger people have sparrow hawks to send against the smaller prey, but the leaders of the sport will wait until they can strike a swift duck or heron. Dogs will race along to flush the game. Horns are blowing, young voices laughing, all the horses prancing. . . . Away they go—racing over fences, field and fallow, thicket and brook, until fate sends to view a heron. Then all the hawks are unhooded together; there are shouts, encouragement, merry wagers, and helloing as the birds soar in the chase. The heron may meet his fate far in the blue above. Then follow more racing and scurrying to recover the hawks. So onward, covering many miles of country, until, with blood tingling, all canter back . . . in a determined mood for supper.[15]

Farm animals of the period, neither well bred nor well fed, were not the main source of meat in medieval times; venison or boar was preferred with partridge, pheasants, and wild duck adding variety to the tables of the aristocracy. The noblemen and higher clergy set aside forests and parks for their use for hunting, excluding peasants and other lower-class persons from most of the hunting grounds.

Both hunting and hawking epitomized the carefully nurtured idea of the medieval aristocracy—a specially defined way of life requiring a specific code of conduct. Both dogs and hawks were expensive and required trained servants to feed, tend, and train them properly. The restrictions placed on

---

15. William S. Davis, *Life on a Mediaeval Barony* (New York: Harper & Brothers, 1923), p. 62.

FIG. 2.6   Sixteenth-century hunting party with hawks. By Permission of the British Library Board.

land or the defining of hunting preserves by the noblemen or clergy, who were often of noble birth, were made on the basis of social position.

Horse Racing

While horses had been used for hunting throughout this period, their use for racing appears to have been an early seventeenth-century development, again as a sport for the aristocracy. By the middle of the seventeenth century rules had been established, and within a few decades betting had developed, but at the time of the early English migrations to this country, horse racing was not yet a popular sport.

A study of the medieval nobility reveals that the nobleman's sport fulfilled both the function of a necessary daily activity and that of sport. Hunting and hawking provided for the table but both were also engaged in for enjoyment, and the satisfaction of handling the hawks and the horses. While tournaments prepared men for battle, they also provided the contesting of physical prowess against an opponent of similar skill and the thrill of risking oneself in a sport arena. In fact, most of the pleasures found in today's sport were part of the daily life of the medieval nobility.

Sport and Pastimes of the Peasants

The pleasurable life of the nobility was made possible by the hard work of the lower classes. The serf was literally part of the noble's holdings: "He was tied to the land, but the land was tied to him."[16] The lord set aside a small portion of land for a serf, who in return for protection, shared part of his crop with the lord or worked for him. An Act of 1495, just three years after Columbus discovered America, defined the working day from March to September from 5 A.M. to 7 or 8 P.M., and in the winter as the daylight hours. For all the peasants, serf and free, each day was largely filled with the same drudgery and life was restricted to the routine of work and church.

However, even for the peasants, there were sports, pastimes, and dancing—snatched a few hours at a time on Sundays, holy days, and at weddings, fairs, and festivals. The Church prohibited some kinds of work on holy days, which occurred frequently, and the peasants appear to have made the most of these occasions. Chaucer, Froissart, Stow, and other writers recount boisterous, rough games, dancing, and gatherings at fairs and "church-ales." Evidence of rowdiness connected with sports also comes from court records, which document many attempts to control sport.

Perhaps the most important legacies from the peasants to our sport today are the ball games, which were the precursors to baseball, football, soccer,

---

16. G.G. Coulton, *The Medieval Scene* (Cambridge: Cambridge University Press, 1959), p. 26.

golf, and bowling. Although the sports and pastimes of the peasants may seem meager compared to the nobility, it is important in the history of sport that peasants did, on occasion, participate in amusements and sport. It is one of the first times in the history of sport that there is *evidence* that sport was not reserved for the highest social group in a country.

Baseball-type Games

Although medieval manuscripts depict peasants apparently playing with balls and bats or sticks, and references are made to such games in the literature, we have no written, contemporary descriptions of *how* the games were played. The clubs or bats appear to be a straight piece of wood which could strike the balls, which were usually made of leather filled with material such as wool or hemp. Most of the evidence suggests that men played baseball-type games, sometimes parish against parish or married men against unmarried men. Occasionally, there are reports of young women playing these games. At least two types of bat-and-ball games, precursors of baseball, can be identified.

Stool-ball, played near Windsor, England as early as 1330, is thought to be the medieval game most closely resembling baseball. Strutt reconstructs the game as follows:

> [It] consists in simply setting a stool upon the ground, and one of the players takes his place before it, while his antagonist, standing at a distance, tosses a ball with the intention of striking the stool; and this it is the business of the former to prevent by beating it away with the hand, reckoning one to the game for every stroke of the ball; if, on the contrary, it should be missed by the hand and touch the stool, the players change places. I believe the same also happens if the person who threw the ball can catch and retain it when driven back, before it reaches the ground. The conqueror at this game is he who strikes the ball most times before it touches the stool.[17]

Stool-ball is theorized to have developed from one stool to two stools or "home" and one "base," then three stools or "home" and two "bases," and then to "home" and three "bases." During this period the game became known as "rounders," the forerunner of baseball.

Club-ball, the name given to a variety of ball-and-bat activities, is illustrated in thirteenth and fourteenth century manuscripts showing both men and women playing. However, the precise method of playing is not clear.

---

17. Joseph Strutt, *The Sports and Pastimes of the People of England* (London: William Tegg, 1867), p. 97.

FIG. 2.7   Early bat-and-ball game. By Permission of the British Library Board.

Soccer and Football-type Games

As early as the fourteenth century, records exist of games in which the ball was kicked rather than batted or driven with the hands. The major elements of the games, two teams attempting to move one ball across the opponent's goal line, appear to have been present in the very early days. The game was exceedingly dangerous, with a number of injuries reported on both sides, and because of the high incidence of injuries, various attempts were made to prohibit play.

Hockey-type Games

Hurling in Cornwall, knappan in Wales, and shinty in Scotland are ball games in which the ball was hit on the ground with a club or stick in an effort to advance it across the opponent's goal. There were no hockey fields as we know them today, and the entire countryside became the field of play. The teams were large, the play rough, but in spite of bruises, black eyes, and scuffed shins, the players continued to engage in these games.

Golf

Goff, as it was called in the sixteenth century, is distinguished from other ball games in that each player has his own ball. Both Scottish and Dutch people claim that golf originated in their country. Supposedly, the first illustration of golf is found in a Flemish Book of Hours from the early sixteenth century. Some authorities suggest that it developed from the Scottish game shinty when the object of the game changed to each player depositing a ball into a series of holes.

Other Games and Pastimes

Not only did the peasants play at ball games, but also they held contests in foot-racing, wrestling, hurling, and shooting. At fairs, on holy days, "church-ales," weddings, and festivals, contests were part of the festivities. Wrestling, especially in the early medieval period, took place at funerals, possibly a vestige of pagan funeral games. In tavern or pub yards, bowling, quoits, and simple challenge games such as pitching pennies were enjoyed. Many forms of bowling developed around the idea of rolling a ball for accuracy or knocking down a series of upright sticks or pins. The games, varying from locale to locale, were most popular with the men. Amusements which we consider suitable for children were indulged in by adults, as depicted by medieval manuscripts which show adult men walking on stilts, twirling rattles, and riding hobby-horses.

Other ball games undoubtedly were adapted from those described above or from games ordinarily thought of as games for the nobility. However, in manuscript after manuscript, in woodcuts, and in the literature of the period, there are numerous references to peasants and the lower classes of town dwellers playing ball games. By the eighteenth century many of these same people had brought their games to the early colonies of North America, where they eventually developed into our modern ball sports.

Sport and Pastimes of the Villagers and Town Dwellers

Villages grew into towns where tradespeople joined together for protection and commercial advantages. Still, agriculture was as basic to the life of the villages and towns as were the growing trades, crafts, and industries. Fitzstephen wrote of hunting and hawking in nearby forests and, while London and Paris seemed congested, other towns blended into the countryside. The sixteenth-century town encompassed a variety of life styles and occupations, much like today's cities and towns. The merchants and their families, as they acquired wealth, became the upper echelons of town society, but in spite of the fact that money permitted them to live better than many noblemen, they were never considered true "aristocrats." In addition to the merchants, other needs and services of the town dwellers were met by artisans, craftsmen, and skilled workers who formed guilds, much like today's labor organizations. At the height of the guilds' strength, almost every conceivable occupation had its own organization, training apprentices and controlling the occupation and, also, living in the same section of town.

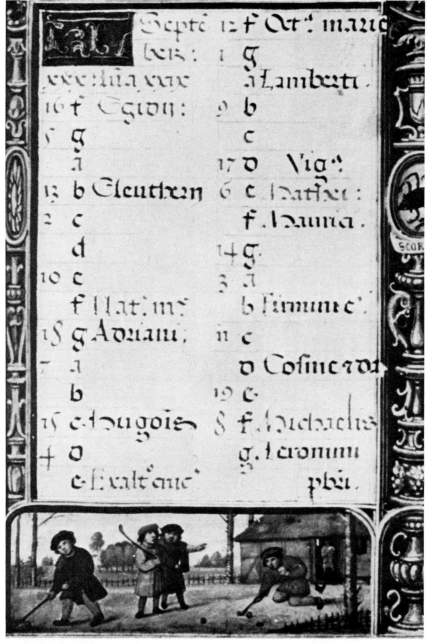

FIG. 2.8 Golf as a sixteenth-century game for peasants. By Permission of the British Library Board.

The sports which emerged in the growing villages and towns were a combination of the sports of the nobility and the sports of the peasants. The variety of social groups in the town—the rich merchants or burghers, the guild members, artisans, students, and laborers—led to adaptations of the country sports of the nobility and the peasants. The villagers and town dwellers, with their lives regulated by their trade and by the Church, found occasions for sport and dance on Sundays, holy days, and festivals.

Animal Sports

Everyone—nobles, peasants, and the town dwellers—enjoyed the animal-baiting exhibitions on Sunday afternoons and the forenoon of holy days. Dogs were trained to attack, torment, and perhaps kill a bear, a bull, badger, or other animal, chained and confined within a pit. While this vicious practice does not seem sport by today's standards, Strutt points out that such "barbarous diversions . . . [were] universally practised on various occasions, in almost every town or village throughout the kingdom, and especially in market towns, where we find it was sanctioned by the law."[18] Even royalty used animal baiting to entertain their visitors:

> Queen Elizabeth, on the 25th of May, 1559, soon after her accession to the throne, gave a splendid dinner to the French ambassadors, who afterwards were entertained with the baiting of bulls and bears, and the queen herself stood with the ambassadors looking on the pastime till six at night.[19]

Writing in the thirteenth century, Fitzstephen reported that school boys were permitted to watch cock fighting on Shrove Tuesday morning.

Mock-noble Sports

As the social groups became more defined, the merchants or burghers who became the upper social group of the city tried to emulate the noblemen in their life style, including their sport and amusements. To protect the citizens, each town had its own group of skilled archers who competed among themselves and who eventually organized intercity festivals:

> Soon, in imitation of the knightly games, the archery festivals developed into great pageantries, boasting parades, heralds on horseback, and jesters who drove in dog carts. In the course of sportive merriment a jester would present the booby prize to the competitor with the poorest showing.

---

18. Joseph Strutt, *The Sports and Pastimes of the People of England* (London: William Tegg, 1867), p. 277.

19. Joseph Strutt, *The Sports and Pastimes of the People of England* (London: William Tegg, 1867), p. 257.

Eager to imitate the practices of the nobility, the burghers organized tournaments of their own in which they approximated all the knightly traditions.[20]

The city fathers also encouraged wrestling and instruction in hand weapons for the young gentlemen of the town. Coaches and teachers were needed for these activities and soon fencing masters formed schools largely organized on a social basis. Thus, barred from the sports of the nobility by birth, the merchants or burghers of the new cities, in imitation of the aristocracy, created their own forms of sport competition.

Pastimes

Townspeople who did not belong to the emerging bourgeois had their own sports and pastimes. Stow's famous account of medieval sports in London describes the pastimes in the language of the day:

Stage playes.

But London for the shows upon Theaters, and Comicall pastimes, hath holy playes, representations of myracles which holy Confessours have wrought, or representations of torments wherein the constancie of Martyrs appeared. Every yeare also at Shrovetuesday, that we may begin with childrens sports, seeing we al have beene children, the schoole boyes do bring Cockes of the game to their master, and all the forenoone they delight themselves in Cockfighting: after dinner all the youthes go into the fields to play at the bal. The schollers of every schoole have their ball, or baston, in their hands: the auncient and wealthy men of the Citie come foorth on horsebacke to see the sport of the yong men, and to take part of the pleasure in beholding their agilitie. Every Fryday in Lent a fresh company of young men comes into the field on horseback, and the best horseman conducteth the rest. Then march forth the Citizens sons, and other yong men with disarmed launces and shields, and there they practise feates of warre. Many Courtiers likewise when the king lieth nere, and attendants of noble men doe repaire to these exercises, and while the hope of victorie doth inflame their minds, do shew good proofe how serviceable they would bee in martiall affayres. In Easter holy dayes they fight battailes on the water, a shield is hanged upon a pole, fixed in the midst of the stream, a boat is prepared without oares to bee caried by violence of the water, and in the fore part thereof standeth a young man, readie to give charge upon the shield with his launce: if so be hee breaketh his launce against the shield, and doth not fall, he is thought to have performed a worthy deed. If so be without breaking his launce, he runneth strongly against the shield, downe he falleth into the

Cock fighting.

Ball play.

Exercises of
warlike feates on
horsebacke with
disarmed Launces.

Battailes on the
water.

20. Nicolaas J. Moolenjizer, "Our Legacy from the Middle Ages," *Quest* 11 (December, 1968): 41.

Leaping, dancing, shooting, wrestling.

water, for the boat is violently forced with the tide, but on each side of the shielde ride two boates, furnished with yong men, which recover him that falleth as soone as they may. Upon the bridge, wharfes, and houses, by the rivers side, stand great numbers to see, & laugh therat. In the holy dayes all the Summer the youths are exercised in leaping, dancing, shooting, wrastling, casting the stone, and practising their shields: the Maidens trip in their Timbrels, and daunce as long as they can well see. In Winter every holy day before dinner, the Boares prepared for brawne are set to fight, or else Buls and Beares are bayted.

Dauncing, Fighting of Boars, bayting of Beares and Bulles.

The Moorefield when there was no ditch by the wall of the Citie. sliding on the yce.

When the great fenne or Moore, which watereth the wals of the Citie on the North side, is frozen, many yong men play upon the yce, some striding as wide as they may, doe slide swiftly: others make themselves seates of yce, as great as Milstones: one sits downe, many hand in hand doe draw him, and one slipping on a sudden, all fall togither: some tie bones to their feete, and under their heeles, and shoving themselves by a little picked Staffe, doe slide as swiftly as a bird flieth in the ayre, or an arrow out of a Crossebow. Sometime two runne togither with Poles, and hitting one the other, eyther one or both doe fall, not without hurt: some breake their armes, some their legges, but youth desirous of glorie in this sort exerciseth it selfe agaynst the time of warre. Many of the Citizens doe delight themselves in Hawkes, and houndes, for they have libertie of hunting in Middlesex, Hartfordshire, all Chiltron, and in Kent to the water of Cray. Thus farre Fitzstephen of sportes.[21]

Hauking and hunting

Strutt provides evidence of at least one highly skilled woman athlete in the fifteenth century:

A French writer speaks of a damsel named Margot, who resided at Paris in 1424, and played at hand-tennis with the palm, and also with the back of her hand, better than any man; and what is most surprising, adds my author, at that time the game was played with the naked hand, or at best with a double glove.[22]

Students' Activities

The sports and pastimes of a medieval city ranged from the exclusive fencing clubs and bear gardens where the baiting of animals could be viewed to rowdy street play. It was into such a climate that students of the period moved when they attended a university. Unlike universities in modern United States, medieval universities had neither recreational nor athletic facilities, nor a program of sports.

---

21. John Stow, *A Survey of London,* reprinted from 1603 (Oxford: Clarendon Press, 1908), pp. 92-93.

22. Joseph Strutt, *The Sports and Pastimes of the People of England* (London: William Tegg, 1867), p. 94.

The students, male, many of them in their early teens, lived away from the university, often in a poor part of town and were exposed to all aspects of city life. They led lives typical of their age and time—snatching some time from studies to play children's games and ball games, to swim in available streams, and to ice skate in the winter. Following the cities' pattern of amusements on Sundays and holy days, the students entered into the town's revelries such as drinking, gambling, and playing ball. Jousting was a favorite entertainment of the students in northern Europe and bullfighting, the local popular sport, was enjoyed by the students in Spain.

Controls on Sport and Dance

Peasant Sport

In the feudal system kings and noblemen held jurisdiction over their vassals, and settled all disputes which arose. In time, various edicts, some of which dealt with sport, became law on the nobleman's estate. These restrictions were the beginnings of laws and regulations affecting sport and, in turn, the use of the people's leisure time. The restrictions on peasants' sport occurred for military reasons, for preventing injuries, and for the convenience of the noblemen.

Prior to the invention of gunpowder, the noblemen relied on the peasants for foot soldiers during periods of war. The one skill required of the foot soldier was accuracy with the bow and arrow. The men were expected to maintain archery equipment and to practice regularly with the bow and arrow. However, many men preferred bowling, football, and other games of their own choosing. Therefore, numerous edicts were issued which prohibited bowling, football, and golf because it interfered with archery practice. Football was forbidden not only because of archery practice, but also because of the number of injuries which occurred in the game. And, only for the convenience of the noblemen, peasants were forbidden to hunt on game preserves and parks set aside for the noblemen's pleasure. Thus, by the sixteenth century the peasants' choice of sport was restricted by the aristocracy in order to provide soldiers for their armies and to maintain their game parks for the use of the noblemen.

Student Sport

The literature of the medieval universities is replete with numerous accounts of controlling the sport of the students. The Scottish Parliament banned football and golf at the University of St. Andrews in 1457. Tennis and other ball games were banned at Cambridge University, and handball and sword play at Oxford. The University of Louvain and the University of Glasgow ruled that students could not bathe in the nearby streams while students at the University of Heidelberg were prohibited from attending tournaments.

The Influence of the Church on Sport

While the Catholic Church was an important influence on medieval life, its position and influence on sport varied from time to time and from locale to locale. Ball games and sports such as tennis appear to have been played in the early monasteries and to have been diffused into secular life. In Elizabethan England, the Church of England became firmly established and, from the beginning of the seventeenth century, the Puritan movement gained strength. Opposing views on sport and pastimes on Sunday developed. While neither the Roman Catholic Church nor the Church of England objected to most amusements and pastimes on Sundays, the Puritans opposed any activities on Sunday except those of a religious nature. King James I found himself caught in the middle of this growing controversy. While travelling through Lancashire, he was handed a petition from citizens complaining that they were barred from all amusements on Sunday. Exceedingly fond of sports himself, the King issued a *Book of Sport* in 1618 expressly approving sport after divine services on Sunday:

> . . . Our pleasure likewise is, That, after the end of Divine Service, Our good people be not disturbed, letted, or discouraged from any lawful recreation, Such as dancing, either of men or women, Archery for men, leaping, vaulting or any other such harmlesse Recreation, nor from haveing of May Games, Whitson Ales, and Morris-dances, and the setting up of Maypoles, and other sports therewith used, so as the same be had in due and convenient time, without impediment or neglect of Divine service.[23]

Thus, the head of the Anglican Church, King James I, stated his official position on sport and pastimes on Sundays. His Declaration was only sporadically enforced; and after King Charles I reissued the *Book of Sport* in 1633, the Puritan Parliament formally ordered it burned. Sabbatarianism, the principle of observing Sundays in a strict Christian way, and disallowing, for everyone, all other activities, whether sport, theater, concerts, or business, became prominent in the seventeenth century in England with the rise of Puritanism. The term derives from *sabat,* Saturday, the seventh day; the principle derives from the Fourth Commandment of the Mosaic Laws. During the Reformation, Sunday rather than Saturday came to be observed. The strict Puritan observance of Sunday envisioned a family attending two church services with long sermons, and also engaging in family prayers and Bible readings. Children might be allowed a few

---

23. L.A. Govett, *The King's Book of Sports* (London: Elliot Stock, 1890), pp. 38-39.

suitably moral tales or Bible games. From this view of life, sport was tolerated elsewhere in the week, but was banned on Sunday.

The European settlers who came to this country left behind turbulent times in which the aristocracy was gradually losing its influence on the growing number of merchants and other middle-class persons. It was from these latter groups that many of the first pioneers came to this country, and it was their amusements and attitudes toward sport, whether Puritan or otherwise, that shaped the pastimes and sport activities in the new country.

The Africans Who Came to America

Culture in West Africa

The first Africans who came to colonial America landed at Jamestown, Virginia in 1619, not as slaves, but as indentured servants. Within two decades the custom of selling West Africans as property was established and the first laws relating to owning slaves were passed in Massachusetts in 1641 and Virginia in 1661. The staple crops grown in the south required a large labor force which could be satisfied neither by the small independent white farmers nor by the native Americans, who were rapidly decreasing in numbers and whose cultural mores did not include the necessary agricultural technology. Also, the native Indians appeared to have less resistance to certain bacterial diseases than the blacks from West Africa. The basis of the West African economy was agricultural. While the men prepared the ground for planting and did the heavy work, the women tended the crops and harvested them when ready. Thus, the Africans were accustomed to both the rhythm and discipline of the agricultural year.

While the first slaves brought to the North American colonies are thought to have come from the mouth of the Niger River, the extent of their origin ranged from the Gambia to present-day Angola, just south of the Congo River. Studying available documents, including ships' manifests, Herskovits suggests that:

—the regions that figure most prominently are "Guinea," which means the west coast of Africa from the Ivory Coast to western Nigeria, Calabar, which represents the Niger Delta region, Angola, or the area about the lower Congo, and the Gambia.[24]

In fifteenth-century Africa, slavery as a condition of life was not unknown. Captives from war were made slaves, but as such were neither

---

24. Melville J. Herskovits, *The Myth of the Negro Past* (Boston: Beacon Press, 1958), p. 47.

subjected to the condition of being property to be bought and sold nor to the hard labor associated later with slavery in the southern part of the United States. For the American slave trade men, women, boys, and girls were usually obtained from African chiefs and merchants, who quickly saw the economic advantages in such trade. Several groups of Africans supplied the demand of slave traders. Persons who had committed crimes for which the punishment was banishment were sold into slavery. Prisoners of war, who might have been condemned as slaves, helped the supply of slaves, but those who ". . . comprised by far the greatest number were those captured by marauding bands of robbers who, with the connivance of native rulers, carried on these raids to satisfy the demands of the European dealers."[25]

Although the area from which most Africans were taken to be brought to the United States was quite large, certain generalizations may be made about life in West Africa during this period. With agriculture as their chief means of support, the Africans traded their surplus crops, using cowrie shells as money. Craft guilds of potters, wood-carvers, basket-makers, and weavers were organized largely by families. The women acted as traders in the market and set prices according to the supply and demand of products.

African families were polygynous, and the marriages carefully planned to the satisfaction of both families. Perhaps the greatest impact on the children was that they realized that they shared their father with a number of other children, but that they shared their mother with only her own children. Each family had its own compound with an individual house for each adult male, married or unmarried. Each wife lived with her children in a single house.

Ancestors, very much revered and sometimes deified, played an important part in the complex forces and cults which were included in the African religions and ceremonies. Religion and ceremony were interwoven into the everyday life of the Africans. "Song and dance are everywhere found to play significant and similar roles in the daily round. . . . Rhythm is invariably complex, and the convention of alternation of leader and chorus in singing likewise the rule."[26] Olaudah Equiano, who published his autobiography in 1789, described his nation as one of "dancers, musicians, and poets."[27]

---

25. Melville J. Herskovits, *The Myth of the Negro Past* (Boston: Beacon Press, 1958), p. 107.

26. Melville J. Herskovits, *The Myth of the Negro Past* (Boston: Beacon Press, 1958), p. 84.

27. E. Olaudah, *The Interesting Narrative of Olaudah Equiano, or Gustavus Vasa, the African* (2 vols, London, 1789), in *Africa Remembered,* ed. P. Curtin (Madison: The University of Wisconsin, 1967), p. 69.

Sport-like Activities

Other sources of information about Africa during this period are the accounts of travelers and explorers. Hugh Clapperton arrived in Kano where he found jugglers and the Hausa boxers, whom he paid 2,000 whydah to fight in an exhibition. About twenty men engaged in the boxing, which was preceded by drummers and a ceremonial show of strength and bravado. The boxers' fists were then bound with cloth and the first pair brought into the ring. The fighters boxed only men whom they did not know. If friends were paired to fight, ". . . they laid their left breasts together twice, and exclaimed, 'We are lions;' 'We are friends.' "[28] When the fighting began, it was a free-for-all technique with blows from the heels as well as the hands. After about six pairs of fighters, Clapperton paid the boxers and the exhibition terminated.

Other travelers described horse racing, which was part of the celebration of the "Bebun Salah" in Kaiama.

The Arab saddle and stirrup were in common use; and the whole group presented an imposing appearance.

The signal for starting was made, and the impatient animals sprung forward and set off at a full gallop. The riders brandished their spears, the little boys flourished their cows' tails, the buffoons performed their antics, muskets were discharged, and the chief himself, mounted on the finest horse on the ground, watched the progress of the race, while tears of delight were starting from his eyes. The sun shone gloriously on the tobes of green, white, yellow, blue, and crimson, as they fluttered in the breeze; and with the fanciful caps, the glittering spears, the jingling of the horses' bells, the animated looks and warlike bearing of their riders, presented one of the most extraordinary and pleasing sights that we have ever witnessed. The race was well contested, and terminated only by the horses being fatigued and out of breath; but though every one was emulous to outstrip his companion, honour and fame were the only reward of the competitors.[29]

Through the autobiography of Equiano we have a glimpse of boyhood in an African tribe before slavery:

I was trained up from my earliest years in the art of war; my daily exercise was shooting and throwing javelins; . . . [and later, as a slave in Africa] my young

---

28. Margery Perham and J. Simmons, *African Discovery* (London: Faber and Faber, 1957), p. 95.

29. Margery Perham and J. Simmons, *African Discovery* (London: Faber and Faber, 1957), pp. 116-17.

master and I, with other boys, sported with our darts and bows and arrows, as I had been used to do at home.[30]

It was from such tribes and small kingdoms that the majority of African slaves came to America. While many kings apparently used the slave trade for their own gains, others did not. In 1526 King Affonso of Congo wrote to the King of Portugal:

. . . merchants are taking every day our natives, sons of the land and the sons of our noblemen and vassals and our relatives, because the thieves and men of bad conscience grab them. . . . So great, Sir, is the corruption and licentiousness that our country is being completely depopulated. . . .[31]

Such abuses continued. As late as 1795 King Naimbanna wrote to a leader in the British antislavery movement that "There are three distant relations of mine now in the West Indies, carried away by one Capt. Cox, captain of a Danish ship. Their names are Corpro, Banna and Morbour. These were taken out of my river Sierra Leona. I know not how to get them back."[32]

For three hundred and fifty years ships from many European countries—Portugal, Spain, England, France, Sweden, the Netherlands, and Denmark—brought West Africans to both South and North America to be sold as property. It is estimated that at least one-sixth of the Africans who left on slave ships perished during the dreaded "Middle Passage," as the voyage across the ocean was called. Some ship captains insisted that the Africans exercise in attempts to keep them healthy:

. . . We often at fea in the evenings would let the flaves come up into the fun to air themfelves, and make them jump and dance for an hour or two to our bagpipes, harp, and fiddle, by which exercife to preferve them in health; but notwithftanding all our endeavour, 'twas my hard fortune to have great ficknefs and mortality among them.[33]

Many slave ships stopped at islands in the West Indies for a period of adjustment of the Africans to the new life on which they were embarking. Eventually, they were brought to the mainland and sold, most of them in the southern states. By 1790 almost 700,000 Africans had been brought to the North American colonies, all but 50,000 to the southern plantations.

---

30. *The Life of Olaudah Equiano or Gustavus Vassa, the African,* Boston, 1837, in *The Negro in American History,* ed. M.J. Adler (Encyclopaedia Britannica Educational Corporation, 1969), p. 382.

31. Basil Davidson, *The African Past* (London: Longmans, 1964), p. 191.

32. Basil Davidson, *The African Past* (London: Longmans, 1964), p. 228.

33. Thomas Phillips, "A Journal of a Voyage to Africa and Barbadoes," in *A Collection of Voyages and Travels,* Vol. 6, ed. Churchill (London, 1732), p. 230.

The Africans were the third of the major groups of people who affected the development of American sport to arrive on the continent. For the majority of these Africans, their lives and amusements were controlled by their new white masters. Some two hundred years later their descendants dominated some sectors of American sport.

The American Colonists

Although the first two colonies on this continent were both established by Englishmen, each had a very different purpose. In 1607 enterprising Englishmen with the hope of quick fortunes—merchants, nobles, clergy, and tradesmen—formed the Virginia Company and sent 120 colonists to Jamestown, Virginia. In 1620 the Pilgrims, intent on founding their own religious community based upon Puritan beliefs, landed in Massachusetts. At about the same time the Dutch West India Company established settlements at Albany, New York, and New York City, and by the end of the century tiny villages and isolated homesteads dotted the eastern seaboard. Nevins and Commager remind us that:

> No real social distinction can be drawn between the settlers of Massachusetts and those of Virginia. The people who made both commonwealths great were drawn from the same large middle-class stratum. . . . The great majority of the emigrants to both Massachusetts and Virginia before 1660 were yeomen, mechanics, shopkeepers, and clerks of modest means; while many in all parts of America were indentured servants, who paid for their passage by a stated term of labor. Their real wealth lay in their sturdy integrity, self-reliance, and energy.[34]

From these new Americans, patterns of sport would evolve which reflected their backgrounds in the European countries, and also their new governments, laws, and daily lives.

The settlers learned to adapt some of their European ways to those of the native Americans, both to survive in the new land and to enjoy its many benefits. Hunting and fishing were no longer pastimes but a means of obtaining food, and the colonists quickly copied Indian methods. Buckskins and moccasins became practical dress for many Americans, as they learned to move quietly and stealthily through the forests as they stalked game. They also learned about the new foods such as corn and tomatoes and the best methods for farming and harvesting the new foods.

The colonists, alike in coming to a new land, were not alike in their modes of life. Different customs developed in different parts of the new world, af-

---

34. Allan Nevins and Henry Steele Commager, *A Pocket History of the United States* (New York: Washington Square Press, 1966), p. 12.

fected by geography, climate, and the purposes of the new settlements. Games and pastimes followed the diverse pattern of the colonies and were different in New England, New York, Pennsylvania, the South, and the western frontier.

New England

The struggle to survive and, in New England, the Puritans' "detestation of idleness" did not permit many pastimes and amusements. There were a few games, there were memories of games played in England, and there were stories of holidays and festivals told by parents and grandparents. The stories were not of tournaments, for few members of the English aristocracy came to America, but of ball games, stool ball, and bowling, the games of the town dwellers. But work and piety were the watchwords in New England and early attempts at sport were immediately suppressed, especially if others were working while some were playing.

> And herewith I shall end this year. Only I shall remember one passage more, rather of mirth then of waight. One ye day called Chrismasday, ye Govr caled them out to worke, (as was used,) but ye most of this new-company excused them selves and said it wente against their consciences to work on yt day. So ye Govr tould them that if they made it mater of conscience, he would spare them till they were better informed. So he led-away ye rest and left them; but when they came home at noone from their worke, he found them in ye streete at play, openly; some pitching ye barr, & some at stoole-ball, and shuch like sports. So he went to them and tooke away their implements, and tould them that was against his conscience, that they should play & others worke. If they made ye keeping of it mater of devotion, let them kepe their houses, but ther should be no gameing or revelling in ye streets. Since which time nothing hath been atempted that way, at least openly.[35]

The Puritans who left England came to America to establish a government in which the church and state would be one. They governed themselves, worked hard in the service of God, and prospered. From Massachusetts, the heart of the Puritan settlements, dissident groups migrated to Rhode Island and Connecticut. The Puritans regulated almost every aspect of their lives, including pastimes, amusements, and sports. On the Sabbath, church attendance was compulsory and amusements forbidden, and on all other days, men were expected to work a full day. In 1633, a court of the Colony of Massachusetts Bay ordered all men to ". . . worke the whole day alloweing convenient tyme for foode & rest . . ." and ". . . that noe person howsehoulder or other, shall spend his time idely or un-

---

35. *Bradford's History "Of Plymouth Plantation"* (Boston: Wright and Potter Printing Co., 1898), pp. 134-135.

profitably under paine of such punishment as the Court shall think meete to inflicte . . ."[36]

In early New England days there were few violations of the many regulations against sport and amusements. The records of the Court of Assistants from 1630 to 1643 list well over 300 crimes and misdemeanors, but only two offenses for sport and amusements. John Baker was ordered whipped for fowling on the Sabbath day and Laurence Waters' wife and others were "admonished to avoyde dancing."[37] New Englanders also attempted to forbid the native Indians from play when in 1646 they stated, "Whosoever shall play at their former games shall pay 10 s."[38]

However, from the middle of the seventeenth century to the end of the eighteenth, additional regulations appeared to be necessary to control the sport activity of the citizenry. From 1657 to 1786 in Boston regulations were passed banning football, sledding, gaming for money, stage plays and theatrical productions, and all Sunday pastimes. In spite of an edict against horse racing, notice of races appeared in Boston newspapers as early as 1715.

The laws, especially those forbidding sport and other secular activities on Sunday, came to be called *Blue Laws,* because the regulation for conduct on Sunday was printed at New Haven, Connecticut in 1781 on blue paper. Sunday ordinances were mostly passed to restrict pastimes and sport, but some did guarantee rights such as fishing and fowling. It was not long before ministers were condoning fishing as a recreation which was both necessary and pleasant. Other "approved" reasons for pastimes and games included physical health and renewal of the soul to return to more productive work. Play was thought to strengthen children, and even adult men could recreate and return to their labors refreshed. In 1739 Armstrong exhorted New Englanders:

When the Body has long wearied with Labour, or the Mind weakened with Devotion, it's requisite to give them ease; then the use of innocent and moderate Pleasures and Recreations is both useful and necessary, to Soul and Body; it enlivens Nature, recruits our Spirits, and renders us more able to set about serious Business and Employment. For to intermix no Gratifications, nor Diversions with our more Serious Affairs, makes the Mind unactive, dull, and useless.[39]

---

36. *Records of the Court of Assistants of the Colony of the Massachusetts Bay,* 1630-1644, Vol. II (Boston: County of Suffolk, 1904), p. 37.

37. *Records of the Court of Assistants of the Colony of the Massachusetts Bay,* 1630-1644, Vol. II (Boston: County of Suffolk, 1904), p. 9 and p. 75.

38. Edward H. Spicer, *A Short History of the Indians of the United States* (New York: Van Nostrand Reinhold Co., 1969), p. 175.

39. J. Armstrong, *A Discourse uttered in Part at Annauskeeg Falls in the Fishing Season, 1739* (Boston: S. Kneeland and T. Green in Queen Street, 1743), p. 1.

As immigrants from other religions and countries settled in New England and mingled with the colonists, the Puritans' attitude toward pastimes softened. By the middle of the eighteenth century, towns had grown and individuals had prospered. Although the Puritan ethic of hard work and sobriety persisted, material comforts and leisure resulting from economic success permitted some pastimes and amusements. However, pastimes, rather than organized sport, were the order of the day.

To meet their religious needs the American settlers erected small clapboard churches, and to meet their social needs they built taverns. Painter calls the tavern, ". . . the most remarkable social center that America has ever produced."[40] Taverns sprang up all over the colonies—just about a day's ride from each other so that travelers could make their way comfortably from Canada to the south and from the east to the western frontier. In Massachusetts a tavern was required in each new village so that travelers, meetings, and other village functions could be accommodated. The Hall Tavern at Charlemont was typical. On the first floor the bar room was reserved for the men. Behind the bar were the regular customers' own mugs, perhaps of pewter, and their marked supply of beer, ale, or rum. The tavern keeper, a highly respected resident, was responsible for being sure that the men did not imbibe too much. The sparsely furnished room centered around the fireplace where the men could warm themselves on cold days. Across the hall from the bar room was the parlor in which the women could gather, since they were excluded from the bar room. In the rear was a large dining room with a long table to accommodate the tavern keeper's family and also travelers. Upstairs were a few bedrooms and the ball room, which was used not only for dancing, but also for other gatherings such as town meetings, town courts, and weddings. The ballroom with its fireplace and small stage or enclosure for musicians usually had benches along each wall. The walls were often decorated with stencilled colored flowers. One tale suggests that young women who were not invited to dance and left sitting on the bench came to be called "wall flowers." Ordinarily the tavern was close to the church, because with services both morning and afternoon and the church probably unheated, the tavern provided a welcome place to have refreshments and get warm between the services.

During the seventeenth and eighteenth centuries the taverns were used for social occasions, entertainment, and a place for diversion. Travelers arrived with news of other settlements or even perhaps of European countries; newspapers sometimes could be found at the tavern and studied; and discussions of important local or regional matters took place. Bowling, billiards,

---

40. Ruth E. Painter, "Tavern Amusements in Eighteenth Century America," *The Leisure Class in America,* ed. Leon Stein (New York: Arno Press, 1975), p. 92.

FIG. 2.9 Frary House, a New England tavern. HISTORIC DEERFIELD, INC., DEER-FIELD, MASSACHUSETTS.

FIG. 2.10 Hall Tavern bar room. HISTORIC DEERFIELD, INC., DEERFIELD, MASSACHUSETTS.

and board games were popular pastimes. Travelers passing through might pause in the village if there were good fishing nearby or might enter local contests of prowess or match their shooting skills against the local villagers. Many such informal pastimes took place in the tavern yard.

Dinners, weddings, and festivals were organized to celebrate special occasions, and these frequently included social dancing. Dancing was considered a necessary skill for ladies and gentlemen and an important part of their training. It was also considered suitable exercise for young ladies, who had few other activities available to them. Dancing masters set up their schools in all the major cities where they taught the fashionable dances of the day as well as manners, a graceful carriage, and deportment in genteel company.

FIG. 2.11 Ballroom in the Frary House. HISTORIC DEERFIELD, INC., DEERFIELD, MASSACHUSETTS.

Sometimes taverns were the destination of pleasure seekers from nearby villages. One such group of young women and men in Massachusetts rode horseback from Palmer to South Hadley, a distance of 29 miles, to view the canal. They spent the night in the publick house in South Hadley and returned the next day by a different route. In the winter sleighing parties traveled to another village for supper or supper and dancing. Ice skating on New England's frozen ponds was a favorite winter pastime.

The tavern was the center for another type of entertainment, at which local residents marveled at wild beasts shown by an itinerant animal trainer. Bear and bull baiting, and also cock fighting, were not uncommon in colonial America and could be found at some taverns.

While the daily lives of the New Englanders were occupied with work and the Sabbath occupied with worship, there were many gatherings at which they combined duty with pleasure. Training Days or Muster Days, Lecture Days, Election Days, and "bees" provided occasions for worthwhile or civic functions accompanied by contests, games, frolics, and balls. Beginning in 1639 the men organized defense units for the towns, assembling on Training Days or Muster Days for artillery practice. The protection of the settlements was serious business, but as the settlements became more established and the Indians removed, amusements, social events, and athletic contests followed the serious business of training.

> Women and children alike looked forward to these days as a holiday, which offered a welcome break in the monotony of New England life. The Puritan tradition prevailed, however, for only an innocent diversion was anticipated. The exercises were always preceded by prayers and the singing of psalms . . At the turn of the century it acquired a more pronounced social complexion and became more and more a day of festivity and merriment. . . . Games, gingerbread, and grog made their appearance . . .[41]

At a 1704 Training Day the winner of the "Olympiak Games . . . has some yards of Red Ribbin presented him [which] being tied to his hatband . . . he is Led Away in Triumph. . . ."[42]

Lecture Days provided the earnest Puritans with opportunities for midweek addresses on religious topics. It also permitted a break in the work week. The thrifty New Englanders might bring extra produce with them to barter or sell. As Lecture Days grew, amusements and pastimes came to be part of the gathering. Election Day was another time when the people assembled to perform a civic duty and remained to make the most of a social occasion.

The "bee" is an American term thought by some to allude to the social or communal character of the bee's work, and by others to have no connection with the insect. In many parts of colonial America a "bee" signified bringing people together for a combination of work and play. Barns were raised, corn husked, apples prepared for cider, sauce, or drying, wood sawed, and quilts quilted. In the early spring "sugaring-off" provided occasions for testing the year's new maple syrup. To make the work time pass

---

41. H. Telfer Mook, "Training Day in New England," *New England Quarterly,* December, 1938, p. 690.

42. *The Journal of Madam Knight,* ed. of 1825 (New York: Peter Smith, 1935), p. 37.

quickly there might be impromptu contests, but after the work there would be more contests, wrestling, and usually dancing.

FIG. 2.12   A barn raising, example of a work "bee." Courtesy of Enoch Pratt Free Library, Baltimore, Maryland.

From the beginning, education was valued and, as early as 1647, just twenty years after the founding of the Massachusetts Bay Colony, every town of fifty householders was required to teach reading and writing. Even earlier, in 1635, the Boston Latin School was established and a year after that Harvard College opened. Other colonies followed Massachusetts' lead and soon public school education was accepted throughout New England. Few schools concerned themselves with anything but the rudiments of a classical education, but some viewed some form of activity as beneficial. One reason for providing exercise programs was a growing concern over the health of the students. Benjamin Rush, for example, suggested that children should exercise every day so that they would be prepared for later life.

Books for children taught proper conduct along with reading. Even *The Little Pretty Pocket Book Intended for the Instruction and Amusement of*

Little Master Tommy and Pretty Miss Polly, published in 1762, described many children's games in rhyme, each with a moral lesson.

Thread the Needle

Here Hand in Hand the Boys unite.
And form a very pleasing Sight:
Then thro' each other's Arms they fly,
As thread does thro' the Needle's Eye.

And the moral:

Rule of Life

Talk not too much; sit down content;
That your discourse be pertinent.

Hop-Scotch

First make with chalk and oblong Square,
With wide Partitions here and there;
Then to the first a Tile convey;
Hop in—then kick the Tile away.

Rule of Life

Strive with good sense to stock your Mind,
And to that Sense be virtue joined.

Marbles

Knuckle down to your Taw.
Aim well, shoot away:
Keep out of the Ring
And you'll soon learn to play.

Moral

Time rolls like a Marble,
And awes every State:
Then improve each Moment,
Before 'tis too late.[43]

Such practical admonitions undoubtedly helped justify the play of children at a time when they were perceived as little adults and generally ex-

---

43. Cited in Margery A. Bulger, "Ali Ali in Free . . . The Games Children Played in Colonial America," *Early American Life,* August 1975, pp. 48-49, 82.

pected to behave accordingly. With or without the moral lesson, however, the children of the new nation played, like those before them and like their own descendants, games such as "I Spy" or "Hide and Seek," "Button Button," "Blindman's Buff," "Prisoner's Base," "Hide the Thimble," "Town Ball," and "One O'Cat, Two O'Cat."

New York

Social life in early New York was much more active and gay than in Puritan Boston. Good food, good drink, and gambling were all part of the lives of the emerging upper class or European gentry who had emigrated to New York. Out on Long Island some of the gentry maintained their own game preserves and deer parks, reminiscent of those in England. Fines were charged if anyone other than the host's guests were found killing a deer in the private parks. In town, shooting matches were advertised with prizes offered such as a gold watch or a house and lot.

The sporting gentry found Long Island ideal for fox hunting and horse racing. Named after its English counterpart, Newmarket, the first course was situated where Garden City now stands. From 1670 to 1775 there were two race-meetings a year at Newmarket and others near Jamaica. In 1736 admission was charged to see a race in Manhattan which brought over one thousand persons to the event. During the eighteenth century English and American horses vied for championships, and just prior to the Revolution the international rivalry was reported at its height, as demonstrated in the following notice from May 16, 1768:

> The Hundred Pounds purse at Upper Marlborough, has been won by Dr. Hamilton's English horse Figure, beating the, hitherto, terrific Salem. As many incidents occur in a four mile heat, and we have no particulars of the sport, it is but justice to the gallant American that the public should suspend its decisive opinion until the champions have met at Philadelphia, next October; when the vanquished may recover, or the victor be confirmed in the triumphant post which, to the astonishment of thousands, he has so successfully contended for. Figure was got by a beautiful horse of that name, the property of the Duke of Hamilton; ran five times in England and won one plate; he also started two years ago against five horses at Annapolis and beat them in four fine heats. Salem, a grandson of Godolphin Arabian, and got by Governor Sharp's valiant Othello, has run about nine times, and till this event proved in every dispute unconquerable. The gentlemen of Philadelphia have raised a purse of £ 100 and two of £ 50 each, to be run for over their course in the Fall. The particulars adapted to the late increase of fine horses in the Northern Colonies will be advertised very soon.[44]

---

44. Cited in Esther Singleton, *Social New York Under the Georges, 1714-1776* (New York: D. Appleton, 1902), p. 268.

In addition to the shooting matches, horse racing, and "animal" sports, the less adventurous city dwellers could enjoy bowling, golf, battledore, tennis or fives and cricket. Boating, fishing, and swimming for pleasure were popular and enjoyed by many. Both gentlemen and ladies were invited to take advantage of the bathinghouse near North River, perhaps wearing a cork jacket proclaimed for its usefulness in saving people from drowning. Other New Yorkers found "Their diversions in the Winter . . . Riding Sleys about three or four Miles out of Town, where they have Houses of entertainment at a place called the Bowery."[45] Dancing was a popular pastime for both ladies and gentlemen. Mr. Hulet, a dancing master who opened his public Dancing School in New York in 1770, taught the minuet, country dances, and arranged " . . . a private class for those gentlemen who had not learned the Hornpipe."[46]

Pennsylvania

Farther south, not far from New York, late in the seventeenth century, William Penn undertook to establish a Quaker community. Before arriving in the New World to assume leadership in his new colony, he devised a code of laws under which the Society of Friends would live in the new land free of religious persecution. These laws, enacted by the Pennsylvania Assembly in 1682, regulated strict Sabbath behavior, and banned many pastimes and amusements. According to Jable:

> . . . Penn placed two provisions in *The Great Laws* which regulated what he considered licentious activities. The first measure banned "rude and riotous sports." Anyone introducing prizes, stage-plays, masques, revels, bullbaits, or cockfights into the colony was subject to a fine of twenty shillings or ten days imprisonment at hard labor. . . . The second measure dealt with lesser evils. Those convicted of playing cards, dice, or lotteries received a fine of five shillings or a five-day sentence in the house of correction.[47]

By the end of the century the Society of Friends, or Quakers, were influenced by other groups who settled in Pennsylvania, and by the prosperity they enjoyed in the new country. A revision of *The Great Laws of 1682* continued to forbid Sunday activities such as stage plays, cock fights, and lotteries, but permitted "innocent diversions" such as ice skating, swim-

---

45. *The Journal of Madam Knight,* ed. of 1825 (New York: Peter Smith, 1935), p. 55.

46. Shirley Wynne, "From Ballet to Ballroom: Dance in the Revolutionary Era," *Dance Scope* 10, no. 1 (1975/1976): 72.

47. Thomas Jable, "Pennsylvania's Early Blue Laws: A Quaker Experiment in the Suppression of Sport and Amusements, 1682-1740," *Journal of Sport History* 1, no. 2 (November, 1974): 109.

ming, hunting, and fishing. As the growing number of wealthy, elite Philadelphians moved to the suburbs, and the city became a mix of nationalities and religions, amusements formerly frowned upon became more and more acceptable. Dancing schools opened; bowling, billiards, bull-baiting, and cock fighting were conducted openly. However, conservative Philadelphians requested bans on the increasingly popular taverns and horse racing.

One famous Philadelphian, Benjamin Franklin, promoted the importance of both education and physical activity. In his *Proposals for the Education of of Youth* he suggested:

> That the boarding Scholars diet together, plainly, temperately, and frugally. That to keep them in Health, and to strengthen and render active their Bodies, They be frequently exercis'd in Running, Leaping, Wrestling, and Swimming, etc.[48]

Franklin called swimming "necessary and life-preserving," and pointed out in *The Art of Swimming Rendered Easy,* "The only obstacle to improvement . . . is fear: and it is by overcoming this timidity, that you can expect to become a master of the preceding acquirements. . . . The exercise of swimming is one of the most healthy and agreeable in the world."[49] The book includes sections on: How to Begin to Swim, Swimming Backwards, Diving, Swimming Like a Dog, To Tread the Water, To Swim Holding Up One Leg, and To Swim on the Belly Holding Both Hands Still.

Out in the suburbs, social clubs which focused on sport provided a variety of activities. One of the early clubs, the Schuylkill Fishing Company, was formed in 1732 and permitted its members to fish and hunt ". . . in the romantic solitudes of the river Schuylkill," thus proving that work and play "may be handmaidens under proper regulations and restrictions."[50] The Gloucester Fox Hunting Club was founded in 1766 by eighteen gentlemen to maintain a kennel of fox hounds which were used in hunting two days a week. Another social sport group active during the Revolution had begun as Troop of the Light Horse of the City of Philadelphia which was founded in the mid-eighteenth century. At times, the social activities of these sport clubs appear to have been more important than the sport, but they did provide opportunity for sport in an elite social setting.

---

48. Benjamin Franklin, *Proposals for the Education of Youth in Pennsylvania, 1749* (Ann Arbor: William L. Clements Library, 1927), p. 10.

49. Benjamin Franklin, *The Art of Swimming Rendered Easy, Dr. Franklin's Advice To Bathers* (Glassow: Printed for the book sellers [184-?]), p. 4.

50. W. Milnor, *Historical Memoir of the Schuylkill Fishing Company* (Philadelphia: Judah Dobson, 1830), p. 2.

The South

If anywhere in colonial America sport was a function of class, it was in Maryland, Virginia, and the south. Many of these immigrants, unlike their New England counterparts, had not left England to establish a different type of society, and thus continued the customs of their families, schools, government, and the Anglican Church. In the new country, the system of large estates, the availability of slaves, and the English system of government made English life and customs possible.

Young southern gentlemen were expected to excel in dancing, fencing, riding, and conversation. Dancing teachers often traveled from plantation to plantation to reach their pupils. In addition to dancing, the master sometimes taught fencing. Hunting was the most popular sport, but had to be adapted to the countryside of the new country. Virginia gentlemen in the first decades of the colony hunted with hawks, as well as hounds, and guns. Horse racing was a popular sport and very much a social occasion, not only in Virginia but in Maryland and all over the south. Kennard reports:

> The early Marylanders reflected British tastes in the pursuits of pleasure, from the running of horse races to the wickets of cricket. In no way was Maryland society better reflected than in its adoration of horse racing. One gets the feeling of the importance of horse racing to the people by the announcement of Race Week in *The Maryland Gazette* which read: "ANNAPOLIS RACES will begin on Tuesday the 6th of October next. There will be Four Days Sport, a particular Account of which will be speedily inserted in this Gazette." Interclass elbow rubbing occurred at the race course, which was dominated by the aristocracy with an intrusion by the common folk.[51]

Sometime between 1730 and 1740 Bulle Rock, a race horse, was imported to Virginia for breeding purposes. After Colonel Tasker of Belair, Maryland, brought over the brood mare Salina, fine racers were produced for the increasingly popular sport. At Williamsburg, Virginia, races were held on the mile-long track each spring and fall. The Virginians at Williamsburg engaged in other pastimes for entertainment and diversion, among which were wrestling, quoits, Pall Mall, battledore and shuttlecock, fives or handball, trap ball, and bowling-type games.

By the mid-eighteenth century Charleston was the center of Carolinian society. While only a third of its almost 7,000 inhabitants were white, only a few of those were in the upper social group of clergymen, lawyers, doctors, and wealthy merchants. They were joined for the winter social season by plantation families who maintained town houses for the malaria and winter

---

51. June A. Kennard, "Maryland Colonials at Play: Their Sports and Games," *Research Quarterly* 41, no. 3 (1970): 392.

season, making Charleston society one of the most glittering in colonial America.

> Plays, balls and concerts enlivened the winter seasons, while the summers offered such diversions as horse races, cock fights, and outdoor musical programs at the Orange Gardens. Then there were the gentlemen's clubs that met regularly at the local taverns.[52]

Broken Traditions Under Slavery

In the American colonies most of the Africans were slaves and led a hard life of drudgery. They did not have command of their own persons and could be sold as a commodity. Some of the southern blacks became fighters or boxers and were set to fight against other slaves, to provide sport and betting opportunities for their white owners. Others became crews and raced for the pleasure and betting opportunities of whites. Kennard reports that black slaves fished and hunted in Maryland, and also attended horse races, and even raced at fairs.

Sundays, holidays, and, perhaps, late summer evenings would be the only time slaves could count their time as their own. In Carolina on Sundays they played pawpaw, huzzle-cap, and pitched pennies. And in Albany, New York the slaves are said to have celebrated the Dutch Pinkster Day by dancing in African dress to eel-pot drums.

The slaves looked forward to Christmas as a time allowing them to stop work for about ten days or, according to Kennard:

> . . . until the yule log burned out. During the holidays visiting, singing and dancing took place. Cabin floors were cleared and participants danced the Juba, a lively dance of African origin. This was accompanied by vigorous shouts, handclapping for rhythm, and a fiddle for melody.[53]

The Frontier

Great contrast existed between the seacoast towns and the frontier. An itinerant Anglican preacher in the Carolina backcountry found industrious but rough settlers who made a social occasion of the minister's visit, ". . . had but a small Congregation the Principal People generally riding abroad ev'ry Sunday for Recreation." He was shocked at "The open profanation of the Lords Day in this Province . . . Among the low Class, it is abus'd by

---

52. F.P. Bowes, *The Culture of Early Charleston* (Chapel Hill: The University of North Carolina Press, 1942), p. 9.

53. June A. Kennard, "Maryland Colonials at Play: Their Sports and Games," *Research Quarterly* 41, no. 3 (1970): 395.

Hunting fishing fowling, and racing—By the Women in frolicing and Wantoness. By others in Drinking Bouts and Card Playing—Even in and about Charlestown, the Taverns have more Visitants than the Churches."[54] This description might be applicable to many of the pioneers who pushed west from the eastern settlements to Kentucky, Indiana, Ohio, and Illinois.

While surviving was the crucial element of the frontier experience, amusements or contests did occasionally occur, sometimes even when the Indians took the frontiersmen captive. Daniel Boone recounts a shooting match which occurred when he was a captive:

> I often went a hunting with them, and frequently gained their applause for my activity at our shooting-matches. I was careful not to exceed many of them in shooting; for no people are more envious than they in this sport. I could observe, in their countenances and gestures, the greatest expressions of joy when they exceeded me; and, when the reverse happened, of envy.[55]

Informal activities such as those occurring around the eastern taverns also took place on the frontier. French and English explorers settled in Illinois in the late seventeenth century. Activities that were planned to meet work needs also met social needs. Barn raisings and quilting bees became social recreation. Hill notes that the English settlers made little distinction between leisure and work.[56] They turned almost any type of task into a contest; corn husking became husking bees, wood to be chopped became chopping bees, and fields were the objects of contests in ploughing matches. The casual activities such as wrestling matches and cock fighting added some zest to an otherwise dangerous and difficult existence.

Summary

The beginnings of sport in the United States were a unique blend of the customs and pastimes of the native Americans who lived on the continent at the time the explorers arrived, of the Europeans who colonized the eastern seaboard, and of the Africans who were brought here as slaves. The

54. Charles Woodmason, *The Carolina Backcountry on the Eve of the Revolution*, ed. R.J. Hooker (Chapel Hill: University of North Carolina, 1953), p. 47.

55. Daniel Boone, "The ADVENTURES of Col. Daniel Boon; containing a NARRATIVE of the WARS of Kentucke, 1798," in *The Discovery, Settlement and present state of Kentucke*, ed. John Filson (New York: Corinth Books, 1962), p. 65.

56. Phyllis J. Hill, "A Cultural History of Frontier Sport in Illinois, 1673-1820," Ph.D. dissertation, University of Illinois, 1966.

newcomers developed their own diversions which, while resembling their European pastimes, were adapted to the new land. Amusements and pastimes also differed from colony to colony. New England's strict laws forbidding all amusements on Sundays and permitting only "necessary" pastimes such as fishing at any time reflected the Puritan work ethic. In the southern colonies life was less restricted and pastimes as well as the sport of horse racing were popular.

In order to survive, the settlers copied the Indians' customs in hunting and fishing. Not so much during colonial days, but later, the Americans adopted native games such as lacrosse, and changed the natives' transportation craft, canoes and kayaks, to pleasure and sport craft. Of the colonial games brought over from Europe, stool ball and rounders evolved into baseball; golf, handball, and bowling survived, and Americans are still avid fans of the turf sports. One of the favorite pastimes of men and women except the pious New Englanders was dancing, whether in a city mansion, a Southern plantation, a tavern ballroom, or at the conclusion of a work "bee." Some African men were used by slave owners as boxers and rowers on which they could wager. The Africans preserved and adapted their dance, which later became the basis of American jazz dance.

Horse racing was the most organized sport prior to the Revolution. Sport-like activities prior to the Revolution provided entertainment at the tracks, a means to accomplish necessary tasks at "bees," and pleasure for the people who engaged in the games, amusements, and pastimes of the period.

Questions for Discussion

1. Select one of the Indian games presented in this chapter which is played in some form in the United States today. As far as possible, analyze the differences and similarities between the Indian game and the modern version of the game.
2. Contrast and compare a medieval tournament with the Tournament of Roses of the last decade.
3. What do all the bat-and-ball games of the medieval peasants have in common?
4. Deduce from what you know about medieval tournaments and other activities of the nobility, the sort of dancing they would be likely to engage in. Consider the sport activities of the peasants and attempt the same kind of educated guess about their dance. Be specific; analyze the kinds of bodily movements involved.

5. What factors contributed to the differences among the American colonists' attitudes toward sport?
6. Is there any element of the work "bee" in today's society? Describe a first-hand experience, if possible, or a newspaper or fictional account.
7. What was the impact of slavery on the experiences in sport and physical activity for the African immigrants?
8. What is the contemporary equivalent of the colonial tavern?

Suggestions for Further Reading

1. Brailsford, Dennis. *Sport and Society, Elizabeth to Anne.* Toronto: University of Toronto Press, 1969.
2. Culin, Stewart. *Games of the North American Indians.* New York: Dover, 1975.
3. Dulles, Foster Rhea. *America Learns to Play.* New York: D. Appleton-Century, 1940.
4. Haley, Alex. *Roots.* Garden City, N.Y.: Doubleday, 1976.
5. Hardy, Stephen H. "The Medieval Tournament: a Functional Sport of the Upper Class." *Journal of Sport History* 1 (1974): 91-105.
6. Strutt, Joseph. *The Sports and Pastimes of the People of England.* London: William Tegg, 1867.

Time Line

HISTORY

1776-1783
War of Independence
1787
Northwest Ordinance, ". . . schools and the means of education shall forever be encouraged"
1812
War of 1812
1821
First public high school, Massachusetts
1823
Monroe doctrine
1825
Opening of Erie Canal
1833
Oberlin College founded as first coed college in United States
1837
Invention of telegraph by S.F.B. Morse
1840
2,800 miles of railway tracks in U.S.

SPORT

1788
Race horse, Messenger, imported
1802
Opening of National Race Course, Washington, D.C.
1810
American boxer, Tom Molyneux, defeated by Britain's Tom Cribb
1814
Georgetown University students played handball
1816
First American yacht, *Cleopatra's Barge,* built
1823
Round Hill School founded
1823
Union Race Course, Long Island; American Eclipse defeated Sir Henry
1831
Catharine Beecher's *Course of Calisthenics for Young Ladies* published
1837
Mount Holyoke Seminary opened with exercise required

3 Pastimes and Sport in a Developing Country, 1776-1840

When tens of thousands, Southerners and Northerners alike, jammed the roads leading to the Long Island race course to see the famous horse American Eclipse race Sir Henry of Virginia in 1823, the United States as a nation had been in existence less than a half century. By this time, however, many Americans, particularly those in the Eastern towns and on Southern plantations, were financially secure and enjoyed the luxuries of the nineteenth century leisure class. Also in the early 1820's John Woods, traveling through the western state of Illinois, described a cornhusking bee.

> [The corn] is gathered in October and November, when they only take off the ears; but as the ears are covered with a large husk, they carry them as they are to the corn-crib, and then all the neighbours collect together to help husk it, and put it into the corn-crib. . . plenty of whiskey is generally found at one of the frolics . . . and they generally conclude with a dance.[1]

And, at about the same time, Joseph Cogswell and George Bancroft opened Round Hill School in Northampton, Massachusetts, with plans to "appropriate regularly a portion of each day to healthful sports and gymnastic exercises,"[2] for they reflected the growing concern of Americans both for education and for exercise, especially for sedentary city dwellers, to attain health.

These three incidents characterize the diversity of pastimes and sport in the United States from 1776 to 1840. With their homes and farms established and a little leisure for their personal interests, more and more early nineteenth-century Americans found time for amusements and sport. Benjamin Franklin, the successful printer, could pursue science, government, education, and swimming. The forceful Abigail Adams discussed

---

1. John Woods, "Two Years' Residence in the Settlement on the English Prairie, in the Illinois Country, United States" in *Early Western Travels, 1748-1846,* Vol. X, ed. R.G. Thwaites (Cleveland, Ohio: The Arthur H. Clark Company, 1904), p. 300.

2. Joseph C. Cogswell and George Bancroft, *Prospectus of a School to be Established at Round Hill, Northampton, Massachusetts* (Cambridge, Massachusetts, 1823), p. 17.

with her husband John, and her friend Thomas Jefferson, her advocacy of increased rights for women and of free public education for all children of Massachusetts, regardless of sex or wealth. In the South, Washington, Jefferson, Richard Henry Lee, and other wealthy planters delved into philosophical studies, politics, education, and also enjoyed a good hunt.

However, it must be remembered that almost all of the United States was rural and relatively underdeveloped. Long, hard days of physical labor were the usual pattern for everyone—men, women, and many children. By 1837 the country numbered 26 states, only three of which were west of the Mississippi. Although five cities—Boston, New York, Philadelphia, Baltimore, and Charleston—served as commercial and social centers, the vast majority of the population east of the Alleghenies were rural folk dwelling on small farms and in towns of no more than a few hundred people. In 1800 Americans, as the citizens of the new country were called, could count only 33 towns numbering 2,500 or more in population, but even in 1840 they could boast of only one hundred more towns and cities over 2,500. With the influx of some 12,000,000 immigrants, chiefly Irish, German, and African, the established families became the "Old American Families," reinforcing and widening distances between social groups. Social classes for white Americans were comparatively fluid, but distinctions *were* made between the Boston Brahmins and the newly arrived Catholic Irish in New England, between the Astors' wealthy group and the European immigrant in New York, and, in the South, among plantation owners, farmers, and slaves.

Sport and pastimes from the end of the Revolution to 1840 reflected the growth of the country, its diverse social groups, and the differences between the settled regions in the East and the frontiers just west of the Mississippi. This chapter will trace the development of certain sports as entertainment, amateur sport clubs, the early fitness movement, social pastimes and dance, college and school sport and physical education, differences between men's and women's activities, and the pastimes and amusements found in western states such as Kentucky, Michigan, and Illinois.

Sports and Pastimes in the Settled Regions

Sporting interests of men living in the settled regions included horse racing, boxing, and cock fighting. Women frequented the fashionable race days at Annapolis, Maryland, and Williamsburg, Virginia, but the boxing ring and cock pit were male domains. The women occasionally joined the socially elite hunting parties, but again it was usually the men and boys who assumed the responsibility for hunting game to supply the family table.

Yachts, rowboats, and other pleasure craft appear to have been enjoyed mostly by men. Children engaged in the timeless games of hop scotch, jump rope, and "base, or goal ball." While life continued to be a struggle for existence for most Americans, especially the first-generation immigrants, the crowds of more than 60,000 who attended a horse race in 1823 give evidence that sport as entertainment was part of early nineteenth-century life in the United States.

Sport as Entertainment

Horse Racing

Before and immediately following the Revolutionary War, Alexandria and Williamsburg, Virginia, and Annapolis, Maryland, were racing centers, attracting the leading citizens of the area. During the war horses belonging to Tories were confiscated and numerous American horses pressed into war service, but, by 1790, horse racing was again a favorite pastime of many Americans. Although the races were sponsored by and contested among the wealthier classes, all sorts of people attended. During the races betting was often heavy, and occasionally small fortunes were won or lost. Jockeys and trainers were drawn predominantly from the ranks of both free and slave black men, particularly in the South. This pattern continued throughout the nineteenth century.

In the late eighteenth century, interest in improving the American horse brought several outstanding English horses to the United States. Two horses, the filly Mambrina, and Messenger, both sired by the famous Mambrino, were purchased in the 1780's for breeding purposes. A third, Diomed, was acquired in 1798 by Colonel Hoomes in Virginia. Thus, before 1800 excellent blood lines had been established for the future of horse racing in this country. Both American Eclipse, who raced in the 1823 match against Sir Henry, and Hambletonian, famous sire of many trotters, were the descendants of Messenger. However, the American horse, Justin Morgan of Randolph, Vermont, became a legend in his own time, and established the popular line, the Morgan horse.

The opening of the National Race Course at Washington, D.C., in 1802 made it possible for the nation's political leaders to leave the affairs of state occasionally and venture out from the new capital to attend the races. In nearby Maryland informal races had been held since the middle of the eighteenth century. The first permanent course was opened in Maryland in 1820 about three miles from Baltimore. In 1821 public racing was legalized in Queens County, New York, and at the Union Course on Long Island. It was there in 1823 that the famous encounter occurred between American Eclipse and Sir Henry of Virginia. It was the first of several North-South

FIG. 3.1 Maryland Jockey Club, Pimlico, 1802. Courtesy of the Enoch Pratt Free Library, Baltimore, Maryland.

horse races, perhaps symbolizing the growing sectionalism in the country, and captured the imagination of thousands of Americans. On the day of the race, the roads leading to the Union Park were clogged with people, probably over 60,000. American Eclipse came home the victor in two out of three races in the first sport event in the United States to attract such a large crowd. Was the interest generated by sectionalism, the identification with a winner, the possibility of gain through wagering, the congeniality of a social gathering, a change in the moral climate of the country, or a combination of these factors?

When the weekly *Spirit of the Times* appeared, local races were advertised and also matches from as far away as Tennessee and Kentucky. In one issue in the 1830's races were announced for Harper's Ferry, Baltimore, Gloucester, Greensburgh, Nashville, Lawrenceville, and Columbia, Kentucky with purses varying from $100 to $500.

Boxing

In the late eighteenth and early nineteenth centuries, a few financially and socially elite men in both the South and the North took up the art of boxing. Many young men of the Southern gentry were familiar with the sport since they had attended college in England where it was popular. In this country, slave owners encouraged the best fighters among their slaves to train extensively and then arranged for them to fight slave boxers from neighboring plantations. The black boxers also fought among themselves for their own entertainment. When the owners planned the fight, there was often heavy betting, and occasionally boxing superiority led to the freedom of the slave.

One successful slave boxer in Virginia, Tom Molyneux, was granted his freedom by his owner because of his expertise as a boxer. He wandered north to New York City where he boxed with longshoremen, noted for their strength and roughness. In 1809 he traveled to England and found the American-born black boxer, Bill Richmond, who coached him and helped arrange matches against some of England's best fighters, against whom Molyneux won. He was then matched with the famous British champion, Tom Cribb, for the unofficial world championship. They met in 1810 under the London Prize Ring Rules and fought forty-four grueling rounds.[3] The December 19, 1810 *Times* of London reported "The battle lasted fifty-five minutes, in which 44 rounds took place, and it was all hard fighting. Both

---

3. The London Prize Ring Rules, not officially promulgated until 1838 by the British Pugilists Protective Association, stipulated that no gloves were to be used; wrestling holds were allowed; a round ended when one or both contestants were knocked down; and at the end of each round, thirty seconds of rest followed. Failure of either man to meet his opponent in the center of the ring resulted in disqualification.

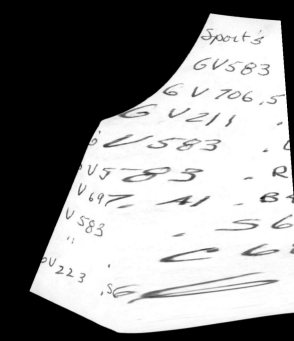

FIG. 3.2   Tom Molyneux: First noted United States boxer.

the combatants were dreadfully beaten; and they were almost deprived of sight. . . . The *Black* gave in rather from weakness than want of courage. He is certainly one of the most promising pugilists that has appeared." A year later Molyneux was defeated by Cribb in eleven rounds.

The first American to win boxing recognition was Bill Richmond, Molyneux's mentor. Born on Staten Island, he went to England as a boy. After he established a reputation as a fine fighter, he became a valet to Lord Camelford, a devotee of horse racing, cock fighting, and boxing. Richmond fought a number of highly publicized matches between 1800 and 1818, one of which, with Cribb, he lost by a decision.

As practiced by these early professional fighters, boxing was neither an art nor a science. Rather, it was a contest of the ability to withstand punishment. Bare-knuckled and physically strong men pummeled one another, sometimes for several hours, until one of them dropped. There were few rules and many matches degenerated into kicking, biting, and gouging free-for-alls, which occasionally ended in the death of one or the other participant. Scorned by many Americans, professional boxing in these years frequently attracted the rougher element in the cities and as a result was banned in local communities and in some states. However, some attempts were made to make the sport respectable. Promoters advertised boxing as "athletic exercise," while others offered lessons to "gentlemen."

Cock Fighting

In city and town, village and rural farm or plantation all over America during this period, cock fighting was one of the more popular sports for men. Although it was not universally approved, many wealthy gentlemen enjoyed the pastime and bred and maintained fighting cocks. Its general popularity carried it past its existence as an early colonial tavern sport, unlike animal baiting which lost favor during the nineteenth century. Cock fighting eventually became almost exclusively associated with the lower classes.

Pedestrianism

Beginning in the 1820's and reaching a peak in the '40's and '50's, pedestrianism or walking races became a craze which attracted many persons in the towns, villages, and at fairs. "Walkers" or pedestrians, moving from town to town and acquiring a reputation, would challenge the best walker of a community to a race, from a quarter of a mile to ten, twenty, or thirty miles. Frequently preceded by an advance man who would promote the contest and arrange the betting, some "peds" attracted crowds of 25,000. Although most races, particularly those over long distances, were conducted on roads, many owners of private race tracks sponsored and promoted pedestrian races. The "peds" were popular until the early 1880's when amateur track and field began to replace the professionals.

FIG. 3.3 Cock fighting, a sport of the early nineteenth century. Courtesy of the Enoch Pratt Free Library, Baltimore, Maryland.

Rowing

By 1811 races among longshoremen in light barges and contests between English and American seamen were held on the Hudson River off Manhattan. On February 18, 1832, the *Spirit of the Times* reported a race between nine boats near Philadelphia. Each boat was manned by a single rower and raced a five-mile course for a prize of $20 "or a new boat of the same value."[4] Rowing was also popular among middle-class young men who began to form their own boat clubs in the 1820's and 1830's in cities such as Savannah, Poughkeepsie, Philadelphia, New Orleans, Mobile, Biloxi, and Detroit. The founding of these clubs and their later introduction onto college campuses established rowing, especially crew, as an upper-middle-class pastime and sport.

---

4. *Spirit of the Times,* 18 February 1832, n.p.

Pastimes and Recreational Sport

Boating and Yachting

Many American cities of this period were located on rivers or lakes or on the Atlantic Ocean, and consequently boating and yachting were important sport activities. According to yachting historians, America's first vessel that might truly be designated a yacht was *Cleopatra's Barge,* built in 1816 in Salem, Massachusetts, by Retire Becket for one of the town's wealthiest citizens, George Crowninshield. As its name implies, the luxurious *Barge* had no purpose but pleasure. It was the forerunner of a class of ship that became more and more a status symbol of upper-class society. Yacht racing began in 1836, when Robert B. Forbes' *Sylph* and Commodore John C. Stevens' *Wave* raced off the Massachusetts coast. Organized yacht racing soon developed with the founding of yacht clubs in a number of major cities.

FIG. 3.4   Detroit Boat Club, circa 1873. Courtesy of Victor H. Wehmeier.

Fox Hunting

The formal hunt was a popular sport among the Southern gentry. George Washington, for example, was proud of his pack of hounds—Pilot, Music,

Countess, and Truelove—and pursued the fox as frequently as he could. Jefferson, too, greatly enjoyed a chase across the rolling Virginia country-side. Elaborate riding outfits for the hunt consisting of waistcoat and buckskin breeches were usually imported from England. The southern states of Maryland, Virginia, and the Carolinas were all well known for their fox hunting, because of the open fields, the climate, and the leisured way of life among the Southern plantation owners. However, there is also evidence of formal fox hunting as far north as New England throughout the eighteenth and nineteenth centuries.

Cricket

By the 1790's, there were cricket clubs in Boston and New York, although Philadelphia, with an influx of English woolen workers, soon emerged as the center for American cricket. Also, cricket was reported in Kentucky and Tennessee in the 1790's, but other than in the large cities, it did not survive, even in communities of English immigrants. One isolated example of cricket-playing, however, was in Albion, Illinois, where the English immigrants regularly played amid much comment from "American" neighbors.[5]

Clubs

In 1828 the United Bowmen, an exclusive Philadelphia men's archery club, organized to provide competition for its members. The membership was limited to 25, and, although it continued to 1859, the promotion of the sport was obviously not one of its goals. The Cincinnati Angling Club also limited its membership to 25 members who enjoyed "good fellowship" as well as the "delightful and healthy amusement of angling."[6] Among other elite sport clubs of Philadelphia was the fishing club on the Schuylkill River. New Yorkers, in contrast to the clubs, sometimes treated themselves to a carriage ride out on the Bowery Road, or further to Harlem for a picnic or feast in a local tavern, inn, or other house of entertainment. Similar trips might be taken in a sleigh in the winter by groups of as many as forty or fifty young people.

While sports such as horse racing provided entertainment for many and sport clubs were popular, especially with the upper class, most pastimes and amusements occurred within the family or with neighbors. Amusements could vary from a formal fox hunt in the South to bowling in the tavern yard in New York. Thus, although sport itself was not a common idea, the

---

5. Phyllis J. Hill, "A Cultural History of Frontier Sport in Illinois 1673-1820," Ph.D. dissertation, University of Illinois, 1966, pp. 81-84.

6. *Spirit of the Times,* 30 January 1832, n.p.

young country in the development of its culture included in its activities pastimes and amusements that would lead to sport.

The children of the period continued to play the traditional games of childhood. There are records of games from England and it is presumed that, as children from other parts of Europe arrived in America, some of their games found their way to the village common or nearby field. *The Boy's and Girl's Book of Sports,* published in 1839, included games such as tag, jump rope, instructions for leapfrog, blind man's buff, and base, or goal ball:

Base, or Goal Ball.—In Base, the players divide themselves into two equal parties, and chance decides which shall have the first innings. Four stones or stakes are placed from twelve to twenty yards asunder, as *a, b, c, d,* in the margin; another is put at *e.* One of the party, who is out, places himself at *c.* He tosses the ball to *a,* in front of whom one of the *in-party* places himself, who strikes the ball, if possible with his bat. If the ball, when struck, be caught by any of the players of the opposite side, who are scattered about the field, he is out, and another takes his place. If none of these accidents take place, on striking the ball he drops the bat, and runs towards *b,* or, if he can, to *c, d,* or even to *a,* again. If, however the boy who stands at *c,* or any of the out-players who may happen to have the ball, strike him with it in his progress from *a* to *b, b* to *c, c* to *d, d* to *a,* he is out. Supposing he can only get to *b,* one of his partners takes the bat, and strikes at the ball in turn. If the first player only get to *c,* or *d,* the second runs to *b,* only, or *c,* as the case may be, and a third player begins; as they get home, that is, to *a,* they play at the ball by turns, until they all get out. Then, of course, the out players take their places.[7]

Mary Livermore remembered children playing on the Boston Common on Saturday afternoon, as well as the contrasting Sabbatarian rigor of the Puritan Sunday in the 1820's.

. . . it was gay and vocal with little girls, attired in sunbonnets and aprons, "keeping house," and "playing school," "hide and seek" and "playing tag," and sometimes, it must be confessed, making "mud pies." It was Saturday afternoon, and the maternal injunction, "Keep your clothes clean!" was not in force on that half holiday, for the clean clothes for the next week were to be donned on Sunday morning . . .

The Sundays of my childhood were not enjoyable days, they were observed with such unnecessary rigor. . . . we children were prepared for the morning Sunday-school at nine o'clock. . . . The Sunday-school ended at half-past ten, when we adjourned from the vestry to the church. . . . When the church service was over we hurried home to the cold dinner. . . . At two o'clock we hurried back to the second session of the Sunday-school, then again to afternoon service in the church, and after that came an interminable prayer-meeting. . . . This

---

7. *Boy's and Girl's Book of Sports* (Providence: Geo. P. Daniels, 1839), p. 19.

prayer-meeting lasted until dark in the winter and until very nearly supper-time in summer.[8]

In the traditionally Dutch areas of New York and Pennsylvania burghers and farmers enthusiastically bowled and played skittles. Bowling on the green was particularly popular. Few were the taverns in New York that did not maintain a green for bowling or a wooden or stone platform for playing at king-pin or skittles. Some citizens would be found playing "kolf," which, it is thought, contained elements of the modern games of golf and hockey. The Dutch residents also were fond of kaetzen, a game possessing the rudiments of handball, in which the horsehair-filled ball was bounced against a nearby post, tree, or wall. Women played the game with a racket. In the winter, families of New York, Pennsylvania, and New England enjoyed ice skating, sledding, and other winter pastimes.

The forests, fields, streams, and lakes of this country, even in settled regions, were easily accessible. Hunters from both North and South enjoyed excursions into the forests, both as a practical means of procuring food and as a pastime. They pursued fowl such as geese, quail, partridge, and grouse, as well as animals ranging from deer and bear to squirrels, woodcocks, and rabbits.

The Early Fitness Movement

Although some people, such as Benjamin Franklin and Benjamin Rush, wrote about the benefits to health of physical exercise, not until the third decade of the nineteenth century was there a significant movement toward regular physical exercise pursued for the sake of physical fitness. Under the leadership of Dr. John E. Warren, Professor of Anatomy and Physiology at Harvard University, several prominent Bostonians promoted a gymnasium for Boston residents. Boston's Board of Aldermen provided land and Dr. Charles Follen instructed in gymnastics. Follen was a German immigrant who had studied with Friedrich Jahn, German patriot and *Turnvater,* or "Father of Gymnastics." After a year Follen was replaced by another German immigrant, Dr. Francis Lieber, who also established a swimming school, probably one of the first in the country.

In part because of the efforts of Catharine Beecher, a member of a prominent American family, public attention was called to the health and the physical needs of women. Four characteristics of "True Womanhood"—piety, purity, submissiveness, and domesticity—were inculcated into young women of the period. These social conventions tended to coerce

---

8. Mary A. Livermore, *The Story of My Life* (Hartford, Conn.: A.D. Worthington, 1899), pp. 37, 53-55.

middle and upper-class women to forego vigorous exercise, physical work, and healthful outdoor exposure, and to wear clothing which restricted circulation and movement. Beecher's 1831 book on the subject, *Course of Calisthenics for Young Ladies,* was intended for use in schools but had a broader application to women of all ages and circumstances. She presented her views on children's play:

> A long merry race upon the snow or sliding upon the ice, will put them in a delightful glow of health.[9]

In other Eastern cities some private gymnasiums were opened in the late 1820's. Intended primarily for men, they proved popular for a few years, but within a decade the "fad" of regular gymnastic exercise in a city gymnasium had waned.

Dance of the Period

Much has been written about the Puritan disapproval of dancing but although this attitude delayed the development of an American theatrical

FIG. 3.5 Dancing in 1798. Courtesy of the Enoch Pratt Free Library, Baltimore, Maryland.

9. *A Course of Calisthenics for Young Ladies* (Hartford, Conn.: H. and F.J. Huntington, 1831), p. 9. No author given; generally presumed to be Catharine Beecher's work.

dance tradition, it did not keep social dancing from flourishing in the period 1776-1840. Ballet, the theatrical dance form of the period, was primarily a French art form and performances like those seen in Paris did not reach the United States during the eighteenth century. Many of the dance teachers also came from Paris, the center of the eighteenth century dance world, in flight from the French revolution, because of their aristocratic associations. Refugees from the Haitian revolution also increased the ranks of American dancing masters, who advertised the latest "Paris dances" and taught and performed in many cities on the eastern seaboard.

The growing popularity of dancing was not without controversy. The Calvinist clergy, for example, frequently preached and wrote against what, to them, was a sinful pastime. Others, too, denounced dance, pointing out that:

. . . dancing was calculated to eradicate solid thought. . . . In fact, versatility of mind, hatred for study, or sober reflection, are the inseparable companions of dancing schools, and the miseries resulting from them are virtually incalculable.[10]

The supporters of dance were equally vocal. "Amelia," a correspondent to the Philadelphia *Minerva,* stated:

Whatever cautious cynics, in the delirium of their spleen, may allege to the contrary, dancing is incontestably an elegant and amiable accomplishment; it confers grace and dignity of carriage upon the female sex . . . it invigorates the constitution, enlivens the role of the cheek, and in its results operates as silent eloquence upon the hearts of men. Nature gives us limbs, and art teaches us to use them.[11]

The fashionable dances of the day included the minuet, courante, galliard, rigadoon, gavotte, cotillion, hornpipe, country dances, reels, and jigs. There were solo dances, dances for couples, and dances for more than one couple. The hornpipe, the only dance which was strictly a solo dance, and a male solo dance at that, was English in origin and was associated with sailors. John Durang, America's first professional dancer, was famous for his performance of the hornpipe as well as other dances.[12]

The courante, galliard, rigadoon, gavotte, minuet, and jig were sometimes performed as solo dances on the stage, but in social dancing they

10. Philadelphia *Minerva,* Dec. 10, 1796, cited in Joseph E. Marks, *America Learns to Dance* (New York: Exposition Press, 1957), p. 33.

11. Philadelphia *Minerva,* Dec. 17, 1706, cited in Joseph E. Marks, *America Learns to Dance* (New York: Exposition Press, 1957), p. 33.

12. Lillian Moore, "John Durang: The First American Dancer," in *Chronicles of the American Dance,* ed. Paul Magriel (New York: Henry Holt and Company, 1948), p. 18.

were couple dances. The minuet, the most popular of these dances, had been danced by the nobility in Europe and a very strict protocol was established for the choosing of partners. The highest ranking gentleman danced the first minuet of the evening with the highest ranking lady, who then chose the next most honored gentleman as her partner for the next dance and so on. The dancers were thus able not only to demonstrate their skill and grace in the dance, but also their rank and wealth.

The steps used in the dances were the same as those used in the ballet but performed in a smaller, less spectacular manner. The steps included *demi-coupe, jeté,* pirouette, balance, chasse, *pas de basqué* and others. The figures of each dance were set and had to be memorized. It is no wonder that dancing masters were in demand.

Once the dances were learned to the satisfaction of the master, the dancers were ready to attend the numerous balls and assemblies in the towns and on the plantations. The term "ball" was applied to any formal social occasion at which dancing was the chief part of the evening's entertainment. An assembly was a gathering sponsored by a group of people who provided dancing on a regular basis for themselves and their guests. There were also some public assemblies—some sponsored by dancing masters—open to anyone who could afford the price of a ticket.[13]

Dance as a social activity was not the exclusive province of the white citizens; the African slaves also danced. The slaves, separated even from those who might have been shipped with them from their African village or country, lost many of their customs. Dance, however, was transplanted and transformed among the slaves. They danced for their own enjoyment and for their masters' entertainment. They danced the buck and wing, cakewalk, and the buzzard lope. The water dance and juba were challenge or competitive dances, and then there were the jigs, cotillions, quadrilles, and reels. The slaves took every opportunity available to them to dance, and the Saturday night dance was a regular occurrence in some places.[14]

Exercise, Dance, and Sport in Colleges and Schools

American colleges, schools, and academies in the first fifty years of nationhood subscribed primarily to a conservative, rigid curriculum geared to the future social roles of the students as dictated by their families. Little

---

13. Joy Van Cleef, "Rural Felicity: Social Dance in 18th Century Connecticut," *Dance Perspectives* 65 (Spring, 1976): 12.

14. Lynne Fauley Emery, *Black Dance in the United States from 1619 to 1970* (Palo Alto, California: National Press Books, 1972), pp. 80-178.

concern was expressed for the health of the students in the colleges, grammar schools, or the academies. There were, however, a few educators who
did envision a broader concept of education, one which included a concern
for the health, vigor, and recreation of those in their charge. Joseph
Cogswell, George Bancroft, Catharine Beecher, and Mary Lyon established
schools with carefully thought out exercise programs. People such as
Beecher and Dr. William A. Alcott promoted physical education through
their writings. Alcott wrote over one hundred volumes and edited five
journals.

> . . . Alcott stressed physical activity for females and encouraged the use of
> physical education for shaping the character of all children. . . . He also em-
> phasized structured exercise for elementary grades such as running, swimming,
> wrestling, walking, skating, coasting, ball playing, and games of physical enrich-
> ment.[15]

Men's Colleges

Georgetown University, founded in Virginia in 1789, appears to be one of
the earliest institutions to concern itself with recreation and sport for
students. Stories are told of a fencing master in 1798 and regulations for the
times and places for swimming in the Potomac River. The 1814 *Prospectus*
of the college announced that "The garden and court where the students
recreate, are very airy and spacious" and that "Cleanliness, exercise, and
whatever contributes to health, are attended to with particular care."[16] The
boys, the youngest to be admitted being eight, began their day at 5:00 A.M.
in the summer and 5:30 A.M. in the winter and had a full day of prayer,
classes, study halls, and three short periods of recreation and one long
period of an hour and a half for recreation after the noon-day dinner. One
student remembered that the study hall was locked during the first hour of
the period, but that the precaution was not really necessary. In 1814 a
backboard for a handball-type game was erected with more courts added
during the next decades. In addition to handball, the students enjoyed fencing and boxing. In 1831 the university announced that dancing was taught
for an additional fee. In contrast to other early colleges, especially in New
England, which observed Sundays in the strict Puritan manner, Georgetown students were permitted to play ball on Sunday. One student wrote to
a friend:

---

15. Paul R. Mills, "William Andrus Alcott, M.D. Pioneer Reformer in Physical Education,
1798-1859," *76th Proceedings,* National College Physical Education Association for Men
(January 6-9, 1973): 32, 31.

16. *Georgetown College,* 1814, p. 2. Georgetown University Library.

. . . the Catholics think it no harm to play Ball, Draughts or play the Fiddle and dance of a Sunday, this will no doubt seem strange to you, it was so to me although I do not pretend to much sanctity, but say nothing of this in your letters home. I have never mentioned it as I know it would only make prejudices stronger, and I know it would make my mother uneasy.[17]

FIG. 3.6   Georgetown University handball court, 1814. Courtesy of the Georgetown University Library.

Other colleges of the period—Harvard, Yale, William and Mary, Liberty Hall (now Washington and Lee), Princeton, and St. John's College—appear to have concerned themselves with the intellectual and moral life of the students rather than with their physical well-being and use of leisure time. In fact, there probably was very little leisure time. The days were long and, in some schools, daily living quite demanding. Dartmouth College students, for example, were responsible for purchasing and cutting wood for the stoves in their rooms. Also, many had part-time jobs to help defray their college expenses.

The college officers expected good deportment and frequently passed regulations such as the one from St. John's in 1833 which "sternly prohibited (the students) from frequenting taverns, billiard or ball rooms."[18]

---

17. Student letter, August 27, 1836. Georgetown University Library.

18. T.F. Tilghman, "An Early Victorian College St. John's, 1830-1860," *Maryland Historical Society* 44, no. 4 (December, 1949): 254.

Diaries of the students from various colleges reveal that the students were serious about their studies, their religious and moral lives, and their families. They found pleasure in the simple tasks of everyday living. Samuel Oliver wrote of his brother Edward, a student at Dartmouth, ". . . he is sixteen years old today, wherefore I have given him 16 slaps on his back he is going to celebrate it by making some molasses candy this evening."[19]

However, many students did find some time for games and sport-like activities. Student letters and diaries from Dartmouth tell of almost daily football contests on the common, ice skating, sleighing, and swinging.

> June 15: . . . After school I went down to Mr. Chadwick's to swing. They have got the highest swing I ever saw. It is probably near 40 feet. It is fine sport to be swung in such a swing.

> December 4, 1835: Took my skates, went down to the river and enjoyed the noble, invigorating sport of skating for three or four hours. The ice was in fine order, . . .[20]

Students of the period were younger than today's students and played games such as town ball, rounders, and one o'cat. In spite of periodic bans, football, more like soccer than present-day football, was a popular activity. The young men also rowed, wrestled, ice skated, danced, swam, played quoits, boxed, and fenced. While some school administrators sought to prohibit such activity, particularly the more violent football games, others encouraged faculty members to join their students occasionally in such play, in order to present a proper example and to prevent rowdiness.[21]

A few colleges between 1825 and 1830 did provide an outdoor or indoor space for gymnastic apparatus but the only faculty supervision was that provided on a volunteer basis by interested individuals. For example, an instructor of German at Harvard College, Dr. Charles Follen, organized a gymnastics program for students in 1825 patterned after a German Turnplatz. Other such "gymnasiums" of the period were located at Brown University, Amherst College, and the University of Virginia.

Women's Colleges

In spite of the name seminary, Mount Holyoke Seminary in South Hadley, Massachusetts was a women's institution which required the students to meet standards similar to nearby Amherst College for men.

---

19. Samuel Oliver, *Journal,* Hanover, N.H., Nov. 25, 1835. Dartmouth College Archives.

20. Cyrus Parker Bradley, *Diary,* 1832. Dartmouth College Archives.

21. Roxanne M. Albertson, "Sports and Games in New England Schools and Academies 1780-1860," paper presented at the North American Society for Sport History, Boston, Massachusetts, April 16-19, 1975, pp. 4-5.

Students were required to be sixteen years of age or older and "of mature character," and able to undertake its rigorous academic curriculum. In 1836, a year before the founding of the Seminary the strong-willed intellectual founder, Mary Lyon, wrote: "When the church early felt her need of the services of young men, she began to found colleges . . . till more than eighty have been reared in our country . . . But what has been the voice of the church to female teachers?"[22] Lyon's own perception of the role of her institution is explicit in a long letter to Catharine Beecher:

> I have not been alone in considering it of great importance to establish a permanent seminary in New England for educating female teachers, with accommodations, apparatus, & somewhat like those for the other sex. Honorably to do this, from twenty to forty thousand dollars must be raised; and such a sum, raised for such an object, would form almost an era in female education.[23]

The financial stability, independent of an individual, sharply distinguished Mount Holyoke Female Seminary from most other female institutions at this time. In the Catalogue, Lyon justified the daily hour of required domestic duties not only as a means of saving money, but also as making the institution independent of the necessity of students' boarding with private families, and relieving it "from another source of depressing dependence—a dependence on the will of hired domestics." She emphasized that the other object of this arrangement is to promote the health of the students "by its furnishing them with a little daily exercise of the best kind."[24] This "daily exercise," although it was publicized enough so that it was sometimes assumed to be the sole kind of exercise expected of the students, was only the beginning of Lyon's struggle to improve female health: "The value of health to a lady is inestimable . . . much has been said on this subject, but enough has not been *done,* in our systems of education, to promote the health of young ladies." Under Lyon's careful eye, much was done. All students were required to walk for a mile every day, or to have a daily hour of "exercise in the open air." Furthermore, the Second Annual Catalogue, 1839, states: "All the members of the school attend regularly to composition, reading, and calisthenics." At 8:30 every evening, each student was on one of the four stairwells in the building, following a teacher's directions and example for twenty minutes of calisthenic exercises. "One girl wanted to be excused from Calisthenics because she wanted more

---

22. Edward Hitchcock, *The Power of Christian Benevolence illustrated in the Life and Labor of Mary Lyon* (Northampton: Hopkins, Bridgman, and Company, 1852), pp. 234-35.

23. Edward Hitchcock, *The Power of Christian Benevolence illustrated in the Life and Labor of Mary Lyon* (Northampton: Hopkins, Bridgman, and Company, 1852), p. 226.

24. Edward Hitchcock, *The Power of Christian Benevolence illustrated in the Life and Labor of Mary Lyon* (Northampton: Hopkins, Bridgman, and Company, 1852), p. 297.

time to read and pray, but Miss Lyon told her exercise was a religious duty."[25]

Schools and Academies for Boys

The advocates of school physical activities, few though they were, were unanimous in their conviction regarding the benefits to health of exercise and sport. The New Haven Gymnasium and the New Haven Classical and Commercial School provided swimming lessons three times a week in Long Island Sound during summer terms. At the Greenfield Hill Academy in Connecticut, Timothy Dwight held morning and afternoon recess periods. The boys were encouraged to take part in vigorous exercise including wrestling, leaping, and running so that they might ". . . find a nervous frame and vigorous mind."[26]

At the Round Hill School in Northampton, Massachusetts, established in 1823, physical education was made an integral part of the curriculum. The founders, Joseph Cogswell and George Bancroft, patterned their new school after the philosophy of European educators Fellenberg and Pestalozzi. In addition to providing a progressive, liberal education in the classics, they announced that they ". . . would also encourage activity of body, as the means of promoting firmness of constitution and vigour of mind, and shall appropriate regularly a portion of each day to healthful sports and gymnastic exercises."[27]

From the beginning they sought to fulfill this pledge by providing three play periods each day. A German immigrant, Dr. Charles Beck, who had been an active *Turner* in his homeland, was appointed to the faculty in January, 1825, with the title of Instructor in Latin and Gymnastics, thereby becoming, perhaps, the first instructor of physical education employed in an American school. In addition to gymnastics, Beck and the other instructors provided lessons in swimming, ice skating, wrestling, dancing, and other games and sports. John Forbes recalled his Round Hill days:

> . . . it was the pleasant and friendly relations of Mr. Cogswell and his masters with the boys, and the gymnastic and out-of-door education, which made Round

---

25. Mary Lyon Memorabilia, p. 61. Mount Holyoke History Room, Mount Holyoke College, South Hadley, Massachusetts.

26. Roxanne M. Albertson, "Sports and Games in New England Schools and Academies 1780-1860," paper presented at the North American Society for Sport History, Boston, Massachusetts, April 16-19, 1975, p. 2.

27. Joseph C. Cogswell and George Bancroft, *Prospectus of a School to be Established at Round Hill, Northampton, Massachusetts* (Cambridge, Massachusetts, 1823), p. 17.

Hill peculiar. The boys were taught to ride, had skating and swimming in their seasons, and wrestling, baseball and football; and, during the summer, excursions on the 'ride and tie' plan, of sometimes over a hundred miles and back, were undertaken, accompanied by Mr. Cogswell, who was himself a great walker.[28]

FIG. 3.7   Sketch of the Round Hill School, Northampton, Massachusetts. Courtesy of the *Daily Hampshire Gazette,* Northampton, Massachusetts.

It is now apparent that Round Hill School, although forced to close its doors in 1834 due to financial difficulties, was one of the most significant institutions in American sport and physical education prior to 1860. It was the first school to provide regular instruction in sport and exercise and to introduce German gymnastics in a school in the United States. While at Round Hill Beck translated Jahn's famous *Deutsche Turnkunst,* which was published in Northampton in 1828.

Schools and Academies for Girls

The seminaries and academies for girls of this period ranged from "finishing schools" teaching embroidery and manners to schools working

---

28. S.F. Hughes, *Letters and Recollections of John Murray Forbes* (Boston: Houghton Mifflin, 1899), p. 44.

FIG. 3.8 Illustration from F.L. Jahn, *Treatise on Gymnastics,* Northampton, Massachusetts, 1828.

toward high academic standards. In 1786, for example, Mrs. Smith of Annapolis, Maryland, announced the opening of a boarding school for young ladies who would be instructed in embroidery, netting, and drawing. Also included in the announcement was a statement about giving "great attention" to the young ladies' health. On the other hand, the Troy Female Seminary, under the influence of Mrs. Hale, provided instruction in substantive subjects.

Some schools approved mild exercise, such as walking, swimming, and horseback riding—sidesaddle, of course. Participation in games and sports was generally limited to mild contests of battledore and badminton, which might promote health through gentle exercise. Bowling contests were held on warm days during the exercise periods at Miss Pierce's Litchfield Academy in Connecticut. In 1829, at the Greenfield High School for Young Ladies in Massachusetts, the teachers and students were urged to join together in such games as battledore.

Through the efforts of Emma Hart Willard, the Troy Female Seminary, which later became Russell Sage College, was founded in 1821 in upper New York State. Willard's sister, Almira Hart Lincoln Phelps, conducted the day-to-day program of physical education, which included calisthenics, dancing, riding, and walking. Dancing, designed to improve "grace of

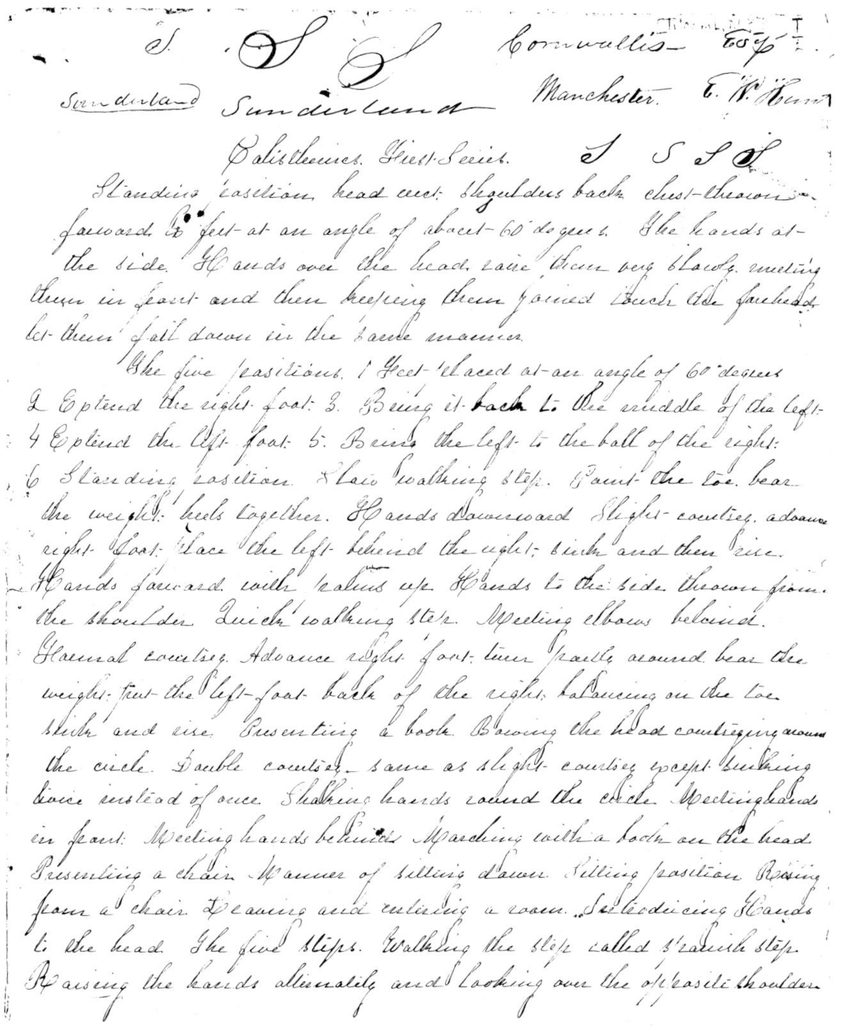
Cornwallis Esq
Sunderland Sunderland Manchester
Calisthenics. First Series.
Standing position head erect shoulders back chest thrown forward feet at an angle of about 60 degrees. The hands at the side. Hands over the head raise them very slowly meeting them in front and then keeping them joined touch the forehead let them fall down in the same manner.
The five positions. 1 Feet placed at an angle of 60 degrees 2 Extend the right foot. 3. Bring it back to the middle of the left. 4 Extend the left foot. 5. Bring the left to the ball of the right. 6 Standing position. Slow walking step. Point the toe. bear the weight. heels together. Hands downward Slight courtesy. advance right foot. place the left behind the right. sink and then rise. Hands forward with palms up Hands to the side thrown from the shoulder Quick walking step. Meeting elbows behind. Formal courtesy. Advance right foot. turn partly around. bear the weight. put the left foot back of the right. balancing on the toe sink and rise. Presenting a book. Bowing the head courtesying around the circle. Double courtesy same as slight courtesy except sinking twice instead of once. Shaking hands round the circle Meeting hands in front. Meeting hands behind. Marching with a book on the head. Presenting a chair. Manner of sitting down. Sitting position. Rising from a chair. Leaving and entering a room. Introducing Hands to the head. The five steps. Walking the step called Spanish step. Raising the hands alternately and looking over the opposite shoulder.

FIG. 3.9 Exercises prepared for use at Mount Holyoke Seminary, 1856. Courtesy of Mount Holyoke College Library.

motion'' and provide healthy exercise, was to be practiced only in the right atmosphere, that is, not in public. The girls were also encouraged to keep a journal in which they made observations about their own health, which would then determine the kind of exercise, food, and general living most suited to their particular constitutions.

In 1823 at the Female Monitorial School in Boston, William Bentley Fowle introduced a program of formal exercises based on German gymnastics, employing exercise, marching, running, jumping, and weight lifting. The program was eventually modified and reduced to dancing because of concern by many parents that the exercises were too similar to those practiced by men. Catharine Beecher, who had called public attention to the health needs of women, founded the Hartford Female Seminary in Connecticut in 1824. In its few years of existence students there followed perhaps the most vigorous and sustained program of exercise available to women in the 1820's. They devoted thirty minutes each half day to Beecher's system of light exercises, which she called Calisthenics. Accompanied by music and sometimes performed with light weights, the program was designed to exercise all the muscles harmoniously. She also encouraged the girls to ride horseback and play other games and sports. From 1833 to 1837, she directed the Western Female Institute in Cincinnati, Ohio, where she employed her educational theories.

Dancing was an important part of the activities of many girls' seminaries.

Merely-ornamental accomplishments will but indifferently qualify a woman to perform the *duties* of life, though it is highly proper she should possess them, in order to furnish the *amusements* of it. Yet, though the well-bred woman should learn to dance, sing, recite, and draw; the end of a good education is not that they may become singers, dancers, players, or painters; its real object is, to make them good daughters, good wives, good mistresses, good members of society and good christians.[29]

Activities of the Rural Areas and Frontier

Physical activities and sport in the frontier regions of early nineteenth century America were strongly affected by the geographic and psychological circumstances of the settlers. West of the Alleghenies most of the population was rural, dwelling on small farms and in towns of no more than a few hundred. The first families in each new region were required to be self-sufficient and to manufacture, build, grow, or do without items which

---

29. *Sentimental Beauties, and Moral Delineations,* cited by Joseph E. Marks, *America Learns to Dance* (New York: Exposition Press, 1957), p. 47.

might be easily purchased by people living in a city, or even in an eastern rural area. The periodic dangers posed by hostile Indians and natural calamities sharpened the settlers' sense of survival. Most families were still extremely isolated, depending for their food upon the game and fish nearby, as well as upon the produce from their own farm and garden.

FIG. 3.10   Wrestling included the practice of "gouging."

Perhaps the isolation and consequent loneliness, more than any other factor, affected the nature, the type, and the scope of sport and other recreational activities found on the frontier of America during the early nineteenth century. The recreational activities primarily served to bring people together and to meet their social needs. Sport-like activities in these regions were largely informal, spontaneous, sometimes rambunctious, and closely related to the daily life of the frontier.

Timothy Flint, sent by the Missionary Society of Connecticut to the Ohio Valley from 1815 to 1825, defended the often-maligned frontiersmen:

. . . it is true there are gamblers, and gougers, and outlaws . . . But . . . the backwoodsman of the west, . . . is generally an amiable and virtuous man. His general motive for coming here is to be a freeholder, to have plenty of rich land, and to be able to settle his children about him . . . His manners are rough. . .when in the woods he has a rifle on his back, and a pack of dogs at his heels . . . But remember, that his rifle and his dogs are his chief means of support and profit.[30]

Pastimes and Sport

Hunting and Fishing

Although many of the pastimes of the pioneers possessed strong elements of competition between individuals, two of the most popular activities were hunting and fishing, in which the competition was more personal and subtle. The rewards, however, were perhaps more obvious. Since the founding of Jamestown the colonial settlers had hunted and fished, as much because of economic necessity as for a recreational outlet.

From the rugged hill country of eastern Tennessee, Kentucky, and Pennsylvania, through the forests of the Ohio Valley, to the very edge of the sprawling Great Plains in western Illinois, the variety and quantity of fish and wild game staggered the imagination. The very earliest reports of this angler's and hunter's paradise were carried east by the explorers, hunters, and other adventurers in the early eighteenth century. Only the British government and the hazardous journey through and over the mountains prevented large numbers of colonists from establishing themselves there prior to the Revolution. Thus, it remained for a century the almost private preserve of the French hunter-trapper-trader and the few hardy frontiersmen from Virginia and the Carolinas who shared the game and the land with the Indians. The succeeding waves of pioneers depended heavily upon fishing and hunting.

Hunting quickly became a recreational as well as an economic factor in frontier life. Basically a solitary, highly individualistic activity, under some frontier conditions it became more efficient through organized group effort. Such an effort was the "ring hunt": "An army of men and boys from near-by settlements would form a vast encircling line of huntsmen around an area of perhaps forty square miles. Gradually they would close in the circle, driving ahead of them all the game they could scare up. When at last the ring was so small that the harried animals began to try to break through, the signal of a huntsman's horn would start a wholesale slaughter. Guns would be used as long as this was reasonably safe, and then clubs, pitchforks, any available weapon."[31] Such hunts often resulted in the slaughter of scores of bear, deer, squirrels, and large and small game birds. While perhaps not sport by today's standards, the hunt provided a winter's supply of meat to

---

30. Timothy Flint, *Recollections of the Last Ten Years,* ed. C. Hartley Grattan (New York: Alfred A. Knopf, 1932), pp. 171-72.

31. Foster Rhea Dulles, *America Learns to Play* (New York: D. Appleton-Century Company, 1940), p. 71.

be salted away in many household cellars. More closely related to competitive sport were the contests between teams of squirrel hunters, who could bring in hundreds and sometimes thousands of animals in one day.

Such organized hunts were, of course, not everyday events. Most hunting was done individually or in small groups. Even here, however, the hunt was usually bound to be successful because of the amount of available game and the unerring accuracy of the hunters. Records of shooting matches prove the frontiersmen's accuracy.

Equally convincing, however, was the practice of "barking off squirrels." The naturalist John James Audubon recounts the demonstration provided by Daniel Boone near Frankfort, Kentucky:

> We walked out together, and followed the rocky margins of the Kentucky River, until we reached a piece of flat land thickly covered with black walnuts, oaks, and hickories. As the general mast was a good one that year, Squirrels were seen gamboling on every tree around us. My companion, a stout, hale, and athletic man, dressed in a homespun hunting shirt, bare-legged and moccasined, carried a long and heavy rifle, which, as he was loading it, he said had proved efficient in all his former undertakings, and which he hoped would not fail on this occasion, as he felt proud to show me his skill. The gun was wiped, the powder measured, the ball patched with six-hundred-thread linen, and the charge sent home with a hickory rod. We moved not a step from the place, for the Squirrels were so numerous that it was unnecessary to go after them. Boone pointed to one of these animals which had observed us, and was crouched on a branch about fifty paces distant, and bade me mark well the spot where the ball should hit. He raised his piece gradually, until the *bead* (that being the name given by the Kentuckians to the *sight*) of the barrel was brought to a line with the spot which he intended to hit. The whiplike report resounded through the woods and along the hills, in repeated echoes. Judge of my surprise when I perceived that the ball had hit the piece of the bark immediately beneath the Squirrel, and it shivered it into splinters, the concussion produced by which had killed the animal, and sent it whirling through the air, as if it had been blown up by the explosion of a powder magazine. Boone kept up his firing, and, before many hours had elapsed, we had procured as many Squirrels as we wished . . .[32]

According to Audubon, such skill was not confined to marksmen of the caliber of Boone, as he witnessed the same feat by many others during the years he lived in Kentucky. He considered such skill very plausible, since ". . . every one in the state is accustomed to handle the rifle from the time when he is first able to shoulder it until near the close of his career."[33]

32. John James Audubon, "Kentucky Sports," from the "Missouri River Journals (1843)," in *Audubon and His Journals*, Vol. II, ed. Maria R. Audubon (New York: Charles Scribner's Sons, 1897), pp. 460-461.

33. John James Audubon, "Kentucky Sports," from the "Missouri River Journals (1843)," in *Audubon and His Journals,* Vol. II, ed. Maria R. Audubon (New York: Charles Scribner's Sons, 1897), p. 461.

Bees

Many necessary tasks were turned into social occasions when neighbors joined forces, with a challenge or contest as part of the work. With a history extending to the earliest colonial settlements, the husking and quilting bees, plowing matches, and cabin and barn raisings were part of life on the frontier. These practical work-oriented activities met some of the social, competitive, and economic needs of the pioneers. Chopping bees in the Illinois territory just after 1800 were held for the practical purpose of clearing land for planting or building. However, in bringing together a number of families, the normally slow, back-breaking task took on elements of play as the men chatted, joked, and contested their relative skills at chopping; the women conversed, enjoying what might be infrequent adult female companionship while the children played with one another. Further emphasizing the competitive aspect of the activity, prizes were frequently given to the person felling the most trees, husking the most ears of corn, or whatever the task might be. [34]

Many social gatherings besides bees, including weddings, holidays, and sleigh rides provided occasions for country dancing. The cotillion and the quadrille were dances for eight dancers in a square formation. The country dances and the reels, performed with one line of dancers facing another line of dancers, could often accommodate many dancers. The unique characteristic of the country dances was that it allowed a number of people to dance together without concern for rank.

Horse Racing

Horse racing moved west with the earliest permanent settlers. Newcomers to Kentucky, Tennessee, and Illinois came largely from the southern and border states of Maryland, Virginia, and the Carolinas, and brought with them their fondness for racing. Tracks were opened in Nashville, Tennessee and in Kentucky in Lexington and Louisville, which had the first circular track west of the Alleghenies. While the permanent tracks were located only in the larger cities, making it almost impossible for rural farmers and frontier residents to attend, the local races, held in conjunction with county fairs and festivals, were followed with keen interest. In Kentucky the breeding of horses became a major pursuit, and jockey clubs were formed, helping to get racing under way.

Matches and Contests

The tavern and inn in the rural areas served several functions. "For villagers and townspeople and many farmers, . . . the inn was indispens-

---

34. Phyllis J. Hill, "A Cultural History of Frontier Sport in Illinois 1673-1820," Ph.D. dissertation, University of Illinois, 1966, p. 82.

able as a social center. It was the theater, the ballroom, the youth center, the restaurant, the bowling alley, the billiard parlor, the saloon, and the sports arena, all in one."[35]

The shooting match similarly served to sharpen skills essential to the frontier while, at the same time, the competition allowed the independent, proud, and self-assured rifleman an opportunity to match ability with and demonstrate prowess to his neighbors. The prodigious shooting skills of the frontiersmen were widely known, partly as a result of the various Indian wars as well as from the accounts of travelers witnessing shooting matches where the contests consisted of snuffing out a candle at fifty yards and driving a nail at eighty yards. The prizes themselves varied in value. Frequently a prize for winning a shooting match was a jug of whisky or a turkey. In prosperous periods the most popular prize was a portion of beef, which was divided among the top several contestants, the choicest portions going to the best marksman.

The popularity of the shooting matches can be illustrated by the fact that these were often the central attractions around which other contests were held. Athletic sports, consisting of throwing, running and jumping contests, were frequently held in conjunction with shooting matches or horse races, or following a court session or some other assemblage. The contests, generally for men and boys, were sometimes planned and sometimes spontaneous. Footraces at distances from fifty yards to a mile or more, jumping for distance, and the throwing of quoits were the most frequent events.

The rough and tumble free-for-all fighting popular in the rural areas was also part of the life of the frontiersmen. Utilizing the various tactics of hitting, kicking, biting, and gouging, the participants gave and received permanent injuries. The not uncommon sight of a man with one empty eye socket or an incomplete ear or lip severed by the teeth was mute evidence of past brawling.

Other activities involving feats of strength which were not quite so dangerous were throwing the long bullet, wrestling, and weight lifting. Physical strength, the basic requisite to pioneer life, was important in these sport-like contests.

Life for the frontiersmen and their families was shared with and frequently challenged by native American Indians, who were first accommodated, then moved, to permit the settlement of the country by the Europeans.

Native Americans

In May, 1830, the President of the United States was authorized to exchange prairie land west of the Mississippi River for Indian lands within the boundaries of the 26 state union. Northern tribes such as the Potawatomi,

---

35. Paton Yoder, *Taverns and Travelers* (Bloomington: Indiana University, 1969), p. 122.

Shawnee, and Iroquois moved west without resistance but the "Five Civilized Tribes" of the southeast—the Cherokee, Chickasaw, Choctaw, Seminole, and Creeks—preferred to remain in their homelands and had to be forcibly removed to the Oklahoma lands reserved for them. During the 1830's some 100,000 native Americans were marched west from the southeast over a route that came to be known as the Trail of Tears. During the same period the painter George Catlin traveled west of the Mississippi River, to paint and record the native Americans in their daily life. He found that the Indians made him welcome and permitted him to paint their daily lives, their ceremonies, and their games.

FIG. 3.11   Racket game, George Catlin. Courtesy of the AMERICAN MUSEUM OF NATURAL HISTORY.

Summary

In its first sixty years the new nation grew rapidly and, while Boston, New York, Philadelphia, Baltimore, and Charleston were commercial and social centers, the country remained largely rural. The period was characterized by diversity in customs and manners from the towns to the country to the westward frontier. The Puritan work ethic endured to control social and

FIG. 3.12 Game of Tchungkee, Hoop and Pole, George Catlin. Courtesy of the AMERICAN MUSEUM OF NATURAL HISTORY.

Sunday customs although the degree of control varied from town to town and colony to colony. Education was available in the few colleges for men, academies and private schools, and in some public grammar schools. Sport and sport-like activities reflected the diversity of the period, and provided entertainment and amusement in the new nation. Dance was a popular pastime, although in some New England seminaries it was used for exercise. Horse racing became firmly established, underscoring entertainment as a major function of sport in the United States. In addition to horse racing, crowds attended pedestrian contests and men patronized boxing matches. A Sunday game of cricket or town ball in Philadelphia or Chicago, a shooting match in Kentucky, or a ball in Charleston were favorite pastimes for the growing numbers of people who found some time for games and recreation. In the rural areas informal social activities centering around the local tavern or work "bees" continued. The first suggestion of organizing sport activities other than horse racing was the fishing and archery clubs which were founded to promote both the sport and fellowship.

By the end of the period educators and social reformers recognized the benefits of exercise and "healthful" pastimes. Two of the more significant programs were the Round Hill School for boys and the Mount Holyoke

Seminary for women. However, the most important development in sport history of this period was the beginning of clubs as a form of sport organization.

Questions for Discussion

1. The three opening incidents represent the diversity of pastimes in the United States during this period. Are there any commonalities among these incidents?
2. What was the attitude toward Sunday sport and occupations at that time in the United States? Does it differ from today's attitude? If so, how and why?
3. Point out the similarities and differences in the activities in the settled and frontier areas. Why precisely did they exist? Are the similarities or the differences greater?
4. In one of the Catlin pictures (Fig. 3.11 or Fig. 3.12) describe exactly what you see and then what you can legitimately infer from that. What do you know about the native American culture from the picture alone?
5. What were the attitudes during this period toward the various sorts of dancing?
6. What was the relationship of Mary Lyon's attitude toward exercise and the development of education for women?
7. What were the contributions of the Round Hill School to the history of sport and physical activity?

Suggestions for Further Reading

1. Audubon, John James. "Kentucky Riflery" in *The Realm of Sport,* ed. Herbert Warren Wind. New York: Simon and Schuster, 1966.
2. Bennett, Bruce L. "The Making of Round Hill School." *Quest* 4 (April, 1965): 53-64.
3. Van Cleef, Joy. "Rural Felicity: Social Dance in 18th-Century Connecticut." *Dance Perspectives* 65 (Spring, 1976):1-45.
4. Wynne, Shirley. "From Ballet to Ballroom: Dance in the Revolutionary Era." *Dance Scope,* 10:1 (Fall/Winter, 1975/76): 65-73.

Time Line

History

1840
Ten-hour work day for U.S. government employees
1844
First telegraph in regular operation
1846
Invention of sewing machine
1848
Revolutions in France, Germany, Austria, Italy & subsequent immigration
Gold discovered in California
Seneca Falls Women's Rights convention
1859
Darwin published *Origin of Species*
1861
Abraham Lincoln inaugurated as president
Civil War
1865
Lincoln assassinated
1867
Marx published first volume of *Das Kapital*
1869
Opening of transcontinental railway
1876
Invention of telephone
1881
Tuskegee Institute founded

Sport

1843
First collegiate rowing club, Yale
1845
Modern baseball game established
1852
First intercollegiate sport contest, rowing, Harvard vs. Yale
1861
First college men's physical education program, Amherst College
1865
First college women's physical education program, Vassar College
1866
First state physical education legislation, California
1868
New York Athletic Club founded
1869
First professional baseball team, Cincinnati Red Stockings
1874
Tennis introduced to United States
1876
National League of Professional Base Ball Clubs founded

4 From Games to Sport, 1840-1885

When Alexander Cartwright and a group of his friends took what was essentially a child's game in 1845 and turned it into an adult, male sport, they initiated the first steps toward today's professional ball sports. When they designed a playing field with standard dimensions, specified equipment to be used, stated the number of players on a team, assigned them responsibilities or positions, and listed the conditions and rules under which the game would be played, baseball was on its way to becoming an organized sport. Thirty years after they adapted rounders and town ball into modern baseball, the National League of Professional Base Ball Clubs was organized in 1876. This change from casual, informal play to organized sport reflects the changes in the society and in sport and pastimes in the United States from 1840 to 1885.

At the middle of the nineteenth century, the United States had coastlines on two major oceans and over three thousand miles of land in between. The country varied from two-hundred-year-old cities and towns in the East to the frontier which constantly pressed westward. In spite of the great internal stresses which culminated in the Civil War, the new nation grew from 17,000,000 people in 1840 to over 50,000,000 in 1880 and became more urban. Discoveries and inventions caused many farmers to become factory workers, changed travel by horses to trips on trains, and vastly accelerated communication, from information transmitted by mail or by word of mouth to news sent almost instantaneously over the telegraph wire.

This was a period of growing social and economic extremes, when some people made fortunes and, in contrast, millions of immigrants barely found a subsistence living. Greatly expanded numbers of industrial laborers worked for twelve to sixteen hours a day, six days a week; even so, their working hours were specified and after work their time was their own. The new living pattern also provided some money to buy manufactured sport goods—balls, bats, roller skates, and perhaps a bicycle.

This was also a period of reform movements. One of those reforms was directed at the increasingly poor health of the people, particularly in the cities. Gymnasiums opened, and philanthropic organizations such as the

YMCA, YWCA, and settlement houses organized exercise programs. In the colleges, especially the women's colleges, physical education programs were instituted to improve the health of the students. Not so much interested in their health, but more interested in interschool rivalry, young men in the colleges engaged in a series of sport challenges which led to intercollegiate athletics.

This chapter will examine the impact of technology on sports, pastimes, and leisure; the development of amateur and professional sport; dance of the period; programs designed to improve health; and the beginnings of intercollegiate athletics.

Impact of Technology on Sport and Leisure

Numerous inventions and discoveries in the mid-nineteenth century combined to change the daily lives of many Americans and also to transform American sport. Elias Howe's sewing machine produced playing uniforms and equipment. The vulcanization of rubber in the 1830's by Charles Goodyear improved the elasticity and resiliency of rubber balls in the 1840's and of golf and tennis balls later in the century. From the early "boneshakers" to the safety bicycle, engineering principles were employed which later found application in automotive and other industries.[1]

As manufacturing developed, machinery and improved techniques ensured balls, bats, and other sport equipment that met specific standards of size, weight, and shape. This was especially important in the rapid growth of baseball, but virtually every sport was affected by new technology, and for the first time all the competitors—in archery and rowing, and later in tennis, croquet, and golf—had standardized equipment. Mass production also made sport equipment less expensive and more available to the average American.

The discovery of electricity and the development of the incandescent bulb in 1879 made a major impact on urban social life. For some time gas lights had been used in armories and arenas such as New York's Madison Square Garden. Although boxers, pedestrians, bicycle racers, and spectators had grown somewhat accustomed to the mixture of gaslight fumes and tobacco smoke, they welcomed the electric bulbs which were installed in the Garden in 1882. By 1885 the Garden was completely electrified. Another early club to install electricity was the New York Athletic Club. By the end of the decade clubs, arenas, and armories from Boston to San Francisco could be lit up after dark. The first hotel to use electricity was the Prospect House,

1. S.S. Wilson, "Bicycle Technology," *Scientific American* 228, no. 3 (March, 1973): 81-91.

Blue Mountain Lake, New York. Altogether, the electric light bulb changed sport from an activity largely carried on in daylight hours out of doors to an enterprise possible by day and night, inside and out.

Rail travel was at first unreliable and sometimes this disrupted sport events. Cars overturned, occasionally injuring passengers and perhaps also horses being transported to a track. For the highly publicized race between Boston and Fashion at New York's Union Course in 1842, the Long Island Rail Road oversold the available space and found five thousand racing fans jamming the trains. To complicate matters the trains failed to arrive on time at the track and the enraged passengers rioted, overturning the cars and demolishing other railroad property.

By the late 1850's, rail service had improved and could be used for reliable transportation to race courses throughout the country, choice fishing sites for a vacation, resort hotels, and for baseball teams traveling during the summer. The Cincinnati Red Stockings' tour from Maine to California in 1869 was a "first," using local rail lines, steam ships, and a large regional rail line, the Union Pacific Railroad. The rise and success of professional "major league" baseball in the 1870's and '80's were dependent on adequate rail transportation. By 1870 collegiate teams, too, traveled by train. Harvard's 1870 baseball team, on a single trip, played amateur and professional teams in New Haven, Troy, Utica, Syracuse, Oswego (Canada), Buffalo, Cleveland, Cincinnati, Louisville, Chicago, Milwaukee, Indianapolis, Washington, Baltimore, Philadelphia, New York, and Brooklyn.

Perhaps equally important was the impact of improved communication on sport. While the speed of news transmission increased with the coming of the steam riverboats and the rail system, it often took weeks before the results of an important fight or race could be known throughout the country. However, with Morse's system of telegraphy in 1844, suddenly the news was received instantaneously over the "magic wires."

The burgeoning newspaper industry immediately saw the advantages of telegraphy and by 1846, both the New York *Herald* and the New York *Tribune* made use of these new inventions. In 1849 citizens in the eastern half of the country received telegraphic accounts of the Hyer-Sullivan fight held at Rock Point, Maryland. During the next decade the wires reported prize fights, horse races, trotting contests, and yachting events. In reporting professional baseball in the 1870's and '80's, the telegraph became practically indispensable in providing the cities news of the home team. In 1866 the Atlantic cable was laid by Cyrus Field, enabling the American public to receive European news quickly.

While sport news did not yet occupy a prominent place in the daily newspapers and in weekly and monthly journals, major events were nevertheless reported. The milestone in early sport journalism came in 1831 when William Trotter Porter published the weekly *Spirit of the Times,* the leading periodical devoted to sport in the mid-nineteenth century. Second only to Porter's *Spirit* was the *National Police Gazette,* founded by George Wilkes in 1845, which became the leading pugilistic journal in America. Also, a sports "extra" was published in Amherst, Massachusetts, in 1859, after Amherst College won the first intercollegiate baseball game, beating Williams College 73 to 32.

By the 1880's the telegraph revolution of the newspaper industry, the increasing use of journalists, and growing interest in sport combined to create the sports page. While some publishers were reluctant to include the topic of sport in their papers, others were not, and by the turn of the century the sports page occupied a permanent place in the daily and Sunday newspapers.

The weekly and monthly magazines and journals were frequently ahead of the newspapers in exploiting the growing public interest in sport. Before the development and popularity of the daily tabloid, editors, not faced with strict deadlines, were able to give thoughtful accounts and interpretations of important sport events.

Sports of the Times

Horse racing, boxing, pedestrianism, and cock fighting remained favorites of the men during this period. While the men supported pugilism and cock fighting, both men and women enjoyed the races. Essentially these sports were based upon a clearly visible competition between one man fighting another or one animal fighting with another, perhaps to the death; or upon competition among horses or men for speed—to see which horse or man was the fastest. Admission charges and the opportunity to wager on the outcome of these events were expected, but the idea of paying to watch one group of men compete against another group in a game of baseball, using balls, bats, and bases seemed remote in 1840. Yet in 1869 over 200,000 persons throughout the country turned out to see the Cincinnati Red Stockings play baseball.

Tracks and Rings

Horse Racing

While harness racing was especially popular at state and county fairs, thoroughbred racing predominated at most of the established tracks throughout the country. Wealthy northern industrialists, southern planters, and western businessmen supported racing stables. Black antebellum slaves and postbellum freedmen were the top jockeys, trainers, and handlers. By the decade before the Civil War the sport was threatened by gambling elements which virtually controlled racing in a number of states. The Civil War destroyed many southern stables and temporarily halted horse racing, but following the War, racing once again began to achieve respectability as interested businessmen and social leaders came to its support. There was, however, continuing opposition by many religious and other reform groups to betting on horses and other forms of gambling.

New tracks were founded and old ones, particularly in the South, were restored. Kentucky's bluegrass country around Lexington, "where limestone soil promoted bone and stamina,"[2] became the home of the thoroughbred. The building of Louisville's Churchill Downs and the first running of the Kentucky Derby in May, 1875, increased the importance of Kentucky in racing. By 1885 thoroughbred racing in the United States had become an extremely popular and prosperous activity.

FIG. 4.1   Union Course, Long Island, 1845. Courtesy of the Enoch Pratt Free Library, Baltimore, Maryland.

---

2. Samuel Eliot Morison, *The Oxford History of the American People* (New York: Oxford University Press, 1965), p. 501.

Boxing

In mid-century America, professional boxing was generally considered a sport of the middle and lower classes. Boxers themselves came from a variety of backgrounds. In 1841 James "Yankee" Sullivan, recently released from twenty years in a British penal colony, began a twelve-year career as the best heavyweight fighter in America. A rough and willing boxer, he finally lost to John Morrisey in 1853. Morrisey actually trained for his fights and retired undefeated five years after his victory over Sullivan. A third champion, John C. Heenan, assumed Morrisey's title and kept it during the next few years. Following the Civil War, boxing was discouraged by respectable upper-class society. Outlawed in many parts of the country, matches were sometimes arranged covertly in barns, warehouses, river barges, and at sea.

However, boxing improved and became more acceptable after adopting the Marquis of Queensberry's code which included: three-minute rounds, a count of ten to rise from the floor after being knocked down, and outlawing certain blows.

It was not until the 1880's and early '90's that the new code was generally adopted in the United States. Beginning in 1881 John L. Sullivan and his eventual conqueror, "Gentleman Jim" Corbett, preferred the Queensberry rules and through their skill and their personal magnetism boxing became a more respectable sport.

From Game to Sport: Baseball

Early forms of baseball, variously called base ball, goal ball, or rounders, had been played regularly by boys and young men in America since the colonial period. While there is some evidence that groups of men occasionally played the game, it was usually considered a game for children or youth. Richter mentions that baseball was played by collegians in 1825.[3] It was clearly unusual, then, for a group of doctors, attorneys, bank tellers, Wall Street brokers, clerks, and small store owners to gather two afternoons a week in a mid-Manhattan meadow to play a game of ball. These men organized the Knickerbocker Club in New York City in 1842, and three years later adopted a clearly written set of rules which became the basis for the modern game of baseball.

While the precise circumstances are unclear, it is generally agreed that Alexander Joy Cartwright, a twenty-five-year-old bank employee, volunteer fireman, and charter member of the Knickerbocker Base Ball

---

3. Frank C. Richter, *Richter's History and Records of Base Ball* (Philadelphia: Francis C. Richter, 1914), p. 12.

Club, played an instrumental role in developing a plan so well thought out that the game's basic form has remained unchanged to the present. The new rules established the design of the field, placement and number of players, and system of outs and innings. The distance between bases, set at ninety feet, was cleverly figured, as a few feet more or less would result in an uneven advantage for either the fielder or the runner. The placement of the infielders at first, second, and third bases, and a fourth player at shortstop, provided adequate coverage of the diamond; and the provision of three outfielders struck a balance between good defensive play and a reasonable chance for the batter to hit safely. The positions of the two roving short fielders and one of the two catchers previously required were abolished, so that a pitcher rounded out a team to nine players. The center of the playing field was set in a ninety-foot square, and the batter was moved from a special box and placed at the fourth or "home" base. Outs could be made by balls thrown to the bases, rather than balls thrown at the runners. The rule of "three hands out, all out" increased the pace of the game, as it was no longer necessary to retire the entire team to end an inning. At first, the game ended when one team scored twenty-one runs or "aces," but later changed to the nine-inning game. It was soon realized that these changes removed the game from the ranks of a children's pastime. "Base-ball, . . . is no longer a boy's game. It requires men to play the game now up to the standard comprehended by the rules in question, and men, moreover, with heads, as well as active limbs and bodies."[4] Hitting, pitching, and fielding skills, as well as individual and team strategies, became important. So appealing was the game that within a few years it dominated the American sport scene and was promoted as the "national" game.

The construction of a suburban railroad through the meadow where the Knickerbocker Club played forced the club to relocate in 1846 at the Elysian Fields across the Hudson River in Hoboken, New Jersey. The next spring they began their first full season as an organized club, playing an occasional match against a "pick-up" team composed of former Knickerbockers who declined to travel frequently to Hoboken for games.

Over the next several years the Knickerbockers continued to play regularly and added new members. Other groups played sporadically in New York, but it was not until 1851 that one of the new clubs felt strong enough to challenge the Knickerbockers. In 1854 two Brooklyn clubs were formed, and the following year three more clubs. During these early years of baseball "clubs," membership was limited by a blackball system and only "gentlemen" were admitted. The game itself was played for enjoyment,

---

4. *De Witt's Base-Ball Guide for 1875*, ed. Henry Chadwick (New York: Robert M. De Witt, Publisher, 1875), p. 12.

and for camaraderie and exercise. Members were fined for swearing, disputing the umpire's decision, and appearing inebriated at a game. The casual attitude toward winning, the insistence upon good manners when playing, the presence of the formally attired umpire, and the traditional post-game party at a favorite hostelry were characteristic of the "gentlemen's" game of baseball.

The Knickerbocker's game used the "New York Rules," which were generally adopted, but in New England, the "Massachusetts Rules" (see p. 133) were played until the 1860's. The "Massachusetts" game was played on a rectangular field measuring sixty feet by forty-five feet, the game itself differing in the shape of the field, ten to twenty players per team, one out, all out, runners out by thrown balls, and the three-foot high stakes used to mark bases. Meanwhile, Philadelphians still played the old game of town ball.

The rapid expansion of the game in the 1850's to all classes and to many parts of the country was a sport phenomenon. In spite of the exclusive membership of the Knickerbockers, the game itself belonged to no one, and with balls, bats, and flat meadows readily available, working men, older men, boys, schoolboys, and college men found the game easily adaptable to their everyday life. Perhaps the first working-class team appeared in New York in the middle 1850's. Captain Frank Pigeon of the Eckfords of Brooklyn wrote:

> A year ago last August a small number of young men . . . were accustomed to meet for the purpose of enjoying the game. Being shipwrights and mechanics, we could not make it convenient to practice more than once a week.[5]

Pigeon continued with careful detail the account of their first match on September 27, 1856, which the Eckfords won.

Teams began forming all over the New York City area—the Mutuals, firemen of the Mutual Hook and Ladder Company No. 1; the Manhattans, a group of New York policemen; the Phantoms, barkeepers; the Pocahontas, employees of a dairy; an unnamed group of clergymen; and the Pastime Club, composed of Long Island workmen. As many as fifty clubs were playing in and around the metropolitan area, and an additional sixty "junior" teams were formed to serve as feeders to the senior clubs. Players rose to practice early in the morning before going to work, and many vacant lots were turned into ball fields. In the summmer of 1858 a series of three contests was played between two Brooklyn and New York City all-star teams. The first of the series, held at the Fashion Race Course on Long

---

5. Cited in Albert G. Spalding, *Base Ball, America's National Game* (New York: American Sports Publishing Company, 1911), p. 60.

Island, attracted over 1500 people, who came by steamboat and railroad and paid fifty cents admission to watch these men struggle to win a bat and ball game.

Prior to the Civil War the game spread across the country, usually introduced by professional or business men. The Buffalo Baseball Club, with city aldermen serving as captains, began games in the late 1850's, and the Franklin Club of Detroit organized in 1857. Several members of the New York Eagles migrated to California in 1859 and soon founded the Pacific Coast Eagles. Likewise, former Knickerbockers William and James Shepard introduced San Francisco to the game in 1861.[6] In New Orleans, the city's first team, the Louisiana Baseball Club, began playing intraclub games in the summer of 1859. By the end of the year, there were seven teams in the city, mostly from the middle and upper classes, and baseball began to displace cricket in popularity.[7] Even after the War this pattern continued. In 1866, Cincinnati's first organized club was founded by a group of Harvard and Yale law graduates, while in Cedar Rapids, Iowa, most of the players were business men and community leaders.

As the baseball craze spread over the country and to all classes, it became a game which no longer was played with the social amenities thought to be essential by the Knickerbockers. Players now emphasized winning, blocked base paths, "rode" opposing players, picked fights, and contested decisions of the umpire—who was, in any case, only an unpaid member of the host club, picked by the visiting team. Unhappy with this turn of events, the older clubs found their influence on the development of the game slipping away. Reluctantly, the Knickerbockers called a meeting in 1858 to discuss the standardization of rules. Twenty-two New York area clubs attended and as a result of the meeting, the National Association of Base Ball Players was established. In succeeding years invitations were sent to clubs throughout the country. Fifty groups attended the convention of 1860 and, while membership dropped during the Civil War, it soared immediately afterward and by 1868, almost 350 clubs attended the National Association meetings.

The Civil War introduced the game to the thousands of soldiers from all over the country who played in army camps and in prison camps on both sides. For example, on Christmas Day, 1862, at Hilton Head, South Carolina, a team from the 165th New York Volunteer Infantry played a team from other Union regiments before about 40,000 soldiers.[8] The game's

---

6. Harold Seymour, *Baseball: The Early Years* (New York: Oxford University Press, 1959), p. 26.

7. Dale A. Somers, *The Rise of Sports in New Orleans, 1850-1900* (Baton Rouge: Louisiana State University Press, 1972), p. 50.

8. Albert G. Spalding, *Base Ball, America's National Game* (New York: American Sports Publishing Company, 1911), p. 96.

tremendous growth in the decade following the War soon gave baseball the appearance of an egalitarian game where everyone, young and old, rich and poor, measured each other only by playing ability. However, certain Americans were still excluded from mid-nineteenth century organized baseball when in 1867 the National Association of Base Ball Players could approve a ban on black players seeking membership. At its convention that year, the Association's Nominating Committee proposed that teams with one or more black players not be admitted to the Association. Their position was based on the belief that some members of the National Association might object to black players and that by excluding them all, no incidents would be created and no one would be "hurt." For the next eighty years the same attitude controlled organized professional baseball, and most black players were restricted to segregated barnstorming teams or "colored" leagues. Occasionally a light-skinned black player was passed off as white, Indian, or Caribbean by a team anxious to capitalize on the individual's playing ability. In essence, this ruling and attitude mirrored American society of the period.

As interest in baseball grew, communities and clubs began to compete for the outstanding players of the period. Despite the strictly amateur, no-compensation policy of the National Association of Base Ball Players, key players *were* hired for important games or induced away from other clubs for a season. The issue of amateurism and professionalism was polarized in 1869 when the young prominent club, the Cincinnati Red Stockings, under the leadership of the dynamic manager/center fielder Harry Wright openly became a professional base ball club and *hired* the best players they could find. Further, they undertook an unprecedented tour through the Middle West, the East, and then the Far West and did not lose a single game.

From a record kept by Harry Wright. . . . Out of 57 games played the Red Stockings won 56 and tied 1. In these games they scored a total of 2,395 runs to 574 for their adversaries. The nature of the batting done is shown in a total of 169 home runs, or an average of nearly three to a game. The number of miles traveled by rail and boat was 11,877, without a serious accident of any kind. Over 200,000 people witnessed the games.[9]

Professional players were more successful than the amateur players of the National Association, and other cities followed the Cincinnati Red Stockings' lead. That fall the National Association changed its position on the prohibition of professional players in match games. At its annual meeting in December, 1869, the rules were revised to recognize professionals as a class of players distinct from amateurs:

---

9. Albert G. Spalding, *Base Ball, America's National Game* (New York: American Sports Publishing Company, 1911), p. 139.

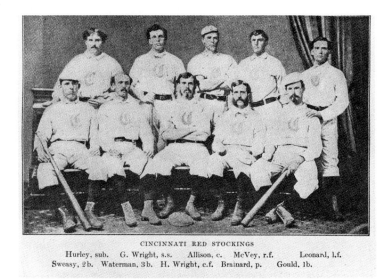

CINCINNATI RED STOCKINGS
Hurley, sub.   G. Wright, s.s.   Allison, c.   McVey, r.f.   Leonard, l.f.
Sweasy, 2b.   Waterman, 3b.   H. Wright, c.f.   Brainard, p.   Gould, 1b.

FIG. 4.2   1869 Cincinnati Red Stockings. Courtesy Spalding Archives Chicopee, Massachusetts.

> Section 7. All players who play base-ball for money, or who shall at any time receive compensation for their services as players, shall be considered *professional* players; and all others shall be regarded as *amateur* players.[10]

Difficulties within the National Association followed and at the 1870 annual meeting a battle was waged between the amateur players and the professional players. The amateurs, composed of seven colleges and ten clubs, withdrew to form their own association, but within a year this group disbanded.

The National Association of Professional Base Ball Players, organized in 1871 to replace the National Association of Base Ball Players, originally consisted of about ten teams. During the period of the amateur-professional controversy the Association grew to eleven clubs, but dropped to eight in 1874. The affairs of the association were loosely organized, with games frequently being called off and some scheduled games not played at all. Attendance dropped; and although thirteen clubs joined in 1875, continuing abuses, particularly in gambling, made the season a disastrous one. There were also difficulties among the teams because of widespread contract-breaking.

These events led to the dissolution of the National Association and the formation of the National League of Professional Base Ball Clubs in

10. *De Witt's Base-Ball Guide for 1869,* ed. Henry Chadwick (New York: Robert M. De Witt, Publisher, 1869), p. 23.

February, 1876, under a constitution constructed by W.A. Hulbert and A.G. Spalding. Rather than being an association of players, the new organization was a league of clubs.

> The function of Base Ball *Clubs* in the future would be to manage Base Ball *Teams*. Clubs would form leagues, secure grounds, erect grandstands, lease and own property, make schedules, fix dates, pay salaries, assess fines, discipline players, make contracts, control the sport in all its relations to the public, and thus, relieving the players of all care and responsibility for the legitimate functions of management, require of them the very best performance of which they were capable, in the entertainment of the public, for which service they were to receive commensurate pay.[11]

The new league, governed by a board of five directors, opened the 1876 season with clubs in Philadelphia, Boston, Chicago, Cincinnati, Hartford, Louisville, New York, and St. Louis. To apply for membership cities had to have a population of at least 75,000. The clubs issued contracts to players which forbade contract-breaking, which in turn discouraged clubs from "raiding" other clubs for players. Other rules forbade gambling and liquor on the club grounds.

Other Sport Clubs and Organized Activities

Morison calls this period an era of "joiners." He suggests that a "desire for distinction in a country of growing uniformity, and a human craving for fellowship drew the Americans into . . . fraternal orders."[12] Perhaps the same wish for identification was the major motivation of the many sport clubs and organizations of the period. Yachting, rowing, archery, and athletics or track and field enthusiasts frequently organized into informal clubs, which later in the period became national sport associations. Organizations were formed in all walks of life, from elite yacht clubs to middle class fraternal orders to ethnic clubs such as the Ancient Order of Hibernians. In the intellectual community the American Association for the Advancement of Science was established in 1848. And the American Humane Association in 1877, the American National Red Cross in 1881, and the National Grange in 1867, were all part of the American "joiners" movement.

Yachting

When John Cox Stevens, member of a prominent New York area family, and an avid yachtsman, called together eight of his friends for a meeting

---

11. Albert G. Spalding, *Base Ball, America's National Game* (New York: American Sports Publishing Company, 1911), p. 194.
12. Samuel Eliot Morison, *The Oxford History of the American People* (New York: Oxford University Press, 1965), p. 787.

aboard his new yacht, *Gimcrack,* on July 30, 1844, they founded the New York Yacht Club. The nine men designated themselves the original members, selected Stevens as the first commodore, appointed a five-man committee to draft club rules and regulations, and planned a club cruise to Newport, Rhode Island, to begin in three days.[13] Other clubs had been organized during this same period but, with the exception of the exclusive Southern Yacht Club in New Orleans, had not been successful. The Civil War interrupted the sport of yachting, but soon after the War clubs sprang up in Detroit, Boston, Marblehead, San Francisco, Oyster Bay, Chicago, and Larchmont. The Southern Yacht Club also reorganized and by 1878 New Orleans once again enjoyed regular racing. Most of the yachting enthusiasts came from the growing number of wealthy Americans who could afford the cost of a yacht and its maintenance and who also had the leisure time in which to sail.

The New York Yacht Club, just one year after its founding, held a formal race on July 17, 1845, ". . . over a course that carried the fleet down through New York's Narrows, around a buoy in the Lower Bay, and back."[14] The cash prize of $225, the total of the entrance fees, was won by William Edgar with his *Cygnet.* The club's fame and tradition became firmly established in 1851, when the yacht *America,* responding to an invitation sent by England's Royal Yacht Squadron, and commissioned by a syndicate headed by Stevens, entered and won an international race around the Isle of Wight. The victorious yacht was awarded the Royal Yacht Squadron Cup and became the first American craft to win in an international race. With this prize, the Royal Yacht Squadron cup, the New York Yacht Club launched the historic *America's* Cup series in 1870.

In New Orleans society before the Civil War, the Southern Yacht Club, founded in 1847, was, like many jockey clubs, ". . . both an exclusive social organization and a regulatory group."[15] Regattas were open to members of yachting clubs and invited guests, and a day's racing often ended, as did a day of horse racing, with a dinner and a ball. The Club's membership included planters, wealthy business men, and other socially elite residents of the Gulf Coast from New Orleans to Pensacola. Pass Christian became the southern summer resort for many of the wealthy, but for those who could not be away from New Orleans, there were the regattas on Lake Pontchartrain.

With the possible exception of New York City itself, summer sailing

---

13. William N. Wallace, *The Macmillan Book of Boating* (New York: Crown Publishers, Inc., 1973), p. 25.

14. William N. Wallace, *The Macmillan Book of Boating* (New York: Crown Publishers, Inc., 1973), p. 27.

15. Dale A. Somers, *The Rise of Sports in New Orleans, 1850-1900* (Baton Rouge: Louisiana State University Press, 1972), p. 44.

flourished primarily at resorts such as Newport, Pass Christian, Lake Pontchartrain, and in the Midwest on Lakes Michigan, Huron, and Erie. The charter members of most clubs were practical amateur sailors, who managed their own expensive craft. With the growing fame and prestige of the yachting clubs and victories in certain races, some wealthy men with no sailing knowledge began to join the clubs to gain social status. Some even purchased yachts and hired professional seamen to sail them so that they could be identified with the sport of yachting.

Rowing

Competitive rowing during this period began with as many professionals as amateurs, but by the end of the period was almost completely amateur. One famous internationally known rower, Canadian Edward Hanlon, was considered by some as the finest North American sculler. The Ward brothers' four-oared crew reigned supreme from 1858 to 1871. While there were also races for six and eight-oared shells, most contests were for single or double sculls, and single scullers such as John Biglin, Josh and Ellis Ward, James Hamill, James Ten Eyck, Charles Courtney, and W.B. Curtis were famous throughout the East.

Perhaps the most important event in rowing was the banding together of several Philadelphia clubs in 1858 to form the Schuylkill Navy. It soon became one of the most influential rowing organizations in the country and in 1872 was instrumental in founding the National Association of Amateur Oarsmen, primarily to preserve amateur rowing for gentlemen and to guard against any form of professionalism. The Association sponsored annual regattas for national championships in several events and classes of boats.

Rowing was popular in New Orleans both before and after the Civil War. When rowing resumed in that city in 1872, it quickly became a favorite in all socioeconomic classes. While the first post-war clubs were composed of, and limited to, middle and upper class ". . . young gentlemen of polish and attainments," there soon followed a profusion of clubs for men of all ranks—cotton press employees, laborers from the metal foundries, and the city's firemen. However, by the early 1890's most of the middle and lower class men had shifted their allegiance to other sports such as baseball and soon the southern rowing clubs were again almost exclusively an upperclass sport. Many clubs, in fact, began to offer fewer races and to expand into social organizations ". . . dedicated to preserving the sport as a pastime for gentlemen and to providing the amenities of an exclusive club."[16]

This pattern in the South appeared to be true in other cities in which rowing was popular. The working class shifted their enthusiasm in sport from

---

16. Dale A. Somers, *The Rise of Sports in New Orleans, 1850-1900* (Baton Rouge: Louisiana State University Press, 1972), p. 152.

rowing to professional baseball. When professional rowing declined, some of the rowers became volunteer or paid coaches for crews in colleges and universities where rowing had become popular.

Track and Field Athletics

The beginnings of track and field in this country came from various ethnic communities. In the schools the Turners promoted gymnastics and track and field athletics. In the adult sport activities, the Scottish community initiated the Caledonian Games which organized, promoted, and stimulated the growth of track and field athletics in the United States. Athletic games had long been an established institution in Scotland, and after several informal annual gatherings in this country to compete in their traditional games, a group of Boston Scotsmen organized the first Caledonian Club in America in the spring of 1853. A social and cultural club for men, the Caledonians held their first official games later that year. In New York a Caledonian Club was founded in 1856 and held its first games the following year. Philadelphia followed suit in 1858 and Newark three years later. The New York club included in its first games the following events: throwing the heavy hammer, throwing the light hammer, putting the light stone, putting the heavy stone, tossing the caber, wheelbarrow race (blindfolded), sack race, standing high jump, running long jump, running high leap, short race, and broadsword dance.[17] The games, which in some cases offered cash prizes, quickly became highly organized and popular affairs which drew large crowds. For the second games in 1858, the New York Caledonian Club advertised the games and levied a twenty-five cent admission fee. The practice was successful and the succeeding years saw increased publicity and crowds of 25,000 attending the games.

Further enthusiasm for track and field sports in New York was evidenced in the early autumn of 1868, when the New York Athletic Club was founded. The founders, William B. Curtis, already a noted weightlifter, and two friends, John C. Babcock and Henry E. Buermeyer, were influenced by the popularity of such sports in New York, and also by the traditional English pursuit of track and field athletics. The club's first indoor meet was held in 1868 at the Empire Skating Rink. A more extensive outdoor meet was held the following spring on a turf track near Central Park. Two years later land was secured north of the Harlem River at Mott Haven, where the club constructed the first cinder track in the United States. The New York Athletic Club began sponsoring annual spring meets, open to male amateur athletes from all parts of the country.

Beginning with the first meet, Caledonian Club athletes were prominent and successful participants in the New York Athletic Club meets. However,

---

17. *Spirit of the Times,* 2 October 1858, p. 69.

the Caledonian Clubs' major efforts concentrated on the annual Caledonian Games, which became an important source of funds for many clubs following the Civil War. The Caledonian Games continued as a significant force in American track and field until about 1880 when the city athletic clubs with their strong amateur traditions became more influential.[18]

By 1879, there were approximately one hundred athletic clubs in the New York City region alone, and many other clubs in cities across the country. There were the American, Manhattan, and Pastime Clubs, all in New York; the Chicago Athletic Club and the Olympic Club of San Francisco, the Detroit Athletic Club and the Indianapolis Athletic Club; there were clubs in Boston, New Orleans, Cincinnati, Philadelphia, Providence, Pittsburgh, Cleveland, St. Louis, and Baltimore. The vast majority of these clubs were for men only. One of the few exceptions was the Ladies Athletic Club on Staten Island in the late 1870's, where tennis, archery, croquet, and darts were played. Until the 1880's the athletic clubs were usually composed of amateur athletes interested in pursuing a regular program of exercise and participating in the track and field athletics. As the clubs became popular and their members wealthier, sumptuous facilities, financial stability, and limited membership characterized more and more athletic clubs, and a greater emphasis was placed on social as well as athletic prominence.[19]

The athletic clubs, wishing to preserve the concept of amateurism, formed the National Association of Amateur Athletes of America (NAAAA) in 1879. For the next several years the NAAAA sponsored national championships and attempted to settle the many disputes about eligibility, professionalism, and other issues. One controversy, for example, concerned the single vote the Intercollegiate Association of Amateur Athletes of America (ICAAAA) accepted to represent all the colleges and universities in the NAAAA. In 1888, under the leadership of the New York Athletic Club and a Philadelphia club, fifteen athletic clubs joined together to form the Amateur Athletic Union of the United States. NAAAA continued to function, but with frequent controversies with the AAU. For example, the AAU Board of Governors passed a resolution that barred amateur athletes from competing in any open games in the United States not governed by the AAU, the penalty to be exclusion from all games under the rules of the AAU. Further, they prohibited AAU athletes from entering the Penn Relays, which were administered under the ICAAAA, which belonged to the NAAAA. Finally the ICAAAA withdrew from the NAAAA and the AAU approved the Penn Relays for their athletes. It was

---

18. Gerald Redmond, *The Caledonian Games in Nineteenth-Century America* (Rutherford, New Jersey: Fairleigh Dickinson University Press, 1971), pp. 42-72.
19. Joseph D. Willis and Richard G. Wettan, "Social Stratification in New York City Athletic Clubs, 1865-1915," *Journal of Sport History* 3, no. 1 (Spring, 1976): 45-63.

PRIVILEGES OF MEMBERSHIP

N. Y. A. C.

Club House, 55th St. and 6th Ave.:

    Gymnasium ; Swimming, Turkish, Russian and Douche Baths ; Reading Room ; Restaurant ; Billiards ; Bowling.

Travers Island, on the Sound :

    Boat House ; Club Houses ; Track ; Boats ; Shower Baths ; Salt Water Swimming ; Lawn Tennis ; Base Ball ; Foot Ball ; Quoits ; Glass Ball and Pigeon Shooting ; Fine Fishing.

COUNTRY CLUB HOUSE : Restaurant ; Bowling ; Billiards ; Finely Furnished Rooms ; Stabling Accommodations.

City and Country Club Houses connected by Telephone.

MEMBERSHIP 2,000 LIMIT.

200 Life, 300 Non-Resident. 2,500 Total. 800 Applications on File.

FIG. 4.3 New York Athletic Club Privileges of Membership. Courtesy Spalding Archives, Chicopee, Massachusetts.

clear that the Amateur Athletic Union had gained control of the track and field athletics in this country.

Popular Sport Activities for Women and Men

Archery

Archery, which had been popular briefly in the early part of the century, boasted more than twenty-five clubs in the East and North by 1879. In the same year the National Archery Association was organized and held its first tournament in Chicago's White Stocking Park. The meet, open to men and women, was heralded by the editors of *Harper's Weekly* as a socially acceptable event:

> The contestants were ladies and gentlemen from the cultured circles of society, and while the rivalry among the shooters was keen to the last degree, an air of such refinement and courteous dignity as is not often witnessed by observers of public games characterized everyone connected with the contest.[20]

Croquet

Croquet was one of several games which brought women outdoors to join men in a mild but enjoyable exercise. First introduced in the mid-nineteenth

---

20. *Harper's Weekly* 23 (September 13, 1879): 73.

century to the upper circles of American society, imported from France, it spread quickly downward to the middle class, while the manufacturers strove to keep up with the demand for equipment. The game continued to be popular as a backyard pastime for several decades and seemed to be a national sport when, in 1882, the National Croquet Association was formed and the first national tournament was held in Norwich, Connecticut. By the end of the century, however, the game was no longer popular and tournament play had become a thing of the past.

Roller Skating

Invented in 1863 by James L. Plimpton, the four-wheeled roller skate created another form of physical activity which was fashionable for a brief period of time in the 1870's and '80's. Although it began with the upper classes, roller skating soon became a popular pastime for the middle classes. Wooden roller-skating rinks were built in many cities and towns, admission fees were modest, the equipment was inexpensive, and the necessary skill was easy to acquire. In addition, roller skating, like croquet and ice skating, was a socially acceptable recreation for men *and* women.

Ice Skating

Women and girls as well as men and boys enjoyed ice skating in the winter months in most northern communities. During the Civil War years the women of Detroit ventured onto the ice in large numbers, and several privately owned rinks were opened to meet the demand. In 1868, the Hook, Dupont and Company Skating Park paid Anna Jagerisky, a well-known local woman, $150 to skate for thirty consecutive hours.[21] The promotion attracted over fifteen hundred spectators. Skating parties at which prizes were awarded for "best costumes" for women and men further promoted skating.

Bicycling

Of all the inventions affecting sport, one of the most dramatic was the bicycle. When the high-wheeled "Ordinary" was introduced in the mid-1870's the machine had been evolving over a sixty-year period. With a front wheel measuring fifty to sixty inches in height, the machine quickly caught on with young male daredevils who were willing to risk "headers" over the high wheel for the exhilaration of a self-propelled speed and the feeling of superiority over those walking below. Strictly a male sport until the development of the safety bicycle in 1888, bicycling grew in popularity at an astounding rate, especially considering the high cost of the instrument—

21. "Remarkable Skating Feats," Detroit *Free Press,* 26 January 1868, p. 1.

$150 to $300. By 1880 the League of American Wheelmen was founded and within six years its membership had reached more than ten thousand. The organization led the way in protesting municipal ordinances which banned bicycles from public parks and main thoroughfares and in lobbying for bicycle paths and good roads. Many cyclists enjoyed Sunday club outings of several miles. Almost immediately, racing attracted large numbers of enthusiasts. As in baseball and rowing, professionalism caused problems in regulating bicycle races. In 1886, the League of American Wheelmen attempted to deal with the problem by declaring as professionals all racers known to have connections with bicycle manufacturers.

FIG. 4.4   League of American Wheelmen Meet, Washington, D.C. from a drawing in *Frank Leslie's Illustrated Newspaper,* May 24, 1884.

In the early years women and less agile men were restricted to the tricycle, a three-wheeled vehicle with a seat between two large rear wheels. The development of the safety cycle in 1888 with its drop bar signaled a major social and psychological breakthrough for women of the gaslight era.

Tennis

The development of the modern game of lawn tennis brought further opportunities for physical activity for women as well as men. By the late nineteenth century there were at least three distinct court games—badminton, court tennis, and rackets—being played in Europe, primarily by the upper classes. Major Walter C. Wingfield, a British cavalry officer, is usually credited with moving the game of court tennis outdoors onto the well-manicured lawns of English estates in late 1873 with a game he patented under the name of Sphairistike. In February, 1874, a young American society girl, Mary E. Outerbridge of Staten Island, New York, while enjoying a winter vacation in Bermuda, observed several British army officers playing Sphairistike. After trying the game herself, she purchased a set of equipment and later that spring introduced it to the United States at the Staten Island Cricket and Base Ball Club.

FIG. 4.5   First National Lawn Tennis Tournament, from a drawing by H.A. Ogden in *Frank Leslie's Illustrated Newspaper*, September 18, 1880.

The game of tennis also began to appear in other sections of the country. After witnessing a contest during a trip to Europe in 1874, James Dwight, now called the "father" of American tennis, procured the equipment and after his return to the United States prevailed upon an uncle to allow him to mark a court on the lawn of his estate at Nahant, Massachusetts. He and his cousin Fred Sears attempted to play the game with no lines and soon became disenchanted. Several weeks later, they again brought out the equipment and gave it another try. Apparently it was more successful, as they played through an afternoon rain in rubber boots and coats.[22] Two years later these two tennis pioneers played in the earliest recorded tennis tournament in the United States, a round robin affair in Nahant. The sport's popularity increased steadily in the East as courts were set up at clubs in Brookline, Massachusetts, Newport, Rhode Island, and Philadelphia during the late seventies.

In the South, the game appears to have had an independent introduction and growth. Shortly after Major Wingfield's original rules for lawn tennis were set forth, a group of New Orleans' English residents began playing the game regularly. In 1876 they founded the New Orleans Tennis Club, the first such organization in the United States. Although the game was played by men and women in the Northeast, ladies in New Orleans were denied access to the club's courts until the mid-1880's.[23]

As was the case with baseball a generation earlier, a lack of standardization of rules and equipment hindered the development of tennis and created numerous problems during its first several years. At what was billed as the first "national" tournament, sponsored in 1880 by the Staten Island Cricket and Base Ball Club, James Dwight and his cousin Richard D. Sears refused to play in the singles matches, after determining that the balls were "lighter, smaller and softer than the regulations provided for."[24] Later in the same year Philadelphia's Young America Cricket Club traveled to the Staten Island Cricket and Base Ball Club and found the net to be six inches lower than the height to which they were accustomed.

Basically the rules being followed were those established by Wingfield— the hour-glass shaped court, fifteen point badminton scoring, wing net five feet high on the sides and slightly over three feet in the center. One could find variations, however, in almost all locales. One club used the hour-glass court while another changed it to rectangular. Other variations affected court size, net height, and scoring procedure. In 1881, the United States National Lawn Tennis Association was formed to standardize equipment, space and court size, and to sanction tournaments as well as sponsor the "national" championships. Although only Eastern clubs were represented, it was a major step toward the development of the game, which by 1900 was played by men and women across the country.

While tennis became popular with the wealthy within a relatively short

22. Parke Cummings, *American Tennis: The Story of a Game and Its People* (Boston: Little, Brown and Company, 1957), p. 34.

23. Dale A. Somers, *The Rise of Sports in New Orleans, 1850-1900* (Baton Rouge: Louisiana State University Press, 1972), p. 211.

24. Parke Cummings, *American Tennis: The Story of a Game and Its People* (Boston: Little, Brown and Company, 1957), p. 35.

period of time, a number of other pursuits vied for their attention. One of these was polo, which after its American introduction by publisher-sportsman James Gordon Bennett, Jr., in 1873, attracted players in clubs as well as on some college campuses.

Swimming for Men and Swimming for Women

Swimming had begun to achieve some popularity in the first half of the century. In the larger cities men and women were strictly segregated in the few bathing houses. When sea bathing became popular, propriety was maintained through the use of bathing machines—small wooden buildings on wheels which were pulled into the water by horses or other swimmers. Bathers changed into their swimming attire in the building and entered the water also from within the structure.

Following the Civil War, as part of a growing concern about the health of women, swimming was considered an appropriate exercise for them. This was not made easier by their bathing costumes; nevertheless, with the construction of large bath houses in the 1870's, more and more women swam. In 1877 the New York Athletic Club sponsored what was possibly the first swimming championship for men in the United States and six years later began to hold scheduled meets.

Dance of the Period

By 1840, New York and Philadelphia had become centers for theatrical entertainment. Both cities supported several theaters where the latest in American and European dance and drama were presented. Performers, at least among the Americans, had to be versatile because an evening's entertainment at the theater usually included drama, opera, and pantomime, as well as dance. The Romantic ballet was in its heyday and was a departure from the dance of the previous era in subject and technique. For the first time in history dancing *en pointe* became part of the ballerina's technique and the dancer became more daring in defiance of the laws of gravity and balance. The female dancer became the center of attention in her tarlatan tunic or tutu, flesh-colored tights, and specially designed soft heelless slippers. Technique for both male and female dancers demanded greater elevation, speed, and agility.

While many European dancers came to the United States on tour, the most celebrated was Fanny Elssler, who arrived in 1840. Elssler, with her partner, James Sylvian, supported by a company of American dancers, toured for two years to enthusiastic audiences: "Champagne was drunk out of her slippers and red carpets were laid at her feet. Congress adjourned because so many of its members were absent, paying homage to the adorable Fanny."[25] Elssler danced a number of *divertissements,* for which she was famous, and staged and danced in eight grand ballets.[26]

Although foreign dancers were preferred, a few Americans rivaled the Europeans in popularity, if not in their formal training in classical dance. They were Augusta Maywood, Mary Ann Lee, and George Washington Smith. Maywood received her early training in Philadelphia with M. and Mme. Paul H. Hazard, French dancers who were then teaching. She made her debut at the age of twelve on December 30, 1837 in a dance titled "The Maid of Cashmere." The following spring she departed for Paris to continue her education. Her career never brought her back to the United States. She gave most of her performances in Italy, where she was ". . . the first and only American *prima ballerina e prima mima assoluta.*"[27]

Mary Ann Lee, another Philadelphia child prodigy, was a rival of Maywood. She made her debut as a dancer in the same production as Maywood. Both young dancers had a loyal following. Lee, who also studied with Hazard, later took lessons from Elssler's partner, James Sylvian, who taught her many of Elssler's solo numbers. In 1844 she went to Paris for a year, where she studied with Jean Coralli and added authentic versions of several Romantic ballets to her repertory, among which was *Giselle.* Upon her return to the United States she formed a company which toured extensively, traveling as far south as New Orleans and Mobile. She retired from the stage in 1854.[28]

George Washington Smith, also a Philadelphian, made his debut at the age of twelve, in 1832. Smith described himself "as a clog, hornpipe, and flatfoot dancer"[29] for this early part of his career. He credits his earliest training in the classical dance to James Sylvian. When Sylvian returned to Europe, Smith replaced him as Elssler's partner. During his long career as a dancer he partnered several other foreign ballerinas as well as the American, Mary Ann Lee. Smith, an excellent dancer, exhibited the versatility demanded of an artist of the period. All during his career Smith was a teacher, whenever time allowed, and in 1881 he opened a studio where he continued his work until his death in 1899.

25. Olga Maynard, *The American Ballet* (Philadelphia: Macrae Smith Company, 1959), p. 18.

26. Lillian Moore, "George Washington Smith," *Chronicles of the American Dance,* ed. Paul Magriel (New York: Henry Holt and Company, 1948), p. 143.

27. Marian H. Winter, "Augusta Maywood," *Chronicles of the American Dance,* ed. Paul Magriel (New York: Henry Holt and Company, 1948), p. 137.

28. Lillian Moore, "Mary Ann Lee," *Chronicles of the American Dance,* ed. Paul Magriel (New York: Henry Holt and Company, 1948), p. 103.

29. Lillian Moore, "George Washington Smith," *Chronicles of the American Dance,* ed. Paul Magriel (New York: Henry Holt and Company, 1948), p. 139.

Ballet was not the only form of dance entertainment on the American stage between 1840 and 1885. Americans developed, toured, and exported a unique form based on the dance heritage of the black population. This new dancing, tap dancing, was a blend of Irish jig, clog, and Afro-American dance tied together by rhythm.[30] Black Americans had long danced for their own enjoyment and the entertainment of others, but when this new dance came to the stage, it was done by white performers in blackface. One early exception, in the 1840's, was William Henry Lane, a free-born black, who appeared under the stage name of Master Juba. Juba's primary rival was Master John Diamond, a white dancer. To determine who was the better dancer of the two, a series of challenge dances was held in 1844, which Master Juba won, being awarded the title of "King of All Dancers." Juba danced with top billing in white minstrel shows in the United States and England.

> The popular minstrel shows had a standard format: . . . "first part" . . . which began with an overture, continued with the comic question-answer period, included some comic and sentimental songs, and ended with a final Walk-Around. The second part was the Olio, in which a variety of singing, dancing, and speaking acts were performed. The final part, the Afterpiece . . . became an extravaganza performed by the entire cast and was usually a burlesque of a serious drama popular at the time.[31]

Social dance also continued during the period. The country dance gave way to the square dance, which added a more lively swing in the form of the buzz step. Dances like the "Spanish Cavalier" consisted of little else. Around 1870, singing calls were in common use.[32] The waltz and the polka, imported from Europe, began to replace the country dance in the fashionable ballrooms of the city. These new dances were denounced as immoral and vulgar, since a lady might whirl around the dance floor in the arms of a man who was not her husband.

The men and women who went west in 1849 in the California Gold Rush took their dancing with them. In California, the new arrivals also found and joined in the dance traditions of the Spanish and Mexican residents, including the Fandango, although the term did not necessarily apply to a specific dance. "Any major event on a Spanish ranchero that featured an

---

30. Lynne Fauley Emery, *Black Dance in the United States from 1619 to 1970* (Palo Alto, California: National Press Books, 1972), pp. 185-190.

31. Lynne Fauley Emery, *Black Dance in the United States from 1619 to 1970* (Palo Alto, California: National Press Books, 1972), p. 191.

32. S. Foster Damon, *The History of Square-Dancing* (Worcester, Mass.: American Antiquarian Society, 1952), pp. 87-92.

informal dancing party or general ball was called a *fandango.*"[33] When a dancing party was given, written invitations were sent to settlers for miles around, and if ladies were available, it was deemed a huge success. The absence of ladies, however, did not preclude the occurrence of such an event. The miners chose each other for partners, sometimes roughly, to dance a quadrille or square dance. It was not unusual for the caller to end the set with a call of "Promenade to the bar and treat your partners." With or without female partners, dancing was a part of the scene in the mining camps.

The Popular Fitness Movement

Social Reformers

During this period, the health of Americans became a growing concern to many leaders of the day, who urged sport and exercise to improve both the health and general outlook of the public. Dr. Oliver Wendell Holmes, *Autocrat* and Harvard medical professor, extolled the virtues of boating, walking, fencing, and even boxing. "Anything is better than this white-blooded degeneration to which we all tend."[34]

Catharine Beecher warned against the poor health of women and against society's conventions, which limited female physical activity. Her famous brother, the Reverend Henry Ward Beecher of Brooklyn, was an American advocate of the English "muscular Christianity movement" which aimed at "breadth of shoulders as well as of doctrines." He encouraged vigorous outdoor recreation and argued that churches and other Christian associations should undertake to provide opportunities for the young men of the city to bowl, play billiards, and exercise in wholesome environments.

One of the most influential voices urging the need for exercise and sport was Thomas Wentworth Higginson, liberal clergyman, author, intellectual, and former military officer. In a series of articles in the *Atlantic Monthly,* he extolled the virtues of the athletic life, and suggested a wide variety of activities from which men might choose. Field sports were lauded as bringing one into touch with nature. Skating was highly recommended, and he agreed with Henry Ward Beecher that bowling and billiards, when rescued from the sordid surroundings of the commercial establishment, were ac-

---

33. Gretchen Adel Schneider, "Pigeon Wings and Polkas: The Dance of the California Miners," *Dance Perspectives* 39 (Winter, 1969): 23.

34. Oliver Wendell Holmes, *The Autocrat of the Breakfast Table* (Boston: Houghton, Mifflin and Company, 1904), p. 171.

ceptable pastimes. Boxing he saw as possessing a tendency to brutalize the mind although he conceded that limited skill and knowledge in the sport might promote desirable qualities of manliness.[35] Others, too, played significant roles in the effort to arouse their fellow citizens to the need for fitness. George Winship, a noted strongman, advocated a system of training with heavy weights. Through lecture-exhibition tours and his Boston gymnasium he urged men to seek health through strength.

In opposition to Winship's use of heavy apparatus and emphasis on strength, Dr. Dioclesian Lewis developed a "New Gymnastics" which incorporated numerous exercises using light wands, Indian clubs, wooden rings, and two-pound dumbbells. Lewis was a popular and dynamic lecturer, perhaps the most effective of the fitness proponents, who in his "observations of people in all sections of the country . . . was so painfully impressed by the prevalence of pale faces, undeveloped and distorted bodies, and nervous debility that he became anxious to arouse the people to active interest in physical culture, and especially to the necessity of making it a part of school training."[36] Concerned for the health of women as well as men, and convinced of the need for systematic exercise suitable for both sexes, Lewis sought to improve not only muscle strength, ". . . but to give flexibility, agility and grace of movement. . . ."[37] Lewis' system achieved widespread popularity in the 1850's, '60's, and '70's, because the heavy, fixed apparatus necessary to some strength-building systems was not required and Lewis' exercises could be performed in the home, the classroom, or other restricted areas. In 1861 he founded his Normal Institute for Physical Education, a ten-week program for training men and women to teach his system. Lewis, a prolific writer, reached many people through books such as *The New Gymnastics for Men, Women and Children* and *Weak Lungs and How to Make Them Strong*.

Private and public gymnasiums opened in many medium-sized and larger cities. In the decade prior to the Civil War a gymnasium opened in Cincinnati, the Tremont Gymnasium started in Boston, and the Metropolitan Gymnasium, the latest in design, began its program in Chicago. The Metropolitan Gymnasium measured 108 × 80 feet, with walls 20 feet high and a center dome 40 feet in both height and diameter. Following the War other privately owned public gymnasiums opened in cities across the nation, including Dudley A. Sargent's Hygienic Institute and School of Physical

35. Thomas Wentworth Higginson, "Gymnastics," *Atlantic Monthly* 7 (March 1861): 283-302.

36. Mary F. Eastman, *The Biography of Dio Lewis* (New York: Fowler & Wells, 1891), p. 70.

37. Dio Lewis, *The New Gymnastics for Men, Women and Children* (Boston: Ticknor and Fields, 1864), p. 9.

Culture in New York. Many organized athletic clubs also included exercise facilities in their buildings.

Societies and Associations

Turner Societies

The German Revolution of 1848 brought thousands of exiles to the United States, many of whom continued their German customs and programs. Among the immigrants were many German Turners, who immediately established Turner societies. The first Turnverein, as the societies were called, was founded in 1848 in Cincinnati by Friedrich Hecker. Within three years the first national turnfest, sponsored by the United Turnverein of North America (the American Turnerbund), was held in Philadelphia and by 1859, seventy-three societies with a combined membership of over 5,000 had been formed. At the end of the Civil War the societies reunited into a North American Turnerbund, testimony both to the popularity of the movement and to the influx of German immigrants to North America in less than two decades. By 1867 there were 148 societies with 10,200 members.[38]

The turnverein, a social center affording a bridge between the old culture and the new, helped preserve traditional customs, language, and celebrations while also offering English language and American citizenship classes. Central to each turnverein, however, was the gymnastics program. Based on Friedrich Jahn's work in Germany, but modified to the new land, each society offered instruction and attempted to provide adequate gymnasium facilities for children, youth, and adults, who were all encouraged to pursue physical fitness through gymnastics. Classes were held during the day, after school, on evenings, and on weekends. Not only did the Turner movement affect thousands of German-Americans, but also it aided the acceptance of physical education in the public schools of several cities with large German-American populations.

The program or system, aiming at a balanced level of fitness, employed marching, free exercises with wands, gymnastic apparatus work, a graded set of games, and dance steps for girls. The activities were taught by age groups, and periodically local turnfests were held where group exhibitions could be seen. Following the Civil War, many other Americans were impressed by the Turner or German system of gymnastics and incorporated it into their programs, usually appointing a Turner to teach the work properly.

---

38. Henry Metzner, *History of the American Turners* (Rochester, N.Y.: National Council of the American Turners, 1974), p. 25.

The Young Men's Christian Association

The Young Men's Christian Association, founded in England by George Williams and introduced to the United States in the early 1850's, sought to provide a wholesome environment for young men newly arrived in the city. Originally organized for Bible study and evangelical work, the "Y" became interested in physical activity programs in the middle '50's. In 1856 the Brooklyn Association's Board of Managers considered the establishment of a gymnasium, but due to financial problems and the Civil War, the plans did not materialize. In 1864, at its annual convention the YMCA received a resolution which formally expressed its commitment to physical education: "Any machinery will be incomplete which has not taken into account the whole man. We must add physical recreation to all YMCAs."[39] Five years later the first two complete YMCA gymnasiums were built, in New York and San Francisco. Slowly, additional associations began to add gymnasiums and to employ physical directors.

The YMCA's in the 1870's and '80's included in their gymnasiums many of the weight implements of Winship, the lighter equipment of Lewis and Beecher, and the new, more scientifically based apparatus of Dudley A. Sargent. "But the gymnasium is only a part of the physical department. . . . In 1884 twenty-three Associations reported various other forms of physical culture, including base-ball, rambling, rowing, as well as swimming clubs and bowling-alleys."[40] The specific programs followed within the gymnasium and outside of it depended upon the training and inclination of the director.

The Young Women's Christian Association

In 1877 the Boston branch of the Young Women's Christian Association began a class in calisthenics, which was taught by one of the residents. Athletics were offered in a nearby park in 1882, and an exercise program was conducted for the residents of the Association's Warrenton Street Home, utilizing a few chest-weights on closet doors and in the corners of hallways. At the same time a class from the Association received free instruction in a private Boston gymnasium. When the YW's new building opened in 1884, it boasted a fifth-floor gymnasium, the first to be incorporated into any American YWCA building. Classes were taught during its first year by Anna Wood of the Wellesley College gymnasium faculty. In

39. M.L. Walters, "The Physical Education Society of the Y.M.C.A.'s of North America," *Journal of Health and Physical Education* 17 (May, 1947): 357.

40. Luther Gulick, "What the American Young Men's Christian Associations are Doing for the Physical Welfare of Young Men," *Annual Autumn Games,* Young Men's Christian Association of the City of New York, October 13, 1888, p. 20. Courtesy of A.G. Spalding Company Archives, Chicopee, Massachusetts.

the next few years light gymnastic classes were reported in a number of other YWCA's. The programs offered were those of the instructor; there was no official YWCA program. Some YW's offered the work of Beecher and Dio Lewis, others offered German or Swedish gymnastics, and still others the Delsarte system.[41]

Physical Education and Sport in the Schools and Colleges

By 1850, public common schools were established in many states and in 1874, the Kalamazoo case upheld the right of local school districts to levy taxes to support high schools. The passage in 1862 of the federal Morrill Act provided for the establishment of land-grant colleges in each state and greatly increased the number of public institutions of higher learning. All levels of education were increasingly accessible to Americans in the latter half of the nineteenth century.

Following the brief period of physical education and gymnasium experiments in the 1820's, colleges and high schools generally ignored the subject for the next three decades. In spite of the earnest pleas from many leaders, only scattered programs existed.

Although German gymnastics were introduced in the Cincinnati schools as early as 1860 and other midwestern cities in the 1860's and '70's, it was not until the middle '80's that programs were permanent and a part of the school system. At San Francisco's Rincon School, John Swett initiated a daily program of play and exercise. He led the boys on ten to fifteen mile hikes as well as in various ball games and insisted that the girls should participate in free gymnastics and work with wands. Funds for equipment were raised through boxing and gymnastic exhibitions.

In 1866, Swett, by this time the California State Superintendent of Public Instruction, was instrumental in the passage of America's first state legislation requiring physical education in the public elementary and secondary schools. The law provided that:

> Instruction shall be given in all grades of schools, and in all classes, during the entire school course in . . . the laws of health; and due attention shall be given to such physical exercises for the pupils as may be conducive to health and vigor of body, as well as mind.[42]

---

41. Elizabeth Wilson, *Fifty Years of Association Work Among Young Women 1866-1916* (New York: National Board of the Young Women's Christian Associations, 1916), pp. 43, 44, 99-101.
42. From Second Biennial Report—State Superintendent of Public Instruction 1866-67, Appendix E, Revised School Law, March 24, 1866, Section 55, cited in Dudley S. DeGroot, "A History of Physical Education in California (1848-1939)," Ph.D. dissertation, Stanford University, 1940, p. 23.

The law specified that the primary schools must allot a minimum of five minutes twice each day for free gymnastics and vocal and breathing exercises.

Women's Programs

Both before and after the Civil War education for women remained controversial and "higher" education for women was almost unheard of. Opponents suggested that "feminine problems" would prevent the women from attending classes regularly and, therefore, they should not be admitted to men's colleges because they would hinder the men's work. Two men, Matthew Vassar and Henry Fowle Durant, disagreed with this position and set out to prove that women could engage in "higher" education equal to that of men. Both included exercise and sport in their plans.

In 1861 Vassar Female College fully committed itself to a physical education program by planning and building a Calisthenium and planning to appoint faculty members to instruct sport and physical training. Feeling keenly the need of women to become more physically active, and eager to demonstrate that they could survive the rigors of academic life, Vassar pro-

FIG. 4.6   Mount Holyoke Seminary students in early 1860's at exercise. Courtesy of Mount Holyoke College Library, South Hadley, Massachusetts.

vided a special School of Physical Training. The school, housed in the Calisthenium, contained a gymnasium 81 × 30 feet, a bowling alley 82 × 30 feet, a music-hall 30 × 52 feet, and riding facilities with accommodations for about 25 horses. Vassar provided facilities for both exercise and sport for his college:

> Recreations, particularly in the open air, will not only be encouraged, but regulated and taught, and, to a certain extent, required of all the students; and the proper facilities will be furnished to render them attractive and useful. For this purpose, in-doors, the spacious and cheerful corridors of the college edifice, and, without, the beautiful college park, will afford unusual advantages. The play-grounds are ample and secluded; and the apparatus required for the Swedish Calisthenics (or Boston Light Gymnastics), and for such simple feminine sports as archery, croquet (or ladies' cricket), graces, shuttlecock, &c., will be supplied by the College.
>
> Every student will be required to provide herself with a light and easy-fitting dress, to be worn during these athletic exercises. It will be left optional with her, whether to wear it or not at other times.

VASSAR FEMALE COLLEGE.

PROSPECTUS.

> The object of this Institution, as stated by its Founder, is "to accomplish for young women what our colleges are accomplishing for young men." This, according to his own interpretation, refers solely to the character of the education it shall seek to impart, and is intended to enjoin, not a feeble imitation of the ordinary college *curriculum*, but a general coincidence in the elevation of its aims and the careful adjustment of its arrangements thereto; with a wise reference, at the same time, to all the peculiar and modifying circumstances of the case.
>
> In their endeavors to carry this idea of the Founder into effect, the Trustees will be guided by the following

General Scheme of Education.

1.—PHYSICAL EDUCATION.

> This is placed first, not as first in intrinsic importance, but as *fundamental* to all the rest, and in order to indicate the purpose of the managers of this Institution to give it, not nominally but really, its true place in their plan.
>
> Good health is essential to the successful prosecution of study, and to the vigorous development of either the mental or moral powers; and without it, whatever attainments are made, will be comparatively valueless as the means of a useful or happy life.[43]

As plans for the college developed, Matthew Vassar heeded the advice of Sara Josepha Hale, editor of the popular *Godey's Lady's Book* and an in-

---

43. *Prospectus of the Vassar Female College* (New York: Alford, 1865).

fluential proponent of women's education, and removed the word *female* from the title. The college opened in 1865. The First Annual Catalogue listed a woman, Dr. Alida C. Avery, as Professor of Physiology and Hygiene and as resident physician. Also listed was Miss Delia F. Woods as Instructor in the Department of Physical Training.

The program consisted of exercises, some of which were based on Dio Lewis' work. The faculty members were evidently sensitive to the students' wishes, for in 1877, Lilian Tappan, an instructor, instituted a plan for sport in physical education. In the spring of the year, she permitted the students to choose an outdoor sport in place of indoor gymnastics. This is the first indication that students were losing interest in regular gymnastic instruction and that other means might have to be found to provide instruction in regular physical activity.

VASSAR STUDENT GAME REGISTRATION*[44]
1876-77

Gymnastics
(November 13-April 13)

Number registered in gymnastics classes   270

Games
(April 23-June 2 or 27)

Ball	25
Boating	94
Croquet	108
Gardening	24
Walking	116
	———
	367*

*Many students selected more than one game.

Henry Fowle Durant, founder of Wellesley College in 1874, followed Vassar's lead and provided for both exercise and sport. The large building on campus, College Hall, housed a gymnasium. Students were required to

44. Lilian Tappan, Report to the President, 1877. Vassar College Archives, Poughkeepsie, New York.

FIG. 4.7   1876 Rowing at Wellesley College, Wellesley, Massachusetts. Courtesy of Wellesley College Archives.

take exercises and to wear looser and shorter dresses than usual—about twelve inches off the floor—for exercise classes. Located on the edge of Lake Waban, Wellesley College took advantage of its setting and provided boats in which several girls could row at one time. In the winter the lake froze over, so that the students could enjoy ice skating. When Durant could not find equipment for the new game of tennis, he sent to England for rackets and nets.

About the same time, in the Middle West, when women were first admitted to the University of Wisconsin in 1873, the University fitted up a gymnasium in Ladies Hall. Similarly, in Boston the women of the "Society for the Collegiate Instruction of Women," later called Radcliffe College, requested Sargent at Harvard to provide gymnastic work for them. He did so and opened the Sanatory Gymnasium for them in 1881.

There was, however, a diversity of opinion regarding dancing as a program in the public and private schools for women. Society, too, had sharply mixed ideas about its place. Matthew Vassar, in a 1867 report, mentions "recent writings pro and con" on the question of dancing, and he specifically mentions an essay by a minister on the "Incompatibility of Amusements with Christian Life." Vassar himself, however, urged that dance be taught in his college, "in view of its being a healthful and graceful exercise."[45] In general in educational institutions, emphasis in dancing was

---

45. Matthew Vassar, "Communications," June 25, 1867, p. 44. Vassar College Archives, Poughkeepsie, New York.

placed upon its value as healthful exercise or as a means of imparting poise and a graceful carriage. Opposition to dancing on religious grounds prevented its widespread practice in the early public schools, so dancing was more likely to be found in the seminaries. In some cases, the objections were overcome by the argument that it was ". . . a healthful recreation and exercise, and that it prevented children from carrying on more harmful activities."[46]

Men's Programs

In 1861 Amherst College, under its progressive president, William A. Stearns, fully committed itself to the concept of physical education in the curriculum by appointing Dr. Edward Hitchcock, a young medical doctor and son of a former Amherst College president, as Professor of Hygiene and Physical Education. A new gymnasium was constructed, and the students were required to attend exercise classes for half an hour four times a week. The gymnasium was fitted out with the equipment of the period. Each class session began with fifteen to twenty minutes of required exercise in uniform, either light gymnastics with dumbbells, or heavy gymnastics with weights for more capable and stronger students, plus formal marching, running or "double-quick" movements. The remainder of the thirty-minute period was devoted to individual, voluntary exercise such as running, tumbling, heavy lifting, or sport activity. Although the only sport facility in the original gymnasium was the bowling alley, the new Pratt Gymnasium, built in 1884, reflected the growing interest in sport by including rooms for billiards, boxing, and baseball practice. Welcoming the increased popularity of sport and athletic activities, Dr. Hitchcock continued to stress the continuing need for the gymnasium exercise program as a necessary foundation for health.

With a medical education and teaching experience only in the areas of anatomy, physiology, and natural history, young Hitchcock began a long tenure at Amherst College and made a lasting impact on American physical education. His physical education program was a model that was transplanted to many other colleges and universities. His original responsibilities at Amherst were to serve as medical officer of the college, instruct in hygiene, and plan and supervise a systematic program of exercise and recreation. By training and interest, Hitchcock was primarily concerned with improving the health of the Amherst College students through hygiene and exercise programs, and again he set a pattern which was followed in

---

46. Richard Kraus, *History of the Dance in Art and Education* (Englewood Cliffs, N.J.: Prentice-Hall, Inc., 1969), p. 125.

other educational institutions, which also appointed medical doctors to direct their physical education programs. The Amherst program was described in an 1869 report to the Board of Trustees:

> The design is, that all the muscles of the body should be exercised in a manner to equalize best the circulation of the blood,—to expand the lungs,—to aid the stomach in the digestion of food,—to strengthen the joints, develop all parts of the body in harmony with the most efficient action of the brain. Thus not only agility and strength of the limbs are acquired, but the vital forces of the system— fed from their natural sources of nutrition, absorption and respiration—are most abundantly supplied. The true course pointed out for physical exercise . . . is, . . . bringing the system into the highest state of physical health compatible with mental exercise.[47]

In addition to these goals, Hitchcock was active in anthropometry, an area of interest to nineteenth century physical educators. Seeking the "average college man," he maintained records on age, weight, height, chest girth, arm girth, forearm girth, lung capacity, and pull-ups on thousands of students. Measurements were taken on all incoming students and an individual program designed for each student to procure bodily symmetry and to correct imbalances and weaknesses. Subsequent readings were made each year to measure the student's progress.

In 1879 Harvard also granted faculty status to a physical educator—to the director of its new Hemenway Gymnasium. Like Amherst College, Harvard appointed a medical doctor, Dudley A. Sargent. In addition to his medical background, he also had practical experience gained as a student Director of Gymnastics at Bowdoin and Yale Colleges. As Assistant Professor of Physical Training and Director of the Gymnasium, Sargent undertook serious studies in gymnastics, anthropometry, and physical education, which he carried on until his retirement in 1919. Although a fine athlete himself, Sargent was primarily concerned with the fitness of the nonathlete. His purpose was ". . . to improve the physical condition of the mass of our students, and to give them as much health, strength and stamina as possible, to enable them to perform the duties that await them after leaving college."[48] To this end he, like Hitchcock, placed great emphasis upon physical examinations as the basis upon which individual programs of exercise would be built. The examination included a personal medical history, strength tests, lung capacity tests, anthropometric

---

47. Nathan Allen, *Physical Culture in Amherst College* (Lowell, Mass.: Stone and Huse, 1869), p. 16.

48. Isabel C. Barrows, ed., *Physical Training, A Full Report of the Papers and Discussion of the Conference Held in Boston in November, 1889* (Boston: George H. Ellis, 1890), p. 68.

measurements, and an examination of the heart and lungs before and after exercising.[49] From this information Sargent prescribed a program of appropriate exercises, always taking care to specify the amount of work and the correct adjustment of the apparatus to be used. In addition he suggested appropriate diet, sleep, bathing, and clothing. He was highly critical of the old heavy apparatus modeled after the German turnplatz, on the grounds that most people could not use it properly. On the other hand, he criticized the Indian clubs, dumbbells, wands, and other light gymnastic equipment as appropriate only for developing suppleness. Sargent ultimately designed over eighty developmental machines: chest-expanders and developers, quarter-circles, leg-machines, finger-machines, high pulleys, inclined planes, travelling parallels, and hydraulic rowing machines. He sought to design equipment based on scientific principles which would be easy to use. By 1885 it was reported that at least forty-eight institutions were using apparatus of Sargent's design. Because Sargent failed to apply for patents on any of his designs, he never received any remuneration from their widespread use.

At about this same time, an Englishwoman traveling in the Middle West visited some colleges with less advanced physical training:

> No suitable provision was made for physical exercise or relaxation at Oberlin College, and no gymnasium existed for either sex. During our ten days' stay we saw no sign whatever of athletic sports or exercises. . . . The utmost physical recreation seemed to consist in a country walk. . . . This absence of desire for physical sports seems more or less common throughout America, and is very strange in the eyes of those accustomed to the exhibition of animal spirits in the English youth of both sexes. . . .
>
> I found, indeed, that at this College [Antioch] somewhat more attention was paid to physical exercise, Mr. [Horace] Mann speaking of "bathing and exercise" as the "religious rites of health," and at the time of our visit short exhibitions of "light gymnastics" (i.e. exercises of arms, &c, without machinery), took place several times a day between the recitations.[50]

Beginnings of Intercollegiate Sport

Intercollegiate sport for men through 1885 centered primarily on casual events in rowing, baseball, football, and track and field. It began slowly as occasional student challenge-matches shortly after mid-century and within thirty-five years was established as a significant part of campus life.

49. Dudley Allen Sargent, *An Autobiography,* ed. Ledyard W. Sargent (Philadelphia: Lea & Febiger, 1927), p. 174.

50. Sophia J. Blake, *A Visit to Some American Schools and Colleges* (London: Macmillan and Co., 1867), p. 33, p. 138.

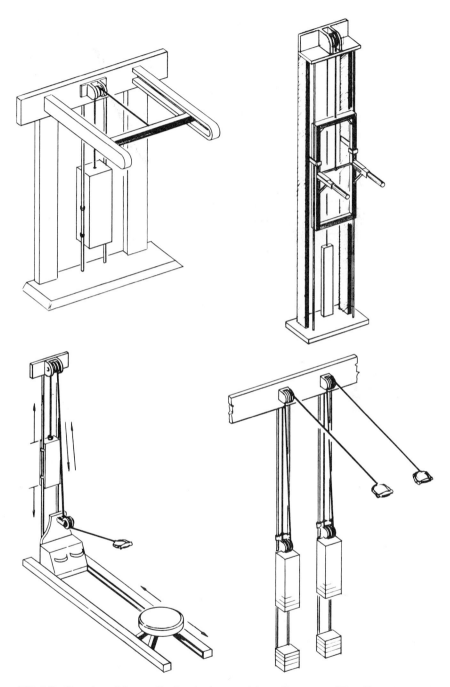

FIG. 4.8   Drawing of Sargent's developing machines. Courtesy of Ron Turmelle.

The growing public interest in sport during the 1840's carried onto the campus. Rowing, one of the most popular sports of the period, began at Yale in 1843 and at Harvard the following year. Rowing clubs were formed both to develop and formalize interest in the activity and to generate funds necessary for the purchase and maintenance of boats and other equipment. The clubs, composed of students and an occasional faculty member, also functioned as social organizations. Officially, however, the clubs had no affiliation with the college or university other than the members being students. The clubs raised funds, purchased boats, constructed facilities, and scheduled matches with other clubs. The rowing clubs were, in fact, student-initiated, student-financed, student-coached, and student-administered. This model set the pattern for the beginnings of inter-collegiate athletics for men in the United States.

The First Events

It is generally accepted that the turning points in establishing inter-collegiate athletics were the 1852 Harvard-Yale crew race, the 1859 Amherst-Williams baseball game, and the 1869 Princeton-Rutgers football contest.

Rowing

August 3, 1852. Harvard, First Place; Yale, Second Place. William J. Weeks, Yale '44, came back to college in the spring of 1843 with a four-oared Whitehall boat and formed a rowing club. The next year the club purchased a six-oared racer, the *Excelsior,* and used it in races with other New Haven clubs. The first Harvard club began with a barge, *Oneida,* which the Harvard men rowed with other amateur crews on the Charles River.

The idea for a Harvard-Yale match appears to have several possible origins. According to one account, "The Yale oarsmen had their eyes on the progress at Harvard and, largely through the efforts of James M. Whiton, '53, a challenge was sent to Harvard. . . ."[51] Another story credits Mr. James N. Elkins, general superintendent of the Boston, Concord and Montreal Railroad with promoting the match to popularize the Lake Winnipesaukee area as a summer resort, which would in turn benefit the railroad as the region's major transportation system. He persuaded the two clubs to send crews to race in eight-oared barges over a two-mile course. Whatever the specific cause, student crews from Harvard and Yale met at New Hampshire's Lake Winnipesaukee in the summer of 1852, and the event marked the inauguration of intercollegiate sport in America.

---

51. Samuel Crowther and Arthur Ruhl, *Rowing and Track Athletics* (New York: The Macmillan Co., 1905), p. 17.

Harvard rowed the *Oneida,* and one of the crew commented that they "had not rowed much for fear of blistering their hands!" Yale had three boats, the *Halcyon, Undine,* and the *Atlanta.* Harvard won the prize, a pair of black walnut sculls mounted on silver.

> There was so much fun in the race that the crews thought they would have another go on the fifth; but that day was very stormy, and the prize was given to the Halcyon as second in the first race.[52]

Hundreds witnessed the event, including the Democratic presidential nominee, Franklin Pierce. Although a New York *Tribune* reporter commented that ". . . intercollegiate sport would make little stir in the busy world,"[53] the event was moderately successful and hinted at the future possibilities of intercollegiate sport as a means of obtaining revenue.

Baseball

July 1, 1859. Amherst-73, Williams-32. The Amherst College Ball Club was established in 1859, with James F. Claflin '59 as captain. A student recalled that Claflin ". . . proposed . . . that a challenge be sent to Williams. After some preliminary negotiation a contest was arranged on July 1, on the neutral grounds of the Pittsfield Baseball Club, each team to provide its own ball. There were thirteen men on a side."[54]

The captains met to agree on the play and chose the Massachusetts Rules with the square playing field and wooden sticks for bases.

The Massachusetts Rules[55]

From *The Baseball Players Pocket Companion*
(Boston: Mayhew and Baker, 1860)

MATERIALS

The only essential materials used in playing the game beside a ball are a bat-stick and four wooden stakes for bases, the form and sizes of which are described in the annexed rules and regulations of the game. The ball is composed of woolen yarn and strips of India rubber wound tightly, forming a complete sphere, and covered with buck or calf skin.

---

52. Samuel Crowther and Arthur Ruhl, *Rowing and Track Athletics* (New York: The Macmillan Co., 1905), p. 18.
53. "Regattas on Lake Winnepiseogee," [sic] New York *Tribune,* 10 August 1852, p. 6.
54. Claude M. Fuess, *Amherst* (Boston: Little, Brown, 1935), p. 197.
55. "One Hundred Years of Baseball," *Amherst Alumni News,* October, 1958, p. 4.

THE GAME

The game is commenced by staking off a square of 60 feet for the bases, and measuring the distance of 35 feet from the thrower's to the striker's stand, as explained by diagram.

The four corners of the square are the bases. The striker's stand is the square of four feet at equal distances between the first and the fourth base. Outside of this square, and the line between the first and fourth base is the catcher's stand. In the center of the square the thrower is stationed, who delivers the ball to the striker, which, if not struck, should be caught by the catcher behind; but if struck by the batsman, he is obliged to run the bases, commencing at 1, so on to 2, 3, and 4; when arriving at 4 or the home base, he is entitled to one tally. After the first player strikes the ball and runs to the base, he is immediately succeeded by the next "in" player, who takes his turn in the order in which he is chosen. The "out" party, besides the thrower and catcher, should be stationed as follows: One player on or within a few feet from each base, who should give strict attention to the game, and be prepared to receive the ball at any time, in order to "put out" an opposite player, while passing from one base to another. One or two players should be stationed a few yards behind the catcher, to stop the ball in case the catcher should fail to do so. The other players should be stationed at different parts of the field, to pass the ball to the thrower when it has been knocked by the striker.

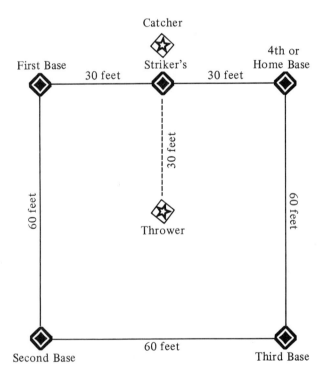

AMHERST EXPRESS.

EXTRA.

WILLIAMS AND AMHERST

BASE BALL AND CHESS!

MUSCLE AND MIND!!

July 1st and 2d, 1859.

FIG. 4.9 "Extra" of newspaper issued after Amherst College won the baseball game.

It was a four-hour game, but apparently did not lag in player and spectator interest. Originally, sixty-five runs had been announced as a limit, but the final score was 73-32. There were no uniforms, gloves, masks, or chest protectors.

The news of the results reached Amherst late that night, and both the college and the town celebrated with bonfires and bell ringing. An EXTRA edition of the newspaper was printed. The next afternoon the victorious team arrived in Amherst to be accorded a hero's welcome.

Football

November 6, 1869. Rutgers-6, Princeton-4. For years there had been an intense rivalry between Rutgers and Princeton. Perhaps in response to the bitter 40-2 baseball defeat of 1866, or for other reasons, when W.J. Leggett '72 was elected the first college football captain, the Rutgers students challenged the men of the College of New Jersey, later Princeton University, to play a series of three football games, beginning November 6, 1869. Princeton accepted the challenge and the two captains agreed on the rules and conditions of play.

The game was played using a round, inflated rubber ball which one player would attempt to advance toward the opponent's goal with short kicks while his teammates surrounded him to keep the opponents away. Players were not allowed to catch or carry the ball, although one could bat a ball in the air using the hands.

There were no uniforms, no padding, or other protective equipment. One account notes:

> . . . a point was the sending of the ball between the goal posts at any height, there being no cross bar. Twenty-five men played on each side. They wore no uniforms. They laid aside their hats and coats and vests, reduced their clothing to serviceable limit, and joined battle.[56]

In all these contests, the students challenged the other team, the students determined the rules, and the students made arrangements for the conduct of the events. At this time the administration and the faculty remained apart from the developing program of intercollegiate athletics for men.

The Development of Intercollegiate Sport

Rowing

Rowing developed earliest as a popular intercollegiate sport. By 1859, the rowing clubs at Harvard, Yale, Brown, and Trinity formed the College

---

56. William H.S. Demarest, *A History of Rutgers College* (New Brunswick: Rutgers College, 1924), p. 429.

Union Regatta Association and in 1860 and 1861, races were rowed on Lake Quinsigamond near Worcester, Massachusetts, with Harvard winning both years. Following a disturbance at the 1860 regatta, Yale students were forced by their faculty to withdraw from all intercollegiate competition. However, in 1864 Yale challenged Harvard to another race, having obtained a professional rower to coach the team and, for the first time in the brief history of intercollegiate sport, the New Haven crew was victorious. The Harvard-Yale series continued for the next seven years.

The race with Oxford University from England against Harvard in 1869 promoted interest in collegiate rowing, and as a result crews were formed at a number of colleges. Following this, the Harvard club initiated a meeting of several New England college clubs. The conference, held on April 15, 1871, at the Massasoit House in Springfield, Massachusetts, was attended by student representatives from Massachusetts Agricultural College (University of Massachusetts), Brown University, Bowdoin College, and Harvard. As a result of the meeting the Rowing Association of American Colleges was formed.

At the Association's first regatta on July 21, 1871, Massachusetts Agricultural College defeated Brown and Harvard, which encouraged other small, less prestigious institutions to enter future competitions with the larger, established schools. The next year Amherst, Bowdoin, and Williams Colleges entered the regatta, as did Yale. Amherst's victory in 1872 again stimulated additional interest and six more colleges entered the 1873 meet.

After Yale's success in 1864, more clubs hired a professional coach to prepare a team for a single event or entire season until, nine years later, the Rowing Association of American Colleges passed a rule prohibiting professional coaches. By 1874 public interest in collegiate rowing had grown to the extent that as a promotional event, the Annual Association Regatta was moved to Saratoga Lake at the invitation of John Morrissey, one of the famous resort's developers. The regattas of 1874 and 1875 attracted thousands of spectators and nationwide newspaper coverage. The mid-1870's marked the height of college rowing, as later baseball, football, and track and field became increasingly popular.

Baseball

Following the Civil War, baseball spread rapidly across the country and play increased at the colleges. By the mid-1870's, baseball was the most popular campus sport outside the Northeast. Amherst College played a series of games with Dartmouth College in the sixties and by 1875 was playing teams as far away as Princeton. A decade later, however, baseball too achieved its greatest popularity and within a decade occupied second place to football at most colleges.

Track and Field

Track and field athletics in colleges and universities began in 1869 when students formed the Columbia College Athletic Association and challenged other student groups. In meets that year events included the 100-yard, 150-yard, and 200-yard hurdle races, mile walk, standing long jump, high jump, and running long jump. Also in 1869, George Goldie, an outstanding Caledonian athlete, was appointed gymnasium director at Princeton University. By 1876 eleven institutions engaged in track and field athletics, and in addition in that year the Intercollegiate Association of Amateur Athletes of America was established—the oldest continuing collegiate athletic organization in the United States.

Perhaps the sudden increased interest in college track and field was partly attributable to the 1873 intercollegiate rowing regatta, when a single two-mile run was included with the rowing events. James Gordon Bennett, Jr., publisher of the New York *Herald* and a noted sport enthusiast, donated a cup to the winner of this race as well as to the rowers, and continued this sponsorship through the next several years. In 1874, five footraces were held: a one-mile run, 100 yards, three miles, seven-mile walking race, and 120-yard hurdles.[57] Eight colleges, including Columbia, Cornell, Harvard, Princeton, Wesleyan, Williams, and Yale took part. Track and field gradually achieved a following and standing of its own, and the ICAAAA assumed the responsibility for hosting an annual championship meet and for regulating the sport on the college level. By 1885 track and field took its place with football, baseball, and rowing as a main feature of the college athletic scene.

Football

Football on the college and university campuses was both exciting and troublesome. It answered the need for a physically demanding activity which the young men found satisfying and enjoyable, but the prevalence of injuries to students, lack of administrative control of the game, and its demands on students' time created problems for the administration. In an effort to codify the rules, Princeton, Rutgers, Yale, and Columbia founded the Intercollegiate Association for Football in 1873. Harvard declined to join the group because of its style of play, in which the player could run with the ball. The following year Harvard played McGill University, using rugby rules. Interest in the rugby-type game continued, and a new Inter-collegiate Football Association, formed in 1876, adopted the rugby rules. In 1881 a graduate student at Yale, Walter Camp, who also had been an

---

57. New York *Herald*, 15 July 1874, p. 6.

undergraduate there, continued to attend the Association's meetings, beginning his long association with the game.

Need for Institutional Control

Faculty reaction to the growing popularity of intercollegiate contests was mixed. Yale faculty assisted the students in the purchase of equipment and some Harvard professors openly acclaimed Harvard's victories. However, the faculty persistently complained that the students in intercollegiate sport, and their followers, missed too many classes. Finally in 1882 Harvard appointed a three-man faculty committee to deal specifically with the complaint regarding the lengthy baseball schedule. Out of this grew a meeting of faculty representatives, the Intercollegiate Athletic Conference, in December, 1883, in New York City. In this first attempt by college faculty to exercise some control over intercollegiate athletics, eight resolutions were passed dealing with subjects such as the prohibition of college teams playing against professional teams; the prohibition of receiving coaching from professional athletes; limiting competition to four years for each student; requiring all games to be played on the home field of one of the competing institutions; and having a standing faculty committee supervise all contests.[58] Only three institutions—Harvard, Princeton, Cornell—ratified the resolutions and thus the problem was not solved. However, the beginnings of change in the control of intercollegiate athletics had begun, and by the turn of the century the administration and faculties of colleges and universities asserted more control over student athletics.

Summary

Although this period was marked by contrasts in almost every phase of life, it was also characterized by a growing identification of "being an American." The Civil War, at a heavy price in lives and long-lasting bitterness, ended legal slavery. The technological improvements in transportation, communication, manufacturing, and urbanization, together with an immense increase in population, changed the towns to cities and created a climate which transformed games into sport.

Alexander Cartwright's organization of a popular game into a formalized sport was a major event in the history of sport. The fascination of men and women for watching other men play a game of ball was not explained, but

---

58. Edward M. Hartwell, *Physical Training in American Colleges and Universities,* Bureau of Education Circular of Information No. 5, 1885 (Washington, D.C.: Government Printing Office, 1886), pp. 125-128.

existed and has persisted. When baseball club owners paid men to play, a new economic component in American life, professional team sport, was initiated.

Another form of today's sport entertainment began in the 1850's and '60's as a series of student challenges. These early contests, planned and conducted completely by students, were the beginnings of intercollegiate athletics for men. However, Amherst, Harvard, and a few other institutions initiated physical education to maintain and improve students' health. On the other hand, women's colleges such as Vassar and Wellesley provided sport as well as physical exercises to promote health.

As life, especially in the cities, settled around "time" to go to work, "time" to leave work, and free "time," men and some women sought vigorous physical activity in and out of doors. Men and women flocked to ice skating, croquet, archery, and some to tennis. Many others tried the new roller skating rinks. Those of the rural regions enjoyed the square or round dances, while more urban people danced in the traditional ballroom styles. In short, people found joy and satisfaction in many forms of physical activity. It was an age of joining and organizing, and almost as soon as a game had several followers, an association was formed. The new sport associations standardized rules of play, promoted their sport, and sponsored national championships.

The growing organization of sport mirrored the developing complexities of urban and industrial life. Within less than half a century, sport moved from an informal, social pastime still somewhat questioned by the Puritan tradition, to an organized component of American life. Some of the significant changes in sport history included the beginning of professional team sports, the first intercollegiate sport events for men, the formation of sport associations, and the use of sport to improve health, especially for women.

Questions for Discussion

1. Are there any technological changes which have occurred recently which are comparable to the ones in this chapter? What are they?
2. What has been the significance of baseball in United States sport history?
3. Why was there such a sudden burgeoning of athletic clubs in the United States?
4. What would Huckleberry Finn (or his equivalent, a very bright, observant provincial boy *with no television!*) have thought of a ballet performance? How might he have described it?
5. If you were a female, 18 years old, in 1862, would you have been

inclined to travel to Poughkeepsie, New York, to attend Vassar College? Why or why not?

6. Was administrative control of college sport for men inevitable or not?

Suggestions for Further Reading

1. Betts, John Rickards. "The Technological Revolution and the Rise of Sport, 1850-1900." *Mississippi Valley Historical Review* 40 (1953): 231-256.
2. Emery, Lynne Fauley. *Black Dance in the United States from 1619 to 1970.* Palo Alto, California: National Press Books, 1972.
3. Higginson, Thomas Wentworth. "Gymnastics." *Atlantic Monthly* 7(March, 1861): 283-302.
4. Lewis, Guy M. "1879: The Beginning of an Era in American Sport." *72nd Proceedings,* National College Physical Education Association for Men (January 8-11, 1969): 136-145.
5. Redmond, Gerald. *The Caledonian Games in Nineteenth-Century America.* Rutherford, New Jersey: Fairleigh Dickinson University Press, 1971.
6. Sargent, Dudley A. *An Autobiography,* ed. Ledyard W. Sargent. Philadelphia: Lea & Febiger, 1927.
7. Willis, Joseph D., and Wettan, Richard G. "Social Stratification in New York City Athletic Clubs, 1865-1915." *Journal of Sport History* 3, no. 1 (Spring, 1976): 45-63.

Time Line

5

The Organizing of Sport and Physical Activity, 1885-1917

When twenty-year-old Francis Ouimet received surprised congratulations on the golf course of The Country Club in Brookline, Massachusetts, on September 20, 1913, he represented a paradox in sport. This former caddy, the son of a Brookline gardener, had just accomplished what was considered impossible; for the first time an amateur golfer from a poor family had won the United States Open Championship. He had defeated not only the best American players but also, in a stirring play-off round, had bested two English professionals for the championship. In that same tournament another golfer, Walter C. Hagen, son of a Rochester, New York, blacksmith, finished in a tie for second place and added further evidence that golf would no longer be the exclusive province of wealthy Americans.

United States society between 1885 and 1917 was filled with paradoxes. The first skyscrapers were built in the cities of the East and Midwest when new settlers on the plains were living in sod houses. Native Americans were facing piecemeal extermination in the West while the city poor were beginning to benefit from the social reforms of organized religion and philanthropists. A few tycoons amassed enormous private wealth and corporate power in industry, mining, and railroads, while millions of workers, flocking from farms and foreign lands, struggled to find subsistence-level jobs in crowded cities.

Sport and physical activity of the period mirrored these paradoxes. The increasing numbers of the very rich and of the upper middle class moved in their own circles and engaged in sports such as yachting, horse racing, polo, riding to the hounds, and the "new" sports of tennis and golf. Some of this group, however, were socially-minded philanthropists who supported playgrounds and settlement houses for the city poor. The growing middle classes during this period enjoyed some active sports and watched others, especially baseball.

Many religious leaders, educators, and doctors recommended exercise, simple play, and sport. Many churches built sport facilities and initiated social services in deprived neighborhoods of many cities and towns. The support of the churches helped make play acceptable to those who disapproved of "time-wasting" recreation and sport. Educators such as G. Stanley Hall, Edward L. Thorndike, William James, and John Dewey praised play and sport as valuable learning tools for youth in a democracy. Jane Addams, who worked among Chicago's poor, strongly asserted the necessity of recreation and attacked a society which did not provide adequate facilities:

> Only in the modern city have men concluded that it is no longer necessary for the municipality to provide for the insatiable desire for play. . . . and this at the very moment when the city has become distinctly industrial, and daily labor is continually more monotonous and subdivided. . . . this industrialism has gathered together multitudes of eager young creatures from all quarters of the earth as a labor supply for the countless factories and workshops, upon which the present industrial city is based. . . . This stupid experiment of organizing work and failing to organize play has, of course, brought about a fine revenge. The love of pleasure will not be denied, and when it has turned into all sorts of malignant and vicious appetites, then we, the middle aged, grow quite distracted and resort to all sorts of restrictive measures. . . . almost worse than the restrictive measures is our apparent belief that the city itself has no obligation in the matter, an assumption upon which the modern city turns over to commercialism practically all the provisions for public recreation.[1]

Doctors increasingly recommended vigorous physical activity for everyone in order to maintain health. In short, Americans began to be told that exercise, sport, play, and recreation were worthwhile aspects of democratic life.

Sport for the very wealthy, for the middle classes, and for the workers differed greatly, however. While some differences could be clearly explained because of available space, facilities, time, equipment, and cost, the greatest difference was in the perceived function of sport in their lives.

Sport and Pastimes of the Wealthy

For the wealthy youth and some men and women, sport was a natural pastime. With families in summer communities in the mountains or on the shore, with riding masters, with private schools or private teachers, children learned to sail, ride, and play tennis and golf. Young men of this group at college might enjoy intercollegiate sports, while the women at college might fiercely contest interclass championships in basketball or field hockey. Whereas Veblen treated sport in the "Gilded Age" as a vehicle for conspicuous consumption, the rich themselves seemed to consider their time on the links, courts, and at the track as an unquestioned part of life.

---

1. Jane Addams, *Spirit of Youth and the City Streets* (New York: Macmillan, 1909), p. 1.

RECEPTION AT 9, SPARRING AT 11, DANCING AT 12.
From "Life."

FIG. 5.1   Boxing, the entertainment at a reception. Courtesy Spalding Archives, Chicopee, Massachusetts.

Yacht racing continued to be a favorite sport of the wealthy. *America's* Cup challenges in 1885, 1886, and 1887 served to stimulate more interest in that sport. By 1889, there were more than 125 yacht clubs. Yacht design improved as each Cup challenge resulted in the construction of a new defender of the title. Edward Burgess designed each of three successful American defenders in the middle eighties and greatly influenced naval architecture during the next several years. In 1893 and 1895, the Earl of Dunraven unsuccessfully challenged for the Cup against American yachts designed by Nathaniel Herreshoff. In 1899 the first of several challenges was made by Sir Thomas Lipton of the Royal Ulster Yacht Club of Belfast. The *Shamrock I,* and two years later *Shamrock II,* were defeated by the Herreshoff-built *Columbia.* Undaunted, Lipton arrived in 1903 with *Shamrock III* and promptly lost to a new defender, *Reliance.* After that there were no more challenges until 1920.

The growing interest in yachting created a demand for a smaller craft, and in 1895 the Seawanhaka Corinthian Yacht Club, of Oyster Bay, Long Island, commissioned the building of a fifteen-foot boat with two hundred square feet of sail, and offered a challenge cup for small-yacht racing. The introduction of the smaller craft broadened the socioeconomic base of the

FIG. 5.2   Sailing in the 1890's.

sport, but until well into the twentieth century most yachting enthusiasts were relatively wealthy.

In the Midwest, yacht racing on the Great Lakes became popular in the 1890's in cities such as Detroit, Chicago, Toledo, Duluth, and Toronto. International races for the Seawanhaka Cup and, beginning in 1896, the Canada's Cup, were events of interest; and in 1898 the first Chicago to Mackinaw race provided Great Lakes sailors with their own prestigious challenge.

Late in the nineteenth century, luxurious steam vessels, which began to appear in Eastern yacht club basins, were used for vacations and transportation more than for racing. The development of the internal combustion engine and its adaptation to boats soon after the turn of the century led to auxiliary power for sailing vessels and power boat racing. Rich yachting enthusiasts now had a new sport and in 1904 inaugurated the Gold Cup Trophy of the American Power Boat Association.

Although following the Civil War thoroughbred racing was revived by respected men of wealth, only constant vigilance by track owners and operators, stable owners, reputable jockey clubs, and the law prevented racing from being controlled by professional gamblers. Millionaires such as

August Belmont and his son, August, Jr., Pierre Lorillard, Senator Leland Stanford, and James R. Keane combined their love of the sport, wealth, prestige, and managerial skills to renew racing success in the 1880's, '90's, and early years of the new century. Except in the economic depression in the first half of the nineties, racing prospered as all classes of people flocked to large new courses around the country. On many racing days crowds of five to ten thousand attended the New Orleans track in the winter of 1890, when the track stopped reserving special seats, sold general admission tickets at fifty cents, and allowed women to enter without charge; however, betting was difficult to control and charges of illegal gambling and fixed races led in 1908 to a six-year suspension.

Betting at horse races was among the many targets of the social reformers of the "progressive era" of the early 1900's. The reformers charged that horse racing existed only for the professional gambler and not for the improvement of the breed as argued by the owners. With Governor Hughes' support, New York state succeeded in ending betting by 1911, but the tracks were virtually deserted in 1911 and 1912. Only with modifications of the law and allowance of limited betting did the fans return to the tracks. By the beginning of World War I racing was again popular.

Bicycling was a particular favorite of many wealthy people. It later became popular with the middle class, but in the mid-eighties the $150 price of the "Ordinary" represented almost a half-year's salary for most Americans. By 1890 bicycle clubs were the fad in most cities and towns. Some clubs required certain social and economic qualifications for membership. For example, New York's elite Michaux Club, organized in 1895, was founded by socially prominent persons who wished a place to ride in the winter. In the rented quarters at Bowman's Hall, the club provided morning lessons, afternoon music rides, tea in one of the club rooms, and gala evening riding parties with grand marches, bicycle dances, and formation rides.[2]

Wealthy individuals did much through their own prestige to promote cycling. John D. Rockefeller, an avid cyclist, presented bicycles to friends and associates whose health he felt was in jeopardy. Other prominent cyclists included William Rockefeller, William O. Havemeyer, president of the sugar trust, Chauncey Depew, president of the New York Central Railroad and United States senator, and Lillian Russell, who rode a jewel-encrusted bicycle given to her by Diamond Jim Brady.[3] However, by the beginning of the century the motor car, a newer, faster, louder, riskier, and

---

2. Robert A. Smith, *A Social History of the Bicycle* (New York: American Heritage Press, 1972), pp. 116-17.

3. Robert A. Smith, *A Social History of the Bicycle* (New York: American Heritage Press, 1972), pp. 117-18.

more expensive mode of transportation, largely superseded the bicycle for this group.

Throughout the eighties and nineties tennis was primarily a game for the upper classes. The national championships were held in a resplendent Newport setting during Tennis Week each year. During these decades Newport was the summer home of some of the nation's wealthy families—the Belmonts, Vanderbilts, Goelets, and Astors among others. During these years "summer Newporters" such as James Dwight and Dick Sears, who was national singles champion from 1881 through 1887, dominated the game. The trophies were often elaborate and expensive, sometimes paid for by entry fees of as much as twenty-five dollars. The play was strictly amateur and, as a matter of course, Dwight, Sears, and other ranking players paid their own expenses to tournaments in the United States and Europe.

In the nineties the game changed to faster, more aggressive play as many college players were all-round athletes, such as Fred Hovey, Oliver Campbell, William Larned, and Bob Wrenn, who was a Harvard football, baseball, and hockey player. All these men were national singles champions in the nineties and early 1900's. Women's singles championships began in 1887 when Ellen F. Hansell took the title. Elizabeth A. Moore was champion three times—in 1896, 1901, and 1903.

In 1900, a well-to-do young man from St. Louis, Dwight Davis, a junior at Harvard and a ranking tennis player, encouraged international play by donating the Davis Cup and establishing this prestigious competition. The first decade of the new century found many outstanding players throughout the country. A Californian, May Sutton, at the age of sixteen won the women's singles championship in 1904 and one year later became the first American to win a British national championship in any sport. The national championship tournament moved in 1915 from the exclusive resort of Newport to New York's West Side Tennis Club, a private organization, but in a more accessible setting.

On a mild February 22nd in 1888, John Reid, a Scottish immigrant living in Yonkers, New York, unveiled a set of golf clubs and balls to a small group of close friends. The party proceeded to lay out three short holes in a nearby cow pasture and Reid and John P. Upham shared the clubs to play a friendly game while the others looked on. Upon the arrival of additional equipment from Britain, the friends played through the summer and fall of that year. In November, Reid gave a dinner party attended by four of the Yonkers golfers at which time he proposed the formation of a golfing club. The group agreed upon the name, the St. Andrews Club of Yonkers, in honor of the famous club in Scotland. After several moves, in 1897 the club made a final move to Mt. Hope and constructed an eighteen-hole course.

Meanwhile, other sportsmen in other cities began to play golf. The Coun-

FIG. 5.3a Longwood Cricket Club. Courtesy Spalding Archives, Chicopee, Massachusetts.

try Club of Brookline, Massachusetts, a suburb of Boston, founded in 1882 by a group of Boston gentlemen seeking a private retreat for riding, tennis, bowling, racing, and dining, added a six-hole golf course in 1893. Ultimately enlarged to twenty-seven holes, it became one of the premier courses in the United States.

Through the efforts of Thomas Havemeyer, the "Sugar King," a group of Englishmen laid a nine-hole course in 1890 in the industrial center of Middlesborough, Kentucky. A few years later the country's first eighteen-hole course was built by the Chicago Country Club in Wheaton, Illinois. So rapidly did the game become popular among wealthy Chicagoans that the city had twenty-six courses by 1900.[4]

The first professionally designed and constructed golf course in the United States was opened in 1891 on the eastern end of Long Island as an incorporated golf club named Shinnecock Hills. In the summer of 1894 the Newport Golf Club hosted a tournament in which both amateurs and professionals competed. Twenty players took part in the thirty-six hole, two-day medal play.

In December of that year the Amateur Golf Association of the United States, later renamed the United States Golf Association, was founded and

4. Will Grimsley, *Golf: Its History, People and Events* (Englewood Cliffs, N.J.: Prentice-Hall, 1966), p. 36.

FIG. 5.3b   R.D. Sears. Courtesy Spalding Archives, Chicopee, Massachusetts.

FIG. 5.3c Belmont Cricket Club of Philadelphia: c. 1885-1900. From left to right: Bertha Townsend, National Singles Champion, 1888-1889; Margaret Ballard, Louise Alderdice, Ellen Hansell, National Singles Champion in 1887. Courtesy Spalding Archives, Chicopee, Massachusetts.

FIG. 5.3d   The Davis Cup. Courtesy Spalding Archives, Chicopee, Massachusetts.

announced plans for the first national championships, the Open and the Amateur, to be hosted during the same week of October, 1895, by the Newport Golf Club. The Association, controlled from the start by influential men, added an aura of social status to the game, and in spite of the growth of public courses and the professional game during the early twentieth century, golf remained an upper-class sport. The first women's amateur championship was won in 1895 by Mrs. C.S. Brown, followed by Beatrix Hoyt in 1896, 1897, and 1898.

For the very rich, fox hunting and polo also were favorite pastimes. The rolling Maryland and Virginia countryside continued to be the center for fox hunting. Polo, first established in the East, also had followers in the West. James Gordon Bennett, Jr., the New York *Herald* publisher, instituted an occasional game in 1876 at a riding academy in New York City. The new game became popular with rich sportsmen and soon had followers and clubs in New Orleans, Los Angeles, Colorado Springs, and other cities. In 1890 the Polo Association, later the United States Polo Association, was founded. America's first international match was played against Britain's Hurlingham Club at Newport in 1886. The superiority of the English players and mounts was readily apparent in the easy defeat of the Americans, but this and later matches were learning experiences for the neophytes. After another defeat in 1902, a quartet led by Harry Payne Whitney finally defeated the British at Hurlingham in 1909 and established American polo as an international sport.

Many sports remained beyond the expectations of most middle-class Americans, who read about events such as the *America's* Cup races, fox hunting, and polo. They did not seem to concern themselves with the fact that many influential men controlled sport organizations such as the AAU and held prominent positions on the committees for the modern Olympic Games. These wealthy upper-class athletes promoted and perpetuated their special concept of the amateur in sport as the person who played for the "love of the game" and did not "taint" that love by accepting money, valuable prizes, or expenses to appear in tournaments.

Sport, Dance, and Pastimes for All

The middle and working classes in the United States by the end of the nineteenth century and at the beginning of the twentieth century included extremes within a seemingly homogenous group. The shopkeeper, the teacher, the factory worker, the secretary, the union organizer, the woman in a sweat shop, the farmer, the rancher, the real estate dealer, the pharmacist, the innkeeper, and the livery keeper were all middle- and

FIG. 5.4   Eleanora Sears. Wide World.

working-class people who were slowly being melded into the average American. Dissimilar in many ways, most were united in wanting a better life and better education for their children than they had had; hoping for some success and a portion of the "American dream."

A phenomenon of sport during this period was the beginning of the diffusion of sport down from the wealthy and socially elite toward the upper

FIG. 5.5 Sports of the period. Courtesy Spalding Archives, Chicopee, Massachusetts.

middle class, the middle class, and even to the working class. While at one time croquet, roller skating, and bicycling had been only for the socially elite, demands for sport equipment increased production which lowered the prices and eventually put even the bicycle in reach of middle-class families. In addition, the introduction of the safety and drop-frame bicycle further popularized bicycling and greatly increased the opportunities for the less daring who still wished to ride.

Sport served many functions for middle class and working people. Sport was entertainment for the crowds who sat in the ballparks together and rooted for hometown teams and their favorite heroes. The advent of public parks and recreation facilities increased the opportunities for sport for working people in the cities. In 1885, facilities for the poor were generally limited to those owned by philanthropic associations, workingmen's clubs, and churches. Three decades later laborers and middle-class people were playing baseball, basketball, football, volleyball, and even tennis and golf on publicly owned and operated courts, fields, and courses.

Sport as Entertainment and Pastimes

Baseball

The early years of organized professional baseball reflected something of the energetic, turbulent times. Not unlike the 1970's, controversies over players' rights and salaries marked professional baseball throughout this period. The newly formed National League of Professional Base Ball Clubs (1876) used many practices common to big business trusts of the period to establish control of the sport. The club owners controlled player contracts and blacklisted players who moved to other clubs between or during seasons. In 1879 came the first introduction of the reserve rule, which provided that each club could "reserve" five men for the following season. The entire system was periodically challenged by independent players who risked blacklisting in order to play for higher salaries in new leagues not affiliated with the National League. Other minor leagues, serving as a source of players for the major teams in an embryonic "farm system," were granted League alliance status by the National League.

The most successful of the early rivals to the National League was the American Association of Base Ball Clubs, founded in 1882 by six clubs: Cincinnati, St. Louis, Louisville, Pittsburgh, Baltimore, and Philadelphia. Promoting their games through 25-cent rather than 50-cent admissions, and through Sunday games and the selling of liquor at games, neither of which was allowed in the National League, the American Association owners were able to achieve modest success which continued through 1891.

The American Association also launched a new round of "trade wars," mutual blacklisting, and the first court suits involving players; one club could still "buy" another club's best players, even in the middle of a season. To bring some semblance of order to the situation, the season of 1883 was ". . . notable for the adoption of the Tripartite Agreement— afterwards the famous National Agreement—by the National League, American Association and Northwestern League, for the purpose of checking the prevailing system of player-piracy and many double-contract transactions."[5] The Agreement was a comprehensive document codifying club relationships, especially the reserve system, which bound a player to the same team for his entire career unless traded, sold, or released; thus ending for a while the wild bidding for players. In another aspect of the game, the same season of 1883 saw the end of the "out on first foul bound catch," so that it became a fly-catch game.

Other rival leagues attempted to compete with the National League and the American Association. The Union Association, opposed to the reserve system, lasted only one season, 1884. Continuing dissatisfaction with contract conditions led to a new organization, this one only for players—the Brotherhood of Ball Players. It was recognized by the National League in the fall of 1887 as an organization, ". . . the Brotherhood agreeing to recognize the Reserve Rule upon condition that the salary of a player should not be reduced while under reservation."[6] However, the next year the League—the owners of the clubs—decided to put all baseball players into an elaborate classification scheme, with tight maximum salaries in each category; this effectively nullified their agreement with the Brotherhood. At that time the top salary was $2,500. The preliminary steps had been taken for a real confrontation between owners and players. It came in the form of a Brotherhood revolt in the fall of 1889, in which most of the players of the Brotherhood, with the assistance of businessmen backers, who sympathized with the players and also desired to be part of organized major league baseball, formed the Player's National League of Base Ball Clubs. Manifestoes were issued by both sides. The Brotherhood said:

> In taking this step we feel that we owe it to the public and to ourselves to explain. . . There was a time when the League stood for integrity and fair dealing. Today it stands for dollars and cents. . . . Players have been bought, sold and

---

5. Frank C. Richter, *Richter's History and Records of Base Ball* (Philadelphia: Francis C. Richter, 1914), p. 57.

6. Frank C. Richter, *Richter's History and Records of Base Ball* (Philadelphia: Francis C. Richter, 1914), p. 61.

exchanged as though they were sheep instead of American citizens. "Reservation" became for them another name for property right in the player.[7]

Two weeks later the National League replied:

> The National League of Base Ball Clubs has no apology to make for its existence, or for its untarnished record of fourteen years. . . . It is to this organization that the player of today owes the dignity of his profession and the munificent salary he is guaranteed while playing in its ranks. . . . And the necessity for such power of preserving the circuit of a League, by approximately equalizing its playing strength, is recognized by the new League, which the seceding players have temporarily organized; for they give this "extraordinary power" of transferring players, with or without consent, and with or without club disbandment, to a central tribunal of sixteen, whose fiat is final. . . . use of such terms as "bondage," "slavery," "sold like sheep," etc., becomes meaningless and absurd.[8]

During the 1890 season the baseball organizations lost large sums of money, as they competed for the same fans in several cities. In addition, press and fans alike became tired of the bickering and name-calling, and this undoubtedly discouraged attendance. At the end of that season, with owners on both sides anxious for some kind of settlement, the Player's League dissolved, with some of its clubs merging into the National League. The following year brought the demise of the once-stable American Association, and the National League again had a monopoly on major league baseball.

The League, however, had trouble even with its monopoly. Factionalism, disloyalty, distrust, and most of all, greedy individualism on the part of the owners, mixed with a tyrannical attitude toward the players, arrogance toward the fans and press, and lack of firm leadership and organization, found the National League in serious difficulty by 1900. In that year Byron Bancroft Johnson, a former newspaperman who had been the successful president of the Western League, organized the American League of Professional Baseball Clubs. After three seasons of successful operation by the new American League, the National League owners, faced with rising competitive player costs and reduced attendance, approached the American League to arrange a plan of accommodation. Thus was born a new and lasting National Agreement, recognizing two major leagues, each with eight teams plus numerous minor leagues. The game was controlled by a three-

---

7. Cited in Albert G. Spalding, *Base Ball, America's National Game* (New York: American Sports Publishing Company, 1911), p. 272.

8. Cited in Albert G. Spalding, *Base Ball, America's National Game* (New York: American Sports Publishing Company, 1911), pp. 273-76.

man National Commission consisting of the president of each major league and a third person selected by them. The 1903 season launched the new system and was climaxed by the playing of the first World Series, in which Boston beat Pittsburgh, five games to three.

By this time the game of baseball was indeed an American institution. Besides its innate excitement and widespread availability, it was promoted by skillful salesmen, one of the most important being Albert Goodwill Spalding. Baseball had been his life since, as a boy of 17 in Rockford, Illinois, he had discovered his powerful pitching arm. His pitching helped Boston win for several seasons; he was pitcher/manager for the Chicago White Stockings; and he helped Hulbert start the National League. Thereafter he identified himself with the owners, and eventually started a sporting goods firm. But his life belonged to baseball. In the jingoistic era of the Spanish-American War, he wanted baseball to be regarded as exclusively American, dismissed its evolution from bat and ball games, and pressured for the appointment of a commission to study the "birth" of the game. On weak evidence, the commission in due course concluded that General Abner Doubleday, a Civil War veteran, had "invented" the game as a young man living in Cooperstown, New York. This conclusion was largely accepted at that time.

Baseball also had its seamy side. Politicians found it financially and politically rewarding either to buy into or otherwise affiliate with the local ball clubs. Boss Tweed and the Tammany Hall machine in New York as well as politicians in other cities found baseball teams excellent means through which to promote themselves, grant favors, and mete out rewards through patronage. On the other hand, owners "in" with politicians could secure special streetcar service to bring spectators to the park and could get favored treatment regarding city police protection and taxes.[9]

"Organized baseball," the term used to identify the established professional major and minor leagues, flourished in the twentieth century. The new National Agreement provided stability to the leagues and player rowdyism was curtailed, especially in the American League where Ban Johnson countenanced no disrespect of umpires. Fans believed in the honesty of the players and umpires; and unprecedented interest was generated by good play, pennant races, and the annual World Series. Fans from all walks of life followed their favorites. An improved ball, somewhat livelier, enhanced the play. Stars of the period were Eddie Collins, Joe Jackson, and Ty Cobb. All these stars, and in fact, all the players in the major leagues, were white.

---

9. Steven A. Riess, "The Baseball Magnate and Urban Politics in the Progressive Era: 1895-1920," *Journal of Sport History* 1, no. 1 (May, 1974): 41-62.

George Stovey, a 35-game winning black pitcher for Newark, was almost signed to a contract by the New York Giants in the 1880's, but objections of other major league managers forced an end to the deal.[10] Four black players appeared on the rosters of important minor league clubs in 1886. Black players continued to play on their own independent teams on an amateur and semi-professional level. In 1885, the New York Cuban Giants were formed by a group of waiters and busboys at the Argyle Hotel in Babylon, New York. Attempts at forming black professional leagues were unsuccessful. One was planned in 1887, the League of Colored Base Ball Clubs, but was never established. Another, which consisted of six white teams and two black teams, was organized two years later but collapsed within a few weeks after the start of the season.[11] Although some black players could be found on white minor league teams through the 1890's, by the turn of the century the color line was set. John McGraw, manager of the New York Giants, attempted to call a black man, Charlie Grant, an Indian, but Charles Comiskey, owner of the Chicago White Sox, objected and the pressure was so strong that even the strong-willed McGraw backed down. No black players were to appear in the major leagues for almost a half century.

Boxing

Baseball, while certainly the most popular sport, was not the only sport providing entertainment. "Gentleman" Jim Corbett, a socially refined heavyweight from San Francisco's Olympic Club, defeated John L. Sullivan in New Orleans on September 7, 1892. Corbett represented careful training and scientific boxing style in contrast to Sullivan's brute strength and aggressiveness, which was typical of the day. While outlawed in most states throughout the 1890's, the sport attracted enough supporters to continue its clandestine staging of fights in rural barns, fields, or on river barges. However, the few fighters at the top were able to arrange important bouts in more public arenas. The championship bout between Sullivan and Corbett, for instance, was held at New Orleans' Olympic Club. Carson City, Nevada, was the scene of Corbett's defeat at the hands of Bob Fitzsimmons in 1897. The latter lost the title two years later to a burly, hard-hitting former sparring partner of the scientific Corbett, James L. Jeffries, in a match at the fashionable New Coney Island Sporting Club.

Despite arguments that boxing was an art and not a public display of

---

10. Jerome Zuckerman, G. Allan Stull, and Marvin H. Eyler, "The Black Athlete in Post-Bellum 19th Century," *The Physical Educato*ʳ 29 (October, 1972): 145.

11. Edwin B. Henderson and The Editors of *Sport Magazine, The Black Athlete—Emergence and Arrival* (New York: International Library of Negro History, 1968), p. 32.

violence, steady opposition to the sport existed in the nineties and continued until 1914. In a number of states the clergy led the anti-boxing crusade and many states passed legislation prohibiting boxing. Frequent knockouts and brutality, accompanied by gambling, corroborated public criticism and the reformers' zeal to outlaw boxing.

In 1910, when Jack Johnson, black and skillful but outspoken and indiscreet, defeated Jim Jeffries for the heavyweight title a new crisis arose. At a time of blatant racism, Johnson flaunted his boxing superiority by demolishing a string of "white hopes," and showed his disdain for white convention by publicly escorting and marrying white women. Jeffries came out of retirement for the fight and the white public pinned their hopes for a white champion on him. Promoted by Tex Rickard, the fight received extensive publicity. When it was learned that Jeffries lost, feelings were so intense that race riots broke out in Pittsburgh, Baltimore, Dayton, and other cities across the country.

FIG. 5.6   Jack Johnson: World Heavyweight Boxing Champion, 1908-1915. Wide World.

Other black boxers also established outstanding records during the period, but were generally denied the opportunity to fight in heavyweight championship matches against whites. Peter "The Black Prince" Jackson, a native of the Virgin Islands, won the black heavyweight championship by defeating American George Godfrey in 1888. Three years later, Jackson fought 61 rounds in five hours for a draw with soon-to-be world heavyweight champion, James Corbett. And yet, in 1892, after challenging all comers, world heavyweight champion John L. Sullivan declined Jackson's acceptance of the challenge with the statement, "I will not fight a Negro. I never have and I never will."[12]

Sam Langford, "The Boston Tarbaby," fought successfully in several weight classifications from 1902-1923 but was denied the opportunity to fight for the heavyweight championship even though Jack Johnson held the title during a major portion of his career. Other boxers such as George Dixon (1890-1903) and Joe Gans, best of the lightweights from 1902-1908, were successful in championship fights at the lighter weights, but many black fighters maintained that they often had to agree to lose a fight in order to be permitted a bout.[13]

Although Governor James N. Gillett prohibited the Jeffries-Johnson bout from being held in San Francisco, in spite of California's law permitting boxing, as the decade progressed more states began to ease their laws banning boxing. By the end of World War I, the country appeared ready to accept boxing as a legal sport.

Golf

As public links were built after the turn of the century, more Americans began to play golf. The professional golfers were usually golf teachers at country clubs, but neither they nor the outstanding amateurs had much appeal for the general public. Thus Ouimet's Open victory in 1913, followed a year later by Hagen's championship, made golf seem more accessible.

Blacks were generally introduced to golf as caddies but occasionally could play in the periodic caddy tournaments sponsored by many golf clubs.[14] Over the strong objections of many, but with the solid support of Theodore Haverman, President of the U.S. Golf Association, one black golfer, John Shippen, entered the second U.S. Open in 1896 and finished in fifth place.

12. John Durant and Edward Rice, *Come Out Fighting* (New York: Duell, Sloan and Pearce, 1946), p. 32.

13. Alexander J. Young, Jr., "Sam Langford, 'The Boston Tarbaby'," *Proceedings,* The Second Canadian Symposium on The History of Sport and Physical Education, May 1-3, 1972, Windsor, Ontario, p. 57.

14. Edwin B. Henderson, *The Negro in Sports* (Washington, D.C.: Associated Publishers, 1949), p. 223.

FIG. 5.7   Walter Hagen at the Los Angeles Open, January 12, 1929. Wide World.

Tennis

   Like golf, tennis developed and gained popularity as more and more public courts were built. In 1909 "Comet" Maurice McLoughlin, a product of San Francisco's public courts, went East and thrilled crowds with his rocket-like serve. In 1912 he signalled the end of an era in American tennis by becoming the first national champion to come from a modest background and to have learned his tennis on public courts. At that time there was separate tennis for black players, who held their first interstate tournament in Philadelphia in 1898 through the efforts of the Rev. W. W. Walker and the Chautauqua Tennis Club. The American Tennis Association was founded in Washington, D.C., in 1916 for the purposes of "fostering and developing the game of tennis among the colored people of the United States. It encouraged the formation of clubs and the building of courts . . . and interested juniors (16-18 years) as well as boys and girls in the possibilities and advantages of this splendid game."[15] The Association sponsored its first national championships in men's singles and men's doubles in Baltimore in the following year.

The Beginnings of Indoor Sport

Basketball

The need for a suitable ball game for use indoors in the winter months was apparent in the YMCA's work with young men. Luther Gulick, Director of the Gymnasium Department of the YMCA Training School at Springfield, Massachusetts, challenged James Naismith, a young instructor in the department, with this problem. Naismith taught a class which had enjoyed outdoor sports in the fall, but rebelled against the normal indoor activities of formal gymnastics, calisthenics, and drill. After trying indoor adaptations of soccer, football, rugby, water polo, field hockey, and even

FIG. 5.8   Dr. James Naismith.

15. Edwin B. Henderson, *The Negro in Sports* (Washington, D.C.: Associated Publishers, 1949), p. 206.

lacrosse, Naismith put together a game utilizing a soccer ball to be passed from man to man, and two goals, which were baskets suspended about ten feet in the air at either end of the court.

The first game was played on December 21, 1891, with Naismith and his colleague Amos Alonzo Stagg captaining the two nine-man teams. The game was instantly popular with the players and several took it back to their respective homes during the Christmas recess and introduced it to others. News of the game spread quickly through the Springfield Newsletter to "Y" physical directors, and Naismith himself toured with a team to Albany, Troy, Schenectady, Providence, and Newport.

Soon other colleges across the country began playing the game. After C. O. Beamis of Geneva College saw a game at Springfield, he introduced it to his classes. H.F. Kallenberg of the University of Iowa learned of the game through the "Y" Newsletter. Basketball grew most rapidly, however, in the YMCA's and high schools. Gulick and Naismith believed they had solved the problem of the unruly class with their new winter sport.

ORIGINAL RULES FOR BASKETBALL

1. The ball may be thrown in any direction with one or both hands.
2. The ball may be batted in any direction with one or both hands (never with the fist).
3. A player cannot run with the ball. The player must throw it from the spot on which he catches it; allowance to be made for a man who catches the ball when running at a good speed.
4. The ball must be held in or between the hands; the arms or body must not be used for holding it.
5. No shouldering, holding, pushing, tripping, or striking, in any way the person of an opponent shall be allowed; the first infringement of this rule by any person shall count as a foul, the second shall disqualify him until the next goal is made, or, if there was evident intent to injure the person for the whole of the game, no substitute allowed.
6. A foul is striking at the ball with the fist, violation of Rules 3, 4, and such as described in Rule 5.
7. If either side makes three consecutive fouls, it shall count a goal for the opponents. (Consecutive means without the opponents in the meantime making a foul.)
8. A goal shall be made when the ball is thrown or batted from the grounds into the basket and stays there, providing those defending the goal do not touch or disturb the goal. If the ball rests on the edge and the opponent moves the basket, it shall count as a goal.
9. When the ball goes out of bounds, it shall be thrown into the field and played by the person first touching it. In case of a dispute, the umpire shall throw it straight into the field. The thrower-in is allowed five seconds. If he holds it longer it shall go to the opponent. If any side persists in delaying the game, the umpire shall call a foul on them.
10. The umpire shall be judge of the men and shall note the fouls and notify the

referee when three consecutive fouls have been made. He shall have power to disqualify men according to Rule 5.

11. The referee shall be judge of the ball and shall decide when the ball is in play, in bounds, to which side it belongs, and shall keep the time. He shall decide when a goal has been made, and keep account of the goals, with any other duties that are usually performed by a referee.
12. The time shall be two fifteen-minute halves, with five minutes rest between.
13. The side making the most goals in that time shall be declared the winners. In case of a draw, the game may, by agreement of the captains, be continued until another goal is made.[16]

The rules against running with the ball were the earliest to be relaxed. In 1893 the pivot was ruled not to be a traveling violation, and by 1896 Yale University added the dribble. By 1897 the number of players was fixed at five. At that time the colleges had one set of rules and the clubs, the Y's, and the AAU played by different rules. Agreement on rules was reached in 1915 when a Joint Basketball Committee was formed with representatives of the NCAA, the AAU, and the YMCA. By the outbreak of World War I basketball began to be the most popular high school sport for boys, and in the colleges, particularly in the Midwest, second only to football. The early barnstorming professional teams which began to appear around 1900 followed their own rules.

In the same winter that Naismith started basketball, Senda Berenson, a physical education instructor at nearby Smith College, adapted the game for her students. The rules for women's basketball also varied during the early years. When women saw the game and tried it, they knew it would be popular. Both the Boston Normal School of Gymnastics (BNSG) and the Sargent School played the game, each with its own set of rules. The graduates of each school then taught the game wherever they went, thus perpetuating two sets of rules. Finally, in 1899 under the auspices of the American Association for the Advancement of Physical Education, a committee of four was chosen at a physical training conference at Springfield to draw up a standardized set of rules to govern the women's game. The committee, composed of Dr. Alice Foster, Director of Physical Training for Women at Oberlin College, Ethel Perrin of Boston Normal School of Gymnastics, Elizabeth Wright of Radcliffe College, and Berenson, established five rules which divided the playing court into three equal areas and restricted players to their respective zones; prohibited "snatching or batting" the ball from the hands of an opposing player; limited each player to a three-bounce dribble; placed a three-second limit on holding the ball; and established the number of players on a team as being not fewer than five nor more than ten.

---

16. James Naismith, *Basketball, Its Origin and Development* (New York: Association Press, 1941), pp. 53-55.

FIG. 5.9 Smith College Basketball. Courtesy the Sophia Smith Collection, The Archives, Smith College, Northampton, Massachusetts.

This committee was the beginning of control of women's and girls' sports in schools and colleges, and today's controlling organization, the Association for Intercollegiate Athletics for Women (AIAW) can be traced to the 1899 Basketball Committee. In 1905 the Committee changed its name to the National Women's Basketball Committee. The Committee set a pattern which was followed as other women's sports needed to be standardized: rules were published and suggestions made for the conduct of events, but the Committee did not regulate or sanction events. It was only by mutual understanding that the committees exerted influence. In 1917 the National Women's Basketball Committee changed to the Committee on Women's Athletics and formed committees on basketball, field hockey, track and field, and swimming.

Volleyball

In an effort to meet the needs of his noon-day businessmen's class, William Morgan, the physical director at the Holyoke, Massachusetts, YMCA developed the game of volleyball. Intended only as a light recreational activity for the group, the game soon became popular. Originally the game utilized the entire gymnasium, the rubber bladder from a basketball, and a six foot six inch high net. The ball was hit back and forth with the hands and an "out" was called if the ball landed out of bounds or hit the floor after more than one bounce. The game of nine innings accommodated any number of players on a team.

Morgan presented his new game, which he called *minonette,* at a YMCA sports conference at Springfield College in 1895. It was received favorably but renamed *Volleyball* because of the techniques involved. The Springfield *Journal* published the rules and within a short time the game was being played at YMCA's around the country. Soon schools and colleges incorporated the game into physical education programs, where it was played by both men and women.

The first rule changes, made in 1900 by the Physical Directors Society of the YMCA, included the elimination of dribbling, the first bounce, and the use of innings. Twenty-one points constituted a game and the net height was raised to seven feet. Finally, balls landing on the side line were "in" and balls rebounding from the walls or other out-of-court objects were out of play. In 1912, court dimensions were established at 35 feet by 60 feet, a player rotation method set, touching the net became a loss of service, two games constituted a match, and the net height was raised to seven feet six inches, width three feet.

In addition to YMCA and school and college play, the game was taken up by the armed services where, during World War I, it was further introduced to the world.

Other Sports and Pastimes

Swimming and Lifesaving

The YMCA initiated the first national program to teach vast numbers of people to swim and ". . . during the years 1909 through 1917 about 376,000 persons were taught swimming and diving."[17] Another broad swimming program started in 1914 when Commodore Wilbert E. Longfellow of the American Red Cross initiated its Lifesaving Service. The "Red Cross" approach emphasized teaching basic techniques to nonswimmers in a carefully developed step-by-step approach.

---

17. C. E. Silvia, *Lifesaving and Water Safety Instruction* (New York: Association Press, 1960), p. 21.

Hunting and Fishing

Hunting and fishing, as always, continued to attract participants from all levels of society, except perhaps the lower classes of the cities. Those with greater means could travel farther and some planned hunting and fishing vacations. Rod and gun clubs increased in number throughout the country and played influential roles in state game and wildlife legislation. Such outdoor sports received added support when Theodore Roosevelt, an exponent of the vigorous outdoor life, moved into the White House in 1901. "Teddy's" strong interests in the American West and big game hunting, as well as in competitive athletics, placed one more stamp of approval on sport as part of the American way of life.

Not only hunting, but also trapshooting and rifle shooting grew in popularity between 1885 and World War I. These were particularly popular among city dwellers for whom time and space made traditional hunting impossible. Trapshooting had begun just prior to the Civil War when improvements in gun making aided shooting on the fly. In the 1860's and '70's, better traps and the manufacture of clay pigeons made possible greater standardization for competition. Local rifle clubs sprang up around the country and stimulated interest and regional competitions. The National Rifle Association, founded in 1871, began sponsoring national rifle shooting tournaments. The National Gun Association, organized in 1885, represented a first attempt to establish national rules and regulations for trapshooting. It was soon replaced by the Interstate Association of Trapshooters in 1889 and in 1900 by the American Trapshooting Association.

Riding and Rodeos

Riding academies in large cities gave the upper and middle classes opportunities for an occasional horseback ride. For the average Americans in small towns or on the farms, horses were very much a part of their lives, providing transportation and riding for pleasure. By the late 1890's the rodeo began to attract participants and spectators in such cities as Denver and Cheyenne. It gave the working cowboy a place to demonstrate his special skills to the world. In the early twentieth century there were fewer opportunities at the national level for the working cowboy, as a new generation of professional riders emerged onto the rodeo circuit.

By the turn of the century, interest in cock fighting was primarily relegated to certain areas of the South and Southwest, due in large part to the efforts of societies for the prevention of cruelty to animals.

Dance of the Period

Melvin Ballou Gilbert, a teacher of dance at the Sargent School of Physical Education and the Boston Normal School of Gymnastics, developed a form of dance variously known as Gilbert dancing, aesthetic dancing, aesthetic calisthenics, or classical dancing. This form of dance emphasized ". . . light simple rhythmic movements of the body and limbs for the cultivation of grace and elegance in form and bearing, figure marching and dance steps."[18]

Free expression was part of the climate of opinion for all the arts, and aesthetic dancing, modern dance, and Isadora Duncan's "free dance" were manifestations of this freedom. Largely self-trained, Isadora Duncan is often credited with being the founder of American modern dance, although the term was not in use during her time and "free dance" was her own term. Duncan's career, beginning in 1899, freed theatrical dance from the constraints of the ballet. She wore a free-flowing Greek style tunic and danced in bare feet. Her movements, which were accompanied by classical music, were free and expressive. Her art and her vivid personality helped establish the right of dancers to develop movements based on their unique personal expression and free of the technical training and vocabulary of the classical ballet.

The nurture and growth of an American non-balletic form of theatrical dance became the task of her contemporaries, Ruth St. Denis and Ted Shawn. Ruth St. Denis had an active career in the theater, spanning some fifty years. Like Duncan, St. Denis had no formal training, but she ventured to New York and by 1906 she had established herself as a solo dancer, creating her own dances based on oriental themes. She toured extensively between 1906 and 1914, when Ted Shawn became her husband and partner.

Ted Shawn served American dance in many capacities: as a dancer in vaudeville and on the concert stage, as choreographer, as teacher, as founder and director of an all-male dance company, and as an impresario. He studied ballet as well as ballroom dancing and later created a dance technique which he considered more suitable for male dancers than the formal classical technique. He also studied the Delsarte system and wrote of its application to dance in the book *Every Little Movement*.

After St. Denis and Shawn were married, they founded a new dance company, Denishawn, which contributed significantly to American dance. In its fifteen years it provided Americans with an exposure to expressive dance, and through its school another generation of expressive dancers gained training and performing experience. The best known of those dancers were Doris Humphrey, Charles Weidman, and Martha Graham.

The presence of expressive dance on the stage was widespread, but it was not the only dance available to the theater-going public. Ballet, vaudeville, and shows growing out of the minstrel style were also presented in the theaters of the day.

---

18. Joseph E. Marks, *America Learns to Dance* (New York: Exposition Press, 1957), p. 101.

Between 1840 and 1909 no prima ballerina of international fame danced in America. However, in January of 1910 the famous Anna Pavlova and Mikhail Mordkin performed at the Metropolitan Opera House in New York. Pavlova was graduated from the Russian Imperial School of Ballet in 1899, where she had been trained in the classical tradition. In Russia she danced many of the leading roles in the classical repertory, and brought to the American public the finest tradition in classical technique and choreography. To many in her audiences, ballet meant Pavlova and Pavlova meant ballet.

Vaudeville was a miscellaneous theatrical entertainment popular in the early part of this century, offering varied dance fare. The most popular forms of dance were clog and tap dancing, which placed primary emphasis on the rhythmic foot sounds of the performer. Clog dancing was primarily Irish in origin and performed with an immobile torso and without arm or hand gestures. Tap dancing, American in origin, grew out of a blending of clog and jazz. As such, tap dance allowed a much freer use of the upper body, arms, and hands. Many of the performers responsible for innovations in the style and technique were black, one of the most famous being Bill "Bojangles" Robinson. The popularity of tap and clog dancing was not confined to the stage; many physical educators found it an exciting activity for boys and girls.

With the decline in popularity of blackface minstrelsy in the early 1890's, black musical comedy provided an opportunity for black Americans to sing and dance. Early shows in the new genre, such as *The South Before the War,* in 1891, and *The Creole Show,* in 1889, were very much in the old style and format. A new musical, *A Trip to Coontown,* produced in 1898, was notable for many firsts: a complete break with the minstrel show format; continuity and plot developed by characterization throughout; and organization, production, and management by blacks.[19]

The development of black musical comedy also had an important influence on the general public. Often dances presented there became the latest popular dance craze. While these jazz dances were being adopted by an urban adult population, boys and girls in school were being introduced to folk dancing and natural dance.

Sponsorship of Sport

For the average American, sport participation prior to World War I was largely limited to the sports available through facilities provided by the local

---

19. Lynne Fauley Emery, *Black Dance in the United States from 1619 to 1970* (Palo Alto, California: National Press Books, 1972), pp. 207-209.

industry, church, municipality, or philanthropist. Educators and social workers began to view sport, especially for boys, as a path to assimilation of the culture and to the socialization of American youth. Out of the social reforms of the nineteenth century and the changing needs of youth, a number of public, private, and government agencies established sport as a part of their programs. Settlement and community houses built gymnasiums and swimming pools. The Boys' Clubs of America began in 1906, the Boy Scouts of America in 1910, and the Girl Scouts in 1912. While these groups planned programs for youth, the YWCA and YMCA answered a different need, that of providing a dormitory or safe city residence for young adults, as well as a place for activities. By 1916, there were over 65,000 women attending YWCA gymnasium classes, and 32,000 in swimming classes.

The YMCA adapted their program to the perceived need for a moral atmosphere for young men in the cities. In 1887 they established a two-year course to train directors of gymnasiums. Luther Gulick stated:

> But the ultimate aim of every department of the Association work, including the physical department, is to lead men to Christ. So corresponding emphasis is laid upon securing gymnasium instructors who are not only thoroughly and scientifically trained, but whose supreme motive in all their work is spiritual.

He recognized the increased interest in sport. "The larger Associations are rapidly securing athletic grounds for the use of their members, and many of the smaller ones, which cannot support gymnasiums, enter heartily into various branches of this work."[20]

Playground Movement

Many philanthropists were concerned about poor city children with no supervision and little fresh air or safe space to play. The poor and middle class were restricted in their choice of recreation and especially in their facilities for play. Particularly hard pressed for space were the children of the poor in the tenement districts of industrial centers. Often left alone all day by working parents, children roamed the streets and sought pleasure in many undesirable and unsafe centers. In addition, very young children needed clean, open spaces where fresh air and room for exercise would create a healthful atmosphere.

The modern playground movement in the United States began in Boston

---

20. Luther Gulick, "What the American Young Men's Christian Associations are doing for the Physical Welfare of Young Men," *Annual Autumn Games,* Young Men's Christian Association of the City of New York, October 13, 1888, pp. 18, 20. Courtesy of A.G. Spalding Company Archives, Chicopee, Massachusetts.

FIG. 5.10   School playground, Detroit, Michigan, about 1910. Courtesy of Detroit Historical Museum.

with the idea of providing sand in which little children could play. In 1885 the Massachusetts Emergency and Hygiene Association opened its first "sand garden" and two years later there were ten such "gardens." During the first two years supervision was provided by volunteers, but soon matrons were employed in such positions. The sand gardens were so popular that in 1901 the Boston School Committee accepted the responsibility for the program, thus acknowledging the supervision of play as an appropriate function of the public schools.[21]

Although Boston pioneered this movement, other cities soon followed and in 1890 New York's Society for Parks and Playgrounds, with the help of churches and synagogues, began a drive for playgrounds. In 1894 at Jane Addam's Hull House, the first playground in Chicago opened. Four years later Chicago gave its first appropriation for playgrounds, $1,000 to the vacation school committee of local women's clubs. Further support was obtained from the Turners, who loaned apparatus for the program. At the turn of the century a group of Detroit women raised money to start a playground in a schoolyard. By 1900, a number of cities from Philadelphia to Denver had opened playgrounds.

In typical American fashion, many of the early playgrounds were initiated by philanthropists and later transferred to the local city governments. Sometimes the land for the playgrounds was donated by a wealthy

21. Clarence E. Rainwater, *The Play Movement in the United States* (Chicago: The University of Chicago Press, 1922), pp. 22-44.

benefactor and sometimes it was set aside by the city. Usually the parks and playgrounds were located in densely populated sections of the city and planned for young children rather than older youth. The early playgrounds were often temporary and maintained only in the summers. Finally, it was customary for policemen to supervise the playgrounds, promoting the concept of child control rather than of guidance and leadership.

In 1906 the Playground Association of America was founded by Dr. Luther Gulick and Dr. Henry Curtis. The formation of such an association, together with the increasing number of parks and playgrounds, substantiates the growing acceptance of play in the life of children.

Sport in Industries

By 1910, some large businesses and industries developed recreation programs for their employees. Some even capitalized on the sport craze and fielded "amateur" teams of talented individuals, often employed as much for their sport ability as for their business or manufacturing skills. By the start of World War I such Eastern organizations as Macy's and Wanamaker's of New York, Johnson and Johnson of New Brunswick, General Electric of Schenectady, Michelin of Milltown, New Jersey, had sponsored athletic clubs. In Akron, Ohio, Goodyear Company formed teams in baseball, football, track, hockey, skating, basketball, volleyball, tennis and cricket.[22]

Physical Education, Sport, and Dance in Schools and Colleges

By the mid-1880's, public and private education in the United States was taken more seriously than at any previous time in the nation's history. Public school facilities for children and youth greatly increased throughout the country between 1885 and 1917. By 1898 thirty-one state and territorial legislatures had adopted compulsory attendance laws, which increased the formal education received by the average American from four years in 1880 to six years in 1910. The national illiteracy rate was reduced from 17 percent in 1880 to 7.7 percent in 1910. On the other hand, most elementary schools limited their curriculums to reading, writing, arithmetic, and other basic subjects. In the 1890's, traditional public school education was challenged by a group of educators led by John Dewey of the University of Chicago, later of Teachers College, Columbia. Under the new influence, the curriculum expanded to include the sciences and subjects such as art, physical education, manual training, cooking, sewing, and commercial skills.

---

22. John Rickards Betts, *America's Sporting Heritage: 1850-1950* (Reading, Mass.: Addison-Wesley Publishing Company, 1974), p. 181.

The colleges and universities changed from required courses with almost no electives to a largely elective system. In addition the liberal arts curriculum added courses in new fields such as physics, political science, economics, sociology, music, fine arts, and advanced modern languages. Technical institutes and engineering programs also revised their curriculums; normal schools raised their standards and the number of land-grant colleges increased; and the founding of several black colleges in the South provided that region with teachers, knowledgeable farmers, and skilled craftsmen among the newly franchised citizens. Finally, graduate programs developed in many of the nation's universities.

College and University Physical Education

The instructional programs for men and women varied considerably, but the general trend of the period was a decrease in gymnastics and an increase in sport instruction. Both the men's and women's programs had been initiated to improve health. With no formal physical education preparation available, medical doctors were appointed in institutions such as Amherst College, Harvard, Yale, and Oberlin to direct the physical education work. The background of these people greatly influenced the courses offered and the research undertaken by the faculty.

The need for teachers of physical education quickly led to programs for training teachers. In 1885 only two programs existed, one in Milwaukee, Wisconsin, and the other in Boston. Having been started by the Turners as an occasional training course in various cities, the North American Gymnastics Union (N.A.G.U.) was established in Milwaukee. By 1891 the course was two years in length and in 1903 it was extended to three years. Because the N.A.G.U. prepared its students for the Turner program, their graduates ordinarily taught in the Turnvereins or in Midwestern public schools. The N.A.G.U. emphasized German gymnastics, German and English, and other cultural subjects. The other teacher training institution of the mid-1880's was the Sargent School, opened in 1881 to train those interested in becoming teachers of physical education.

By 1890 three additional schools which also greatly influenced the development of physical education had been established in this country. In 1886 William G. Anderson opened the Brooklyn Normal School to both men and women; the following year the YMCA Training School at Springfield, Massachusetts, created a department to train physical directors for the YM programs; and in 1889 the Boston Normal School of Gymnastics opened, originally to provide teachers of Swedish gymnastics for the Boston public schools.

While the curriculum and offerings of these schools differed according to their educational philosophy, they all offered anatomy and physiology and all but N.A.G.U. taught anthropometry and sciences such as physics. An examination of the early curriculums reveals that a rigorous search was made for a curriculum that would be particularly relevant to physical education. Courses offered included physiological psychology, the relation of body and mind, mechanics of the body, and sphygmography. On the other hand, a description of one "health education" course in the 1890-91 *YMCA Training School Catalogue* reads: "Personal Purity—physiology of the reproductive organs. Effects of violation of the laws of purity; in the body, on the mind. Intellectual licentiousness, cause, effects. Hygienic treatment. Quack doctors and their methods."[23]

The Boston Normal School of Gymnastics (BNSG), modeled after the Royal Gymnastics Central Institute in Stockholm, reflected a carefully supervised two-year course. The students studied their basic sciences at the Massachusetts Institute of Technology and heard lectures by selected Harvard professors. In 1909 the BNSG became affiliated with Wellesley College and, beginning in 1917, admitted only graduates from recognized colleges.

The sports offered during this period at the various institutions also varied with the philosophy of the school. The YMCA school offered an extensive sports program. Anderson included as many sports for which he had facilities while the others offered a limited sports program.

While the Sargent School and the BNSG were opened originally to both women and men, both became schools for women only. They were both popular and educated many of the early women leaders. In 1904 Sargent had graduated 261 students and BNSG 312. Among the leaders graduated from Sargent were Delphine Hanna, Elizabeth Burchenal, Helen Putnam, and Lucille Eaton Hill. The graduates in BNSG's early days included Senda Berenson, Ethel Perrin, J. Anna Norris, and Blanche Trilling. In the first class graduated from Wellesley were Mabel Lee and Mary Channing Coleman. Others who were graduated in the early Wellesley years prior to World War I were Florence Lawson, Gertrude Manchester, Gertrude Baker, and Elizabeth Halsey.

Mrs. Mary Hemenway, a Boston philanthropist who founded the Boston Normal School of Gymnastics, named Amy Morris Homans as its director. Born and educated in Maine, Homans joined the thousands who went South following the Civil War to aid in the Reconstruction. She taught in Wilmington, North Carolina, in a school which Hemenway helped support. Hemenway brought Homans North to direct her various philanthropic enterprises. An energetic perfectionist, Homans, not trained in physical education, immediately involved herself in the new field and became active in the AAAPE. Hemenway died in 1894, leaving funds to support BNSG

---

23. *YMCA Training School Catalogue, 1890-91,* Springfield, Massachusetts, p. 19.

for fifteen years. By that time Homans had negotiated an affiliation with Wellesley College and planned for a new gymnasium for the college. This act fulfilled one of Hemenway's dreams, which was to see the professional work in physical education based on a liberal arts background.

Other colleges and universities soon began to offer teacher preparation programs. Beginning in 1885 at Oberlin, Dr. Delphine Hanna first prepared teachers by offering a single course to a selected group of undergraduate men. They in turn taught the physical training courses for the other men on campus because there was no director of the men's program. From this effort came three early leaders of the profession, Thomas Wood, Luther Gulick, and Fred Leonard. In 1892, Oberlin College instituted a two-year Normal Course in Physical Training which in 1900 became a four-year course leading to a Bachelor of Arts degree. During this decade George Wells Fitz, M.D., organized the first formal studies on the physiological effects of physical activity at the Physiological Laboratory in the Lawrence Scientific School at Harvard. He also taught in the Department of Anatomy, Physiology, and Physical Training. "Under Fitz's direction, this department offered and awarded the first four-year degree in physical education in the United States."[24] By the turn of the century, only three other institutions had established degree programs: Stanford University, University of California, and the University of Nebraska.

Beginning in the 1880's, early teacher training efforts also included summer school courses. In 1886, William G. Anderson and Dr. Jay Seaver began the Chautauqua Summer School for Physical Education. Sargent, with the approval of Harvard's President Eliot, instituted the Harvard Summer School of Physical Education in 1887, and attracted, over the years, hundreds of teachers who used this unique school to help improve physical education.

Between 1900 and 1917, the Eastern private normal schools continued to be the most important source of qualified physical education teachers. Early in the second decade of the new century, however, four-year colleges and universities, both public and private, superseded the normal schools.[25] Graduate work was initiated and the first master's degree was awarded by Teachers College of Columbia University in 1910.

One of the major interests of the period was anthropometry. Influenced by the work of Hitchcock and Sargent, college gymnasium faculty members measured and meticulously recorded individual statistics on size, growth, strength development—all to seek the "typical" college man and woman.

---

24. Walter P. Kroll, *Perspectives in Physical Education* (New York: Academic Press, 1971), p. 194.

25. Wilbur P. Bowen, "Seven Years of Progress in Preparing Teachers of Physical Education," *American Physical Education Review* 27 (February, 1922): 64.

Between 1885 and 1900 thousands of students were charted at Harvard, Amherst, Yale, Oberlin, the University of Nebraska, Beloit College, and Wellesley. Sargent constructed life-sized statues of the "typical" college man and woman and exhibited them at the World's Columbian Exposition in Chicago in 1893. The new association to advance physical education, the AAAPE, established a Department of Anthropometry and Statistics with Dr. Hitchcock serving as chairman. Two years later a Committee on Vital Statistics was established, chaired by Senda Berenson of Smith College and in 1897, a Committee on School Anthropometry was formed with Henry P. Bowditch of the Harvard Medical School as its chairman. The data from the anthropometrical studies were used to prescribe specific exercises and activities to correct deficiencies and develop strength, body symmetry, and health.

Another general issue during the beginning of this era was the so-called "battle of the systems." At this time a variety of specific exercise systems had the support of certain groups or individuals. The Turners promoted German gymnastics, Dr. Sargent tested and prescribed individual exercises, Dr. Hitchcock used both mass exercises and individual exercises, and the BNSG promoted Swedish gymnastics. In 1889, Hemenway, a strong proponent of Swedish gymnastics, hosted the "Conference in the Interest of Physical Training" to bring the various systems to the attention of the public. The conference was held at the Massachusetts Institute of Technology on November 29 and 30 with over two thousand people attending. Papers were read by a number of outstanding physical educators, the various physical training systems were explained and debated, and the entire proceeding was presided over by William T. Harris, the United States Commissioner of Education. The so-called "battle of the systems" abated as play and sport became the dominant components in the changing field of physical education.

As interest in physical education increased in various sections of the country, state legislation began to require it in the public schools. By the start of World War I, however, only seven states had enacted such legislation.

In the early 1890's various forces combined to alter the programs of college physical education. First, the growing popularity of men's intercollegiate sport introduced thousands of students to the fun and stimulation of vigorous games and athletics. The relatively dull routine of exercise programs palled in comparison to participation in sport. Second, sport developed in the curriculum as perceptive instructors such as Tappan at Vassar and Naismith at Springfield recognized student interest in games and sport. Many of the women's colleges had long included sport instruction in their curriculum.

Berenson of Smith College had been the first to modify the rules of basketball for women. Recognizing that Naismith probably did not envision women playing the game, she stated:

> However, directors of gymnasia for women saw at once that it was, perhaps, the game they were eagerly seeking—one that should not have the rough element of foot ball, yet should be a quick, spirited game—should cultivate strength and physical endurance, and should be interesting enough to become a part of physical training for women as foot ball and base ball are for men.[26]

A third factor affecting the shift from formal gymnastics to sport was the "new psychology" of William James, G. Stanley Hall, Edward L. Thorndike, William Kilpatrick, and John Dewey. Believing that to be effective centers of learning, schools must be interesting, Dewey emphasized the role of play in the education of the child. His teaching and writing influenced generations of physical educators and was, perhaps, the most significant factor in the growth of the play movement in physical education for young children. One of the first physical educators to support a play orientation was Thomas Dennison Wood. By 1910 Wood, head of the Department of Physical Education at Teachers College, Columbia University, had articulated his ideas in the *Ninth Yearbook of the National Society for the Study of Education*. Known as the "new physical education," Wood's philosophy emphasized the "natural" programs of play, games, and sport for teaching intellectual awareness and moral and social behavior. Clark Hetherington, Wood's student at Stanford, exemplified this philosophy with particular energy. As Professor of Physical Training and Director of Athletics at the University of Missouri from 1900-1910, he struggled for ethics in athletics, sport for men and for women, and for statewide recreational opportunities for the people of Missouri.

Luther Halsey Gulick also was firmly committed to games and sport as a major educational force. As Superintendent of the Department of Physical Training at the YMCA Training School in Springfield, Massachusetts, from 1889 to 1900, and as Director of Physical Training in the public schools of New York City from 1903 to 1908, and through his leadership in the Playground Association of America and the Camp Fire Girls, Gulick was in a position to demonstrate his belief in the value of play and sport. He particularly stressed the role of sports in the ". . . toughening of the individual for the achievements of life."[27]

Two other physical educators also illustrate the change from formal gym-

---

26. Senda Berenson, "Editorial," *Basketball for Women* (New York: American Sports Publishing Co., 1903), p. 7.

27. Luther Halsey Gulick, *Physical Education by Muscular Exercise* (Philadelphia: P. Blakiston's Son & Company, 1904), p. 47.

nastics to the "new physical education." Jessie Hubbell Bancroft began her career devoted to systematic exercise and postural development. In 1909, after working closely with Gulick as Assistant Director of Physical Training in the New York Public Schools since 1903, she wrote *Games for the Playground, Home, School, and Gymnasium,* perhaps the most comprehensive book of games in its time. Ethel Perrin, a graduate of the Boston Normal School of Gymnastics, and a proponent of Swedish gymnastics during her fourteen years as a faculty member there, taught at the University of Michigan for one year. The following year, 1908, she became the director of physical training at Detroit's Central High School. One year later she was named Supervisor of Physical Culture of the Detroit Public Schools. Over the following fourteen years she encouraged the growing program of play-based physical education from elementary through high school that became a nationally renowned model.

During this period the curriculum in both colleges and high schools reflected the changes in student interest and educational philosophy. These changes resulted in more games and sport in the instructional program. A subtle reenforcement of the sport and athletic programs for high school boys was the growing acceptance of intercollegiate athletics for men. More and more high school athletes became the sport stars of the college campus.

Programs for Men

By 1890 intercollegiate sport for men was entrenched on most campuses in the East and in a growing number in the South, Midwest, and Far West. Football was played at a number of colleges across the country but its real growth in terms of spectators and new teams came in the nineties. West Point formed its first team in 1890 and by 1900 the Army-Navy game was an annual spectacle drawing military and governmental officials as spectators. Intersectional play increased as Midwestern teams such as Michigan, Minnesota, and Chicago challenged the traditionally strong elevens in the East. In 1892 Stanford University and the University of California began a rivalry that soon drew capacity crowds. The Oakland Athletic Club, in 1895, traveled East to play teams in Chicago and also the University of Michigan and Cornell. By the end of the century, Thanksgiving Day games had become an annual tradition, and in 1902 New Year's Day became another football holiday with the Rose Bowl game and the Tournament of Roses in Pasadena, California.

While the Eastern teams continued to dominate the game through the nineties, the quality of play in other parts of the country improved as former star players from Yale, Princeton, Harvard, and other gridiron powers were hired to coach in the newer colleges. President William Rainey Harper brought former Yale and Springfield All-American, Amos Alonzo

Stagg, to the University of Chicago in 1892 where he coached for the next forty-one years. Yale star Mike Donahue went to Auburn University while John Heisman assumed coaching duties at Georgia Institute of Technology. Glen "Pop" Warner left Cornell to coach at the Carlisle Indian School, Pittsburgh, and later Stanford University.

The first reported game between two black teams involved Biddle University (now Johnson C. Smith) and Livingstone College on Thanksgiving

FIG. 5.11   Fielding Yost, Football Coach and Athletic Director, University of Michigan. Courtesy of University of Michigan.

Day, 1892. Howard University, Lincoln University of Pennsylvania, Tuskegee and Atlanta Universities all began play in 1894.

As early as 1890 a limited number of black players were members of predominantly white college football teams in the North. William H. Lewis and William Tecumseh Sherman Jackson were teammates at Amherst in 1889, 1890, and 1891 and Lewis served as team captain in the second year. Lewis then played the 1892 and 1893 seasons at Harvard, meriting All-American honors both years. Other black players included George A. Flippen at Nebraska, Joseph H. Lee at Harvard, George M. Chadwell at Williams, and William Washington at Oberlin. Through the first decade of the new century, the number of black football players at these and similar institutions increased slightly. After graduating from Harvard Law School in 1895, Lewis returned in 1898 to help coach the Harvard line for one season. In 1904, Matthew Bullock, a black Dartmouth player from 1901-1903, was hired by Massachusetts Agricultural College to coach the football team, thus becoming the first black man to serve as a head football coach at a predominantly white college. He again filled that position in 1907 and 1908 after an absence to attend Harvard Law School.

The style of play in the nineties was increasingly rough and dangerous, emphasizing mass formation plays, in which players surrounded their own ball carrier and moved forward with great speed and force toward the opponent's goal. In 1894, the "flying wedge" was outlawed on kickoffs but it was not until after the season of 1905 that serious steps were taken to reduce the violence that had become a tragic part of the game. In that season, eighteen players were killed and more than one hundred seriously injured. Because of the brutality, Columbia and Northwestern, among others, dropped the sport entirely and Stanford and California changed to rugby. Following the 1905 season, authorities representing thirteen universities met in New York City with the full support of President Theodore Roosevelt, an avid college football fan, to deal with persistent problems in football such as injuries and excessive absence from class. The meeting resulted in the formation of the Intercollegiate Athletic Association of the United States. The association sought to conduct college athletics on a high ethical plane and to assume whatever control was necessary. In 1910 the name was changed to the National Collegiate Athletic Association to describe its role more accurately.

The forward pass helped to open up play but mass formation plays continued. Despite changes in rules to make the game safer, football still caused many injuries. Some defended the game as a rallying point for the student body and as a character builder for the players. Further reforms by the Intercollegiate Athletic Association and stars such as Jim Thorpe of the Carlisle School and Gus Dorais of Notre Dame helped quiet critics, and college football became extremely popular. By 1917, the game was played in small southwestern colleges, black colleges and white universities in the South, prairie colleges in Oklahoma, Kansas, Nebraska, and the Dakotas, as well as in the established schools of the East and the large state universities of the Midwest and Pacific Coast. Large stadiums were constructed and expansions planned as the "business" of college football became a revenue-producing enterprise.

FIG. 5.12   Jim Thorpe. Wide World.

Football was not the only sport the students played, but it was the one that drew thousands of spectators and the press. Baseball continued to be popular with the players and track and field grew steadily. Exciting dual meets took place in the East among Harvard, Princeton, Yale, Pennsylvania, and Columbia. Michigan, Chicago, Illinois, and Wisconsin had track teams in the Midwest, and California and Stanford in the West. In 1894 the University of Pennsylvania established the University of Pennsylvania Relays and Drake University in Des Moines, Iowa, initiated the Drake Relays.

The first intercollegiate basketball game is not known. There is a record of Hamline University losing to Minnesota State School of Agriculture on February 9, 1895 and of Haverford College defeating Temple University several weeks later. The first known game to use five-man squads was played between student teams from the University of Chicago and the University of Iowa on January 16, 1896. While some intercollegiate play continued through the late 1890's, most college teams filled their schedules with YMCA clubs and even high schools. In the East, football conference rivalries were separate from basketball leagues such as the Intercollegiate League and the New England League, which were formed in 1901. On the other hand, the Western Conference adopted basketball but it was not until about 1903 that intercollegiate conference basketball began to be stable. By the beginning of World War I, it was clear that basketball was an integral part of intercollegiate sport for men.

Control of Intercollegiate Sport

Of major importance to all of men's intercollegiate sport in this period was the trend away from volunteer student-run athletic associations to college-controlled administration. The rise of football played a significant role in this move. Its increasing popularity and financial complexity required administrative and faculty control. Hired coaches and larger stadiums represented major investments, and the colleges saw the need to appoint "athletic directors" to supervise their interests.

At the same time, conference and league affiliations brought interinstitutional stability and increased faculty control over schedules, eligibility standards, and rules of play. The first faculty-controlled athletic conference was the Intercollegiate Conference of Faculty Representatives formed in 1895 by Chicago, Illinois, Michigan, Minnesota, Northwestern, Purdue, and Wisconsin. Also known as the Western Conference and later, the Big Ten, the league adopted twelve resolutions, including the following points: participants on intercollegiate teams must be bona fide students enrolled in a full program of studies; students having played on an intercollegiate team at one college must, upon transferring to another college, matriculate at that institution six months before becoming eligible to compete on its athletic teams; no one may receive any gift, remuneration, or pay for his services on the college team; students delinquent in studies become ineligible for intercollegiate play; and each institution must appoint a committee to take general supervision of all athletic matters on its campus.[28] The growing number of such conferences resulted in increasing control over college sport. However the pressure for winning teams at many schools proved to be more than a match for even well-intentioned university administrators and faculty. Questionable recruiting practices, the use of invalid academic records, and financial relationships with players became endemic problems which plagued college and university athletics.

Programs for Women

Competitive sports for women were organized in a variety of ways depending upon the institution, the leadership, the facilities, and the desires of the students. There were clubs, all-college tournaments, interclass tournaments, interclass competitions, varsity programs, field days, pageants and festivals, and athletic associations.

A number of institutions fostered interest in sports through clubs. California organized a tennis club in 1890 and a boating club in 1901. The University of Wisconsin women had several sports clubs—a tennis club, a pedestrian club, and a bowling club. Tournaments among the women students were popular and frequently satisfied the desire of the women to compete. Goucher College held its first archery tournament in 1894 and awarded the winner a blue and silver hat pin. California's tennis tournament was held with nearby Mills College. When Oberlin College held a basketball tournament in 1900 six teams entered.

Basketball was immediately popular and played in all parts of the country either in campus tournaments as at Oberlin, in class games, or as a varsity sport. In 1894 an English instructor at the University of Nebraska served as the manager, coach, and a player for the girls' varsity basketball team. The University of Wisconsin girls' team played varsity ball briefly, but found that:

> The inter-class program of competition, however, became highly organized and enthusiastically supported. After 1900 each class fielded a team in the major sports and the class winning the most tournaments throughout the year was honored at the conclusion of the sports season.[29]

---

28. Kenneth L. Wilson and Jerry Brondfield, *The Big Ten* (Englewood Cliffs, N.J.: Prentice-Hall, Inc., 1967), p. 52.

29. Nancy Struna and Mary L. Remley, "Physical Education for Women at the University of Wisconsin, 1863-1913: A Half Century of Progress," *Canadian Journal of History of Sport and Physical Education* 4, no. 1 (1973): 21.

When the women's basketball team at California played Miss Head's School on November 18, 1892, "it was the first women's team to officially represent the University (and the first basketball team of either sex). . . ."[30] In 1915-16 California changed from a varsity-type program to an interclass program, but finished the season with an interclass intercollegiate competition with Stanford University in which each school entered four teams. One type of activity which included a variety of sport and dance activities was the May Day pageant and physical education demonstration. Such festivals might include marching, mass exercise drills, demonstrations of folk dancing, and perhaps a game of some type.

Also during this period student associations, usually called Women's Athletic Associations, developed. Although the associations were "student" organizations, most were carefully advised and directed by a woman faculty member. The first year of the Winthrop Recreation Association was successful:

> . . . already it is becoming one of the strongest and most influential organizations at Winthrop. At the close of the school session for 1913-14 we adopted a constitution and elected officers for the year 1914-15. At the beginning of this session the Athletic Association took up its work and our officers have faithfully performed their duties. For a number of years there has been need for an organization to systematize athletics and to aid in arousing an interest in all outdoor and indoor sports. The Athletic Association is meeting this long-felt need of the student body, and we prophesy for it even greater influence and more rapid growth during the coming year.[31]

In 1917 Blanche Trilling of the University of Wisconsin called a meeting of Women's Athletic Associations and assisted the students in organizing the Athletic Conference of American College Women. The purposes of the organization can be summarized:

> The efforts of the Federation are devoted to those activities which might be sponsored by the Women's Athletic Association, and which open to the student opportunity for useful recreational pursuits and the development of outdoor hobbies.[32]

Competitive sports for women in this period differed from those for men in several significant ways. First, from the beginning the women's programs

---

30. Roberta J. Park, "History and Structure of the Department of Physical Education at the University of California with Special Reference to Women's Sports," unpublished paper, 1976, p. 5.

31. *The Tatler* (Rock Hill, So. Carolina: Winthrop College, 1915), p. 147; cited in Rhonda K. Fleming, "A History of the Department of Physical Education at Winthrop College," M.S. thesis, University of North Carolina at Greensboro, 1973, pp. 53-54.

32. Marguerite Schwarz, "The Athletic Federation of College Women," *Journal of Health and Physical Education* 7 (May, 1936): 297.

FIG. 5.13   Field hockey at Wellesley College. Courtesy Wellesley College Archives, Wellesley, Massachusetts.

were organized and conducted largely in Departments of Physical Education for Women in coeducational institutions or in Departments of Physical Education in women's colleges. Second, the philosophy on which the programs were planned carefully avoided the problems created by the men's programs. The women were not permitted to engage in games where injuries were numerous. Also, they excluded the public from watching their contests so that they could not be accused of fostering some of the "evils" of men's athletics. Third, the philosophy on which the women's program was based encouraged the participation of many students rather than a few for a varsity team.

In spite of this philosophy, the women's programs continued to be criticized as too strenuous, possibly damaging to the women, and encouraging unladylike behavior. However, by carefully controlling the type of activity, by supervising all matches, and by planning types of activities which were different from the men's, the women physical educators were able to provide opportunities for many women to pursue sport in acceptable surroundings and to enjoy the new games of the period. It is also true that the "acceptable surroundings" often lacked adequate space and facilities, and the new games were often played with makeshift equipment, as women struggled for minimal programs.

Interscholastic Sport for Boys

Early interscholastic programs for boys were modeled after those of the colleges as student-directed athletic associations were formed. By the late 1890's, however, many of the public school systems which offered physical education employed physical education teachers who could also coach interscholastic teams. Because most early physical training teachers had been prepared only for the teaching of gymnastic classes, those with sport experience were highly sought after.

Interscholastic sport first developed in the cities. A Detroit High School football team existed in 1888, and in 1890 a school periodical reported that the same school's baseball team had defeated Grosse Isle, 33-3.[33] By 1892, the Detroit High School traveled as far as Ann Arbor for baseball games. The Ann Arbor High School boasted a baseball team in 1888, although no record of games is available until 1892 when thirteen games were played, nine of which were with class teams at the University of Michigan, two with University fraternity teams and two with Ypsilanti High School. Athletic field days, consisting of various track and field events between two or more high schools, were reported in Michigan in the eighties and nineties.[34] Wisconsin appears to have been the first state to organize a high school athletic association and by the turn of the century, three other midwestern states—Michigan, Illinois, and Indiana—had similar associations. In 1903, Dr. Luther Gulick established the Public School Athletic League in New York City, and provided an outstanding model of faculty-directed athletics. However, two years later, Dr. James Huff McCurdy's national study of public school physical education concluded that most interschool competition in the United States was still student-directed. Within the next decade the growth in interest and participation brought about increased faculty control.

Interscholastic Sport for Girls

At the high school level basketball was the most popular sport across the country. Lansing High School in Michigan played four games against Michigan Agricultural College in 1898 and Detroit's Central High School played in an intramural league from about 1900 to 1908. In New York City a Girl's Branch of the Public School Athletic League was formed by Elizabeth Burchenal in 1905, although until 1909 the program was run by a group of prominent women in the city rather than by the school system. It should also be noted that the program excluded inter-school contests. In

---

33. *The Argus,* October 1890, p. 13.
34. Lewis L. Forsythe, *Athletics in Michigan High Schools: The First Hundred Years* (New York: Prentice-Hall, Inc., 1950), pp. 38, 49.

1909, Burchenal became Inspector of Girl's Athletics and the program was brought under the full control of the school system.

Great concern was raised over the issue of interscholastic sport for girls. The major criticism focused on basketball and what was perceived as an increasing emphasis on "winning at all cost." Senda Berenson, long a leader in women's basketball, wrote in 1901: "The greatest element of evil in the spirit of athletics in this country is the idea that one must win at any cost— that defeat is an unspeakable disgrace."[35] Other objections centered on specific issues such as men coaching girls' teams, men officials, spectators of both sexes, "sensational" reporting in the press, and possible physiological harm to the health of the participants. By 1917, steps were being taken by professional educators to control and de-emphasize interscholastic sport for girls. In that year Illinois formed the first state high school athletic association for girls.

Dance in Education

The work of Francois Delsarte, which influenced dance in education and in theater, was first presented in the United States by Steele MacKaye. The Delsarte system originally developed as a method of training actors and singers in expressive gesture. Although the system was limited in popularity and short-lived among physical educators, it was widely used by teachers of elocution and singing. Its emphasis on grace and poise received considerable attention in the educational institutions of the period. Melvin Gilbert's aesthetic dancing, which had similar emphasis, was carried into the educational system by the many teachers who received their preparation in professional schools in Boston. Among Gilbert's students who were later to become known for their contributions to dance in education were Gertrude Colby, Mary Wood Hinman, and Elizabeth Burchenal.

Isadora Duncan may have been the inspiration for natural dance, but it was Gertrude Colby who was responsible for its development and practice in the public schools. Colby had been a student of Gilbert but when she was called upon in 1913 to evolve a rhythmic movement program for children, she found that formal dance was not suited to the goals of the new program. She based her teaching on the natural movement of children, which permitted the individual expression of the children. Her philosophy of natural dance was based on the desire to make the children, ". . . free instruments of expression, rhythmically unified . . . enabled to express in bodily movements the ideas and emotions which come from within."[36] For

---

35. Senda Berenson, *Basket Ball for Women* (New York: American Sports Publishing Company, 1901), p. 20.

36. Gertrude Colby, *Natural Rhythms and Dances* (New York: A.S. Barnes Company, 1922), n.p.

educators the value of natural dance lay in the opportunity to introduce creative activity into the physical education program.

Folk dance, inaugurated by Elizabeth Burchenal in 1905, is still widely used in the public schools. In order to provide suitable dances for recreational activity, she learned the dances first hand from the immigrant groups in the United States and she also studied in Europe. As a result of her research and teaching, many United States children learned the dances of England, Scotland, Ireland, Norway, Finland, Denmark, Sweden, Germany, and Switzerland. In 1916 she became president and director of the newly formed American Folk Dance Society, which was active in the world movement for the study and preservation of folk arts of all countries.

Summary

Between 1885 and 1917 the United States experienced continued growth in the cities, increased industrialization, improved transportation, and a widening gap between the rich and the poor. Educators and philanthropists instituted reforms to better the lot of the urban poor. While sport differed greatly for the various economic classes, the greatest difference was in the way they perceived sport as part of their lives. Many wealthy families vacationed in resorts where they enjoyed tennis, golf, sailing, and polo. It was men from these groups who had leisure time who were largely responsible for organizing and maintaining amateur sport in the United States. Also, many of today's sport organizations—AAU, USLTA, USGA, and others— can trace their beginnings to this period. The sport associations set standards for eligibility, rules of play, and playing etiquette. Professional major league baseball was a source of entertainment for all classes.

Baseball, as the "national" game, encouraged thousands of immigrant boys to embrace it as a means of acceptance in their new country. Basketball and volleyball were invented to answer the need for indoor winter sport as gymnastics and exercise programs became less and less popular. During the beginning of this period, physical educators argued the "battle of gymnastic systems" while the students continued to conduct their own intercollegiate sport program. After the NCAA had been established, and after the institutions had formally adopted intercollegiate athletics for men, the need for coaches and other administrators led to a change in curriculums in the men's programs from gymnastics to sport. As soon as sports such as basketball and field hockey were available, the women added them to their program. At the turn of the century, control of women's collegiate sport began with the appointment of a Committee on Women's Basketball. Departments of physical education for women also included the new forms of classical or aesthetic dancing.

The seminal figure in the new form of dance was Isadora Duncan, who freed dancers from rigidly devised techniques. Modern dance was initiated in this period, ballet revived in popularity, and black musical comedy evolved from the minstrel shows.

This was a period of rapid development in sport and physical activity. By the beginning of the twentieth century, sport had become institutionalized in American life as a major entertainment industry, both professional and amateur, as a means of socializing youth into American customs, both in school and out, and as an acceptable use of leisure time.

Questions for Discussion

1. Are there other examples in this chapter of "paradox in sport" (p. 143 of this chapter), especially disparities between sport and society?
2. Compare the beginnings of tennis and of golf in this country in terms of technology, social class, geography, and organization of the sport.
3. What was the impact of Jack Johnson on the concept of the American sport hero?
4. It has been said that basketball and volleyball are invented sports. Why are so few brand-new games invented?
5. How do you account for the popularity of basketball and field hockey among college women in the 1890's?
6. What issues were responsible for the development of institutional control of intercollegiate sport?
7. What kinds of contemporary dance movements have their roots in this period? Give specific examples, drawing on dance you have seen in concerts, television, and film.

Suggestions for Further Reading

1. Riess, Steven A. "The Baseball Magnate and Urban Politics in the Progressive Era: 1895-1920." *Journal of Sport History* 1, no. 1 (May, 1974): 41-62.
2. Smith, Robert A. *A Social History of the Bicycle*. New York: American Heritage Press, 1972.
3. Spears, Betty. "The Emergence of Women in Sport," in *Women's Athletics: Coping with Controversy*, ed. Barbara J. Hoepner. Washinton, D.C.: American Association for Health, Physical Education and Recreation, 1974.
4. Swanson, Richard A. "The Acceptance and Influence of Play in American Protestantism." *Quest* 11 (December, 1968): 58-70.
5. Terry, Walter. "The Legacy of Isadora Duncan and Ruth St. Denis." *Dance Perspectives* 5 (Winter, 1960): 1-60.
6. Zuckerman, Jerome; Stull, G. Allan; and Eyler, Marvin H. "The Black Athlete in Post-Bellum 19th Century." *The Physical Educator* 29 (October, 1972): 142-146.

Time Line

6 The Growth of Sport and Physical Activity During Social Change, 1917-1945

Following World War I, as the nation's attention turned toward prohibition, women's suffrage, and the flapper age, the country's sport world was rocked by a major scandal. Eight members of the Chicago White Sox baseball team were accused of "fixing" the 1919 World Series and were promptly dubbed the "Black Sox." After the scandal and the reorganization of baseball with Judge Landis as Commissioner, sport entered an era frequently referred to as the Golden Age of Sport. Along with the traditional baseball, boxing, and horse racing—tennis, golf, and numerous other sports prospered. Superstars such as Babe Ruth, Bill Tilden, Helen Wills, Bobby Jones, Babe Didrikson and many others became familiar names in millions of households. As college football grew from a casual, campus sport to a major entertainment business, players such as Red Grange from the University of Illinois and the "Four Horsemen" from the University of Notre Dame were the heroes in the stadiums. One indication of the popularity of sport is newspaper coverage. In 1921 about twenty sports were reported in the New York *Times,* whereas just prior to World War II, almost fifty sports received attention in the paper.

The Golden Age of Sport reflected the economic and technological boom of the twenties. Henry Ford made the family car a reality and the car made the beaches, golf courses, stadiums, and parks accessible. The radio brought sport events into the living room; daily newspapers devoted several pages to sport and the bulging Sunday papers an entire section; sportscasters and sports writers became part of the sport world. When the Depression hit, many sports were affected, but overall, sport increased. Again, during World War II sport was affected drastically, but was never dropped or banned. All in all, between World War I and World War II, the United States became a nation in which sport was firmly woven into the fabric of its life—as entertainment, as an integral part of education, and as an accepted and worthwhile way to spend time.

Not only did professional sport expand dramatically, but also amateur sport and men's intercollegiate athletics increased rapidly. About the only sport program which declined during this period was the women's intercollegiate varsity athletics, which was viewed by many women physical educators as undesirable for women. On the other hand, many departments of physical education for women supported the new "modern" dance which was characterized by a search for forms that were uniquely American. What we now know as modern dance emerged in both educational institutions and in the theater during this period. This chapter will seek to explain the rise of sport and dance as entertainment, the phenomenon of sport stardom, the differences in the development of men's and women's sport and physical education programs in educational institutions, and the acceptance of sport as an integral part of the American way of life.

Sport as Entertainment

The shortened workday, the new time-saving devices such as more efficient furnaces, electric stoves, and vacuum cleaners, and better trains, trolleys, and more family cars created time and mobility to attend sport events. In 1923 almost 150,000 automobile racing enthusiasts watched the Memorial Day Races at Indianapolis, and more than 300,000 saw the World Series. Even during the Depression, in 1934, 80,000 crowded in to see a double-header baseball game in St. Louis. Under Tex Rickard's promotion, three boxing matches drew 200,000 in 1923, and although horse racing suffered in the Depression, when Santa Anita opened in 1937, 50,000 Americans attended and bet $790,000.

Professional Sport

Professional football and basketball were almost unheard of in the early twenties, but by 1934, a crowd of 37,000 watched the New York Giants and Detroit Lions football teams in a National Football League championship game. On the other hand, in basketball two strong teams developed in New York City, the white Original Celtics and the black New York Renaissance ("Rens"). By the middle thirties water shows and ice shows provided family entertainment, and other sports such as wrestling and cycling attracted sport fans with special interests. But it was the national pastime, baseball, that had become the favorite of the sport fan.

Baseball

Perhaps the most important change in professional sport was the adoption of the Commissioner form of organization, which resulted from the 1919 scandals. Allegations of a "fix" had circulated from the time of the 1919 World Series between the Chicago White Sox and the Cincinnati Reds, which was won by the Reds. Rumors continued to persist not only about the Series, but also regarding other games, and finally, in 1920, a grand jury was appointed to investigate the situation. The investigations did, indeed, reveal that the 1919 Series had been "fixed." The gamblers had used a go-between, Billy Maharg, who in turn finally involved eight players—Eddie Cicotte, Joe Jackson, Fred McMullin, "Swede" Risberg, Oscar (Happy) Felsch, Claude Williams, George (Buck) Weaver, and Arnold (Chick) Gandil. The men had promised to lose the series in return for a substantial amount of money in several payments, although the only payment actually paid was after the White Sox lost the first game. The plan almost backfired when Kerr, *not* one of the eight players, pitched and won the third game. The eight men, called the *Black* Sox by the press and people alike, were indicted, tried, but acquitted when the confessions of Cicotte, Williams, and Jackson disappeared.

FIG. 6.1   Byron Bancroft Johnson, Judge Landis, Charles Comiskey. Courtesy Spalding Archives, Chicopee, Massachusetts.

This incident, along with internal problems in the National Commission, led to the reorganization of professional baseball and the appointment of a Commissioner with complete responsibility for the integrity of the sport. Judge Kenesaw Mountain Landis of the United States District Court in Chicago was named the first Commissioner. In accepting the position he explained:

It came like a flash to me, thinking of my boy, what baseball meant to him when he was young; what it means to him to-day. And I knew that is what baseball means to every kid in America. And then I realized that I could not refuse the responsibility and decided that if there were anything I could do to keep that game clean and honest, and to make it so that the kids of the United States never shall lose their ideals of the sport, it was a bit more than my duty to do it.[1]

To make good his promise to clean up baseball the eight White Sox players who had been involved in the Black Sox scandal were banned from professional baseball for life. Baseball was again the subject of a court case in 1922 when the United States Supreme Court declared that organized baseball did not constitute commerce among the states, thus upholding the reserve clause in players' contracts.

After it was reorganized under a commissioner and the disgraced players were ousted, baseball continued to grow, enhanced by improved equipment, the attention of the mass media, and the emergence of the sport hero. A new ball, more tightly wound, produced more home runs and more lively play. The year the new ball was introduced, Babe Ruth's home runs increased from 29 to 59. Not only did such feats please the fans, but the increased coverage in the papers and over the radio enabled them to follow the sport more closely. Men such as John Drebinger of the New York *Times,* Shirley Povich of the Washington *Post,* and Paul Gallico of the New York *Daily News* chronicled the game each summer, reported the play of the stars, and analyzed the increasing body of statistics. Although the sports page was by now a regular feature of the newspaper, the possibility of broadcasting the games over the radio made baseball owners fear that attendance in the ball parks would fall. But when "sportscasters" like Graham McNamee recreated the game for eager listeners, interest in the live game did not diminish but to everyone's surprise, increased.

The popularity of radio continued to grow, and its consumer market expanded to include 250,000 auto radios by 1932. By then radio's overwhelming appeal crushed its oppositon. Certainly owners welcomed the offer of networks to pay for the privilege of broadcasting games. Late in 1933, owners let bids for the exclusive rights to broadcast Series games. Landis represented baseball at the annual bargaining sessions, and in 1936 he signed a $100,000 contract for exclusive broadcasting rights.[2]

The sports writers and sportscasters had exciting games, thrilling Series, and star players to report during the two decades between the wars. While the New York Giants and New York Yankees dominated the play, teams from many parts of the country stimulated unexpected interest. Washington won its first pennant in 1924 with the President of the United States, Calvin

---

1. H.S. Fullerton, "Baseball—the Business and the Sport," *American Review of Reviews* 63 (April, 1921): 420.

2. David Voigt, *American Baseball,* Vol. II (Norman: University of Oklahoma Press, 1970), pp. 233-234.

FIG. 6.2 George Herman (Babe) Ruth. Courtesy Spalding Archives, Chicopee, Massachusetts.

Coolidge, joining the welcome celebration. In 1926 Rogers Hornsby led the St. Louis Cardinals to their first pennant and in 1934 the Detroit Tigers won the American League pennant. But the thirties was the Yankees' decade when they won five World Series.

This was also the period of the sport star. From Babe Ruth's 59 home runs in 1921 to his total of 714 career runs, the Babe outshone them all. Between 1920 and 1925, Rogers Hornsby led the National League in batting and from 1921 to 1925, averaged .397, .401, .384, .424, and .403. Ty Cobb, one of the greatest hitters of all times, retired in 1928. The two Deans, Dizzy and Paul, pitched the St. Louis Cardinals to victory in the 1934 World Series. Also in 1934, Lou Gehrig set a new record for consecutive games played. Toward the end of the period new superstars such as Joe DiMaggio and Lefty Gomez appeared.

George Herman (Babe) Ruth (1894-1948). Born in Baltimore, Ruth spent most of his boyhood at St. Mary's Industrial School for Boys. In 1914 he left St. Mary's to join a minor league team, the Baltimore Orioles. By the end of the season he had moved to a major league team, the Boston Red Sox. In 1919 he went to the Yankees where his career soared. Many of his records stood for years and some still stand today. He made money and he spent it, but he continued to play superstar ball. During his twenty seasons with baseball he made the game livelier, set records, and was a major box office attraction. The stories of his life away from the diamond were not often flattering, but in spite of them, and in spite of his rough manner and speech, his soft round face, slightly pudgy body and tapered ankles, he played baseball brilliantly, he played it joyously, and the fans loved it.

He met an elemental need of the crowd. Every hero must have his human flaw which he shares with his followers. In Ruth it was hedonism, as exaggerated in folklore and fable.

. . . The combination of great skill on the field and a shared flaw off the field made him the most admired and theatrical man in the game.[3]

At forty years of age, his last year with the Yankees, he hit 22 home runs. The following year he moved to Boston where he did not finish the season. Ruth appeared two more times in front of his beloved fans—on Babe Ruth Day in the Yankee Stadium on April 27, 1947 and again, just two months before he died, in June, 1948.

When the Atlantic City Bacharach Giants and the Lincoln Giants of New York played at Brooklyn's Ebbets Field in 1920 it marked the first time two black teams played in a National League ball park. The Negro National

---

3. Marshall M. Smelser, "The Babe on Balance," *The American Scholar* 44 (Spring, 1975):299.

League comprised nine teams—the Detroit Stars, Cleveland Browns, Cuban Stars, Kansas City Monarchs, Birmingham Black Barons, Chicago American Giants, St. Louis Stars, Memphis Red Sox, and Indianapolis A. B. C.'s. The Hilldale Club, Bacharach Giants, Lincoln Giants, Washington Potomacs, Baltimore Black Sox, Cuban Stars, Harrisburg Giants, and Brooklyn Royal Giants played in the Eastern Colored League. At that time black baseball had nothing comparable to the World Series and it was not until 1924 that a black World Series could be arranged between the Negro National League in the west and the Eastern Colored League. That year the Hilldale Club in Darby, Pennsylvania, won the Eastern League and the Kansas City Monarchs captured the Western title to play in the first black World Series. Kansas City won in a ten-game series played in Philadelphia, Baltimore, Kansas City, and Chicago, during which over 45,000 paid $52,114 to see the games.

The black World Series was never an outstanding success, but the black All-Star game was. Like the white leagues, the black league introduced an All-Star game between the East and the West in 1933. The following year the white All-Star game drew 48,363 and the black All-Stars 30,000. The black All-Star event continued to be popular and, in 1939, two All-Star Games were played, one before 40,000 in Chicago's Comiskey Park and one with 20,000 in attendance at Yankee Stadium in New York. The black All-Star game overshadowed the white All-Star game in 1939, the black game attracting 46,247 and the white game 29,589.

Pressure to admit black professional ball players into the major leagues increased during World War II. In 1943 New York State Senator Charles E. Perry introduced a resolution in the New York Senate, pointing out the state's antidiscrimination laws. The resolution was sent to Judge Landis, who in response declared that each club could employ any players of their choice. In April of 1945 United States Congressman Marcantonio from New York introduced a resolution in the United States House of Representatives calling for an investigation of racial discrimination in baseball. New York City Mayor Fiorello LaGuardia appointed a committee to study the situation and Branch Rickey, president of the Brooklyn Dodgers, was a member of the committee, though he later resigned. According to the committee's report black players were excluded from professional baseball because of tradition and because of prejudice. The report further concluded that there was no rule excluding Negroes from organized baseball and no reason that Negroes and whites could not play together on a team.

By this time Branch Rickey had initiated plans to sign Jackie Robinson for the Montreal Royals and, later, to bring him to the Brooklyn Dodgers. Many agreed that during this period the caliber of play among the best of the black leagues was as good as, if not better than, that of the white leagues. In reply to a counter-charge that the black players preferred to play in their own league, "Dr. J.B. Martin, president of the Negro American League, said that the league had no intention of standing in the players' way 'if they had a chance to advance.' "[4]

Josh Gibson (1911-1947). Josh Gibson did not live to see Jackie Robinson break the color line in white major league baseball. Born in Buena Vista, Georgia, he had moved to Pittsburgh by 1929 where he worked in a steel mill and played semipro ball with the Crawford Colored Giants. On July 25, 1930, he attended the game between the Homestead Grays and the Kansas City Monarchs during which the Gray's catcher was injured and Gibson, well known locally, was pressed into service. Gibson quit the steel mills and played black pro baseball for the next sixteen years and was considered one of the hardest hitters of all time, chalking up 89 home runs in one season. In 1931 he hit 75 homers and 61, 72, and 69 in the next three years. Playing 123 games for the Pittsburgh Crawfords, he had 441 putouts, 49 assists, and batted .379.

Players in black leagues moved from team to team, depending on which team could offer the most money. In 1937, along with "Satch" Paige and others Gibson was lured to San Domingo, which paid higher salaries. When Josh returned to finish the season with the Grays, he was fined a quarter of a month's salary for the escapade. Because of further salary problems he played with Vera Cruz in the Mexican League in 1940 and 1941. However, Gibson returned to the black pro teams and played many All-Star games. Josh Gibson, one of the great players in black baseball, played his last season in 1946, batting .331 and knocking in 27 home runs.

Boxing

When Tex Rickard, who had promoted the Jeffries-Johnson fight in 1910, saw Jack Dempsey fight Jess Willard, he recognized another champion. He proceeded to launch a decade of champions, earning for boxing the approval of many who had questioned the respectability of the sport. He promoted the 1921 Dempsey-Carpentier match and turned the 1926 Dempsey-Tunney fight into a $2,000,000 venture. Gene Tunney, a quiet, scientific boxer, and the slugging Dempsey met again the following year in a controversial fight in Chicago. After six rounds, Dempsey caught Tunney off guard and knocked him down. A delayed, but legal count gave Tunney a few seconds more time to recover, regain his feet, and go on to win the fight. For a time interest in boxing declined until Joe Louis, the Brown Bomber from Detroit, began his series of victories. Having been thoroughly

---

4. Ocania Chalk, *Pioneers of Black Sport* (New York: Dodd, Mead, and Co., 1975), p. 78. More detailed information on black sport of this period can be found in this work.

FIG. 6.3   Josh Gibson, all-star catcher in the Negro Leagues. Wide World.

defeated by the German Max Schmelling before he captured the crown from James J. Braddock in 1937, Louis fought Schmelling again the second time. In the era of Hitler's speeches about the purity of the Aryan race, the fight had overtones of a black American fighting an Aryan Nazi. Louis, the black American, won in only two minutes and four seconds. In 1942 Louis defeated first Max Baer and then Abe Simon, donating the first purse to the Naval Relief Fund and the second to the Army Relief Fund. Inducted into the army in February, 1942, Lewis was not required to defend his title until after the war.

Horse Racing

Among the more popular "heroes" of the Golden Age of Sport was a two-year-old horse named Man O'War. Running only as a two- and three-year-old in 1919 and 1920, he won all but one of his twenty-one races, and lost that one to a horse appropriately named Upset. Like other sports, racing grew during the years between the two wars, and even though the sport was hard hit by the Depression, it increased from 1022 racing days in 1920 to 2228 days in 1942. In 1937 Man O'War's son, War Admiral, won the triple crown—the Kentucky Derby, the Preakness, and the Belmont Stakes. In the same year famous Sea Biscuit was the year's leading money winner. But the horse of the era was still Man O'War who, in 1950, was voted by the Associated Press as one of the greatest athletes of the first half of the twentieth century.

Football

Towns such as Green Bay, Wisconsin, Canton, Ohio, and Hammond, Indiana, nurtured the beginnings of pro football. The American Professional Football Association first met in Canton, in 1921, naming Jim Thorpe president. To get the league under way, franchises sold for a hundred dollars that year, and the next year, as further inducement, they were lowered to fifty dollars. In 1922, the Association changed its name to the National Football League as the young sport slowly established itself. When the University of Illinois star Red Grange left the university and joined the Chicago Bears in 1925, the fans followed and success for pro football seemed assured. Although by 1927 teams such as the New York Giants broke even, many pro teams continued at a subsistence level. By 1934 crowds of 50,000 attended some of the games, and by the end of the period, the pro game had become firmly entrenched in the sport world. However, it was football in the college stadiums which attracted the crowds.

Basketball

The Original Celtics, with Nat Holman as the star, toured the country in the early twenties, winning over ninety percent of their games. Characteristic of the pro game of the day was a net which hung from floor to ceiling, separating the players from the audience, and keeping the ball in bounds and the fans off the court. Although attempts were made to establish league play in 1925, it was not until 1938 that the National Basketball League was organized.

The Rens and the Harlem Globetrotters were two very strong black pro teams. The Rens, short for the New York Renaissance, were organized by Robert Douglas in 1923. In the 1925-26 season they split a six game series with the Original Celtics. During the Depression the Rens' popularity flourished, as they beat the Celtics in 1932. The Rens then won 88 games in a row, but were finally defeated by the Celts the following year. Throughout the thirties the Rens continued to win and to attract crowds. In March 1939 the Rens accepted the invitation of the National Basketball League to play in a League tournament, which the Rens not only won, but which brought them national recognition. This season was the height of their success as a team. They continued to play, but as other black teams improved, they lost some of their appeal, and in 1941 were defeated in the NBL tournament by the Harlem Globetrotters, whom Abe Saperstein had organized in 1927. In the beginning the Globetrotters played remote towns scattered over the country but later became an integral part of the basketball world. They were highly skilled basketball players and also extremely clever at trick shots, rapid ball handling, and clowning, which they inserted into their game to please the audience. Some sport critics have likened the Globetrotters' carnival atmosphere to the minstrel shows of the South, pointing out that middle-class Americans accepted blacks as entertainers, but not as athletes.

Other Professional Sport

While baseball dominated the professional sport world between the two wars, other sports reflected the increased interest in and growth of sport in general. When the New York Rangers, Detroit Cougars, and the Chicago Black Hawks were all admitted to the nine-year-old National Hockey League in 1926, professional ice hockey was assured a place in United States sports. The speed of the game was one of hockey's attractions and seemed to reflect the fast-paced twenties. By 1942 six teams had emerged in the League—the Montreal Canadiens, Toronto Maple Leafs, Boston Bruins, New York Rangers, Detroit Red Wings, and Chicago Black Hawks. America's fascination with speed was further mirrored in bicycle racing and automobile racing, especially the Memorial Day Race at the Indianapolis Speedway.

Beginning in 1916, the Professional Golf Association of America held pro championships, but many of the better players continued to compete in the Open championships. Tennis turned from an elite amateur sport to a professional one when the theatrical French woman, Suzanne Lenglen, the American Mary K. Browne, and four men, Vincent Richards, Harvey Snodgrass, Howard Kinsey, and Paul Peret of France successfully toured the country in 1926. The biggest indoor sport in the United States, bowling, offered prize money for men under the auspices of the American Bowling Congress and for women under the Women's International Bowling Congress. Such sports as wrestling accounted for another area of interest in sport as entertainment.

There were also sport spectaculars such as the ice shows and aquacades, which were particularly popular in the middle and late thirties. Since the days of Annette Kellerman before World War I water shows had existed, but it was Norman Ross who invented the term "synchronized swimming" for the 1933 Chicago World's Fair entertainment and initiated the elaborate aquacades of the period. Later at New York City's Jones Beach, Minneapolis, and many other cities the summer aquacade became an annual affair.

Thus, professional sport during the period between World War I and World War II increased in the number and variety of sports. Before World War I most people attended baseball, boxing, and horse racing events but by the late 1930's the sport fan could see a tennis match, a football game, a six-day bicycle race, an aquacade, or many other sport events.

Amateur Sport

If professional sport made rapid progress between the wars, the growth of amateur sport was astonishing. Although college football was the greatest attraction, golf, tennis, swimming, field hockey, track and field, polo, rowing and other amateur sports also thrived. By 1925 the United States had reached international prominence in several sports. Five Olympic Games were held from 1920 to 1936, and in all of these the United States athletes, especially in track and swimming, turned in superior performances. In the 1920's Duke Kahanamoku and Johnny Weismuller dominated men's swimming, and in 1932 19-year-old Mildred "Babe" Didrikson appeared as a one-woman track team and won the National Women's AAU Track Meet. Sports such as rowing, lacrosse, squash rackets, handball, badminton, curling, and table tennis beckoned more and more enthusiasts. By the late thirties skiing, tobogganing, and other winter sports lured thousands out of doors in northern United States. Amateur sports had their sport stars just as the professional sports did, and the public responded enthusiastically to Bobby Jones, Bill Tilden, Gertrude Ederle, and Helen Wills.

Golf

Walter Hagen, Gene Sarazen, Glenna Collett, and Bobby Jones dominated the game of golf. The Walker Cup competition between the United States and British men's teams began in 1922. Robert Tyre Jones, Jr. from Atlanta, Georgia, performed the seemingly impossible task of achieving the "Grand Slam" when, in 1930, he won the United States Open, the United States Amateur, the British Open, and the British Amateur. From 1922 to 1935 Glenna Collett was the consistent winner in women's golf. She entered her first major competition at seventeen and dominated the women's field for the next seventeen years. In 1929 she set a record when she won her fourth national title.

Robert Tyre Jones, Jr. (1902-1971). Bobby Jones began playing golf at five and at nine won his first championship, the junior cup at the Atlanta Athletic Club. He was graduated from Georgia Institute of Technology, received a law degree from Harvard University, and was admitted to the bar. He played on five Walker Cup teams, won five United States Amateur titles, four United States Opens, three British Opens, and one British Amateur in 1930, the year he won the Grand Slam. Paul Gallico called him:

. . . a born golfer. Everything about the game suited his body, his character, and his competitive spirit. . . . Jones played so beautifully, he was such a joy to watch in action—the quiet elegance and smooth rhythm of his stride, the arc and pattern of the flight of his ball, that he reached the heart of even the sourest or most misanthropic old pros.[5]

Jones was described as the epitome of the amateur athlete, interpreting the rules strictly and calling strokes on himself, even those which cost him matches. After winning the Grand Slam he retired from golf competition, but continued to play and in 1934 helped plan the Masters Tournament. In 1958 he received the distinctive honor of the Freedom of the City of St. Andrews, Scotland—the second American to be so honored. The first was Benjamin Franklin.

Tennis

The tennis stars of the twenties and thirties were dramatic, flamboyant, and superb players. Suzanne Lenglen and Big Bill Tilden have been equaled by few players since their day. The French player, Lenglen, was theatrical on the court, and a superior player who defeated the best women players. One of the most dramatic events in her career was her default to Molla Bjurstadt Mallory in 1921. Vincent Richards teamed with Tilden that same year to take the national doubles. In 1923 the young Helen Wills won the women's national crown from Mallory and also in 1923 Hazel Hotchkiss Wightman, a top player in the United States, donated a trophy for world competition among women, which in actuality turned out to be contests between the United States and England. After six years, Tilden was finally

---

5. Paul Gallico, *The Golden People* (Garden City, N.Y.: Doubleday, 1964), p. 279.

beaten by Henri Cochet of France. While both Tilden and Wills, later Helen Wills Moody, continued to dominate tennis on both sides of the Atlantic, other stars such as Helen Jacobs, Alice Marble, and Donald Budge made their appearance. In 1938 Budge achieved the Grand Slam in tennis. He was the first to win the British, French, American, and Australian titles in one year. A new men's star, Bobby Riggs, made his appearance in the tennis world just prior to World War II.

FIG. 6.4   Representatives of the first Golden Age of Sport in the U.S.: Bobby Jones, golf; Bill Tilden, tennis; Gertrude Ederle, distance swimming; Johnny Weismuller, swimming. Wide World.

William Tatem Tilden 2nd (1893-1953) Big Bill Tilden, six foot one and 165 pounds, transformed the game of lawn tennis, sometimes considered not a game for the manly, to today's complex, highly skilled, hard-fought contest. He dominated first amateur tennis and then professional tennis from the time he won the men's outdoor national singles championship in 1920 until he turned pro and retired in 1935. Theatrical in his game, controversial on and off the courts, he was a superb player noted for ". . . power hitting, a booming cannon-ball service, cunning volley, and smashing net game. . ."[6] Tilden's string of championships included seven American National Turf Court Championships, three Wimbledon singles titles in 1920, 1921, and 1930, one Wimbledon doubles, five United States doubles, and fifteen Davis Cup singles. He was the first American man to win the men's singles at Wimbledon. After turning pro in 1931 he continued to reign as the King of the Courts for the next four years, beating players such as Richards, Cochet, and Vines.

Helen Wills Moody (1906-   ). The daughter of a Los Angeles physician, Helen Wills played at the Berkeley Tennis Club in Berkeley, California, won the national junior girls championship at fifteen and entered her first women's nationals the following year. She was defeated in the finals by Molla Mallory but returned in 1923 to take the title. During her first years of play she continued studying and was admitted to Phi Beta Kappa. Her serious attitude and the predilections of the press gave her the nickname "Little Miss Poker Face." Her brilliant play brought her twelve Wimbledon titles, eight singles and one mixed doubles, seven United States singles titles, four United States doubles championships, the French singles championships, and membership on ten Wightman Cup teams. She had the distinction of winning two gold medals in the 1924 Olympic Games, the women's singles and the women's doubles, in which she teamed with Hazel Wightman. From 1922 when she won the United States women's doubles with Mrs. Marion Jessup to 1938 when she captured her eighth Wimbledon singles title, Helen Wills Moody was "Queen of the Nets."

Swimming

Like many other sports, swimming experienced a tremendous growth both as an amateur sport and as a recreational activity. During this period competitive swimming was commanded by Duke Kahanamoku from Hawaii, Johnny Weismuller, and several women, most of whom swam under L. deB. Handley at the Women's Swimming Association (WSA) in New York. Ethelda Bleibtry, Gertrude Ederle, Helen Wainwright, Aileen Riggin, and Eleanor Holm were all WSA swimmers. In 1926, 19-year-old Gertrude Ederle amazed the world when she swam the English Channel from Cape Gris-Nes to Dover in 14 hours and 31 minutes.

---

6. Paul Gallico, *The Golden People* (Garden City, N.Y.: Doubleday, 1964), p. 124.

Gertrude Ederle (1906-   ). At seventeen Gertrude Ederle, daughter of a New York delicatessen owner, earned a gold medal and two bronze medals in the Paris Olympics, and held the AAU championship in the 880-yard freestyle. There appeared to be no further challenges in the swimming world for Trudy, as she was known, but she announced that she was ready to swim the English Channel, which only five men had done—and which was considered impossible for a woman. However, the publisher of the New York *News*, Captain Patterson, sensed a good story and underwrote the venture and arranged for a coach, Thomas Burgess, who was one of the five men who had completed the difficult swim. Also he sent a woman reporter to keep the United States public informed of events, and her sister Margaret to be her companion on the trip.

The swim began as planned, but about two hours before the finish the seas became rough, and Trudy was seasick. Although her coach suggested she stop, she would not give up. When she reached shore, she was not only the first woman to swim the English Channel, she was also the record holder as her time was two hours faster than the existing men's record. Before Trudy could capitalize on her fame, a second woman swam the Channel, making Trudy's victory not quite so impressive to the public. On her return to New York, Trudy received a "ticker tape" welcome, but not the professional contracts for which she hoped. Thirty-nine years later, she was inducted into the International Swimming Hall of Fame.

John Weismuller (1904-   ). At the age of fourteen Johnny Weismuller was spotted at a Chicago YMCA by Burt Bachrach of the Illinois Athletic Club in Chicago and persuaded to swim for the club and a year later he won his first national event. His coach utilized his natural talent and long, lean body to develop a style which revolutionized freestyle swimming. He developed a smooth relaxed style with a long arm pull and great drive, which kept him high in the water. His stroke became the model for most swimmers of the period. Overall, Weismuller set 67 records, of which 24 were world records. He won gold medals in the 100 meters and 400 meters in both the 1924 and 1928 Olympic Games. His complete mastery of swimming and his good-natured personality helped to popularize the sport.

Field Hockey

Amateur field hockey for women developed through clubs in the major cities of the country and in localities near colleges and universities. By 1922 there was sufficient interest to form the United States Field Hockey Association. In that same year M.K. Constance Applebee of Bryn Mawr College opened her famous Pocono Hockey Camp on the grounds of Camp Tegawitha in Pennsylvania. After the children left the camp for the summer, Miss Applebee, or the "Apple" as she was affectionately called, opened the camp for one week to school girls, college and university students, teachers, and club players. At what was possibly the first "sports" camp, the "Apple" prodded, chided, and goaded women and girls into improving their games and into aspiring after English standards of field hockey. In 1924 and again in 1933 a selected team of United States women toured European countries playing other field hockey clubs. In 1936 the United States women, in turn, welcomed teams from Australia, Wales, England, Scotland, and South Africa. After a tournament in Philadelphia, each team toured the country playing at colleges, universities, and city clubs. Outstanding United States players of the period included Anne Townsend of Philadelphia and Betty Richey, a faculty member of Vassar College, who played with the Stuyvesant Club in New York.

FIG. 6.5   Constance Applebee. Courtesy of Bryn Mawr College Archives.

Track and Field

Men's track and field was dominated by university and college students such as Charlie Paddock, Glenn Cunningham, Jesse Owens, and Don Lash. In the early twenties Paddock, a University of Southern California student, starred as a sprinter. In 1923 for the first time, there were three national championships, the AAU, ICAAAA, and NCAA. The crowd of 30,000 which watched the 1924 Olympic tryouts demonstrated the increased interest in track and field events. The ICAAAA celebrated its thirtieth anniversary with a meet at Harvard. When Sabin Carr of Yale pole-vaulted 14 feet in the 1927 ICAAAA meet, the track world was amazed. In the thirties Glenn Cunningham of Kansas and Jesse Owens of Ohio State were among the stars. In 1935 Owens starred in both the NCAA and AAU championships and in 1936 won 4 gold medals in the Berlin Olympics.

FIG. 6.6   Jesse Owens setting one of four world records at the Big Ten Meet, May 25, 1935, Ann Arbor, Michigan. Courtesy of University of Michigan.

In 1923 the AAU formally adopted track and field championships for women. Back in 1915 the Union had assumed control of women's swimming, but had not added any additional women's sports. Cautiously, in 1922 it appointed a committee to investigate the possibility of assuming control over women's track and field. This was the summer of the First Women's Olympic Games, to be held in Paris under the auspices of the Fédération Sportive Féminine Internationale (FSFI) and the AAU accepted an invitation to send a team to the Paris meet. The team, coached by Dr. Harry Stewart, finished second in the meet. The following year the AAU officially announced its control over women's track and field in this country. Under the AAU, women's track grew steadily, with stars such as Babe Didrikson contributing to its increasing popularity.

FIG. 6.7   Mildred "Babe" Didrikson (far right) on her way to victory in the 80-meter hurdle event at the 1932 Olympic Games.

Mildred "Babe" Didrikson Zaharias (1914-1956). Born in Port Arthur, Texas, and raised in Beaumont, Texas, Babe possessed the necessary traits of a champion—natural ability, the desire to win, and the perseverance to pursue a goal—but she lacked the necessary money for good coaching and the time to practice. In her junior year in high school her basketball marksmanship reached the local sports pages and captured the interest of Col. M.J. McCombs, who was in charge of the Employers Casualty Company's women's athletic program. He arranged an office job for Babe and immediately put her on the company's basketball team. After basketball season, the company's athletic program included swimming, diving, track, and softball. Babe practiced the track events and entered the 1930 AAU nationals, winning two events. In 1932 the company sent Babe to the Olympic trials and national AAU meet in Chicago where she won five events, tied for a sixth and placed in two other events, thereby capturing the team title. She won national fame for her performance in the 1932 Olympics, winning two gold medals and one silver.

After the Olympics, Babe remained in sport, performing and playing many sports, but it was golf which eventually captured her imagination and interest. Having been disqualified as an amateur, Babe stopped all sport competition until she was declared an amateur again and then between 1940 and 1950 won every major golf tournament open to her. In 1946 and 1947 she had 17 consecutive wins. In 1950 she was voted the greatest woman athlete in the first half of the present century.

Dance as Entertainment

In the early 1920's, Martha Graham, Doris Humphrey, and Charles Weidman left the Denishawn organization to make their own personal statements as artists. They searched for dance forms which were uniquely American without borrowing the styles of other peoples as St. Denis and Shawn had done. In their explorations they evolved new techniques for training the dancer's body to interpret the dances. Their early choreographic efforts were not understood or accepted by many. In fact, some were repelled by the new use of the body and by the dances. Through touring and teaching they were able to educate more people to their ideas, which are now accepted as basic to American dance.

Sport, Dance, and Physical Activity in Educational Institutions

During the period between the two World Wars, sport, exercise, dance, and physical activity became integral parts of the educational system in the United States. Although programs were distinctively different for men and

FIG. 6.8   A summer class at Denishawn receiving instruction from Ruth St. Denis and Ted Shawn. *The Denishawn Magazine,* vol. I, No. 1 (undated—about 1923).

women, physical education for graduation came to be required in more and more colleges and universities.

For the men, intercollegiate athletics became firmly established in the administrative structure of the institution, and sport replaced gymnastics in most physical education programs. Student sport, especially football and basketball, became important as entertainment and as a focal point for student and alumni loyalty. Many institutions provided financial aid for men student athletes, some of whom would not otherwise have been able to attend college.

The women, already teaching a variety of activities such as sport, gymnastics, body mechanics, and dance, emphasized activities in which large numbers of women could participate and effectively avoided intercollegiate varsity programs. Most women physical educators emphasized the importance of choosing a college or university on the basis of academic offerings rather than on financial inducements through athletic programs, and they neither approved of nor permitted financial aid to women based on their athletic ability.

Sport in Colleges and Universities

The Men's Program

College football was the nation's most popular fall sport. Not only college students, but alumni and the general sports fan packed the stadiums across the country. By 1921 intersectional contests produced additional enthusiasm among the fans. In the East, Penn State dominated the game; in the Middle West, Iowa and Notre Dame stood out; in the South, Centre College; and in the West, California. McGeehan reported that ". . . intercollegiate football in season draws more spectators than the national pastime."[7] The New York *Times* reported 1934 as one of the best football seasons because of ". . . spectacular play, increased attendance, decreased fatalities, and the brilliant Minnesota eleven."[8] By 1937, 20,000,000 people attended college football games.

The crowds required stadiums and other facilities for which the university itself might have little need. To accommodate football within the university, stadiums were financed in a variety of ways. For example, Ohio State University's first stadium was partially paid for by donors who were then assigned special seats. October 18-23, 1920, was declared Stadium Week with parades, pageants, demonstrations, and appeals for money. An "Ohio State Day," celebrated nationally on November 26, 1920, produced over $900,000, and finally, two years later, the stadium opened. From the beginning the athletic facilities of many universities developed parallel with, but not necessarily from, the institution's budget.

Such games as the Army-Navy game and the Harvard-Yale contests were sellouts and the "Galloping Ghost" and the "Four Horsemen" became familiar in ordinary households far from Indiana. The Four Horsemen, Knute Rockne's famous backfield, helped the University of Notre Dame achieve national prominence. Under Rockne's leadership, Notre Dame from 1920 to 1930 won 96 games, lost three, and tied three. Innovations such as intersectional and post-season play increased interest in the game. The Orange Bowl was initiated in 1933 followed by the Sugar Bowl and Sun Bowl in 1936 and the Cotton Bowl in 1937.

Gallico credits Red Grange with beginning the competition for football talent in the major football programs which resulted in the adoption of the semiprofessional model:

> . . . in their frantic attempts to acquire similar attractions [to Red Grange], the universities impaled themselves front, back, and sideways on the horns of the dilemma that had been created—how to coax, lure, rent, hire, or buy football stars who would be drawing cards, while at the same time managing to keep their fingers off the swag. During this process they fractured amateur codes into so many pieces that no one has yet been able to put them together again.[9]

7. W. O. McGeehan, "Our Changing Sports Page," *Scribner's Magazine* 84, no. 1 (July, 1928): 58.

8. "20,000,000 Saw College Games as Football Scaled New Heights," New York *Times,* 26 December 1937, p. S3.

9. Paul Gallico, *The Golden People* (Garden City, N. Y.: Doubleday, 1964), p. 259.

FIG. 6.9 Harold "Red" Grange, the University of Illinois' "Galloping Ghost."
Courtesy of University of Illinois.

Whether or not undergraduate sport should be used to entertain fellow
students, alumni, faculty, and the public became a controversial issue
throughout the country. Usually expressed as a discussion of the value of
athletics to the athletes rather than of the desirability of entertaining others,
arguments for and against men's intercollegiate athletics appeared in
periodicals such as the *Atlantic Monthly, Harper's* and *Forum.* In the
November 1926 issue of *Forum,* for example, one article favored intercollegiate athletics and one article opposed it.

Aspects of the programs most frequently criticized were commercialism
and professionalism. In 1929 the Carnegie Foundation for the Advancement of Teaching published the results of a study of athletics in colleges and
universities. Over 130 institutions were included in the investigation, which
came to the following two conclusions.

1. . . . a change of values [is needed] in a field that is sodden with the commercial and the material and the vested interests that these forces have created. Commercialism in college athletics must be diminished and college sport must rise to a point where it is esteemed primarily and sincerely for the opportunities it affords to mature youth . . . to exercise at once the body and the mind, and to foster habits both of bodily health and . . . high qualities of character . . .

2. The American college must renew within itself the force that will challenge the best intellectual capabilities of the undergraduates.[10]

The report met with mixed reactions, many agreeing with it and many believing that the report did not assess the values of athletics to the participants. In the early thirties the NCAA made some attempts to restructure recruiting and appointed committees to study the association's policies. In reality, the report had little effect on the athletic programs.

In spite of the disputes, the fall Saturday afternoon spectacles continued. During this period, however, more direct control of the men's intercollegiate athletics programs was assumed by institutional departments such as a Department of Athletics or a Department of Physical Education for Men. This administrative shift was one of several factors which combined to complete a change begun prior to World War I, in which the content of the men's physical education program became predominantly sport. The change was consistent with the current educational philosophy which focused on social and citizenship goals. Organizations such as the NCAA, the National Amateur Athletic Federation, and the Playground and Recreation Association supported the new philosophy. It was thought that the objectives of men's physical education could best be met through a "sports for all" program. In response to these factors the curriculum shifted from the goal of health through gymnastics to character and sportsmanship through sport. Underlying the change in curriculum was the practical need for coaches rather than gymnastic teachers. According to Lewis:

Well-intentioned administrators, assisted by a tremendous increase in the number and size of physical education programs, forced physical educators to adopt the sports program. From this point formulation of a philosophy was merely a practice in justifying the existence of programs already sanctioned by higher authority. Accommodation, then, of varsity athletics was the key factor in the transformation of the profession. The status of competitive athletics established the location of physical education in high schools and colleges; facilities, equipment, and staff secured for varsity sports determined the content of the curricula and the nature of the programs.[11]

10. H.J. Savage, *American College Athletics* (New York: The Carnegie Foundation for the Advancement of Teaching, 1929), p. 310.
11. Guy M. Lewis, "Adoption of the Sports Program, 1906-39: The Role of Accommodation in the Transformation of Physical Education," *Quest* 12 (May, 1969): 42.

The "sports for all" philosophy was reflected in increased intramural programs, which were also possible due to the expansion of facilities. College basketball attracted national attention with the 1934-35 invitational tournament in Madison Square Garden. Interchange of play across the country brought a number of changes to sport. Players and coaches alike were exposed to different styles of play and the general level of play improved as a result. The interpretation of the rules became more uniform and officiating improved as a result of these interactions. Thus, before World War II a casual campus endeavor, college football, had ceased to be a nineteenth-century student enterprise and had become a semiprofessional sport for the entertainment of the campus, the alumni, and the public. Other intercollegiate sports and also intramural sport programs expanded. Men's physical education, originally an exercise program to improve students' health, now offered instruction in a variety of sports.

FIG. 6.10   Pioneering intramural sport at the University of Michigan.

The Women's Programs

Housed in separate Departments of Physical Education for Women or in separate institutions such as Wellesley College in the East or Lindenwood College in the Midwest, the women carefully developed programs which promoted the philosophy of "A sport for every girl and every girl in a sport." Women physical educators continued to build on the statements voiced by Lucille Eaton Hill in 1903, that athletics should be planned for the greatest good to the greatest number and should avoid the "evils" of men's athletics. At the 1920 meeting of the Conference of College Directors of Physical Education the group went on record as disapproving women's intercollegiate athletics for the following reasons:

1. It leads to professionalism.
2. Training of a few to the sacrifice of many.
3. It is unsocial.
4. Necessity of professional coaches.
5. Physical educators, both men and women, of our leading colleges find results undesirable.
6. Expense.
7. Unnecessary nerve fatigue.[12]

Two years later women physical educators took more direct action to control competition for women through the Committee on Women's Athletics of the American Physical Education Association, which now included committees on basketball, field hockey, track and field, and swimming. Some women physical educators served on the AAU committee to investigate track and field competition for women (See p. 211), and objected to the AAU's acceptance of the invitation to the 1922 First Women's Olympic Games in Paris. The AAU did not hold jurisdiction over women's track and field, and there were certain aspects of the meet which the women physical educators questioned. When the AAU decided to send a team to the Paris track meet in spite of the women's objections, and named Dr. Harry Stewart to coach the team, many women physical educators strongly objected.

By this time, the leaders of the National Amateur Athletic Federation, founded to promote sport for men, approached Mrs. Herbert Hoover to organize the women in the United States as part of the Federation. At her suggestion a national conference was called to determine the position and program of sport and athletics for women. In April, 1923, women and men

---

12. *Bulletin* (1920-21), Mary Hemenway Alumnae Association, Department of Hygiene, Wellesley College, Wellesley, Mass., p. 48.

representing a variety of organizations and institutions met in Washington. The participants included Marjorie Bouvé, Boston School of Physical Education; Eline von Borries, Goucher College; Dr. William Burdick, Playground Athletic League; Rosalind Cassidy, Teachers College, Columbia University; Katherine F. Lenroot, Children's Bureau, U.S. Department of Labor; Emma Dolfinger, American Child Health Association; Commodore W.E. Longfellow, American Red Cross; and Helen McKinstry, Central School of Hygiene and Physical Education. After two days of meetings four actions were taken: (1) a Women's Division of the NAAF was established; (2) 16 resolutions prepared by a committee chaired by Dr. J. Anna Norris were adopted; (3) a committee chaired by Blanche Trilling reported the conference; and (4) Mrs. Hoover was elected permanent chairman and Blanche Trilling, University of Wisconsin, named vice-chairman. The Women's Division began its activities with two purposes in mind, to establish the standards set forth in their platform statements and to act as a clearing-house for problems in athletics for girls and women.

B. ORIGINAL RESOLUTIONS

As Adopted by the Conference on Athletics and Physical Recreation for Women and Girls, April 6-7, 1923

I. *Resolved,* That it be noted that the term "athletics" as used in this Conference has often included the problems connected with all types of noncompetitive as well as competitive physical activities for girls and women.

II. WHEREAS, The period of childhood and youth is the period of growth in all bodily structures, and
WHEREAS, A satisfactory growth during this period depends upon a large amount of vigrous physical exercises, and
WHEREAS, The strength, endurance, efficiency, and vitality of maturity will depend in very large degree upon the amount of vigorous physical exercise in childhood and youth, and
WHEREAS, Normal, wholesome, happy, mental, and emotional maturity depends in large part upon joyous, natural, safeguarded big-muscle activity in childhood and in youth.
Be It Therefore Resolved,
(a) That vigorous, active, happy, big-muscle activity be liberally provided and maintained and carefully guided for every girl and boy; and
(b) That all governments—village, county, state, and national—establish and support adequate opportunities for a universal physical education that will assist in the preparation of our boys and girls for the duties, opportunities, and joys of citizenship and of life as a whole.

III. *Resolved,* That there be greater concentration and study on the problems and program of physical activities for the pre-pubescent as well as for the adolescent girl.

IV. *Resolved,* in order to develop these qualities which shall fit girls and women to perform their functions as citizens:

   (*a*) That their athletics be conducted with that end definitely in view and be protected from exploitation for the enjoyment of the spectator, the athletic reputation, or the commercial advantage of any school or other organization.

   (*b*) That schools and other organizations shall stress enjoyment of the sport and development of sportsmanship and minimize the emphasis which is at present laid upon individual accomplishment and the winning of championships.

V. *Resolved,* That for any given group we approve and recommend such selection and administration of athletic activities as makes participation possible for all, and strongly condemn the sacrifice of this object for intensive (even though physiologically sound) training of the few.

VI. *Resolved,*

   (*a*) That competent women be put in immediate charge of women and girls in their athletic activities even where the administrative supervision may be under the direction of men.

   (*b*) That we look toward the establishment of a future policy that shall place the administration as well as teaching and coaching of girls and women in the hands of carefully trained and properly qualified women.

VII. WHEREAS, A rugged national vitality and a high level of public health are the most important resources of a people,

   Be It Therefore Resolved, That the teacher-training schools, the colleges, the professional schools, and the universities of the United States make curricular and administrative provision that will emphasize

   1. Knowledge of the basic facts of cause and effect in hygiene that will lead to the formation of discriminating judgments in matters of health.

   2. Habits of periodical examination and a demand for scientific health service.

   3. Habits of vigorous developmental recreation.

   To this end we recommend:

   (*a*) That adequate instruction in physical and health education be included in the professional preparation of all elementary and secondary school teachers.

   (*b*) That suitable instruction in physical and health education be included in the training of volunteer leaders in organized recreation programs.

   (*c*) That definite formulation be made of the highest modern standards of professional education for teachers and supervisors of physical education and recreation, and the provision of adequate opportunity for the securing of such education.

VIII. *Resolved,* That in order to maintain and build health, thorough and repeated medical examinations are necessary.

IX. *Resolved,* That since we recognize that certain anatomical and physiological conditions may occasion temporary unfitness for vigorous athletics, therefore effective safeguards should be maintained.

X. WHEREAS, We believe that the motivation of competitors in athletic activities should be that of play for play's sake, and
WHEREAS, We believe that the awarding of valuable prizes is detrimental to this objective,
Be It Resolved, That all awards granted for athletic achievement be restricted to those things which are symbolical and which have the least possible intrinsic value.

XI. *Resolved,* That suitable costumes for universal use be adopted for the various athletic activities.

XII. WHEREAS, We believe that the type of publicity which may be given to athletics for women and girls may have a vital influence both upon the individual competitors and upon the future development of the activity,
Be It Resolved, That all publicity be of such a character as to stress the sport and not the individual or group competitors.

XIII. WHEREAS, Certain international competitions for women and girls have already been held, and
WHEREAS, We believe that the participation of American women and girls in these competitions was inopportune,
Be It Resolved, That it is the sense of this Conference that in the future such competitions, if any, be organized and controlled by the national organization set up as a result of this Conference.

XIV. *Resolved,* That committees be appointed for study and report on the following problems:
   (*a*) Tests for motor and organic efficiency
   (*b*) The formulation of a program of physical activities adapted to various groups of the population
   (*c*) The relation of athletics to the health of pre-pubescent and post-pubescent girls
   (*d*) Scientific investigation as to anatomical, physiological, and emotional limitations and possibilities of girls and women in athletics, and a careful keeping of records in order that results may be determined.

XV. *Resolved,* That the sincere and hearty thanks of the members of this Conference on Athletics and Physical Recreation be extended:
   (*a*) To the National Amateur Athletic Federation for its suggestion that this Conference be called; and
   (*b*) To Mrs. Herbert Hoover for her vision and devotion in organizing this Conference and in making possible the vitally significant achievement of co-ordination of the various agencies for women's athletics.

XVI. *Resolved,* That the National Amateur Athletic Federation be requested to publish these Resolutions and distribute them:
   (*a*) To all members of this Conference
   (*b*) To all present members of the National Amateur Athletic Federation
   (*c*) To the Associated Press and the United Press
   (*d*) To the American Physical Education Association, with the request that they be copied and distributed to all members at the Springfield Convention.[13]

13. Alice A. Sefton, *The Women's Division, National Amateur Athletic Federation* (Stanford: Stanford University Press, 1941), pp. 77-79.

Within two days after the Washington, D.C., conference many of the same women such as Blanche Trilling, Helen McKinstry, and Agnes Wayman traveled to Springfield, Massachusetts, to attend the annual meeting of the American Physical Education Association. As part of the APEA program the Committee on Women's Athletics received a report of the Washington conference creating a Women's Division of the NAAF. The newly created platform for women's athletics was endorsed by the CWA. Thus, within a year after their objections to the United States women's participation in the Paris track meet, the women leaders in physical education had promoted their principles of athletics through the CWA and the newly formed Women's Division of the NAAF.

FIG. 6.11   Mabel Lee, Blanche Trilling, and Agnes Wayman. Courtesy American Alliance of Health, Physical Education and Recreation.

The women's philosophy, emphasizing a broad program of sport, medical examinations, women leaders, and protection from exploitation was promoted by both associations through national programs. Through both the NAAF and the APEA the women collected data, wrote articles and books on athletics, broadcast over the radio, spoke to professional associations, and met with local clubs. They coined phrases implying that in intercollegiate athletics girls would receive more "physical straining than training." Data collected from fifty colleges revealed that intercollegiate athletics for women ". . . does not exist in the colleges of the United States except in a very limited number and percentage" and that "There is little tendency on the part of physical directors to change their opinions on this subject. . . . Of those who have changed of recent years, the majority have changed from an attitude of approval to one of disapproval."[14]

---

14. Mabel Lee, "The Case for and Against Intercollegiate Athletics for Women and the Situation Since 1923," *Research Quarterly* 2, no. 2 (May, 1931): 122-23.

One plank in the Women's Division of the NAAF, to promote competition, appeared inconsistent with the women's position on varsity athletics. However, the women devised several forms of competition which they believed promoted their philosophy. The most popular were play days and sports days. Play days were designed for women from several different colleges to be assigned onto teams organized solely for the play day. The events were usually informal and the program planned for mass participation. The Triangle Day in Central California, held in 1927, was typical.

TRIANGLE SPORTS DAY IN CENTRAL CALIFORNIA

A Triangle Sports Day was held at the University of California November 6, 1926, with three neighboring colleges (Mills, Leland Stanford Jr. and the University of California) taking part.

Each college had been invited to send at least 60 girls (and as many more as possible) to participate. These 180 girls were divided into squads of 30 each, 10 from each college. There were 6 carefully chosen squad leaders, 2 from each college. Each squad was given a number and a color (1. yellow, 2. red, 3. purple, 4. green, 5. blue, 6. pink).

From 9:30 to 9:40 the squads were given opportunity to select a name and compose a yell.

At 9:40 the contests began with informal games—shuttle relay and pass ball relay. Then followed 3 games of net ball (squads 1 & 3, 2 & 4, 5 & 6). Hockey was played in five minute halves with no time between halves (squads 1 & 2, 3 & 4, 5 & 6). Tennis was played on 6 courts, 4 players each, in progressive fashion. The winners of 2 out of 3 games moved to the next higher court and the losers stayed. While the tennis was going on, impromptu games of hop scotch and marbles were played. A swimming meet ended the day (1. 25 yard relay, 2. surface diving for discs, 3. medley relay race for form and speed).

Awards throughout the day were a blue ribbon for first place and red for second place with the name of the event in gold letters.

At 12:30 a luncheon was served, at which there was an interesting program of speaking.

Those who participated in this sports day bore testimony to the value of meeting new college women and to the gaining of new ideas of sportsmanship. They had great fun without the feeling of intense college rivalry.[15]

Sports days, in which each school participated as a team, usually included several sports adapted to the sports day concept. Playing periods might be shortened, round robin competition employed, and novelty events interspersed with sports. The closing event was a tea or social hour which provided a time when students from the various colleges could compare their institutions or talk with each other. Other types of approved competition included swimming and archery "telegraphic" meets in which each institution held the competition on its own campus and mailed the results to the hostess institution, who determined the ratings and mailed them back to the com-

15. *Bulletin* (March 1927), Mary Hemenway Alumnae Association, Graduate Department of Hygiene and Physical Education, Wellesley College, Wellesley, Mass., pp. 28-29.

peting colleges. The Women's Division also suggested field days and carnivals. Intramurals, under the women's program, increased and in many colleges and universities students engaged in keen interclass competition.

It was clear that the women's philosophy did not include the idea of women in the Olympic Games, and the women physical educators actively protested the women's events in the 1928 and 1932 Games. One year after their unsuccessful petition to exclude track events for women in the 1928 Games, the Women's Division adopted two resolutions; one of which opposed women in the 1932 Games and one which addressed itself particularly to the track and field events in 1932. It was the latter resolution which was sent in 1930 to M. Baillet-Latour, President of the International Olympic Committee, and M.J.S. Edström, President of the International Amateur Athletic Federation. Copies of the petition and letters together with a request to adopt similar resolutions were sent to the International Council of Women, Women's Pan-Pacific Conference, Sixth Pan-American Congress on the Child, a committee of Great International Associations, and the National Council of Women in the United States. Not because of the petitions, but for other reasons, the IOC did delete the 800 m. race in 1928. As late as 1938 the Women's Division requested that girls under sixteen be barred from the Olympic Games.

The women's curriculum in physical education, already strong in sport instruction, also included other activities such as body mechanics and dance. It was not unusual to have requirements within the physical education requirement such as swimming and, perhaps, one team sport and one individual sport. For example, at the University of Minnesota in 1927 the freshmen selected sports such as field hockey, tennis, baseball, archery, track or outdoor basketball in the spring, but in the winter the freshmen all took the same course consisting of exercise, folk dance, apparatus, and games.[16]

The sports included in the women's programs followed the rules established by sport committees of the CWA. In 1932 that group reorganized to become the National Section on Women's Athletics. The number of sport committees increased to over twelve by the end of the period. The sport committees determined which rules would be followed, made changes in the rules, proposed ratings of officials, published the results of meets such as telegraphic meets, and published helpful articles for teachers. One of the major changes in a women's sport which came about during this period was the change in basketball from the three-court to two-court game.

16. Helen W. Hazelton, "The University of Minnesota Plan for Freshmen Work," *Bulletin* (September 1927), Mary Hemenway Alumnae Association, Graduate Department of Hygiene and Physical Education, Wellesley College, Wellesley, Mass., p. 7.

After careful study the official NSWA game changed to two-court basket-ball in 1936.

A study of the thirties reveals four major trends in women's physical education and sport: (1) an increase in opportunities for sport for women and an increase in numbers participating; (2) a growing use of research as a basis for planning and improving sport and athletic programs; (3) a greater acceptance in society of the concept of women in sport; and (4) a reexamination of the position limiting intercollegiate athletics. By the end of the thirties some women physical educators such as Bernice Moss and Gladys Palmer had proposed competitive programs for the skilled woman athlete, and even Mabel Lee, a strong opponent of women's intercollegiate athletics, had somewhat changed her views on the subject. During the latter part of the period certain experiments were undertaken such as the Ohio State University invitational golf tournament which was initiated in 1941.[17]

One of the most influential groups of women physical educators organized officially as the National Association for Physical Education of College Women in 1924. Between 1910 and 1915 Amy Morris Homans had invited certain directors to visit Wellesley College to exchange views on cur-rent problems, and in 1915 this group became the Association of Directors of Physical Education for Women. Two years later midwestern women organized as The Middle West Society of College Directors of Physical Education for Women. In 1921 the Western Society for Physical Education of College Women was organized, and in 1922 there was a move to form a National Society. The actual organizational meeting took place in 1924 when the Association of Directors of Physical Education for Women in Colleges and Universities became a reality. Membership was limited to directors or chairwomen of departments and thus any resolution or action was influential. It was not until after World War II that membership was opened to faculty from all ranks.

Dance in Colleges and Universities

The first dance major in the United States was started by Margaret N. H'Doubler in 1926 at the University of Wisconsin, Madison. After H'Doubler completed her undergraduate work at the University of Wiscon-sin with a major in biology, she was invited to become a member of the women's physical education faculty at the university. In 1916, she studied in New York at Teachers College, Columbia University. Part of her purpose was to find a new dance form suitable for the Wisconsin program because

---

17. Judith Davidson, "Sport for Women in the Thirties," unpublished paper, University of Massachusetts, 1977.

H'Doubler did not feel that the natural dance which was being taught suited her needs. She studied dance with Bird Larson, Porter Beegle, Alys Bentley, and at the Isadora Duncan School.[18] Upon her return to Wisconsin she set about developing a dance form which emphasized the creative nature of the dance experience based on a sound understanding of the biological nature of the body and its capacity for expressive movement. Through her work with students and teachers she exerted a great influence on dance in American colleges and universities.

In the summer of 1934, the Bennington School of the Dance opened at Bennington College in Vermont. The faculty included, among others, Graham, Humphrey, Weidman, and Hanya Holm, an exponent of the German modern dance. Here these artists choreographed and taught college and university teachers, who came from all parts of the country to study at Bennington and who then returned to their institutions to teach the new dance on their campuses. Many departments of physical education for women invited dancers such as Graham, Humphrey, Weidman, and Holm to perform on their campuses. Through the summer programs and the winter dance tours, early modern dance was nurtured on college campuses.

The Bennington program continued and in 1939 the school was moved to Mills College on the west coast, and then returned to Bennington where it remained through the summer of 1942. After that it moved to Connecticut College, New London, Connecticut, where it offered summer study with the leading dancers.

Sport and Physical Activity in the High Schools

With public education a responsibility of the state and local government, the extent, content, and development of sport and physical activity differed from state to state, city to city, and town to town. In the early twenties, following World War I, many states passed laws requiring physical education in order to improve the physical condition of the children and youth. However, according to the state and the availability of facilities, many high school programs could not be implemented, while other programs, especially those in the cities, tended to follow a program similar to the colleges and universities.

The program for boys usually included interscholastic sports, ordinarily under the jurisdiction of a state high school athletic association. In 1931 forty-seven states conducted their associations with an executive board and usually had full control of the program. The sports for which state championships were conducted included football, basketball, baseball, and track, with basketball tournaments most frequently held.

18. "Margaret N. H'Doubler," *Dance Encyclopedia,* ed. Anatole Chujoy and Phyllis W. Manchester (New York: Simon and Schuster, 1967), p. 449.

The picture for girls was quite different. In 1928, twenty-one states had some form of organization and twenty had none. Twelve states controlled athletics for both boys and girls and five states had an association solely for girls. In 1925 the National Association of Secondary School Principals indicated they would use their influence against interscholastic athletics for girls. In some states girls played boys' rules, while in others they followed the rules proposed by the Women's Division of the NAAF. Eight states with special programs for girls were North Carolina, Illinois, Iowa, Nebraska, Kansas, Oklahoma, and Colorado.

Further west in Oregon, high school physical education was planned to furnish opportunities for "normal physical development, . . . learning activities and health standards which will 'carry over' and be of use . . . in later life, and . . . for the development of leadership, responsibility, loyalty, team-play, and sportsmanship."[19] The program to meet these objectives included remedial gymnastics, gymnastics, dancing, self-testing activities, individual athletics, organized sports, and games. Across the country in Brookline, Massachusetts, the program started in kindergarten, permitting each child to develop large-muscle activities, imagination, and self-expression. The child was allowed "protected freedom" in the gymnasium to invent exercises and activities which were not superimposed by an adult. The progressive school movement suggested that in the upper grades teams be organized by boys and girls themselves.

High school physical education in the twenties and thirties is difficult to describe in generalities. Some cities and towns had excellent programs, others mediocre to poor programs, and many no programs at all. During the Depression physical education was frequently curtailed or dropped entirely as budgets were cut. On the other hand, the high school football and basketball programs helped to occupy unemployed people's time during the Depression, to entertain the public, and to provide a sense of community.

The Study of Sport and Physical Activity in Higher Education

During the 1920's and 1930's higher education expanded rapidly as did education at all levels, and better-trained teachers were in greater demand. Proponents of a child-centered curriculum and progressive education initiated the study of education as a proper field of study. The one, two and three-year "normal" schools in which many physical educators had been trained were reorganized into four-year colleges and universities or affiliated with existing four-year institutions. R. Tait McKenzie warned that graduate work in physical education would be essential. By 1917 graduate

19. Gertrude B. Manchester, "Physical Education in the High School," *Bulletin* (1924-25), Mary Hemenway Alumnae Association, Graduate Department of Hygiene and Physical Education, Wellesley College, Wellesley, Mass., p. 13.

work was offered by The Normal College of the American Gymnastic Union, Wellesley College, the University of Southern California, and the University of Oregon. Zeigler reports that "Between 1926 and 1949, some fifty-four colleges and universities began Master's degree programs in physical education . . ."[20] The first Ph.D. programs in education with a major in physical education were initiated in 1924 at New York University and Teachers College, Columbia University. Five years later the Ed.D. with a concentration in physical education was offered by the University of Pittsburgh and Stanford University.

The curriculum varied considerably from institution to institution and reflected the growing trend in physical education toward sport and social values. Dramatically increasing needs for physical education and sport teachers and responses to the changing educational philosophy led to a broad program of courses rather than a clearly defined field of study. First, the rapid growth of public education and the rapidly increasing state laws requiring physical education created a need for teachers. In 1920, 311,266 girls and boys were graduated from high school in the United States. Twenty years later the figure was 1,221,475. Second, the medical education of many early leaders in physical education was no longer seen as appropriate professional training, partly because of the growing emphasis on sport. The physical educators with a medical background were well qualified to prescribe and conduct gymnastics, but they were not prepared to teach sport or coach athletics. While the early programs, especially for men, had been largely gymnastics, by the twenties sport was the dominant component in the curriculum. For some institutions there no longer appeared to be an urgent necessity for the grounding in biological and physical sciences basic to a thorough understanding of gymnastics; rather the need was for sport teachers and coaches. Further, the first doctorate programs were developed in schools of education. Kroll asserts:

> The slim chance that physical education might have followed a path closer to the biological sciences, or at least a parallel course of professional education and a biological science orientation, quickly dissipated under the influence of such a close association and identification with college departments of education. Having been accepted in education departments, physical education was rightly expected to conduct itself in accordance with educational doctrine.[21]

Thus, depending upon where graduate programs were conducted in each institution and on the interests and professional position of the administrator and faculty, the courses and requirements for degrees in physical education varied.

20. Earle F. Zeigler, ed., *A History of Physical Education and Sport in the United States and Canada* (Champaign, Ill.: Stipes Publishing Company, 1975), p. 279.

21. Walter P. Kroll, *Perspectives in Physical Education* (New York: Academic Press, 1971), p. 71.

There was even a suggestion that the central focus of physical education be sport. In 1931 Seward Staley pointed out that the old mind-body dualism on which the concept of physical education had been based was no longer plausible within the context of modern psychological and educational theories. He made the case that the content of the physical education program was big-muscle activity and that the most appropriate title for sports in educational institutions was "Sports Education." He defined it as "that phase of education concerned with directing individuals in the learning of sports," and sports as ". . . all relatively vigorous activities that individuals engage in for fun, joy, or satisfaction." He pointed out that the major portion of the class work was sports education and that the title "Sports" was in agreement with the ideas of Wood, Hetherington, Williams, and Nash. Staley further noted that "sports" education would ". . . undoubtedly produce interested, intelligent spectators at sport contests, but . . . the vital objective and outcome should be the production of participants."[22]

Physical educators in the thirties were engaged in a series of controversies, confrontations, and debates over definitions and objectives. The situation was further complicated by three outstanding and influential men, each of whom proposed a different direction for physical education. According to Gerber, Jesse Feiring Williams defined physical education as "education *through* the physical rather than *of* the physical"; Charles Harold McCloy saw physical education as "the adequate training and development of the body itself"; and Jay Bryan Nash believed that physical education was ". . . all the experiences children have in neuromuscular activities which are directed to the desired outcomes." Under Williams' definition, the objectives of physical education were to develop character and learn activities that could be utilized later in the student's leisure time. McCloy believed in organic power, physical development, strenuous exercise, and the mastery of physical skills. Nash, on the other hand, believed that children should be educated for their leisure-time activities as well as for a vocation. These men were all dynamic, and developed a following among their students and colleagues. Gerber points out that physical educators attempted the impossible task of accommodating all three positions:

. . . physical educators adopted all three modes and believed they could effectively conduct all three types of programs simultaneously. Although there were vague ideas advanced which suggested that in the lowest grades body development and fundamental skills should be the basis of curriculum followed in the middle school years by games and team sports, and culminating in individual activities, in actual practice a little of everything was done at almost every

22. Seward C. Staley, "The Four Year Curriculum in Physical (Sports) Education," *Research Quarterly* 2, no. 1 (March, 1931): 82, 90.

FIG. 6.12   Jesse **Feiring Williams** and Jay Bryan **Nash**. Courtesy, Mary Roby, University of Arizona. Dr. Harold McCloy. Courtesy of University of Iowa Photographic Service.

level. . . . As a result, physical education projected itself into the anomalous situation of holding classes in accord with McCloy's suggestion, of advocating the activities urged by Nash, and of committing itself to accomplishing the social goals delineated by Williams.[23]

Thus, prior to World War II the study of physical education, of which sport in schools was a major component, was diffused and varied. Not every student studied the same courses and materials in every institution in every part of the country. However, there were many carefully focused programs that produced consistently excellent scholars and teachers. More research in masters theses had been completed in the twenties in the area of physiology of exercise and tests and measurements than in other areas.

23. Ellen W. Gerber, "The Ideas and Influences of McCloy, Nash, and Williams," in *The History of Physical Education and Sport,* ed. Bruce L. Bennett (Chicago: The Athletic Institute, 1972), pp. 98-99.

The American Physical Education Association also reflected the developing interest in research, establishing the *Research Quarterly* in 1930. At that time, the Association also initiated the *Journal of Health and Physical Education.* A year later, 1931, Mabel Lee became the first woman president of the Association. That same year the Association recognized a number of outstanding women and men in physical education. Ten women and thirty-eight men were honored, including Amy Morris Homans, Delphine Hanna, Elizabeth Burchenal, Ethel Perrin, Thomas D. Wood, William G. Anderson, Clark Hetherington, and James Naismith.

Sport—An American Way of Life

By the end of the third decade of the twentieth century sport had become an integral part of the American way of life. Many Americans possessed to some degree the two conditions necessary for sport—some leisure time and some money beyond that required for basic needs—and many had transportation in the form of a bicycle or family car. Public transportation on the trolleys and trains made travel much easier and faster than in earlier days. The money Americans spent on sport equipment, toys, and other amusement-related goods almost doubled between 1921 and 1929. To attend sport events they spent $30,000,000 in 1921 and $66,000,000 in 1929. In the same period the number of passenger cars sold jumped from 1,905,500 to 4,455,100. As education and conditions of employment improved and the standard of living rose, Americans discovered more and more sports available to them.

Further, the social upheaval of the twenties fostered changes in fashions for both women and men, making sport clothing available to all. Special costumes for tennis, winter sports, basketball, and swimming made the sports more enjoyable, especially for women. The increase in public school education acted as a catalyst to what Betts called "The Melting Pot of the Playing Fields."

After the early 1920's the flow of the foreign-born to this country declined as a result of the new immigration acts, and the problem of the immigrant in our national life soon centered on children who comprised the second or third generation. . . . Nowhere was the process of Americanization more in evidence than in sport.

. . . Families whose chief recreation had been folk dancing or the beer garden found the children enthusiastic over athletic games. Many parents failed to understand these games and called them "foolish, wasteful, ridiculous and immoral," while the child rebelled against European forms of play and resented the parent's antagonism toward American games.[24]

---

24. John Rickards Betts, *America's Sporting Heritage* (Reading, Mass.: Addison-Wesley Publishing Company, 1974), p. 330.

Everywhere, it was clear that sport had become a part of American society—the daily newspapers reported sport, everyday language used sport phrases, excursions were often to a sport event, and neighborhood parks provided a place for sport.

Sport and the Depression

The big Depression, which swept the country during the thirties, altered sport in the United States, both favorably and unfavorably. Tunis disputed the generally accepted theory of the "Boom of the Twenties" and proposed that the thirties launched the real sports boom.

> Today there is a more intelligent appreciation of the values of real sport, there are more persons of average ability competing, there are more participants who are interested in the game for the game's sake, more people playing than ever before in our history. Not merely is this a greater period for athletics than the era of the super-champion, but there is every likelihood of greater times ahead.[25]

The stark reality of massive unemployment with its accompanying humiliation and fear left millions of persons with nothing to do and little money for travel or amusements, but by the end of the Depression sport in all sectors of society had survived and, in many cases, prospered. While elite sports such as golf and tennis were the hardest hit during the Depression, family sport, youth sport, and informal sport activities increased. Both men's college and professional sport responded to a number of promotional devices, but perhaps the greatest impact on sport was the time, money, and personnel expended by the federal government. By the end of the Depression over ten federal agencies had recreation or sport-related programs and services. These included the National Park Service, Forest Service, Tennessee Valley Authority, Public Works Administration, National Youth Administration, the Civilian Conservation Corps, and the Works Progress Administration. A brief examination of the last three will illustrate various ways by which federal programs affected sport.

Both the National Youth Administration (NYA) and the Civilian Conservation Corps (CCC) were planned for youth. Over 1,500,000 young adults were being added to the labor market each year with the prospect of neither full-time nor part-time employment. The youth programs hoped to reduce the size of the labor market and at the same time provide training for future jobs. The NYA, part of the Emergency Relief Appropriation Act of 1935, supplied part-time work to high school and college students and to former students between the ages of 18 and 25. High school students worked three

---

25. John R. Tunis, "Changing Trends in Sport," *Harper's Monthly Magazine* 170 (December, 1934): 86.

hours a weekday and seven on Saturday, while college and university students could be employed eight hours a day. Employed as construction workers, they built and repaired stadiums, swimming pools, tennis courts, and other recreational facilities. Further, the fact that they were able to remain in school also permitted them time to participate in intramural and other sport programs.

The Civilian Conservation Corps, largely directed toward conservation and forest protection, opened its first camp in Luray, Virginia, in April, 1933 and by August, 1935 over 500,000 men were enrolled in the program. Men between the ages of 18 and 25 whose families were on relief had preference and could enroll for no more than two years. For many, the CCC meant three meals a day, clothing, and purposeful work, and they gladly sent the required $22 to $25 of their $30 a month pay home. As part of their planned program the men improved national and state parks, built swimming pools, and other recreation and sport facilities. Their major goals were reforestation and other conservation projects and only incidentally sport. The CCC men lived in barracks built in rows, military style, with recreational or sport facilities nearby. When camps were close enough, inter-camp as well as intramural events were planned. The CCC was part of the Indian Emergency Conservation Work and these camps also included sport. Rather than being planned in military-type rows, the Indian camps were built in the shape of a horseshoe with room for a softball diamond in the center.

The Works Progress Administration (WPA), begun in 1935, sought to employ people in the field of their expertise. The projects were of a great variety but included stadiums, swimming pools, gymnasiums, and other sport facilities. In Kansas alone 344 public buildings were erected including auditoriums, swimming pools, and gymnasiums. In New England and other northern states ski facilities were constructed, which helped skiing become a popular winter activity. A number of universities added to their athletic and physical education facilities through the use of the WPA program.

During the thirties, informal activities such as swimming, picnicking, and miniature golf also flourished. In an effort to occupy young people, youth agencies such as the Boy Scouts, Girl Scouts, YMCA, YWCA, and others utilized sport programs. Many religious organizations also initiated social, recreational, and sport activities. In 1930 the Catholic Youth Organization was founded and immediately launched basketball and boxing tournaments. Little League baseball originated in 1939 in Williamsport, Pennsylvania, and similar youth sport programs followed.

The emergence of softball as a popular sport was a phenomenon of the thirties. By 1934 an estimated 2,000,000 Americans were playing the new game under the auspices of the American Softball Association. Gerber reports that 1,000 women's teams played the 1938 season in California.[26] Betts explains the phenomenon:

> Softball, more adaptable to both sexes and to all ages, less expensive to maintain and lacking little of the dash and drama of baseball, rapidly attained the position of one of America's favorite recreations. By 1940 there were some 300,000 organized clubs and the Amateur Softball Association claimed at least 3,000,000 affiliated players. Veterans of Foreign Wars posts promoted junior softball, and a "Cripple A League" of oldsters who played a simplified version reputedly had 2500 teams in Chicago. A new support of the diamond world had been found and at the end of the Depression interest in baseball seemed as keen as ever.[27]

In addition to the promotion of softball and youth baseball during the Depression years, professional baseball introduced night baseball and opened a Hall of Fame. The Babe finished his amazing career in 1935, but other players such as Lou Gehrig, Lefty Gomez, Joe DiMaggio, and Dizzy Dean became the new heroes of American boys. While night lighting for sport had been developed for several years, it was first used in major league baseball in 1935 when Cincinnati played Philadelphia. Many industries and merchants sponsored semipro teams or local teams in twilight leagues. A native of Cooperstown, N.Y., Stephen C. Clark, proposed a national baseball museum and saw his dream become a reality when the National Baseball Hall of Fame and Museum opened in Cooperstown in 1939.

The pervasive mood of futility during the Depression was somewhat lifted by the extravaganzas of water shows and ice carnivals. After Sonja Henie's final Olympic appearance in 1936 she turned professional and her tours launched a series of ice show entertainments.

As the thirties drew to a close the United States, recovering from the Depression and swinging into a defense industry economy, had accepted sport for men and for many women as an important use of leisure time. During the prosperity of the twenties middle-class Americans had been introduced to the world of sport and, during the Depression, had helped build their own playing fields and develop their own patterns of sport participation.

> . . . millions of urban workers—men, women, and children—were finally enjoying the organized sports that had been introduced by the fashionable world half a century and more earlier. Democracy was making good its right to play the games formerly limited to the small class that had the wealth and leisure to escape the city. No exact totals can possibly be given as to the number of active sports

26. Ellen W. Gerber et al., *The American Woman in Sport* (Reading, Mass.: Addison-Wesley Publishing Company, 1974), p. 117.

27. John Rickards Betts, *America's Sporting Heritage* (Reading, Mass.: Addison-Wesley Publishing Company, 1974), p. 279.

participants in comparison with attendance at sports spectacles in the 1930's . . . there is every reason to believe that in the 1930's the public was spending far more of its leisure . . . on amateur than on professional sports.[28]

Sport and World War II

A general European war began in 1939, and by the summer of 1940 most of Europe was controlled by German and Italian armies. The United States became the "arsenal of democracy" until December 7, 1941, when Japan attacked Pearl Harbor and the United States declared war on Germany, Italy, and Japan.

In 1940 a Selective Service bill was passed and millions of men were drafted into the army or volunteered for other branches of the armed services. To free men for active duty, women's armed services were created: WAVES (Navy), WAC (Army), SPARS (Coast Guard), and women Marines. "Including voluntary enlistments, over 15 million people served in the armed forces during the war; 10 million in the army, 4 million in the navy and coast guard, 600,000 in the marine corps. About 216,000 women served . . ."[29] as nurses and in the women's branches.

After the passage of the Selective Service Act almost four million dollars was set aside for sport activities and equipment by the War Department. Former athletes were called into service and coached soldiers, to help develop tough, hard fighters out of young men who had been reared to believe in peace. Gene Tunney bacame a naval commander in charge of physical fitness. One-time wrestling champion Ed Don George, Art Jones of the Pittsburgh Steelers, and others combined to instruct young American men how to be rough and tough in battle. Football, boxing, wrestling, track, and swimming were adapted to train soldiers, not to provide fun and enjoyment through the sport. Major Theodore P. Bank commented:

> We Americans are all aware of the obvious physical benefits derived from participation in competitive athletics, but we sometimes forget the intangible benefits the soldier receives from competitive athletics. Sports like boxing, or other sports involving bodily contact, rapidly develop in the individual man the sense of confidence, aggressiveness and fearlessness that is always desirable in a trained soldier. Sports like football, basketball and other team-play sports also develop the principles of coordination between groups of men that are invaluable on the battle field.[30]

The women's branches had their own fitness and sport programs.

28. Foster Rhea Dulles, *America Learns to Play* (New York: D. Appleton-Century, 1940), p. 349.

29. Samuel Eliot Morison, *The Oxford History of the American People* (New York: Oxford University Press, 1965), pp. 1007-1008.

30. Theodore P. Bank, "Army Athletics," *Hygiea* 19 (November, 1941): 876.

The campuses of the nation were the training centers for many special programs for all the armed forces. Civilians on campuses and in the cities and towns added their efforts in planning social and sport activities for the men and women in the services. Lincoln, Nebraska, for example, converted a skating rink to an area for badminton, archery, shuffleboard, volleyball, and table tennis, as well as occasional square dancing. In Hartford, Connecticut, the citizens converted a school building into a recreation area for black soldiers.

While sport moved into the background of American life, it remained a small but significant part of the war effort. Early in 1942 President Roosevelt expressed his belief that professional baseball players of service age should be expected to enlist or serve their country, but that baseball itself could provide recreation and help keep morale high. Other leaders felt men overseas would welcome the normalcy of the baseball seasons and would like to hear how their favorite teams were performing. Professional baseball never stopped but many of the players did volunteer or were drafted, and former players were called back or minor league players brought up from the farm clubs. Because of travel restrictions the teams trained in the north and made other adjustments to the wartime life. Baseball became the vehicle for selling millions of dollars worth of war bonds, and the ball parks became collection points—in 1943, for example, a million pounds of scrap metal, 23,000 pounds of rubber, and 12,000 pounds of waste fat were collected at the ball parks for use in the war effort.

In case baseball could not survive the 1943 season, the Chicago Cubs owner, Philip K. Wrigley, organized the All-American Girls Baseball League to keep his park open. The women played modified softball rules which moved more and more toward major league rules, until the only difference was a five foot shorter basepath. Most players were between 18 and 25 years of age, and to assure complete acceptance of the teams by the public and to reassure parents that their daughters would be cared for properly, each team was supervised by a chaperone. The chaperones were responsible for the players off the field and for enforcing league rules such as being sure that the players did not wear slacks, shorts, or jeans in public and that they did not wear their hair too short.

Professional personnel administered the regularly scheduled games in Chicago and other midwestern cities such as Kalamazoo and Muskegon in Michigan; South Bend and Fort Wayne, Indiana; Peoria, Illinois; and Racine and Kenosha, Wisconsin. The women played well, were greatly admired, and the teams' standings were followed with interest by their fans. The end of the war brought a change in the internal management of the league, and the advent of television contributed to the close of the league in 1954. However, for over ten years a successful professional women's league existed. The nonprofit status, carefully supervised players, and slogans such as "Recreation for the War Worker" and "Family Entertainment" created an "All-American Girl" reputation for the league and its players.[31]

Elsewhere members of sport organizations such as yacht clubs helped instruct naval officers. The AAU promoted an extensive fitness program. Sport during the war tried to provide quality entertainment for the armed services, war workers, and the general public. Leaders encouraged physical fitness and utilized sport events to increase the sale of War Bonds.

By September, 1945, World War II was over. The country was both jubilant and sorrowful—grateful that the Allies had won, saddened by the millions who would not return home, and weary of the four years of high-pitched effort. As the country moved to a post-war boom, sport was part of the new decades to come.

Summary

In the period between the two wars, 1918-1945, sport became firmly woven into the fabric of American life. The economic boom of the twenties partially accounted for the growing acceptance of sport in American society. In addition, changes in social behavior, such as more informal clothing, dance crazes such as the Charleston, greater use of the automobile, and shorter working hours created a climate in which sport flourished.

Baseball, still hailed as the national pastime, recovered from the "Black Sox" scandal of 1919 and was reorganized under a commissioner, a form of sport organization in use today. This was the period of sport superstars such as Babe Ruth and Josh Gibson in baseball. Other sports also had their stars, created by their playing style and their charismatic personalities, as well as by the reporting of sports writers and sportscasters.

Perhaps one of the most paradoxical situations of the twenties was the growth of college football, which became the most popular fall sport in the United States, and on the other hand, the controlled development of collegiate sport for women. College men stars turned student sport into public entertainment with intersectional play and post-season "Bowl" games. The semiprofessionalism and commercialism accompanying the use of student sport as public entertainment was criticized but accepted by most institutions. Women physical educators safeguarded the women from such professionalism by promoting programs which encouraged the "greatest good to the greatest number" through play days and sports days. By this period

31. Merrie A. Fidler, "The Development and Decline of the All-American Girls Baseball League, 1943-1954," M.S. thesis, University of Massachusetts, 1976.

sport had become the dominant component in physical education in all levels of education. Physical education for women nurtured and developed modern dance as the winter tours to the college and university campuses and the summer schools sustained the early dance companies.

Overall, sport and physical activity increased during the great Depression. During the boom of the twenties many people had become involved in sport, but during the Depression more and more people engaged in sport. Although in the previous period, prior to World War I, sport had made its greatest strides, it was in this period between the wars that it became an integral part of American life.

Questions for Discussion

1. A number of sport superstars were cited in this chapter. What common characteristics do they demonstrate? In addition to their sport achievements, what factors contributed to their stardom?
2. What major changes took place in baseball during this period? Explain the events leading to each change.
3. Analyze the impact of the Depression on sport in the United States.
4. In educational institutions the men's philosophy was characterized as "Sports for all" and the women's philosophy as "A sport for every girl and every girl in a sport." What similarities and differences occurred in each program as a result of these philosophies?
5. Is "American Dance" a valid phrase? What does it mean?
6. In a magazine of November, 1926, there were articles on both sides of the question, "Whether or not undergraduate sport should be used to entertain." Write the opening argument for or against this position, to be published in 1926 and/or now.

Suggestions for Further Reading

1. Betts, John Rickards. *America's Sporting Heritage: 1850-1950.* Reading, Mass.: Addison-Wesley Publishing Company, 1974.
2. Gerber, Ellen W. *Innovators and Institutions in Physical Education.* Philadelphia: Lea & Febiger, 1971.
3. Lee, Mabel. "The Case for and Against Intercollegiate Athletics for Women and the Situation Since 1923." *Research Quarterly* 2, no. 2 (May, 1931): 93-127.
4. Lewis, Guy M. "Adoption of the Sport Program 1903-39: The Role of Accommodation in the Transformation of Physical Education." *Quest* 12 (May, 1969): 34-46.

5. Lockhart, Aileene S., and Spears, Betty. *Chronicle of American Physical Education*. Dubuque, Iowa: Wm. C. Brown Co., 1972.
6. Zeigler, Earle F., ed. *A History of Physical Education and Sport in the United States and Canada*. Champaign, Ill.: Stipes Publishing Company, 1975.

Time Line

7 Sport and Physical Activity for Everyone, 1945-1975

In the first three decades following World War II sport changed from a popular activity to a pervasive force in American society. The mid-century civil rights and women's movements, which made a great impact on society, also affected sport. In 1946 Jackie Robinson became the first black in the twentieth century to be signed to a major league baseball club. That same year Kenny Washington signed with the Los Angeles Rams of the National Football League and four years later the Boston Celtics drafted Chuck Cooper of Duquesne and the New York Knicks acquired basketball star "Sweetwater" Clifton from the Harlem Globetrotters. In 1949 the Ladies Professional Golf Association was formed and by the early 1970's sports fans were following the careers of top golfer Judy Rankin and tennis professional Chris Evert as well as those of Jack Nicklaus and Jimmy Connors. For the first time blacks, women, and other minorities played more than a token part in sport.

Since World War II not only have racial and sexual barriers been infiltrated, but civil rights legislation, the twentieth century women's movement, and a re-examination of professional players' rights as persons have lent support and credence to the "sport for everyone" ideal. In addition, post-war technology has further improved sport equipment, transportation to sport events, and most important, has brought sport into millions of homes through television. Sport has also grown into a major sector of the economy, with hundreds of professional sport performers, thousands of student athletes, more thousands of amateur sportsmen and sportswomen, hundreds of thousands of sport participants, and millions of sport fans. The production and marketing of sport had become a multi-billion dollar industry by the mid-1970's. In addition the manufacture and selling of sport-related goods and the operation of sport- related businesses were other areas of the sports world.

The civil rights movements of the fifties and sixties challenged the myth about sport as the most democratic institution in society. By the sixties professional and collegiate teams were charged with maintaining race quota

---

The authors are indebted to Albert G. Applin for his help in the preparation of this chapter.

systems, with "stacking" of black players in certain team positions to restrict their numbers in a game at any given time, with inadequate academic counseling for black intercollegiate players, with discrimination in off-season employment and endorsement contracts for professional players, and with the lack of black coaches, managers, and athletic administrators in predominantly white institutions. In addition, black athletes entered the civil rights movement, lending their name and influence to the cause. The threat of a boycott by black members of the 1968 United States Olympic team was the most dramatic of several incidents in which the athletic arena was used to publicize problems of black athletes.

The civil rights cause involved not only black athletes, but also white players who spoke out on issues which they perceived as unfair or improper. Stimulated by the timely writings of Jack Scott and players such as Dave Meggyssey, George Sauer, and Chip Oliver, some athletes increasingly criticized the autocratic approach to athletics at a time when they and their peers were protesting an undeclared war in Vietnam and other civil inequities. For most Americans, however, the American dream of "sport for all" persisted, and they refused to acknowledge the accusations against sport.

The women's movement, too, supported equal opportunity on the playing field for women and men. In the 1960's and '70's several forces interacted to produce a climate in which women's sport in general *exploded,* and women's professional sport in particular made rapid strides in numbers, organization, prize money, press coverage, and general acceptance. This explosion, the twentieth century women's movement, civil rights legislation, and the impact of individual athletes such as Mildred "Babe" Didrikson Zaharias, and Billie Jean King, all contributed to a growing support of equality of opportunity for women in sport. Golf and tennis became the major professional sports for women, but there were also professional women bowlers, ice skaters, softball players, jockeys, basketball players, track and field performers, and football players. Women athletes became an important and integral part of sport in every aspect: girls seeking equal chances in youth sport such as Little League; college women asking for a greater number of sports and more competition and more support; professional women golfers and tennis players demanding and obtaining a greater share of prize money. Federal legislation of the 70's mandated equal opportunity in programs and in institutions supported by federal funds and hastened the growing concept of "sports for all." Special segments of the population of orthopedically impaired, physically handicapped, and mentally and emotionally disturbed persons also began benefiting from more sport and physical activity programs.

Professional football and baseball players contested the "reserve" clause in their contracts through lawsuits. The owners also took refuge in the courts as they sought immunity from anti-trust laws. The use of the law court in sport soon became an accepted manner of business.

Post-war technology in communication, fabrics, physiology, and transportation all affected traditional sports and created new ones. By 1960, television had become a major force in presenting sport to Americans. More than twice as many people watched a single World Series baseball game in 1975 (76 million for the seventh game) than attended all the major league games played in that year (more than 29 million). Transportation from continent to continent took only a few hours and made international competitions and world championships an established part of world-wide sport. In the United States teams traveled by air, and intersectional events became commonplace. A prosperous economy encouraged more participants in sport, more spectators, more television coverage, and a growing acceptance of sport and physical activity as a pervasive force in American life.

This chapter will examine the social and technical changes that occurred after World War II as they affected professional sport; amateur sport and physical activity; youth sport; and sport, dance, and physical activity in educational institutions.

Professional Sport

Following World War II the professional teams became the dominant component of American sport. Changes in amateur and school sport and games frequently resulted from alterations in professional programs. Organized sport for children and youth was modeled after professional organizations, and the professional athlete became the sport hero for millions of youngsters. Professional sport was promoted through advertising, books, and especially television, which became the key to financial success for entire leagues and was a major marketing agent for sport.

The growth of professional sport was largely a phenomenon of technological society. Sport on television entertained millions, super jets transported teams across the country and to other continents, manufactured goods supplied athletes, and computers assisted in recruiting athletes and scheduling league games. Fifty million Americans watched the Super Bowl football game in 1975, and regular sports on television changed the eating habits of millions of families. In addition, crowds turned out to watch men and women of various racial and ethnic backgrounds compete professionally in games and contests unheard of at mid-twentieth century.

Ski resorts offered hotdog skiing and lake resorts water skiing. The development of professional sport in this period will be traced by examining changes in "the big three," baseball, football, and basketball, and other popular pro sports.

The Big Three

In spite of the great increase in professional sport baseball, football, and basketball remained the most popular pro sports. Both football and basketball expanded rapidly following World War II and were thought by many to replace the traditional national game of baseball. However, baseball responded to the times and continued to be a very popular if not the most popular game.

Baseball

The years 1947 and 1948 marked the end of one era and the beginning of another in baseball. On April 11, 1947, Jackie Robinson played in his first regular season major league baseball game, paving the way for hundreds of black players in professional sport. Signed by Branch Rickey of the Brooklyn Dodgers in 1945 and carefully groomed in the club's Montreal farm team for two years, Robinson made his debut without the predicted race riots and, further, withstood the suspicions, taunts, and threats of players and fans alike. His selection as "Rookie of the Year" in 1947 and as "Most Valuable Player" for the Dodgers in 1949 insured the success of the "noble experiment." In the next few years the Dodgers signed other talented black players such as Joe Black, Don Newcombe, and Roy Campanella.

In 1948 the sports world mourned the death of George Herman "Babe" Ruth, the man who had brought unprecedented popularity to baseball. At the time of his death many of Ruth's records remained and were lasting testimonies to his greatness. New stars such as Ted Williams, Stan Musial, Jackie Robinson, Willie Mays, and Micky Mantle, while perhaps lacking the theatrical qualities of the early star, nevertheless responded to changes in the game and provided new thrills and records. The New York Yankees began their string of victories which led them to five consecutive World Series championships from 1949 through 1953 and a total of ten World Series Championships and 15 American League pennants between 1947 and 1964.

By the beginning of the sixties, two of Ruth's most hallowed records—sixty home runs in one season and 714 career home runs—still stood. In 1961, Roger Maris of the New York Yankees broke the first record by one in a season that was six games longer than the Babe's 1927 year, thus creating a controversy over whether or not the record was actually broken. The second record fell on April 8, 1974 when Henry (Hank) Aaron of the Atlanta Braves hit his 715th home run.

In spite of the success of the Yankees, or perhaps even because of it, baseball attendance dropped from 20,972,601 in 1948 to 16,616,310 in 1955. Although television had been accepted by the 1950's, the owners at first blamed it for the drop in attendance. The Boston Braves of the National League drew only 281,278 spectators in 1952. The following year an experiment changed the structure of baseball from a few cities in the East to a nation-wide network. In 1953 the Boston Braves moved to Milwaukee and had instant success with 1,826,397 in attendance. In 1954, the St. Louis Browns became the Baltimore Orioles, and in 1955 the Philadelphia Athletics were the Kansas City Athletics. The West Coast acquired major league teams in 1958 when the New York Giants moved to San Francisco and the Brooklyn Dodgers switched to Los Angeles. League expansion in 1961, '62, and in '69 resulted in four divisions, each league consisting of two divisions, the champions of which competed in a play-off to determine the league pennant winner. The expansion brought more cities into the national structure of the game and more demand for baseball on television. Cities with regional television markets became desirable home cities for baseball franchises, and television rights meant economic survival of major league clubs. The widespread televising of major league games did, however, mean the doom of many minor leagues, who were unable to attract spectators and fans. By the 1970's both the All-Star game and the World Series were major television attractions.

In 1962, when the Yankees gained their 27th American League pennant, another New York team, the Mets of the National League, began a losing streak which became as much a box office attraction as winning. During one losing season, 1963, they drew a million fans. They had finished last five times, and placed second to the last twice in their league, when they shocked and delighted the sports world in 1969 by winning both the pennant and the World Series. Arthur Daley of the New York *Times* explained:

> The Mets did far more for baseball than just bring championship banners to Shea Stadium. They gave a shot of adrenalin to the entire baseball establishment with an injection of renewed life, vitality, interest and excitement, all woefully diminished of recent years.[1]

The players expressed their growing concern about the conditions of their employment as baseball players. Voigt points out that "Many players now saw themselves as workers and seemed more interested in money and pen-

---

1. Arthur Daley, "Sports of the Times," New York *Times,* 21 December 1969, Section 5, p. 2.

MAJOR LEAGUE BASEBALL EXPANSION 1952-1977

American League

1952	1955	1961
Boston Red Sox	Baltimore Orioles (1954)	Baltimore
Chicago White Sox	Boston	Boston
Cleveland Indians	Chicago	Chicago
Detroit Tigers	Cleveland	Cleveland
New York Yankees	Detroit	Detroit
Philadelphia Athletics	Kansas City Athletics (1955)	Kansas City
St. Louis Browns	New York	Los Angeles Angels (1961)
Washington Senators	Washington	Minnesota Twins (1961)
		New York
		Washington

National League

Boston Braves	Brooklyn	Chicago
Brooklyn Dodgers	Chicago	Cincinnati
Chicago Cubs	Cincinnati	Los Angeles Dodgers (1958)
Cincinnati Reds	Milwaukee Braves (1953)	Milwaukee
New York Giants	Philadelphia	Philadelphia
Philadelphia Phillies	Pittsburgh	Pittsburgh
Pittsburgh Pirates	New York	St. Louis
St. Louis Cardinals	St. Louis	San Francisco Giants (1958)

( ) Year franchise changed name or entered league.

* Divisional winners play off for pennant in each league; winners compete in World Series, established in 1903.

MAJOR LEAGUE BASEBALL EXPANSION 1952-1977

American League

1969   1977

Eastern Division   *Eastern Division*   *PLAYOFFS**
Baltimore   Baltimore Orioles
Boston   Boston Red Sox
Cleveland   Cleveland Indians
Detroit   Detroit Tigers
New York   Milwaukee Brewers (1970)
Washington   Toronto Blue Jays (1977)

                                                                  American League
                                                                     Pennant

Western Division   *Western Division*
California Angels   (1965)   California Angels   (1965)
Chicago   Chicago White Sox
Kansas City Royals   Kansas City Royals
Minnesota   Minnesota Twins
Oakland Athletics   (1968)   Oakland Athletics
Seattle Pilots   (1968)   Seattle Mariners   (1977)
                                 Texas Rangers   (1972)

                                                                            World Series

National League

Eastern Division   *Eastern Division*
Chicago   Chicago Cubs
Montreal Expos   (1962)   Montreal Expos
New York Mets   (1962)   New York Mets
Philadelphia   Philadelphia Phillies
Pittsburgh   Pittsburgh Pirates
St. Louis   St. Louis Cardinals

                                                                  National League
                                                                     Pennant

Western Division   *Western Division*
Atlanta Braves   Atlanta Braves
Cincinnati   Cincinnati Reds
Houston Colts/Astros (1962)   Houston Astros
Los Angeles   Los Angeles Dodgers
San Diego Padres   (1969)   San Diego Padres
San Francisco   San Francisco Giants

sions."[2] In 1946, the owners averted formation of a players' union by allowing player representatives to attend meetings and help construct more equitable contracts. The Major League Baseball Players' Association was formed in 1966. Three years later the players boycotted the opening of spring training because of a dispute over owner contributions to the pension fund. In 1972, major league players staged a thirteen-day strike, again over the issue of the pension fund, and delayed the opening of the season ten days, causing the cancellation of 86 regular season games.

In 1973, the owners agreed that a player with ten years of major league experience, the last five with the same club, could not be traded without his consent. The players began to acquire more rights. Over the years several players had tested the tight control of the players by the owners. After arbitration had been accepted by baseball, Andy Messersmith of the Los Angeles Dodgers, who had played a year without signing a contract, contested the proposed renewal of his contract. The arbiter declared Messersmith a free agent. "The practical effect of *Messersmith* was to allow all players currently under contract to play out their option year and become free agents."[3]

During this period baseball was again investigated in relation to anti-trust laws. In 1953, a congressional committee repeated an investigation into baseball's exemption from anti-trust laws. Again in 1970 the Supreme Court confirmed earlier decisions that baseball was not subject to anti-trust laws.

The game itself changed in this period. In 1930, 66 players with 400 or more times at bat had batting averages over .300 while in 1968 Boston's Carl Yastrzemski won the American League batting title with .301. In an effort to bolster the hitting, which had declined steadily, the American League instituted the "designated hitter" position to replace the pitcher in the batting order in 1973. As the hitting became less important, pitching came to dominate the game due to the development of relief pitchers, greater emphasis on home run hitting, larger ball parks, and more night games.[4]

The opening of the Houston Astrodome in 1965, with its artificial turf on which the ball moved faster and players fell harder than on conventional grass, sparked a period of new stadium construction in cities with

---

2. David Q. Voigt, *American Baseball,* Vol. II (Norman: University of Oklahoma Press, 1970), p. 289.

3. *Professional Sports and the Law* (Washington, D.C.: United States Government Printing Office, 1976), p. 13.

4. Associated Press Sports Staff, *A Century of Major American Sports* (Maplewood, N.J.: Hammond Inc., 1975), p. 59.

established teams as well as those with new franchises. A number of new stadiums installed artificial turf which was economical, easily maintained, and readily adapted to a variety of sports and other events. The number of night games increased to draw the people unable to attend afternoon games and to adapt to prime time on television.

Football

The growth of professional football from 1949 to 1977 was a modern sport phenomenon. In a twenty-year period the National Football League (NFL) expanded from 13 teams to 28 teams. In a series of moves to exploit the potential market of football fans, rival leagues formed, then merged with the old NFL, reorganized, and again merged. World War II decimated the young National Football League but by 1946 it had recovered, and the All-American Football Conference (AAFC) formed as a rival to the older league. The AAFC signed some NFL players and drafted top college talent, including players from Southern black colleges, helping to integrate professional football. In 1949 the AAFC merged with the NFL, awarding franchises to the Cleveland Browns, the San Francisco 49er's, and the Baltimore Colts. The other teams were disbanded and the players distributed among the remaining clubs. In 1950 the NFL reorganized into conferences, the National and the American, and also in that year held a playoff to determine a championship team.

A second rival league, the American Football League (AFL), was organized in 1961 by a number of wealthy businessmen led by Texan Lamar Hunt. The new league raided NFL and college teams, escalating player salaries at a rate alarming to owners and fans alike. In 1966, a merger of the NFL and the AFL was negotiated to begin in 1970. The name National Football League was retained and the League organized into two conferences, the American and the National, each with three divisions.

The phenomenal growth and popularity of pro football was attributed largely to television. Like their peers in baseball, the football owners were at first opposed to the concept of free viewing of games on television. The NFL's policy of televising only games away from home and blacking out the home games on local television seemed to build interest and encourage ticket sales. By 1957, games were telecast into 175 cities and millions of people watched young Jim Brown of Cleveland begin his career by winning "Rookie of the Year" honors, and in 1958 over 20,000,000 watched the championship games.

In the early sixties the National Broadcasting Company (NBC) signed a contract to televise American Football League games, infusing enough

PROFESSIONAL FOOTBALL EXPANSION 1946-1977

National Football League

1946	1950	1961
Eastern Division	**American Conference**	**Eastern Conference**
Boston Yanks	Chicago Cardinals	Cleveland
Philadelphia Eagles	Cleveland Browns (1950)	Dallas Cowboys (1960)
Pittsburgh Steelers	New York Giants	New York
New York Giants	Philadelphia Eagles	Philadelphia
Washington Redskins	Pittsburgh Steelers	Pittsburgh
	Washington Redskins	St. Louis Cardinals (1960)
		Washington
Western Division	**National Conference**	**Western Conference**
Chicago Bears	Baltimore Colts (1950)	Baltimore
Chicago Cardinals	Chicago Bears	Chicago
Green Bay Packers	Detroit Lions	Detroit
Detroit Lions	Green Bay Packers	Green Bay
Los Angeles Rams	Los Angeles Rams	Los Angeles (1961)
	New York Yanks	Minnesota
	San Francisco 49ers (1950)	San Francisco

All American Football Conference 1946-1949	American Football League 1961-1970
Eastern Division	*Eastern Division*
Brooklyn Dodgers	Boston Patriots
Buffalo Bisons	Buffalo Bills
Miami Seahawks	Houston Oilers
New York Yankees	New York TItans/Jets
Western Division	*Western Division*
Chicago Hornets/Rockets	Dallas Texans
Cleveland Browns	Denver Broncos
Los Angeles Dons	Oakland Raiders
San Francisco 49ers	San Diego Chargers (1961)

( ) Year franchise changed name or entered league.

* Six division winners plus wild card team in each conference compete for Conference Championships. Conference champions compete in Super Bowl. First Super Bowl was in 1966.

PROFESSIONAL FOOTBALL EXPANSION 1946-1977

National Football League

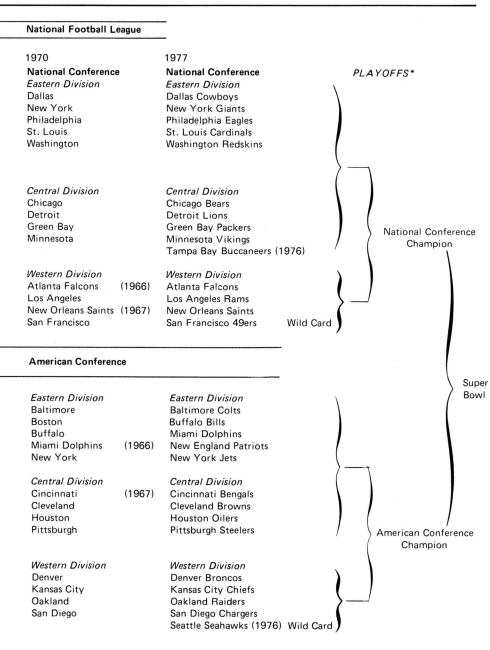

1970	1977	
National Conference	**National Conference**	*PLAYOFFS**
Eastern Division	*Eastern Division*	
Dallas	Dallas Cowboys	
New York	New York Giants	
Philadelphia	Philadelphia Eagles	
St. Louis	St. Louis Cardinals	
Washington	Washington Redskins	
Central Division	*Central Division*	
Chicago	Chicago Bears	
Detroit	Detroit Lions	
Green Bay	Green Bay Packers	National Conference
Minnesota	Minnesota Vikings	Champion
	Tampa Bay Buccaneers (1976)	
Western Division	*Western Division*	
Atlanta Falcons (1966)	Atlanta Falcons	
Los Angeles	Los Angeles Rams	
New Orleans Saints (1967)	New Orleans Saints	
San Francisco	San Francisco 49ers Wild Card	

American Conference

Eastern Division	*Eastern Division*	
Baltimore	Baltimore Colts	
Boston	Buffalo Bills	
Buffalo	Miami Dolphins	
Miami Dolphins (1966)	New England Patriots	
New York	New York Jets	
Central Division	*Central Division*	
Cincinnati (1967)	Cincinnati Bengals	
Cleveland	Cleveland Browns	
Houston	Houston Oilers	
Pittsburgh	Pittsburgh Steelers	American Conference
		Champion
Western Division	*Western Division*	
Denver	Denver Broncos	
Kansas City	Kansas City Chiefs	
Oakland	Oakland Raiders	
San Diego	San Diego Chargers	
	Seattle Seahawks (1976) Wild Card	

Super
Bowl

money into the league to save its faltering franchises. Throughout the decade the television contracts grew more lucrative until league owners considered those revenues necessary to meet spiraling personnel and other operating expenses. By 1970 all three major networks—NBC, CBS, and ABC—were televising regular season games on Saturdays, Sundays, and Monday evenings.

As important as television was to the popularity of professional football, the game itself was well suited to telecasting. The camera was able to pick up developing plays and the commentators analyzed them between downs. The isolated camera and "instant replays," introduced in the late 1960's, added to the enjoyment of the telecasts. The initiation of the free substitution rule in the early fifties allowed increased specialization by players and thus more highly skilled performances. The new rule permitted greater recognition of players such as the defensive linemen, long the unsung laborers of the game. Stars such as Joe Schmidt of the Detroit Lions and Dick Butkus of the Chicago Bears became football heroes. Offensive position stars such as Tom Groza, Bob Waterfield, Johnny Unitas, Jim Brown, Gale Sayers, Joe Namath, and O.J. Simpson brought additional excitement to the game. The superb coaching of Paul Brown, George Halas, Vince Lombardi, and Don Schula gave football scientific precision, which appealed to millions of "armchair quarterbacks" across the nation. Many argued that the game had passed baseball as the nation's most popular sport.

Basketball

At the beginning of the 1976-77 basketball season, the National Basketball Association (NBA), having merged with the American Basketball Association (ABA), consisted of 22 teams in 21 cities ranging in size from Portland, Oregon (398,000) to New York City (7,895,000).

This completed a cycle which began in 1949 when the National Basketball League and the Basketball Association of America merged into the National Basketball Association with 17 teams in cities such as Anderson and Indianapolis, Indiana, Syracuse and Rochester, New York, Sheboygan, Wisconsin, and Waterloo, Iowa, as well as larger cities such as St. Louis, Chicago, and New York. In 1953, professional basketball averaged only 3,000 spectators per game. By 1959, the NBA drew over 2,000,000 in attendance, relocated most teams from small cities to major population centers, reduced itself to eight teams and operated on a fiscally sound basis. With the increasing popularity of professional basketball, not only did the NBA expand in 1961 but a rival, the American Basketball League, was founded with eight teams. The ABL folded in 1963, but four years later the American Basketball Association started with George Mikan as Commissioner.

FIG. 7.1   Bill Russell (6) and Wilt Chamberlain (13), popular professional basketball players. Wide World.

PROFESSIONAL BASKETBALL 1949-1977

National Basketball Association

1949-1950*
Merger: BAA & NBL
Eastern Division
Baltimore Bullets
Boston Celtics
New York Knicks
Philadelphia Warriors
Syracuse Nationals
Washington Capitols

Central Division
Chicago Stags
Fort Wayne Pistons
Minneapolis Lakers
Rochester Royals
St. Louis Hawks

Western Division
Anderson Packers
Denver Nuggets
Indianapolis Olympians
Sheboygan Redskins
Tri-Cities Blackhawks
Waterloo Hawks

1961-1962
Eastern Division
Boston
Philadelphia
New York
Syracuse

Western Division
Cincinnati Royals   (1957)
Detroit Pistons   (1957)
Los Angeles Lakers (1960)
St. Louis

1967-1968
Eastern Division
Baltimore Bullets   (1963)
Boston
Cincinnati
Detroit
New York
Philadelphia

Western Division
Chicago Bulls
Los Angeles
St. Louis
San Diego Rockets   (1967)
San Francisco Warriors (1962)
Seattle Supersonics   (1967)

	American Basketball League 1961-1962	American Basketball Association 1967-1976
	Eastern Division Chicago Cleveland Pittsburgh Washington	*Eastern Division* Indiana Pacers Kentucky Colonels Minnesota Muskies New Jersey Americans Pittsburgh Pipers
	Western Division Hawaii Kansas City Los Angeles San Francisco	*Western Division* Anaheim Amigos Dallas Chaparrals Denver Nuggets Houston Mavericks Oakland Oaks New Orleans Buccaneers

( ) Year franchise changed name or entered league.

  * The Basketball Association of America and the National Basketball League merged to form National Basketball Association.

** Six best teams (record) in each conference compete in playoffs with division winners receiving a bye into quarter finals; the winners in each conference compete for World Championship.

PROFESSIONAL BASKETBALL 1949-1977

National Basketball Association

1976-1977

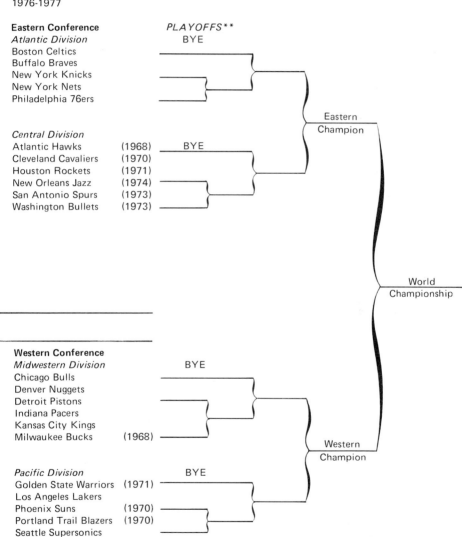

Eastern Conference — *PLAYOFFS***

Atlantic Division — BYE
Boston Celtics
Buffalo Braves
New York Knicks
New York Nets
Philadelphia 76ers

Central Division — BYE
Atlantic Hawks (1968)
Cleveland Cavaliers (1970)
Houston Rockets (1971)
New Orleans Jazz (1974)
San Antonio Spurs (1973)
Washington Bullets (1973)

Eastern Champion

World Championship

Western Conference
Midwestern Division — BYE
Chicago Bulls
Denver Nuggets
Detroit Pistons
Indiana Pacers
Kansas City Kings
Milwaukee Bucks (1968)

Pacific Division — BYE
Golden State Warriors (1971)
Los Angeles Lakers
Phoenix Suns (1970)
Portland Trail Blazers (1970)
Seattle Supersonics

Western Champion

The competition for players forced contracts into multi-million dollar figures with "Dr. J" Julius Erving in 1977 contracting $3,500,000 over a six year period. These conditions led to a merger of the two leagues in 1976, completing a 25-year cycle of merging, expanding, rivaling, and merging.

Professional basketball, like football, experienced phenomenal growth beginning in the fifties and continuing into the seventies. George Mikan in the late forties, and Bill Russell and Wilt Chamberlain in the fifties and sixties, established the importance of the "big man" in championship basketball. Fans found the agile, aggressive giants exciting as they scored and scored and scored. Mikan, of the Minneapolis Lakers, signaled the coming of the super-tall center but the seven-foot Chamberlain demonstrated in his play the importance of the position and beginning in 1959-60 led the league in scoring for seven straight years. In 1961-62 he reached a high of 4,029 points and later became the first player to pass 25,000 points in his career. Although Chamberlain took individual honors, Russell's Boston Celtics won the team titles in eight consecutive league races from 1959 to 1966.

As with other professional sports, television helped both to popularize the game and to provide a major source of income. In addition to the influence of television on basketball, the black players became a major factor in its success. In 1950 there were only a few black players in the NBA but by 1966 they comprised over 65 percent of NBA player personnel. In 1967 Bill Russell was named player-coach of the Boston Celtics, the second black manager in a major league sport. The first was John McLendon, a former coach of a black college, who had been hired by the Cleveland club in the short-lived American Basketball League in 1960. The 1975-76 NBA and ABA All-Star teams included 13 black players out of 20 positions.

Other Professional Sports

Ice Hockey

Until 1967 the National Hockey League consisted of six teams located in northeastern United States and eastern Canadian cities—Montreal, Toronto, Boston, New York, Detroit, Chicago—with Canadian players greatly outnumbering Americans. That year the NHL doubled the number of its franchises and, by 1972, had expanded to 16 teams. Also in 1972, the World Hockey Association was organized with twelve teams. With artificial ice making possible indoor rinks, major league hockey, traditionally a cold climate sport, was played all over the United States. To introduce hockey to the Southern cities a massive education program was undertaken, beginning with teaching young people to play the game. However, it appeared that the followers of the new franchises were generally transplanted Northerners.[5]

---

5. Roy Blount, Jr., "Losersville U.S.A.," *Sports Illustrated* 46 (March 21, 1977): 85.

Horse Racing

The "sport of kings" generated excitement in 1946 when Assault won the Triple Crown and two years later Citation repeated the feat. It was to be another twenty-five years, in 1973, before another horse, Secretariat, again took the Triple Crown.

In 1946 member tracks of the Thoroughbred Racing Association organized the Thoroughbred Racing Protective Bureau to ". . . insure that the public is furnished an honest, clean racing spectacle, as well as to protect their patrons from undesirables," and the following year they adopted a code of racing standards.[6] State governments not only welcomed the industry's efforts to police itself but also were pleased with the revenue from parimutuel betting. Between 1940 and 1962, New York State alone collected $1,100,000,000 in taxes from this source. In 1965 in the twenty-six states allowing betting a record forty million people wagered $3,351,000,000 on thoroughbred racing.

One of the outstanding jockeys of the period was Willie Shoemaker, who at 22 rode 485 winners in 1953, a record at that time. Other top jockeys were Eddie Arcaro, who retired in 1961 with 4,779 victories, and Johnny Longden, who rode 6,026 winners in a forty-year career ending in 1966.

Harness racing moved out of the small towns and state fair arenas to large cities following World War II. In 1948 almost 5,500,000 attended trotting races in the United States, and the purses totaled nearly $10,000,000. By 1974, attendance had jumped to approximately 27,000,000 and the purses to over $134,000,000. Harness racing had joined other sports in the business of entertainment.

Boxing

During World War II the world heavyweight title remained in the hands of Joe Louis who, as a member of the United States Army, conducted exhibitions for troops around the world. In 1946 he defeated Billie Conn and retired in 1949 after holding the title for thirteen years. In 1950, in an attempted comeback to pay income tax debts, he was defeated by Ezzard Charles and was forced to retire. A succession of heavyweight titleholders followed: Charles (1949-51), Jersey Joe Wolcott (1951-52), Rocky Marciano (1952-55), and Floyd Patterson (1956-59, 60-62). The leading middleweight was the brilliant stylist, "Sugar" Ray Robinson.

During the fifties boxing suffered from overexposure on television, and many small clubs where young boxers honed their skills were forced to close. Rumors of fixed fights led to a United States Senate Committee to Study Organized Crime. Later, on March 8, 1957 a federal court judged

---

6. Frank G. Menke, *The Encyclopedia of Sports,* 5th ed. (New York: A.S. Barnes and Company, 1975), p. 594.

that boxing promoter J.D. Norris, the International Boxing Club, and Madison Square Garden were in violation of the Sherman Anti-trust Act. After that, public interest in boxing dropped until colorful Cassius Clay wrested the title from ex-convict Sonny Liston in 1964. Given to boasting, impromptu poetry, and an entertaining style in the ring, Clay was the most controversial fighter since Jack Johnson. Immediately following his title victory Clay announced himself as a member of the Black Muslim sect and changed his name to Muhammad Ali. After successfully defending his title several times in 1965 and 1966, he refused to be drafted for military service in 1967 because he had become a Muslim minister. He was the object of great controversy and the World Boxing Association stripped him of his title. Uncertainty prevailed about the title holder even after the World Boxing Association held an elimination tournament with little-known Jimmy Ellis emerging victorious. Joe Frazier, who had been recognized as champion in six states, had refused to enter the WBA tourney. Early in 1970 Frazier defeated Ellis and the matter appeared settled. However, Ali, in the midst of legal battles over his draft status, declared that he remained the champion. Finally, in 1973 he was allowed to return to the ring and on October 30, 1974 he defeated George Foreman, establishing his clear right to the title.

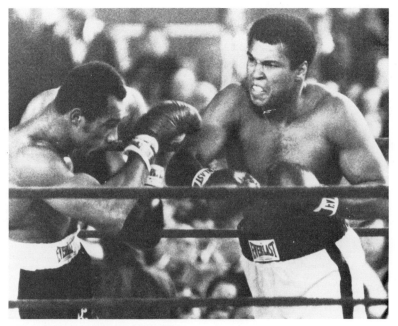

FIG. 7.2   Muhammad Ali. Wide World.

Golf

In 1946 Ben Hogan earned $42,556 on the pro golf tour, while in 1975, Jack Nicklaus led the winners with a total of $298,149. This sevenfold increase reflects the growth of professional golf from the early 1940's to the mid-seventies. Through the efforts of promoter Fred Corcoran in the early 1940's the prize money increased and professional golf expanded. Under the Professional Golfer's Association (PGA) Tournament Player's Division the number of tournaments, the course standards and the players themselves improved the image of pro golf. As with some other sports, television exposure increased the attendance at tournaments and, in turn, the number of golfers. The affluent fifties found more and more players who not only played more golf but followed the professional players closely.

The golfers themselves contributed to the continuing success of the game with their improving performances and lower scores. In the late forties and early fifties, fiercely competitive Ben Hogan and swinging Sam Snead were in top form, and at the end of the fifties and early sixties Arnold Palmer's aggressive, daring style of play led the professional game. In 1962, young Jack Nicklaus' superb strength, accuracy, and concentration defeated Palmer. By 1963, both Palmer and Nicklaus earned more than $100,000 in prize money. In 1975 fourteen players earned more than $100,000 and the top sixty players all surpassed Hogan's 1946 winnings.

The first opportunities for women to earn money through golf were through the endorsements of golf equipment and apparel. Zaharias reported ". . . I signed up with the Wilson Sporting Goods Company, to be on their advisory staff and have them market Babe Zaharias golf equipment. . . . I also signed with the Serbin dress manufacturers, who made a golf dress that I designed."[7] During World War II, in 1943, an amateur golfer, Betty Hicks, a physical education teacher, Ellen Griffin, and a golf professional, Hope Seignious, organized the Women's Professional Golf Association to promote golf for women, including professional golf. An early supporter of the association and active from the beginning was Babe Didrikson. Immediately after the war they initiated the United States Women's Open Championship, but the association was uncertain of its future and was reorganized in 1949 as the Ladies Professional Golf Players Association, and a year later incorporated under its present name, the Ladies Professional Golf Association.

As the Women's Professional Golf Association, the group sponsored the U.S. Women's Open from 1946 to 1953 when the United States Golf Association assumed the responsibility for the Open. In the first Open, Patty

<hr>

7. Babe Didrikson Zaharias, *This Life I've Led* (New York: A.S. Barnes & Co., 1955), pp. 180-81.

Berg beat Betty Jameson; Babe Zaharias won the championship in 1948 and 1950; and Louise Suggs repeated the double victory in 1949 and 1952. The LPGA tour grew slowly and, even with Fred Corcoran appointed to conduct the tournaments, the prizes were small and the situation difficult. By 1950 the tour included just nine tournaments. From 1953 to 1975, the players conducted their own affairs, but in 1975 appointed a commissioner to administer the LPGA.

The LPGA experienced a spurt of growth in the fifties and has continued to expand. Both the number of events and the prize money have increased from 26 events and a purse of $140,447 in 1956 to 33 events and a purse of $3,000,000 in 1977. The individual earnings have also increased from Mickey Wright's high of $20,000 in 1962 and Kathy Whitworth's $65,064 in 1972 to Judy Rankin's over $130,000 in the first nine months of 1976.

Growth of the Ladies Professional Golf Association[8]

Year	Purses	Number of Events
1956	140,447	26
1961	288,750	24
1966	509,500	37
1971	558,500	21
1976	2,527,000	32

The LPGA included two types of membership: those who played on the tour, and those certified as teachers by the Association. The latter taught or coached at colleges, golf clubs, or other golf facilities. According to Theberge, in 1976 ". . . the teaching division numbered 141 players and the touring division included 136 active touring players."[9]

Tennis

Tennis, the conservative stronghold of the pure amateurs, changed little in patterns of competition from about 1875 to the mid-1960's. Since that time the world of tennis has undergone a drastic revolution which resulted in open championships, increased professional play, and more prize money for women. Through the 1940's, '50's and most of the '60's tennis generally followed the pattern of the thirties. In 1947 Jack Kramer, singles champion

8. Nancy Theberge, "Analysis of Women's Professional Golf," Ph.D. dissertation, University of Massachusetts, 1977, p. 36.
9. Nancy Theberge, "Analysis of Women's Professional Golf," Ph.D. dissertation, University of Massachusetts, 1977, pp. 39-40.

at Wimbledon and of the United States, and Bobby Riggs toured North America and, in 1949, "Pancho" Gonzales toured with Kramer. The following year a combined men's and women's tour featured Kramer, "Pancho" Segura, "Gussie" Moran, and Pauline Betz Addie. In 1954 Kramer stopped playing to promote world professional tennis tours. Much to the consternation of countries competing in Davis Cup matches, he signed many top amateurs from around the world. Australia was hard hit in 1957 when Ken Rosewall signed with Kramer for $55,000 and Lewis Hoad agreed to a 25-month $125,000 contract.

For years amateurs in tennis received expense money for tournaments but were excluded from playing against professionals. The All-England Club proposed that the Wimbledon championships be made open to professional and amateur players alike. The international tennis governing body, International Lawn Tennis Federation (ILTF), rejected such proposals until 1967 when the British Lawn Tennis Association recognized no difference between amateur players and professional players. In return, the International Lawn Tennis Federation announced that each country must determine the status of its own players. In 1968 for the first time Wimbledon was an open tournament when Rod Laver for the men and Billie Jean King for the women were victorious. By 1970 the ILTF recognized three classes of players, amateurs recognized by their country's national association, professionals recognized by their country's national association, and professionals who played under contract.

In 1968 two organizations in this country controlled professional tennis, National Tennis League and World Championship Tennis. Texas millionaire and sportsman Lamar Hunt sponsored the latter group and in 1970 bought control of the former and combined the two groups. For women, the breakthrough came in 1970 when eight women refused to compete in the Pacific Southwest Open at Los Angeles in which the men's prize was $12,500 and the women's $1,500. Instead of playing in Los Angeles the women—Billie Jean King, Kerry Melville, Peaches Bartkowicz, Kristy Pigeon, Valerie Ziegenfuss, Rosie Casals, Nancy Gunter, and Judy Dalton—entered the first Virginia Slims tournament in Houston, Texas. The Houston Eight, as they came to be called, braved the wrath of the United States Lawn Tennis Association, but led the way to greater purses for women's tennis. In 1971 the Virginia Slims tournaments averaged $16,590 and grew to $81,818 in 1975. Also, the women, with King in the lead, pressured Wimbledon to better the women's purses.

In 1974 a new concept, World Team Tennis, in which co-ed teams based in a number of cities played five sets at an event, again changed professional tennis. The sets—women's doubles, men's doubles, women's singles, men's singles, and mixed doubles—were scored and the team that won the most games won the match. Unlike traditional tennis, spectators were encouraged to cheer, hoot and whistle for their favorites.

Throughout this period interest was sustained because of colorful players. Jack Kramer's ability to combine playing with selling helped establish post-war professional tennis. The temperamental but brilliant play of "Pancho" Gonzales kept him near the top throughout the fifties, and Rosewall and Hoad added international interest to the tours. The featured player of the seventies was controversial Jimmy Connors who by the age of twenty-two was ranked the number one player in the world. Calm, steady, black Arthur Ashe provided additional interest to the pro men players.

Billie Jean King, the first woman tennis player to win more than $100,000, crusaded for women in tennis and women in sport. Women's tennis received an unexpected boost when King played Riggs. After having defeated Margaret Court, Riggs scheduled a match with King. Billed as a "Battle Between the Sexes," amid pageantry, pomp, and commercial ballyhoo, there was some question as to whether it was spectacle or sport. However, when the play began, it was clearly a serious match. King soundly trounced Riggs:

> . . . what began as a huckster's hustle in defiance of serious athleticism ended up not mocking the game of tennis but honoring it. This night King was both a shining piece of show biz and the essence of what sport is all about.[10]

Chris Evert became the leading woman tennis professional in 1976. In a relatively short time she captured two Wimbledon crowns, two United States Opens, two French Opens, two Italian Opens, and three Virginia Slims Championships. In 1976 the four women following Evert were Evonne Goolagong, Virginia Wade, Rosemary Casals, and Martina Navratilova.

Soccer

Soccer, long the number one team sport in the world, was generally played by ethnic clubs and a few colleges and secondary schools in the United States. While a number of professional and amateur organizations existed prior to 1967, the formation of two professional leagues that year greatly increased the interest in soccer. The new soccer leagues signed many European players, but rarely attracted crowds over 20,000 and lost five million dollars the first year. The next year the leagues merged to form the North American Soccer League. The League dropped to five teams at one point and then increased to fifteen teams by 1974 and added five more in 1975. Stars such as Pelé and Kyle Rote helped increase interest in the game.

---

10. Curry Kirkpatrick, "There She Is: Ms. America," *Sports Illustrated* 39 (October 1, 1973): 32.

FIG. 7.3   Billie Jean King, first woman athlete to earn $100,000 in a single year. Wide World.

Other Areas in Professional Sport for Women

Many other sports opened to women during the period following World War II. Some sports, such as bowling and ice skating, had had professional women for many years. Bowling, for instance, continued to attract its own audience. Many ice skating professionals, such as Norwegian Sonja Henie, were former Olympic medalists. Recent skaters such as Barbara Ann Scott, Peggy Fleming, and Dorothy Hamill have become stars of ice shows. But skaters of lesser billing, the cast of skaters in ice shows, came from the growing number of women ice skaters who skate professionally.

The All-American Girls' Baseball League, begun in World War II, continued until 1954 under the auspices of Philip K. Wrigley. According to Fidler, "Several factors can be cited to account for the league's decline.

FIG. 7.4   Robyn Smith, jockey. Wide World. Kathy Whitworth, professional golfer. Wide World.

Among these were discontent among team administrators, changes in league administration, a reduction in promotional budgets and programs, the growing popularity of television, and changes in the game itself."[11]

Affecting the gimmick of red hair, the Red Heads, a women's professional basketball team, played as much to entertain as to display a skilled game. One of the few pro teams in the country, they played over 200 games with local teams in a seven-month season.

Diane Crump became the first woman to ride in a regular thoroughbred horse race at a major track on February 7, 1969 at Hialeah. The next year she became the first woman to ride in the Kentucky Derby. Perhaps one of the most publicized breakthroughs for women in a professional sport, however, was Robyn Smith's hard-fought battle to obtain mounts as a jockey. Smith's first victory in 1969 paved the way for some sixty women who rode at tracks in 1974, although at that time only Smith and Mary Bacon were considered important jockeys.

Women have earned prize money and their livelihood in sports such as roller derby and football. In 1972 a New York city lawyer, Jim Eagen, formed the Fillies of New York, while later a Cleveland theatrical agent started a Woman's Football League. In 1976 the Women's Professional Football League held its first Superbowl in which the Toledo Troopers beat the Oklahoma City Dades, 13-12.

Amateur Sport

Era of Expansion

Not only did professional sport grow after World War II, but amateur sport expanded almost beyond belief. Participation increased, the general level of performance improved, records were broken, championships increased, and international competition became commonplace. By the mid-1970's over thirty national sport championships took place. The term "world-class athlete" became an accepted concept. Such people devoted many hours each day to practice and entered a regular program of events, including regional, national and world championships. They also spent a great deal of money in order to participate in the sport of their choice. Financing the amateur was solved in several ways: sometimes the athlete's family provided the money; sometimes grants-in-aid permitted college men and, after 1973, college women to continue their sport during their education; and sometimes sport organizations provided expense money for meets.

---

11. Merrie A. Fidler, "The All-American Girls' Baseball League, 1943-54," *Proceedings, North American Society for Sport History, 1975, p.36.

When Don Schollander demonstrated unusual promise in swimming by the end of his freshman year of high school he left his family in Oregon and entered a California school to swim with the Santa Clara Swim Club.

> In Oregon I had done well just training an hour a day because everyone else was training an hour a day, too: but in California, where everyone was training three hours a day, I was in another league. At Santa Clara I began two-a-day workouts, something entirely new for me; an hour and a quarter in the morning before school, two hours after school.
>
> . . . .
>
> At Santa Clara we arrived at the pool at 6:30 A.M., and George Haines, striding up and down with a megaphone, would order a 500-meter warm-up swim. Five hundred meters is a third of a mile. Then we would swim another 500 meters "pulling," using only the arms. Next, 100-meter repeats, probably five. Another long swim, more repeats, breathing drills, turning drills, starting drills, one more long swim and we had worked an hour and a quarter and were through for the morning. In the afternoon we were back for more of the same. At the peak of training we were swimming about eight miles a day.[12]

Women became a significant component of amateur sport following World War II. Some of the same factors which contributed to women's greater participation in professional sport also led to an increase in amateur sport. The post-war affluence permitted time for sport, money for equipment and instruction, and a growing social acceptance of sports such as horseback riding, tennis, golf, swimming, and gymnastics. Greater numbers of girls and women were struggling with changing concepts of femininity in work and play. They were ". . . finding their own images of woman at her utmost in many . . . forms of sport. And in both work and sport, their choices reflect their own definitions of the feminine image which is currently acceptable within their own social milieus."[13] However, if women wished to compete at the national or international level many had to make a choice between sport and a college education. Because of educational philosophy, eligibility rules, and financial aid regulations, many women were unable to combine a sport career with their college or university education.

The federal government became involved in amateur sport due to the growing emphasis on international competition. During the Cold War of the fifties, it became clear that Communist nations were using the amateur sport arena to promote their ideology. Since 1950 the United States State Department has sponsored "good-will" tours including athletic competi-

---

12. Don Schollander and Duke Savage, *Deep Water* (New York: Crown Publishers, Inc., 1971), pp.13-14.
13. Eleanor Metheny, *Movement and Meaning* (New York: McGraw-Hill Book Company, 1968), p.77.

tion and instruction. International amateur sport has become, then, not only the measure of a nation's amateur athletes, but also a reflection of the socio-political system.

Golf

Amateur golf since World War II was conducted largely in the shadow of the professional game. While media coverage was primarily devoted to the latter, the amateur game thrived with thousands of new golfers. The National Amateur Championships sponsored by the United States Golf Association served not only to determine the nation's best amateur players, but also to facilitate joining the professional ranks. The Amateur Public Links Championship grew in importance as municipal, county, and state-owned courses increased. By the early 1970's entries for the regional quali-fying rounds were running into the thousands. In Walker Cup play from 1947 through 1975, only once, in 1971, did the men lose to Great Britain. In the same period, approximately from 1948 through 1976, the American women won the Curtis Cup thirteen times. As in the case of the men, amateur golf tended to be the route for women to become professional golfers. Pros Louise Suggs and Mickey Wright were both United States Golf Association women's amateur champions before joining the Ladies Professional Golf Association. While the USGA women's amateur tourna-ment had been held since 1895, the United States Open began in 1946. In 1967 amateur Catherine Lacoste had the distinction of winning the Open, beating all the pros.

Tennis

Amateur tennis in the United States from 1946 to 1968 was marked by conflict, controversy, and charges of hypocrisy. Conflict over the profes-sional versus the amateur game, with Jack Kramer frequently cast in the role of villain, rocked the tennis circles. After first Kramer and then other players turned professional, the Americans managed to win only three Davis Cup championships between 1950 and 1967: 1954, 1958, and 1963. Vic Sexias in 1954, Tony Trabert in 1955, and Arthur Ashe in the sixties were among the well-known men tennis players.

In 1947 and 1948 the United States took the Wightman Cup with Margaret Osborne duPont and Louise Brough as the leading players. In 1950 Althea Gibson was the first black in the national grass court cham-pionships. Although Maureen "Little Mo" Connally was ranked the number one woman in tennis in 1952 and 1953, Gibson continued in the championship race, winning the French crown in 1956. Also that year she undertook a Far Eastern tour arranged by the State Department, reached the finals at Forest Hills, and won the doubles at Wimbledon. In 1958 she took the United States and British championships, was named the Associated Press woman athlete of the year, and was honored by a ticker-tape parade on her return to the United States.

Beginning with Ashe's victory in the 1968 U.S. Open, a number of world-class men and women players emerged, including Billie Jean King, Jimmy Connors and Chris Evert, each of whom turned professional. More significant, perhaps, was the fact that by the mid-1970's millions of Americans had discovered the game. Indoor tennis facilities sprang up at a record pace and the demand for equipment, playing time and space was unprecedented.

Sports Organized by the Amateur Athletic Union (AAU)

The AAU controlled many amateur sports in the United States such as basketball for men and basketball for women, boxing, track and field, synchronized swimming, wrestling and many others. Although the AAU and NCAA signed an "Articles of Alliance" in 1946 in an effort to reconcile their differences, the dispute between the two organizations continued. In the early 1950's athletes, coaches, and the NCAA charged the AAU with dictatorial attitudes regarding established policy, ignoring requests by athletes for hearings, denying foreign trips to athletes and coaches who criticized the AAU, managing AAU track meets unsatisfactorily, inadequately preparing teams for foreign competition, and failing to coordinate and process applications for national and world records.[14]

By the end of the decade the complaints intensified until, in 1960, the NCAA cancelled the "Articles of Alliance" with the AAU, refusing to honor any suspensions imposed upon college students by that organization. In 1962, NCAA-related coaches and administrators attempted to form new federations in basketball, track and field, gymnastics, baseball, and wrestling. Collegiate, military, religious, recreational, and scholastic personnel were part of the proposed organization.[15]

The struggle over sanctioning contests, particularly in track and field, continued with the athletes caught in the middle of a crossfire of boycotts and threats of suspension between the NCAA and the AAU. In order to insure an Olympic team in 1964, United States Attorney General Robert Kennedy mediated a temporary reconciliation in 1962 and General Douglas MacArthur another in 1963.

---

14. Eric Danoff, "The Struggle for Control of Amateur Track and Field in the United States—Part I," *The Canadian Journal of History of Sport and Physical Education* 6, no. 1 (May, 1975): 58-59.

15. Arnold Flath, "A History of Relations between the N.C.A.A. and the A.A.U., 1905-1968," in *A History of Physical Education and Sport in the United States and Canada,* ed. Earle F. Zeigler (Champaign, Ill.: Stipes Publishing Company, 1975), p. 211.

After the NCAA barred college men from participating in the 1965 U.S. track and field team trials in San Diego, and the men's team lost to the Russians in an international meet, a Sports Arbitration Board was appointed by U.S. Vice President Hubert Humphrey to attempt to resolve the conflict. A reluctant and uneasy truce was made which lasted through the mid-1970's with only a few serious sanctioning disputes.

Aside from the political struggles for jurisdiction, track and field athletes achieved major gains in the first decade following World War II. At the summer Olympic Games in 1948 seventeen-year-old Bob Mathias won the decathlon. Harrison Dillard, a high hurdler from Baldwin-Wallace College, won eighty consecutive races in the sprints and hurdles during 1947 and 1948.

In the fifties, American track and field stars broke many barriers. In 1951, Bob Richards became the second man to clear fifteen feet in the pole vault. Two years later, Wes Santee of Kansas threatened the four-minute mile as he ran 4:02.4. That same year Parry O'Brien, with his revolutionary shot-put style, came within striking distance of sixty feet and Walter Davis cleared 6 ' 11-1/2 " in the high jump. Of these three, only O'Brien reached his goal by putting the shot 60 ' 10 " in 1954. It was Roger Bannister who broke the four-minute barrier in 1954 at Oxford, England, when he ran 3:59.4. Charles Dumas finally surpassed the seven-foot barrier with a high jump of 7 ' 1/2 " in 1956. A third important record was broken, also in 1956, when Glen Davis of Ohio State University ran the 440-yard intermediate hurdles in 49.9 seconds and the 400-meter intermediate hurdles in 49.5 seconds. In 1958, the first United States-Russia track and field meet was held in an effort to promote a cultural exchange between the two countries.

Technological improvements such as the fiberglass vaulting pole, which revolutionized the event, resulted in unprecedented performances in the 1960's. Instead of the fast, strong athlete of the aluminum pole days, the new vaulters required exceptional gymnastic ability. The world record in the pole vault soared from 15 ' 10-1/4 " in 1961 to 18 ' 8-1/4 " in 1976.

Other changes included foam landing pits for the vault and high jump, composition tracks, jumping and throwing pads, lighter, more comfortable running shoes and uniforms, and electronic timing devices. The softer landing pits removed much of the discomfort of landing thus encouraging better performances. The composition tracks required less maintenance and provided more consistent surfaces for varying weather conditions.

In 1964 Jim Ryun became the first high school boy to break the four-minute mile. Two years later, with a time of 3:51.3, he became the first American in over thirty years to hold the world record in that event. Perhaps most significantly, United States distance runners achieved international status when Billy Mills and Bob Schul became the first Americans to win the Olympic 10,000- and 5,000-meter runs in 1964 and Frank Shorter captured the marathon title at Munich in 1972.

Track and field had not been among the more acceptable sports for women until the late 1960's and the 1970's brought a burst of popularity and excellent performers. However, certain institutions had been noted for their excellent programs and dominated the field for many years. Foremost was the Tennessee A & I State University program which provided the core of the U.S. women's international teams through the 1950's and '60's. The Mayor Daley Youth Foundation in Chicago also provided a needed organization, beginning in the late fifties, for non-college girls and women.

The indomitable Stella Walsh continued to compete after World War II. At 42 years of age in 1953 she won the pentathlon in the western region of the AAU. Both Stella Walsh and Olga Fikotova Connolly competed for other countries in the Olympics, but Connolly, who competed in the discus for Czechoslovakia in 1956, married Hal Connolly, a hammer thrower, and became a star for the United States at the national and international level.

Wilma Rudolph, known as the "darling of the Rome Olympics," was a black American from Clarksville, Tennessee who had been crippled after an illness while a young child. After two years she began to walk again and by the time she reached high school had become an all-state basketball player. Spotted by the Tennessee A & I State University coach, Ed Temple, Rudolph began running in high school and made the 1956 Olympic team. But 1960 was the year when she won three gold medals and in 1961 she received the Sullivan Award. Another outstanding black woman, Wyomia Tyus Simburg, also attended Tennessee A & I and earned one gold and one silver medal in the 1964 Olympic Games. At Mexico City, when she again won the 100-meter sprint, she supported the black athletes' protest. When the Professional International Track Association was formed Tyus Simburg ran in the only event for women, the 60-yard dash. In international track the United States women surprised the Russian women in 1969 by winning the meet 70-67. The following year, Chi Ching from Taiwan, who was training in America, was the outstanding woman athlete, taking three individual AAU titles.

Perhaps the greatest change in women's track and field has been the reinstatement of longer distances, the addition of cross-country events, and the marathon. Having given up the longer distances at the time women's athletic events were added to the Olympic Games, it was over 50 years before women again ran the 1500-meter race. They were assumed to be unable to compete in the longer distances. However, as interest in women's track developed, the athletes demonstrated excellent performances at the longer distances. Training and practice showed that women had remarkable stamina. The American record in the women's 1500-meter run was lowered to 4:02.1 by Jan Merril in 1976. Even the Boston Marathon admitted women by 1972, when a Women's Division was established. In the mid-70's, Sara Mae Berman held the women's record.

Following the War, American men reasserted themselves on the international swimming scene. At the 1948 Olympic Games they made an unprecedented sweep of the swimming events. Challenged briefly by the Australians in 1956, the American men continued to dominate throughout the 1960's and '70's. Highlights included Schollander's four victories in the 1964 Olympic Games, Mark Spitz's unbelievable seven gold medals at Munich in 1972, and the eleven of twelve victories by the U.S. men's team at Montreal in 1976 in the face of a strong East German team.

The United States dominated international swimming meets for women from the early 1950's to 1976. In fact, the young women, sometimes referred to as the United States "water babies," were considered a sport phenomenon. Record after record fell as thirteen- and fourteen-year-old girls became world record holders. Ann Curtis began this trend, although she was an older seventeen when she set her first records. At eighteen she was the first woman to receive the Sullivan Award. Curtis broke the minute barrier in the 100-yard freestyle for women with a time of 59.4 seconds.

In the 1950's the AAU age-group swimming program paid off handsomely for the women. In the 1960's swimmers such as Chris von Saltza, Sharon Stouder, and Debbie Meyer set national and Olympic records. Meyer, who won the Sullivan Award in 1968, was the second woman swimmer to receive this honor. Other young women swimming stars of the period included Donna deVarona, Melissa Belote, Sandra Neilson, and Shirley Babashoff.

Other Amateur Sports

The fifties belonged to the United States figure skaters. Dick Button was the first American man to capture the world title, which he held from 1948 through 1952, and was also the first skater to win the Sullivan Award. Button was followed by two American brothers, Hayes Allan Jenkins, who won the title from 1953 through 1956 and David Jenkins, title holder from 1957 through 1959. Tenley Albright became the first American to win the women's world championship in 1953. She captured it again in 1955 and then another American, Carol Heiss, took the title from 1956 to 1960. In 1966 Peggy Fleming, another American, held the title from 1966 to 1968 and Tim Wood took the men's title in 1969 and 1970. Many skaters such as Peggy Fleming in 1972 and Dorothy Hamill in 1976 joined ice shows as skating stars after winning gold medals in the Olympics.

The game of field hockey reflected the growing interest in women's sport. By 1972 an estimated 65,000 girls and women played in both school play and club hockey. The practice of announcing all-star or nationally selected teams continued, as did the teams touring other countries. In 1963 the eighth International Field Hockey Association's tournament was held in the United States with 22 countries represented. Following the tournament, fourteen teams toured the United States. Constance M.K. Applebee, the staunch promoter of field hockey for United States women, celebrated her 100th birthday in 1973 and was recognized by greetings from all over the world.

Although the United States Women's Lacrosse Association was organized in 1931, its greatest growth was after World War II. International competition began with the United States team touring the British Isles in 1935. As in field hockey, the teams were honorary and the top women players were picked for each position. The outstanding player of the period was Betty Richey of Vassar College, who was selected for 21 teams from 1933 to 1954.

Softball continued to grow as a sport for all. In women's softball the Raybestos Brakettes dominated play for much of the period with Joan Joyce the leading player. In 1975 Joyce joined the International Women's Professional Softball Association, a new venture into women's pro sport.

As prosperity increased following World War II, more and more Americans skiied and enjoyed the many resorts which opened in New England, the northern Midwest, and Western mountain regions. In 1950 the Federation Internationale de Ski held the world championships in the United States for the first time. Four years later the National Ski Association Hall of Fame opened in Ishpeming, Michigan. Although a few champions such as Andrea Mead Lawrence emerged in the early 1950's the United States was not one of the top international skiing contenders. The United States Ski Educational Foundation hired a professional coach to work with the National Alpine team in 1965. By the 1970's skiers such as Barbara Cochran and Billy Kidd competed successfully in international competition.

Boating became a major recreational pursuit for millions. In 1972 approximately thirty million Americans participated in some type of recreational boating activity.[16] Sailboats, canoes, power boats, kayaks, and rowboats filled the lakes, streams and inland waterways. Sailing, with thousands of small regattas, was, perhaps, the most popular aquatic activity, although by actual count, the fishermen undoubtedly outnumbered the sailors. World-class rowers in the United States rowed both for colleges and for private clubs. In international competition usually the eight-oared shells were college crews, while the fours, doubles, and singles were club rowers. However, in 1964, Philadelphia's famed Vesper Boat Club proved the exception by defeating Harvard and California in the Olympic trials.

---

16. *Statistical Abstract of the United States, 1976,* U.S. Department of Commerce, p. 217.

In 1975 a President's Commission on Olympic Sports was appointed to construct a plan for conducting amateur sport in the United States. Composed of athletes, athletic administrators, business people, United States senators and representatives, the Commission completed its task in late 1976. The report proposed to establish a non-profit Central Sports Organization in place of the present United States Olympic Committee with broad powers to reorganize United States Olympic policy on developing, funding, and promoting amateur athletics. Affiliated with this body would be some forty national governing bodies representing a specific sport or group of sports, each of which would elect five members to an annual congress, which would then be the legislative body for amateur athletics in the United States.

Many Americans increasingly turned away from sports which led to competitive events and national championships, and found their enjoyment and satisfaction in informal activities which took them out to woods, lakes, mountains, and back roads. Backpacking, mountain climbing, bicycling, and cross-country skiing grew rapidly after the mid-1960's. Outdoor pursuits were perceived by many to be truly re-creational for the participants.

> The growing popularity of wilderness sports may thus be viewed as part of a wider search for emotional and spiritual contentment, a search which has spawned American interest in and approval of such phenomena as Transcendental Meditation, yoga, Zen, est, and a host of other "True Ways."[17]

FIG. 7.5 Interest in wilderness sport increased dramatically in the 1960's and '70's.

17. Wayne Wilson, "Social Discontent and the Growth of Wilderness Sport in America: 1965-1974," *Quest* 27 (Winter, 1977):56.

Youth Sport

While adults were turning to sport in increasing numbers, they were also organizing youth sport into a complex network of Little League Baseball, Inc., Pop Warner Football, Biddy Basketball, Pee Wee and Midget Hockey, and AAU age-group swimming, wrestling, skiing, and track and field. All these developed and expanded during the 1940's, 1950's, 1960's, and 1970's. By 1976 the state of Michigan alone reported some 93,000 children between the ages of 6 and 16 were participating in some agency-sponsored sport program.[18]

Credit for the superiority of both men's and women's swimming in the United States was given to the AAU age-group swimming, which identified future stars as early as ten years of age. In thousands of swimming clubs throughout the country, children trained in programs comparable to those of adults of the 1920's and 1930's. The programs produced a number of record holders, many of whom were in their teens.

In centers of great hockey interest such as Detroit, Minneapolis, and Boston, hockey games among four- and five-year-olds were televised on local stations in the early 1970's. Indoor hockey arenas built by cities and private entrepreneurs scheduled both professional adult hockey and youth hockey in their programs.

Youth sport was controversial from the beginning. In the early 1950's critics questioned the physical and emotional impact on youth of highly organized sports with state, national, and even world championships. Dr. Creighton Hale, president of Little League, Inc., cited his own research findings which alleged no adverse physical or emotional effects when programs were properly supervised.[19] Reports of problems such as unqualified coaches, excessively long seasons, improper medical advice, inadequate equipment, injuries, and undue pressures to adopt a "winning" philosophy continued to be leveled at Little League, but the programs continued to be popular.[20]

From its inception in the mid-60's the American Youth Soccer Organization attracted thousands of boys and girls. Based on a philosophy of "everyone plays" and intent on keeping the competition without undue pressure, the organization was sufficiently successful to send a team to tour and play in West Germany in 1975.

Although the soccer organization was established for both boys and girls,

18. State of Michigan, Joint Legislative Study on Youth Sports Programs: *Agency Sponsored Sports, Phase I* (November 18, 1976), p. 56.

19. Creighton J. Hale, "What Research Says About Athletics for Pre-High School Age Children," *Journal Of Health, Physical Education and Recreation* 30 (December, 1959): 19.

20. Terry Orlick and Cal Botterill, *Every Kid Can Win* (Chicago: Nelson-Hall, 1975); James A. Michener, *Sports in America* (New York: Random House, 1976), Chapter IV.

and the AAU age-group swimming had always been co-ed, most youth sports excluded girls. In general, the attitudes reflected common American values regarding women and girls in sport. With increased national interest in sports, however, little girls too wished to play. Many city programs did not offer girls' sports on the assumption that they were not appropriate and that little girls were not interested. However, when Carol Mann, the golf pro, held a clinic for girls in Baltimore in 1972, over 150 attended. Since the early 1970's many softball leagues, called Little Leaguerettes or Lassie Leagues, have been successful. Carolyn King, Ypsilanti, Michigan, on the other hand, wanted to play in the national Little League and had to go to court to be admitted. When Little League, Inc. in New Jersey made efforts to exclude girls from the league the court ruled that girls must be allowed to play.[21]

Youth sport was characterized as a trend ". . . which led to changes in the American family structure and in many instances added a new dimension to the socialization of children . . . the degree to which children's sports became organized mirrored an often proclaimed American characteristic of being overly regimented, businesslike and competitive."[22]

Sport for everyone increased at a rapid pace after World War II. From young swimmers interested in world-class competition to members of the new judo club in a midwest town, from the families with a bicycle for everyone, to the joggers for both sport and health—sport was an integral component of society by the mid-1970's. The coming of television seemed to reinforce the sport trend—the more people saw the more they participated. The more they participated the more they became involved in sport for their entertainment.

Dance of the Period

The expansion of dance after World War II paralleled the increased interest in the United States in all forms of physical activity. Modern dance, ballet, and dance in musical comedy expanded and experimented until each form found itself accommodating elements of the others' techniques. Renewed interest in Isadora Duncan's dances and her attempts to codify movement led to the increasing awareness of her seminal contributions to modern dance.

---

21. Jan Felshin, "The Social View," in *The American Woman in Sport* by Ellen W. Gerber, Jan Felshin, Pearl Berlin, and Waneen Wyrick (Reading, Mass.: Addison-Wesley Publishing Company, 1974), pp. 217, 218.

22. Jack W. Berryman, "From the Cradle to the Playing Field: America's Emphasis on Highly Organized Competitive Sports for Pre-adolescent Boys," *Journal of Sport History* 2, no. 2 (Fall, 1975): 131.

After her retirement in 1945, Doris Humphrey became the artistic director for Jose Limon and Weidman continued to work alone. Choreography during the period for the established dancers such as Humphrey, Limon, Weidman, and Graham focused on broad social problems expressed through movement. In the sixties Graham, the most significant United States modern dancer, employed religious themes in works such as the 1962 *Legend of Judith.* Some of the younger dancers experimented with new themes and several of Graham's outstanding students broke away to establish their own companies. Eric Hawkins, Pearl Lang, Paul Taylor, and Merce Cunningham were part of the new group who focused on pure movement of the body, improvisation, and multimedia experiences. Cunningham, sometimes described as avant-garde, choreographed with such unusual ideas that the term contemporary dance was used for his dances rather than modern dance. Alwin Nikolais presented "total theater" with equal emphasis on dancers, properties, music, and costume. Alvin Ailey, a student of Lester Horton, employed components of ethnic dances from the West Indies and Africa.

As the newer dancers searched for movements to express their ideas, they incorporated certain elements of ballet in their works, while, at the same time, choreographers for ballet, in their search for new movements, found that they had adopted some modern dance techniques. George Balanchine, the most influential choreographer in ballet, used abstractions and movements rather than narrative as the basis for some of his works. After existing in temporary theaters, two of the major ballet companies acquired permanent locations in the 1960's and 1970's. The New York City Ballet became part of the Lincoln Center for the Performing Arts in 1964 and in 1971 the American Ballet Theater moved to the John F. Kennedy Center for the Performing Arts in Washington, D.C.

Dance in musicals, in which the dance is an essential component of the narrative, developed into a popular form after World War II. Ballet dancer Jerome Robbins choreographed and directed the musical *West Side Story,* and modern dancer Hanya Holm, *My Fair Lady.* The impact of dance in films, too, was important. Through movies and television the routines of Fred Astaire, Ginger Rogers, Gene Kelly, and many others became familiar to millions of people. Dance throughout the period was an exciting and important performing art in the United States.

Sport and Physical Activity in Educational Institutions

With the exception of a few Western institutions, physical education for men and women was organized in separate departments on most campuses.

The programs and their administration highlighted the major philosophical differences between physical education for women and physical education for men. On the one hand, departments of physical education in women's colleges and departments of physical education for women in the universities had common goals, similar programs, and similar problems. Gerber points out:

> Few departments of physical education for women separated their three functions of teacher preparation, general physical education and extra-curricular physical recreation or sport into different staff responsibilities. The same people who ran the sport programs conducted the teacher education programs and thus indoctrinated the teachers-to-be in the national philosophy.[23]

In keeping with the philosophy developed early in the century most women's departments supported strong instructional programs, majors' programs firmly based in biological and kinesiological sciences, a limited extramural or intercollegiate program, strong intramural or interclass competition, sports days, and club programs. In both women's colleges and coeducational institutions, highlights of a "typical" year might consist of a sports day in the fall, basketball class competition, and a field day in the spring, as well as annual concerts or shows presented by the modern dance club and synchronized swimming club. Women physical education majors provided the leadership for department activities and by graduation were well trained in the proper conduct of programs for physical education of women.

The departments for men, on the other hand, demonstrated no such uniformity of purpose among institutions. In many of the large universities with major intercollegiate athletic programs there was some philosophical conflict between the faculty which primarily taught in the men's physical education teacher preparation program and those whose primary assignment was coaching. In smaller institutions or those with less ambitious athletic programs, the physical education teaching faculty and coaching staff were usually the same people.

Through the mid-1960's, many institutions maintained physical education course requirements for all undergraduate students. By the end of that tumultuous decade, however, a number of colleges and universities had eliminated required courses in a number of disciplines, including physical education, even while professional association meetings and faculty senates continued to debate the relative merits of required versus elective programs.

As the social climate was altered by forces such as the mid-twentieth cen-

23. Ellen W. Gerber, "The Controlled Development of Collegiate Sport for Women, 1923-1936," *Journal of Sport History* 2, no. 1 (Spring, 1975):9.

tury women's movement, economic constraints in the 1970's, and federal legislation, many institutions combined departments of women and men while others reorganized. The Ohio State University combined departments in 1971, the University of Nebraska in 1974, the University of Georgia in 1975, and Purdue University in 1976. In 1973 one example of reorganization was the School of Physical Education at the University of Massachusetts, which changed departments from Physical Education for Women, Physical Education for Men, Leisure Studies, Exercise Science, and Athletics to Athletics, Exercise Science, Sport Studies, and Professional Preparation in Physical Education. Sometimes programs on campuses which had two departments had only one program at the graduate level. Graduate programs tended to focus on areas of specialization such as exercise science, teaching behaviors, aesthetics, and sport studies.

Women's Programs in Colleges and Universities

The Instructional Program

Always the backbone of the women's program, the instructional program responded to the tenor of the times in several ways. In reaction to the war, great interest was expressed in a re-examination of democratic processes and ideals. Emphasis on developing goals and objectives of physical education classes by involving students in decision-making was believed to reflect and teach the democratic process. Students were encouraged to participate in instructional classes of their own design. These procedures created a climate in which the less skilled woman could be comfortable, but, in many instances, the time spent in this group process lessened the actual time for instruction and frustrated the highly skilled woman.

Many programs in women's physical education responded to the trend of relieving women of their rigorous wartime duties and fostering the idea of the American woman in the home. Expressive activities such as modern dance, synchronized swimming, movement education, and gymnastics grew in popularity. Fitness, posture, carriage, and proper daily body mechanics were the post-war modes for optimal personal development. Team games were taught, sometimes for the cooperation thought to be inherent in team play, but they were not as popular as the growing list of other sports in which women participated. As interests expanded, so did programs— tennis, archery, many forms of aquatics, canoeing, ballet, jazz dancing, and skiing could be found in many programs by the late 1950's and early 1960's.

The development of physical education for women in black colleges was somewhat slower than in many white institutions. About the time of World War II most teacher education colleges required physical education. In 1946 Xavier University in New Orleans offered a wide range of activities including field hockey, tennis, archery, handball, speedball, folk dancing, recreational activities, soccer, and track and field.[24]

Club, Intramural, and Extramural Programs

In addition to the instructional program, departments of physical education for women administered a number of other programs. These included clubs, intramural activities, and extramural activities. There were also conferences or associations of college women interested in a specific sport such as skiing or sailing. Students with specialized interests such as modern dance and synchronized swimming frequently were organized as a club with a member of the physical education faculty assigned as an adviser, sometimes as part of her departmental responsibilities. The programs varied but the typical dance or swim club met regularly to practice, choreograph, and produce special performances or concerts once or twice a year. The clubs were usually organized and run by students with strong faculty support.

Intramural activities varied according to the size and type of institution. In coeducational institutions sports might be organized according to housing units such as dormitories or sororities or other planned teams. In smaller institutions and women's colleges interclass rivalry was the important competitive pattern for women. Individual tournaments in sports such as badminton or tennis might be organized on an event basis.

Extramural as a descriptive word became widely used to explain the slowly developing patterns of inter-institution competition. Programs and extramural events followed closely the carefully developed "Desirable Practices in Athletics" published by the National Section on Women's Athletics (formerly the CWA).

Standards for Desirable Practices[25]

The program of athletic activities should:

1. Be based upon the recognition of individual differences (age, physique, interests, ability, experience, health) and the stage of maturity (physiological, emotional, social) of the participants.
2. Be determined by,
   (a) The evaluation of the activity in its present and its future use.
   (b) The classification of individuals in ability from beginner to expert.
   (c) The development from simple to complex activity.
3. Provide opportunity for each player to lead according to her merit and to follow according to her willingness and ability to adapt herself to others and to a common end.

---

24. Ruth E. Spear, "A Study of the Needs and Provisions in Physical Education of Women Students in Selected Negro Colleges," M.S. thesis, Smith College, 1950, p. 19.
25. National Section on Women's Athletics, "Desirable Practices in Athletics" (Washington, D.C.: American Association for Health, Physical Education, and Recreation, 1949), n.p.

The Synchronized Swimming Group

of

The Women's Recreation Association

of

Brooklyn College

presents

"Alice in Waterland"

An aquatic version of Alice's Adventures

DECEMBER 1955

ANNUAL . . .
Spring Dance Concert

BY THE

WAYNE UNIVERSITY
DANCE WORKSHOP

assisted by the

STUDENT DANCE GROUP

Friday, May 23, 1952
8:30 p. m.
UNIVERSITY THEATRE

. . Program of Dances . .

1. Trio of Dances
   France . . . . traditional folk music
   Polka . . . . music by Elizabeth Walberg
   Schottische . . . . music by Elizabeth Walberg
   Student Dance Group

2. Patterns of Celebration . . . . music by Wallingford Riegger
   Dance Workshop
   assisted by John Angry and Charles King

3. Nuptial Prelude . . . . music by Maurice Ravel
   Norma Gillette

4. Silly Stuff . . . . traditional American folk songs
   (recording by Tom Glazer)
   Goodbye, Liza Jane
   What Are You Made Of?
   Taddle Diddle, Dink-Dink
   Dance Workshop

5. Pensée de Jeunesse . . . . . . music by Bela Bartok
   Student Dance Group

6. A Ceremony of Carols . . . . music by Benjamin Britten
   (recording for treble voices and harp by RCA Victor Chorale,
   Robert Shaw conducting)
   Procession   Spring Carol
   Wolcum Yule!   Deo Gracias
   Res Miranda   Recession
   The words of these carols are in Latin and Middle English
   suggesting a medieval source. All of them have some religious
   significance.
   Dance Workshop

INTERMISSION

7. Three Faces of Fear . . . . . . music by Bela Bartok
   Agitation   Apprehension   Panic
   These dances show the cumulative effects of fear first show a pervasive
   tension and restlessness, then a foreboding of impending disaster, and finally
   a reaction to catastrophe.

8. The Old Chisholm Trail . . . traditional American folk song
   (accompanist—Richard Berk)
   Harriet Berg

9. Two Nocturnes . . . . music by Alex North
   Dusk . . . . Norma Carter
   Midnight . . . . Jeanette Malick

10. Feminine Rituals: The Shower
    Dance Workshop
    assisted by Thomas Andrus

11. "Ways to Say Goodnight" . . . . poem by Carl Sandburg
    Student Dance Group

12. Festival Dance . . . . . music by Alexander Tansman
    Dance Workshop
    assisted by Arthur Chebet, Dennis Knight, Nicholas Michalakis

Choreography for most of the group dances is by the performing group, assisted by the Directors. Solo dances were
choreographed by the performers.

FIG. 7.6 Synchronized swimming program, Brooklyn College. University dance concert program, courtesy of Wayne State University.

4. Promote the acquisition of skill by using sound and varied methods.
5. Schedule regular play periods of limited length, at frequent intervals, at a time of day when energy is at a high level.
6. Provide for the selection of members of all teams so that they play against those of approximately the same ability and maturity.
7. Be taught, coached and officiated by qualified women whenever and wherever possible.
8. Provide officials whose decisions are sound, consistent, and impartial.
9. Include the use of official rules authorized by the National Section on Women's Athletics of the American Association for Health, Physical Education and Recreation.
10. Stimulate the participants to play for the enjoyment of playing and not for tangible rewards or because of artificial incentives.
11. Include a variety of sports, both team and individual, and provide opportunity for all girls wishing to participate to be a member of a team in those sports for which teams are organized.
12. Promote informal social events in connection with competition.
13. Secure written parental permission for minors engaging in any extramural competition.
14. Educate girls and women concerning appropriate costume for sports.
15. Limit extramural competition to a small geographic area.
16. Provide safe transportation in bonded carriers.
17. Provide a program of competition for girls separate from that arranged for boys (eliminating such events as double-header games or "curtain raisers") except in those activities in which boys and girls are encouraged to play together on mixed teams.
18. Limit the total length of sports seasons and the maximum number of practice periods and games to be played in a day or a week.

The first "experiment" in extramural tournaments was a highly successful intercollegiate golf championship, initiated by Dorothy Palmer at Ohio State University in 1941. Although there was some protest in the beginning, the tournament was held annually under exemplary conditions and a college woman was named national collegiate champion. Betsy Rawls, later a golf pro, was a winner of this tournament. By 1956 Ohio State felt that it could no longer continue to sponsor the golf event and sought other institutions to sponsor the tournament. By this time the increasing extramural competitions and the desire of college women for competitive opportunities began to concern women physical educators. Three associations created a tripartite committee to deal with the situation. The Division for Girls and Women's Sport, formerly the National Section on Women's Athletics, the National Association for Physical Education of College Women, and the Athletic and Recreation Federation of College Women, an association of students, formed the National Joint Committee on Extramural Sports for College Women in 1957. The committee planned to develop standards for the conduct of extramural events for college women and to sanction tournaments.

Also about this time individual sport enthusiasts began to form regional and national associations to provide organized competitions. By the mid-1960's New England women skiers competed in the Women's Intercollegiate Skiing Conference, women sailors in the New England Women's Intercollegiate Sailing Association, fencers in the Intercollegiate Women's Fencing Association, the squash players joined and competed in the United States Women's Squash Racquets Association, and by the 1970's the rowers had their own association.

The 1960's proved to be a period of rapid change in women's collegiate sport. The philosophy of the DGWS, reflecting the women physical educators of the time, impelled a revision of their "Statement of Policies and Procedures for Competition in Girls and Women's Sports."

> For the college woman and high school girl who seek and need additional challenges in competition and skills, a sound, carefully planned, and well-directed program of extramural sports is recommended.

DGWS further outlined standards for collegiate competition such as conducting the program in the women's physical education department, and being sure that the program did not interfere with the student's academic program. It was also made clear that "Girls and women may not participate as members of boys and men's teams."[26] They again affirmed the philosophy that student athletes should not receive financial aid for superior skill alone. Athletic scholarships were not approved, but financial aid for needy students was acceptable.

By this time a groundswell of interest in women's sport was forming. Also in 1963 the DGWS, in cooperation with the United States Olympic Development Committee, sponsored the first of five institutes to promote Olympic sports. For the first time in almost fifty years the Olympic movement was directly promoted by women physical educators. After fifty years of promoting a sport for every girl rather than high-level sport for a few, many women were not prepared to coach students or teams at expert levels. The institutes planned to work with selected teachers from every state who, in turn, would return to their states and hold additional clinics to spread Olympic sports and to improve girls' sport performance in general.

The structure of the National Joint Committee on Extramural Sports for College Women proved unwieldy and the administrative procedures difficult. After eight years, in 1965, the associations which started the NJCESCW agreed to disband the committee and to have DGWS assume the

---

26. Division for Girls and Women's Sports, "Statement of Policies for Competition in Girls and Women's Sports," *Journal of Health, Physical Education, and Recreation* 34 (September, 1963): 31-32.

DGWS—USODC Institutes in Women's Olympic Sports

Institute	Year	Sports Included
First	1963	Gymnastics, track and field
Second	1965	Gymnastics, track and field Kayaking, fencing, diving
Third	1966	Skiing, figure skating
Fourth	1966	Basketball, volleyball
Fifth	1969	Gymnastics, track and field, Basketball

control of women's intercollegiate athletics. The women's movement of the mid-sixties, to the delight of some and consternation of others, chose sport as one of the suitable arenas for equal rights struggles. The remainder of the decade of the sixties and the early seventies was fast-moving, full of radical changes for women.

In response to a number of pressures, including inquiries from the National Collegiate Athletic Association, the Board of Directors of the American Association of Health, Physical Education, and Recreation, under whose auspices DGWS operated, announced national championships for college women beginning in 1967. Consequently, the DGWS formed a Commission on Intercollegiate Athletics for Women in 1967 for the purpose of proposing appropriate intercollegiate athletic programs for women, of sponsoring national championships, and of organizing women's inter- collegiate competition under one structure. Still further reorganization was found necessary and, in 1971, the Commission was terminated and the Association for Intercollegiate Athletics for Women (AIAW) was estab- lished with Carole Oglesby as the first president.

The explosion in women's and girls' athletics was given further impetus by an amendment to the Civil Rights Act of 1964, Title IX of the Educa- tional Amendments of 1972, applicable to institutions receiving any federal funds:

> No person in the United States shall on the basis of sex be excluded from participation in, be denied the benefits of, or be subjected to discrimination under any educational program or activity receiving Federal financial assist- ance. . ."[27]

In a release on June 3, 1975, Secretary of Health, Education, and Welfare Weinberger declared that the law affected the nation's 16,000 public school

---

27. U.S. Department of Health, Education, and Welfare, *HEW Fact Sheet*, June, 1975, p.1.

Association of Intercollegiate Athletics for Women
Championships 1972/73-1975/76

	1972-73	1973-74	1974-75	1975-76
Badminton	Pasadena City College	California State U. Long Beach	Arizona State University	Arizona State University
Basketball	Immaculata College	Immaculata College	Delta State University	Delta State University
Golf	U. of North Carolina/Greensboro		Arizona State University	Furman University
Gymnastics	University of Massachusetts	Southern Illinois University	Southern Illinois University	Clarion State University
Swimming and Diving	Arizona State University	Arizona State University	University of Miami	University of Miami
Track and Field	Hayward Texas Woman's Univ.	Prairie View A & M University	University of Cal.-Los Angeles	Prairie View A & M University
Volleyball	California State U.-Long Beach	California State U.-Long Beach	University of Cal.-Los Angeles	University of Cal.-Los Angeles
Cross Country				Iowa State University
Field Hockey				West Chester State College

Junior Colleges/Community Colleges

	1972-73	1973-74	1974-75	1975-76
Basketball	Mississippi Gulf Coast Jr. College	Anderson College S. Carolina	Anderson College S. Carolina	Anderson College S. Carolina
Volleyball		Eastern Arizona College	Ricks College Idaho	Mesa Community Arizona
Softball				Golden West College Cal.
Tennis				Indian River Com. College, Florida

Small College

	1972-73	1973-74	1974-75	1975-76
Basketball			Phillips Univer. Okla.	Berry College Georgia
Volleyball				Texas Lutheran College

systems and nearly 2,700 post-secondary institutions. The effective date of the regulation was July 1, 1975 with elementary schools allowed one year to comply with the regulations, high schools two years, and institutions of higher learning three years. Covering a wide range of topics such as admissions and treatment of students, employment, and services to students and employees, the law included several sections which dealt specifically with physical education and athletics.

Section 86.33 Comparable facilities.

A recipient may provide separate toilet, locker room, and shower facilities on the basis of sex, but such facilities provided for students of one sex shall be comparable to such facilities provided for students of the other sex.

Section 86.34 Access to course offerings.

A recipient shall not provide any course or otherwise carry out any of its education program or activity separately on the basis of sex, or require or refuse participation therein by any of its students on such basis, including health, physical education, industrial, business, vocational, technical, home economics, music, and adult education courses.

(a) With respect to classes and activities in physical education at the elementary school level, the recipient shall comply fully with this section as expeditiously as possible but in no event later than one year from the effective date of this regulation. With respect to physical education classes and activities at the secondary and post-secondary levels, the recipient shall comply fully with this section as expeditiously as possible but in no event later than three years from the effective date of this regulation.

(b) This section does not prohibit grouping of students in physical education classes and activities by ability as assessed by objective standards of individual performance developed and applied without regard to sex.

(c) This section does not prohibit separation of students by sex within physical education classes or activities during participation in wrestling, boxing, rugby, ice hockey, football, basketball and other sports the purpose or major activity of which involves bodily contact.

(d) Where use of a single standard of measuring skill or progress in a physical education class has an adverse effect on members of one sex, the recipient shall use appropriate standards which do not have such effect.

Section 86.37 Financial assistance.

(a) *General.* Except as provided in paragraphs (b), (c) and (d) of this section, in providing financial assistance to any of its students, a recipient shall not: (1) On the basis of sex, provide different amount or types of such assistance, limit eligibility for such assistance which is of any particular type or source, apply different criteria, or otherwise discriminate; . . .

Section 86.41 Athletics.

(a) *General.* No person shall, on the basis of sex, be excluded from participation in, be denied the benefits of, be treated differently from another person or otherwise be discriminated against in any interscholastic, intercollegiate, club or intramural athletics offered by recipient, and no recipient shall provide any such athletics separately on such basis.

(b) *Separate teams.* Notwithstanding the requirements of paragraph (a) of this section, a recipient may operate or sponsor separate teams for members of each sex where selection for such teams is based upon competitive skill or the activity involved is a contact sport. However, where a recipient operates or sponsors a team in a particular sport for members of one sex but operates or sponsors no such team for members of the other sex, and athletic opportunities for members of that sex have previously been limited, members of the excluded sex must be allowed to try-out for the team offered unless the sport involved is a contact sport. For the purpose of this part, contact sports include boxing, wrestling, rugby, ice hockey, football, basketball and other sports the purpose of major activity of which involves bodily contact.

(c) *Equal opportunity.* A recipient which operates or sponsors interscholastic, intercollegiate, club or intramural athletics shall provide equal athletic opportunity for members of both sexes. In determining whether equal opportunities are available the Director will consider, among other factors:

(i) Whether the selection of sports and levels of competition effectively accommodate the interests and abilities of members of both sexes;
(ii) The provision of equipment and supplies;
(iii) Scheduling of games and practice time;
(iv) Travel and per diem allowance;
(v) Opportunity to receive coaching and academic tutoring;
(vi) Assignment and compensation of coaches and tutors;
(vii) Provision of locker rooms, practice and competitive facilities;
(viii) Provision of medical and training facilities and services;
(ix) Provision of housing and dining facilities and services;
(x) Publicity.

Unequal aggregate expenditures for members of each sex or unequal expenditures for male and female teams if a recipient operates or sponsors separate teams will not constitute noncompliance with this section, but the Director may consider the failure to provide necessary funds for teams for one sex in assessing equality of opportunity for members of each sex.[28]

As part of the procedures, each institution underwent a self-study to evaluate the existing situations and developed plans for compliance with the law. Local, regional, and national publicity and debates raged in the months following the signing of the law. Although the legislation covered a wide range of topics, the debate and public interest centered on athletics. Nationally recognized football coaches met with the president of the United States in efforts to maintain their control over intercollegiate athletics. Leading newspapers and magazines featured discussions both for and against the proposed changes. Some immediate improvements in women's programs resulted, partly related to Title IX and partly related to the increased interest in women in sport.

The case of Kellmayer vs. the NEA, AAHPER, DGWS, AIAW, NAPECW, and the Florida Association for Physical Education of College Women, the Southern Association for Physical Education of College Women, and the Florida Commission of Intercollegiate Athletics for Women in 1971, represented a group of students from Marymount College in Florida who had been awarded "tennis" scholarships and were denied the right to participate in an AIAW tournament. On the advice of attorneys the AIAW statement regarding financial aid based on women's athletic ability was deleted from their regulations. Thus, the possibilities of women to receive "athletic scholarships" increased, at first modestly, and then

---

28. *Federal Register*, 40, no. 108 (June 4, 1975): 24141-24143.

dramatically. By 1974, Arizona State University, which had awarded 20 athletic scholarships for women the previous year, increased the number to 70. Budgets for women's athletics jumped at the University of Georgia from $15,000 to $80,000 and at the University of California at Los Angeles from $60,000 to $180,000. While most women's budgets did not equal that of the men's, many were much greater in the mid-1970's than ever before, which in turn meant better programs.

Men's Programs in Colleges and Universities

The Instructional Program

Throughout the forties, fifties and early sixties traditional team and individual sports predominated in programs for men. Touch football, volleyball, basketball, softball, swimming, tennis, golf, badminton, and handball were taught in most institutions. In the East, soccer, lacrosse, and fencing were frequently offered, and by 1960 were included in many other universities across the country.

The variety of courses broadened in the late sixties and early seventies as students demonstrated a marked interest in recreational sport such as backpacking, scuba diving, mountain climbing, orienteering, bicycling, and skiing. Other popular activities included the oriental martial arts, personal defense, and aerobic conditioning. Professional preparation programs generally contained a strong biological science base and an emphasis on secondary school physical education and coaching.

The Intramural and Sport Club Programs

As the major college intercollegiate programs prospered during the forties, fifties, and sixties, they often provided the funds to construct recreational facilities and to underwrite a wide range of intramural and competitive athletics. On other campuses student activity fees provided funds for the construction of intramural and recreation buildings. By the 1970's many programs in large universities were removed from departments of physical education and athletics and placed under the control of Offices of Student Services.[29] Activities offered to the students ranged from the traditional football, basketball, baseball, and track to handball, squash, coed team sports, frisbee, and bowling.

The late 1950's and early '60's brought a resurgence of the sports club movement that had existed in the pre-intercollegiate days of the mid-nineteenth century. The enormous increase in student population of this period played some part in the growth of sports clubs. Not only were there

29. Harry R. Ostrander, "Financing Intramural Programs," in *Intramural Administration: Theory and Practice,* ed. James A. Peterson (Englewood Cliffs, N.J.: Prentice-Hall, Inc., 1976), pp. 261, 262.

FIG. 7.7   Intramural coed activities. Courtesy, Department of Athletics, University of Massachusetts.

thousands of students interested in activities, but they were sufficiently affluent to support a club sport. Further, the intramural directors did not add the new activities, nor did the athletic directors always add new varsity teams to accommodate some of the club interests. Club activities ranged from formal teams in soccer, rowing, lacrosse, skiing, volleyball or other sports not included in the varsity program, to sailing, backpacking, and rock climbing.

Competitive activities such as skiing, sailing, soccer, and lacrosse often included regularly scheduled contests with clubs from other institutions. The non-competitive pursuits usually involved only the club members themselves, and their popularity reflected the contemporary societal interest in individual recreational sport.

Intercollegiate Sport

Following the war, the nation's colleges and universities experienced a period of unprecedented growth as thousands of servicemen took advantage of the educational benefits of the G.I. Bill of Rights. The pre-war enrollment high for all institutions of higher education in the United States was 1,494,203 in 1939-40.[30] By 1946 that figure was 2,078,095 and by 1950 had reached 2,659,021.[31] With this influx, hundreds of small colleges that had

---

30. U.S. Office of Education, *Biennial Survey of Education in the United States, 1944-46,* p. 8.

31. U.S. Office of Education, *Annual Report of the Federal Security Agency, 1947,* p. 205; Garland G. Parker, *The Enrollment Explosion* (New York: School & Society Books, 1971), p. 40.

FIG. 7.8   Expanded athletic facilities at the University of Michigan. Courtesy of University of Michigan.

found it difficult or impossible to field men's varsity athletic teams from 1942 through 1945 enjoyed restored intercollegiate programs and a new group of talented athletes. "Big-time" programs in colleges and universities shared in student growth and in the enthusiasm of Americans to put the war behind them with sport entertainment. The tradition of college football and basketball, well established during the first half of the century, became a major facet of the entertainment industry beginning in the late forties. In the 1946 football season four teams—Michigan, Notre Dame, Ohio State, and UCLA—played to over 500,000 spectators each. That same year, seventeen post-season bowl games drew 478,000 fans and $1,765,000. Two years later, front-ranked Michigan regularly played to 80,000 at its home games. In 1949, 102,000 were on hand for the Army-Navy game, and two teams in the midst of winning streaks—Oklahoma and Notre Dame—captured national interest and thousands of spectators. By 1955, the Big Ten Conference drew a total of 3,121,649 to its football games and in 1976, top-ranked Michigan averaged over 100,000 spectators at each of seven home games.

Football alone made major college sport a big business. However, following the post-war years, college basketball also emerged as an important business enterprise. In the East, the major attractions were the Madison Square Garden college doubleheaders and tournaments. Teams from all over the country coveted the chance to play in the Garden against the top-ranked New York City teams—City College of New York, New York University, Long Island University, St. John's University, Fordham

University, and Seton Hall University. In 1947, 655,676 spectators saw the Garden's college program, which included twenty-eight doubleheaders and post-season National Invitation Tournament (NIT) games.

Outstanding basketball was played throughout the country by teams such as University of Kentucky, Bradley University, Ohio State University, University of Utah, and Stanford University. Bill Russell of the University of San Francisco in 1955 and '56 and 7 foot Wilt Chamberlain of Kansas in the late fifties drew more fans and by the early 1960's the NCAA Championship tournament finals were a prime-time television attraction. The success of Coach John Wooden's UCLA teams from 1964 through 1975 and the play of stars such as Cassie Russell (Michigan), Lew Alcindor and Bill Walton (UCLA), Pete Maravich (Louisiana State), Jerry Lucas and John Havlicek (Ohio State), and Oscar Robertson (Cincinnati), built an unprecedented television audience. Large universities built new basketball arenas in the sixties and seventies to accommodate ten to twenty thousand spectators. Basketball had joined football as a major source of financial support for the athletic budgets of many large institutions.

The spectacular growth in the popularity of college athletics was not without problems. The pressure to win in order to sell tickets to meet expenses necessary to recruit athletes, which were required in order to win, produced a climate conducive to cheating, scandal, and hypocrisy. In the late forties the NCAA found it necessary to assume an enforcement role because of repeated reports of recruiting violations among its members. In July of 1946 a "Conference on Conferences" was held for the purpose of determining "Principles for the Conduct of Intercollegiate Athletics." In 1948 the NCAA adopted as a "sanity code," five points from this conference: (1) Principle of Amateurism, (2) Principle of Institutional Control and Responsibility, (3) Principle of Sound Academic Standards, (4) Principle Governing Financial Aid to Athletes, and (5) Principles Governing Recruiting.[32] In 1950, seven schools were cited for non-compliance with the code, but a motion to suspend the institutions failed to receive a two-thirds endorsement. In 1952, new legislation was adopted dealing with academic standards, financial aid, ethical conduct, and out-of-season practice in football and basketball.

Throughout the fifties the NCAA strengthened its enforcement powers and penalized offending institutions. Continuing reports of wrong-doing through the sixties, however, prompted the organization to expand its enforcement arm. By 1976, eleven full-time investigators were on the staff with the responsibility of following up on every serious charge of illegal pro-

---

32. U.S.A. 1776-1976, NCAA 1906-1976 (Shawnee Mission, Kansas: National Collegiate Athletic Association, 1976), p. 17.

cedure by member institutions.[33] Penalties for violations ranged from a warning of suspension from post-season bowl games, championships, and television appearances to limiting the number of allowable grants-in-aid in the sport at issue, to outright dismissal from the NCAA.

The most serious crisis in college sport was one which threatened its very credibility, one which involved gambling and basketball. Because of the practice of giving "point spreads" to equalize the betting chance, certain gamblers approached individual players on favored teams to persuade them to "shave" points and keep the winning margin within the predicted range. The first reported instance of such tampering occurred in 1945 when rumors of a fixed game between Brooklyn College and the University of Akron caused a significant fluctuation in the point spread and cancellation of the game. All five Brooklyn players admitted taking bribes to throw the contest.[34]

A major scandal occurred in 1951 when more than thirty players from seven schools—City College of New York, Long Island University, Manhattan College, New York University, University of Kentucky, Bradley University, and University of Toledo—were found by the New York District Attorney to have conspired to fix game scores during the 1949 and 1950 seasons. The coaches of the indicted colleges claimed no knowledge of the schemes, which affected both the schools and the players. The National Basketball Association issued a lifetime ban on all of the implicated players whether or not they had been found guilty in the courts. The University of Kentucky was suspended for one year by both the NCAA and the Southeastern Conference and sat out an entire season. Long Island University, where the highly respected coach Clair Bee accepted blame for not knowing about the fixing, and for failing to instill his standards in his players, dropped intercollegiate basketball for six years. CCNY de-emphasized the sport and moved out of the "big time." Manhattan, New York University, Bradley and Toledo carried on their programs through the troubled years. Many colleges, sensing a tie between Madison Square Garden and the gamblers, ruled the Garden off limits for their basketball teams, and the golden age of New York doubleheaders was over. Basketball historian Neil Isaacs disputed the connection between New York City and gamblers by pointing out that traditionally the betting lines had been established in cities such as St. Louis, Cincinnati, Kansas City, Minneapolis, and more recently, Las Vegas.[35] The fact that "point shaving" scandals occurred again in 1961

33. Larry Van Dyne, "College Sports Enforcement Squad," *The Chronicle of Higher Education* 7 March 1977, pp. 1, 14.

34. Neil D. Isaacs, *All the Moves* (Philadelphia: J.B. Lippincott Company, 1975), p. 104.

35. Neil D. Isaacs, *All the Moves* (Philadelphia: J.B. Lippincott Company, 1975), p. 106.

and 1965 involving thirty-nine players and twenty-three schools was evidence that New York City and the Garden were not the sole causes of basketball fixing.

As both college basketball and football moved into the 1970's, cries of overemphasis, winning-at-all-costs, recruitment abuses, transcript fixing, and illegal financial support continued to surface. Coaches such as Penn State's Joe Paterno and Arkansas' Frank Broyles asserted that recruiting violations in college football were at an all-time high.[36] Institutions such as Minnesota and California State University, Long Beach, were placed on probation after the coaches, under whom the offenses in the basketball programs had occurred, had left for other positions. The latter situation prompted many, including college presidents, to call for punishment of guilty coaches rather than singling out the institution or players.

While "big-time" college football and basketball continued to dominate the news throughout the period, other sports also drew the attention of the public. The NCAA initiated National Championship Tournaments in baseball (1947), ice hockey (1948), and skiing (1954). In addition, a College Division was established in 1956 for those institutions not wishing to pursue major programs in football and basketball. In 1973, the NCAA approved a major reorganization into three divisions: Division I (major institutions), Division II, and Division III, with separate national championships in many sports. The smaller National Association for Intercollegiate Athletics (NAIA), founded in 1938 to conduct athletics in small colleges, increased to about 500 member institutions in 1973.

Baseball, through most of the period in many sections of the country, labored as a spring sport with little attention given to it by the public or the professional leagues. Beginning in the 1960's, however, the colleges became a valuable source of experienced players. As developmental costs for the minor league system continued to rise through the mid-70's there was widespread speculation that college baseball, like basketball and football, would become the primary "feeder" to the major leagues.

Ice hockey, in areas with strong traditions in that sport, also became a self-supporting activity through sell-out crowds in modern ice arenas. College track and field and swimming programs continued to provide the basic vehicles for training world-class athletes for international competition. In 1967, the United States Collegiate Sports Council was formed by the NCAA, NAIA, AAHPER, and the National Junior College Athletic Association to select representative teams of men and women from the United States for participation in the World University Games.

The major problem facing intercollegiate sport during the 1970's was

---

36. Richard Starnes, "An Unprecedented Economic and Ethical Crisis Grips Big-Time Intercollegiate Sports," *The Chronicle of Higher Education* 24 September 1973, pp. 1, 6.

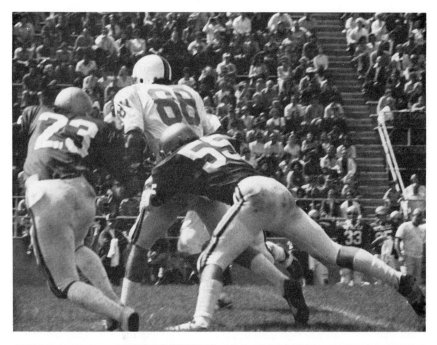

FIG. 7.9   Contemporary intercollegiate sports.

financial. As the economy declined during the recession of 1974-75, the cost of goods and services rose and the nation's colleges and universities found operating funds diminished. Some schools dropped football, while others found themselves raising ticket prices, eliminating other sports, and limiting grants-in-aid, recruitment budgets, and travel expenses. Efforts were made to curtail costs on a national level through NCAA-enforced limits on travel squad size, on-campus visits by recruits, visits by coaches to recruits, and total grants-in-aid. Such efforts, favored by the weaker Division I and II schools, were vigorously opposed by the stronger schools, who threatened to leave the NCAA and form a new association. By 1976, college sport was extremely popular, but except for those few institutions who conducted profit-making "big-time" programs, it was becoming an increasingly costly luxury.

Secondary and Elementary School Programs

The Instructional Program

Physical education for junior and senior high school boys and girls continued with a strong emphasis on games, sports, and dance. The boys' program through the 1950's generally emphasized the major team sports, although those schools with proper facilities often included such individual activities as tennis, golf, and swimming. Girls' programs tended to focus on the team sports of field hockey, basketball, volleyball, and softball, and other sports such as badminton, tennis and golf, and modern dance. This pattern was somewhat affected in the mid-1950's when the Kraus-Weber test results indicated that American children were less fit than European children. Public and official concern resulted in a temporary emphasis on physical fitness-producing activities in school programs.

In the mid-1960's there was increased interest in activities which sought to equip boys and girls with recreational sport skills, such as tennis and golf, which could be pursued throughout life. In the early 1970's these were expanded in a few schools to include skiing, backpacking, canoeing, and other outdoor recreational pursuits. Further, under the influence of Title IX guidelines, coeducational participation became increasingly prevalent in many activities.

Elementary school physical education, largely confined to the major cities through the 1950's, became a "new frontier" in the sixties as fast-growing suburban communities as well as small to medium cities developed broader curriculums. The American Association for Health, Physical Education and Recreation encouraged the movement through publications, workshops, and numerous sessions at national, district, and state conventions.

FIG. 7.10   Physical education activities in an elementary school.

Largely through the efforts of women physical educators who had studied in England, the English approach to "movement education" was suggested as a model for American elementary schools. The methodology stressed learning and understanding the fundamentals of body movement through problem-solving activities related to space, time, and flow of movement. These qualities of movement were believed to enhance body awareness. Usually found in elementary programs, movement education also had some influence in secondary and college courses. In spite of the increasing use of movement education, the traditional methods of teaching were employed by most teachers.

Recent research in the perceptual-motor development of children has brought renewed attention to fundamental movements and the importance of orderly skill acquisition. Psychiatrists, motor-learning specialists, and reading specialists suggested that the child's motor development was central to self-perception, motor behavior, and some aspects of social behavior. An increasing number of public schools have provided special training in this area.

Interscholastic sports

Under Title IX the high schools were allowed two years to comply with the law. The high schools generally reflected the philosophy of the colleges, with one major difference—there was only one governing body for inter-scholastic athletics for both boys and girls. However, there was, as in the colleges, a major change in the philosophy of many high school physical education teachers regarding interschool athletics for girls. The increased participation of girls at the high school level was more dramatic than at the college level. Statistics from the 1974 Sports Participation Survey of the National Federation of State High School Associations revealed:

> The increase in girls participating has been nothing less than phenomenal. From 1971 to 1973 it grew by over 530,000 and from 1973 to 1975 by over 480,000. Thus, there was an increase of over 1,000,000 from 1971 to 1975 in the number of girl participants. In 1973 there were 26 activities listed for girls. Participation increased in 14 of those categories and there were three new activities listed for the 1974-75 school year.[37]

In spite of the significant increase, financial support remained a problem. In 1972 New Brunswick, New Jersey, budgeted $3,700 for boys' track and $1,000 for the girls' track team. At a small school in Pennsylvania $460 of a $19,800 sport budget was allocated to the girls' program.[38] On the other hand, Iowa had a well-developed program with over ten state championships in sports. Thus, as with other subjects and activities in United States high schools, the quality and quantity differed from state to state, city to city, and town to town. In the early part of this period, many segregated high schools attended by blacks lacked gymnasiums, especially if the school had a small population. In a 1950 study of over 400 black college freshmen in three different geographical areas, Spear found:

> For the most part, students from schools of under 1000 reported a lack and/or inadequacy of facilities and outdoor areas in comparison with those of over 1000. . . . Gymnasiums, locker rooms, and shower facilities were lacking in a majority of the segregated schools represented, and while some schools which lacked gymnasiums made other arrangements for indoor physical education, a large number did not.
>
> . . . Girls from segregated schools were, in large part (60.5 per cent), dissatisfied with physical education activities available in preparatory schools. Tennis and swimming were the most desired activities and basketball, softball, and volleyball the most popular available sports.[39]

37. Memorandum, C.B. Fagan to College and University Athletic Directors, Commissioners of Conferences, and League Directors, National Federation of State High School Associations, November 13, 1974, p 2.

38. Bill Gilbert and Nancy Williamson, "Sport is Unfair to Women," *Sports Illustrated* 38, no. 21 (May 28, 1973): 90-91.

39. Ruth E. Spear, "A Study of the Needs and Provisions in Physical Education of Women Students in Selected Negro Colleges," M.S. thesis, Smith College, 1950, pp. 137-139.

Iowa's girls' basketball was both a phenomenon and a source of state pride. As late as March, 1977 *Time* magazine reported:

> Tournament week is an official holiday for many schools, and the players, their chaperones and supporters checked into hotel rooms that had been booked for a year. They commandeered entire floors, lugging hair curlers, stereo tape decks and stuffed mascots. One coach brought along a toaster to ensure breakfast for his flock. Between forays to Frankel's clothing store to gawk at the array of trophies—including the 3-ft.-high bronze totem for the winning team—the girls decorated hallways with flowers and telegrams sent by fans back home.[40]

However, it should be noted that the Iowa girls played "two-court" basketball, with the players limited to action in half the court. The DGWS, in recognition of the increasing stamina of women and the changing times, had changed its rules in 1971 to the five-player, full-court game.

The boys' programs continued to grow in popularity throughout the period. By 1976 the National Federation of State High School Associations reported over four million boys from all fifty states competing on interscholastic teams in thirty-one sports. Over one million competed in football and almost 700,000 in basketball but other activities ranged from pentathlon (75) to outdoor track and field (644,813).[41]

The greatest controversy during the 1940's and 1950's raged over elementary and junior high school athletics. For the most part, few interscholastic programs were maintained for children under the sixth grade in the public schools. Many school systems declined to allow contact sports below the seventh grade and others restricted all junior high school athletic programs to intramural status.

The Civil Rights Movement and Educational Sport

The Brown vs. Topeka decision of the U.S. Supreme Court in 1954 was the first blow in the battle to eliminate "separate but equal" educational programs. The black civil rights movement over the next two decades brought an end to many segregated school systems and high school athletic associations throughout the South. Many small Southern towns found themselves consolidating into one integrated high school and faced the problem of integrating the faculty as well as the student body. In numerous instances charges were made that the white head coaches retained their positions while the black coaches were relegated to assistant roles or dismissed.

In other parts of the country segregation based on housing patterns was

---

40. "Hooping it Up Big in the Cornbelt," *Time* 109 (March 28, 1977): 85.

41. "1976 Sports Participation Survey," The National Federation of State High School Associations, n.p.

more difficult to overcome. By the mid-1970's, the city school systems were becoming increasingly black while the suburban areas remained predominantly white. Racial conflicts among spectators at interscholastic sport contests involving the two types of schools were not uncommon. At the collegiate level the 1950's brought larger numbers of black student athletes to predominantly white campuses in most parts of the country. It was not until the 1970's, however, that numbers of blacks were recruited by large southern universities.

The late 1960's brought to the attention of the public many of the frustrations of the black student athlete on the nation's campuses. Charges of inadequate academic counseling were leveled by many students at those coaches who advised black students into a program of "easy" courses which did not lead to degrees. In support of this accusation many critics pointed to the 1966 NCAA championship basketball team in which not one of the five black starting players graduated. Other protests were lodged against practices of position-stacking, the intrusion of coaches into athletes' dating practices, inadequate medical attention for black athletes, the absence of black coaches and athletic directors, and discrimination in part-time and summer employment. Protests included walkouts and strikes by black student athletes at numerous institutions. By 1976 many colleges and universities had black head and assistant coaches, and black quarterbacks and linebackers were no longer novelties on football teams. The 1976 football rosters of the Southeastern Conference were roughly one-third black compared to none a decade earlier.

The increasing opportunities for black student athletes in predominantly white institutions did, however, have an adverse effect on the small black colleges. Athletic powers such as Grambling State University, Southern University, Jackson State University, Texas Southern University, and Kentucky State University suddenly found themselves competing with the larger institutions for the black high school athlete. The black colleges, during the 1960's and the early 1970's, provided the professional football leagues with talent far out of proportion to their size. In 1976 approximately 15 percent of the National Football League's players came from black colleges. The recruiting competition from the larger, more prestigious universities, however, began to result in fewer southern black high school stars enrolling in the black schools.[42] To counteract this trend and to attract a national black following, a few institutions such as Grambling State University began scheduling games on neutral sites in major cities around the country. In spite of the stronger competition, however, Grambling's

---

42. Larry Van Dyne, "The South's Black Colleges Lose a Football Monopoly," *The Chronicle of Higher Education* 15 November 1976, p. 1.

famous head football coach and athletic director, Eddie Robinson, was willing to view the situation from a larger perspective:

> In places like Runston [a nearby town], it used to be that blacks went to their games and whites to theirs . . . now the kids are mixed on the teams and everybody goes together.

> I look at the crowd going in together, sitting together, eating hot dogs together. It's football and athletics that's really got them together. If that means I maybe lose a boy, is that more important than the schools being together—and that black kids may come out with a better degree?[43]

FIG. 7.11   Coach Eddie Robinson brings Grambling State University football to Houston's Astrodome. Courtesy of Grambling State University.

The Study of Sport and Physical Activity

The organization of a Department of Sport Studies at the University of Massachusetts in 1973 represented a first fruition of a concept that had been

---

43. Larry Van Dyne, "The South's Black Colleges Lose a Football Monopoly," *The Chronicle of Higher Education* 15 November 1976, p. 8.

slowly evolving for forty years. From the early physical fitness research efforts of the 1930's and '40's to the attitudinal and behavioral studies of the fifties, the serious investigations of the many dimensions of sport and physical activity had steadily progressed. Through their writings and their courses in physical education curriculums, scholars such as Delbert Oberteuffer, Eleanor Metheny, and many others exposed two generations of students to the theoretical foundations of sport and physical activity.

In 1965, two sport sociologists at the University of Wisconsin, Gerald Kenyon and John Loy, called for American scholars to join them as they moved "toward a sociology of sport."[44] Shortly thereafter Bruce Ogilvie and Thomas Tutko popularized the work of sport psychologists.

Many working in these fields were physical educators with some training and more than a little interest in the questions raised through such study. A few were scholars trained exclusively in psychology, history, philosophy, or sociology with an interest in sport. Within a few years an examination of university catalogues revealed an array of courses in each of these subdisciplines. Primarily housed in departments of physical education, these courses began to be grouped together to form majors or specializations, generally at the graduate level. Such specialization developed first at the doctoral level and then moved downward, perhaps as these new degree holders assumed college teaching positions. In 1970, the State University of New York, College at Brockport reported the development of an undergraduate major in sport science. The new program was described as ". . . the study of man as he develops and participates in the social institutions that supply his varied needs and wants for competitive physio- cognitive behavior."[45] The University of Massachusetts introduced its program in sport studies three years later. Many universities followed with diversified major programs in physical education at the undergraduate and graduate levels with specializations such as sport psychology, sociology, history, and philosophy, sport management, exercise physiology, biomechanics, and athletic training.

Professional Associations

The growing interest in the academic study of sport brought scholars together into new associations. In the early 1960's those interested in sociological concerns joined with already productive European sociologists in the Committee for Sociology of Sport of the International Council of

44. Gerald Kenyon and John Loy, "Toward A Sociology of Sport," *Journal of Health, Physical Education and Recreation* 36 (May 1965): 24-25, 68-69.

45. Clark V. Whited, "Sport Science, The Modern Disciplinary Concept of Physical Education," *Proceedings, 74th Annual Meeting,* National College Physical Education Association for Men (December 27-30, 1970): 227.

Sport and Physical Education, within UNESCO. In 1966 the North American Society for the Psychology of Sport and Physical Activity was formed. Six years later the Philosophic Society for the Study of Sport was founded and in 1973 the North American Society for Sport History held its first annual convention on the campus of The Ohio State University. Finally the Association for the Anthropological Study of Play was organized in 1974-75. Each of these associations provided scholars with outlets for the dissemination of their research and writing. Further, they gave visibility to the field of study and a sense of common effort to their members.

The National Association for Physical Education of College Women (NAPECW) and the National College Physical Education Association for Men (NCPEAM) joined forces in 1963 to publish *Quest,* a semi-annual monograph of scholarly papers. From the beginning, *Quest* encouraged high-quality manuscripts on a wide variety of subjects, from professional preparation in physical education to sport theory. In addition, the two associations further encouraged scholarly productivity through the presentation of papers at their annual meetings. In 1974 the NCPEAM and NAPECW initiated further combined efforts, among which was the first joint meeting, at Orlando, Florida, in January, 1977.

The American Association for Health, Physical Education and Recreation, until 1937 the APEA, provided physical educators with a broad program and a national voice. Its annual national, district, and state conventions offered programs relevant to current issues. Special task forces and workshops considered subjects such as elementary physical education, drugs and sport, desirable practices in elementary, junior high school, and senior high school athletics, women in sport, and the interpretation of research. Through the *Research Quarterly* and the *Journal of Health, Physical Education and Recreation,* the AAHPER provided professional physical educators with the means to report research into the theoretical foundations of sport and physical activity.

In 1974 AAHPER reorganized into seven associations: American Association for Leisure and Recreation; American School and Community Safety Association; Association for the Advancement of Health Education; Association for Research, Administration, Professional Councils, and Societies; National Association for Girls and Women in Sport; National Association for Sport and Physical Education; and National Dance Association. At that time the name was changed to the American Alliance for Health, Physical Education, and Recreation.

The World of Sport

The third quarter of the twentieth century witnessed sport permeating every aspect of life in the United States. Professional, intercollegiate, and amateur sport continually attracted new spectators. In spite of critics who saw nothing but a "nation of spectators," more and more Americans became active participants in recreational and competitive sport. The development of the federal interstate freeway system in the 1950's encouraged millions to travel and acquaint themselves with the countryside. In 1972 alone more than twenty-five million people engaged in some type of camping activity. By 1976 many national parks, such as California's popular Yosemite Park, were forced to limit access because of overwhelming crowds of visitors. Sales of recreational camping vehicles, trail bikes, and other off-road vehicles such as snowmobiles and water craft soared. Even wilderness areas felt the onslaught as many people discovered backpacking, rock climbing, and cross-country skiing.

The increased interest in tennis brought entire families into clubs, as new indoor tennis facilities mushroomed across the country. In the early 1970's outdoor courts became filled from early morning until late evening. Golf courses in major metropolitan centers experienced logjams of players at each tee on weekends. The Amateur Softball Association of America reported a 57 percent increase in participants from 1970 to 1975.[46] In 1976 Americans spent nearly 146 billion dollars on leisure time activities and equipment. According to one popular news magazine, "This is not only a record for spending on the good life, but far exceeds annual outlays for all home building—or for national defense."[47] Many of the sport activities pursued by Americans required some free time and at least a moderate level of affluence. Time is generally required to travel to recreational sport sites for skiing, hiking, and camping. Money is necessary to purchase club memberships, $50 tennis rackets, $300 golf clubs, $8 greens fees, $40 warm-up suits, and $30-$75 athletic shoes.

Certainly sport participation in the 1970's was seen as a part of the "good life," which has been pursued by Americans in various ways for two hundred years. How else does one explain the phenomenal growth in the numbers of people playing and watching sport? Clearly Americans have elected to spend a great portion of their leisure time and money on these activities. Whether motivated out of simple enjoyment or perceived status, a great many Americans seem to associate sport with "the pursuit of happiness." As long as this perception continues, the future of sport in the United States appears assured.

The major uncertainty is the possible direction it will take. Present trends suggest a continued balance between sport entertainment and sport par-

---

46. "Statistical Abstract of the United States 1976," U.S. Department of Commerce, Bureau of the Census, pp. 217-18.

47. "Americans: Splurging in Big Ways, Cutting Back in Small Ones," *U.S. News and World Report* 82 (April 25, 1977): 27.

ticipation, with the latter experiencing the greatest growth. Technology will presumably continue to play a major role in the development of new sport forms and in the alteration of established activities. Certainly the continuing need to conserve energy-producing resources will affect sport and other leisure pursuits, as it will affect all aspects of life.

Developments of the final quarter of the twentieth century may well determine the form, the role, and the substance of American sport in the twenty-first century.

Summary

The period following World War II was marked by major technological and social changes. The automobile continued to increase in importance as Americans depended on it as their main transportation. Television altered America's lifestyle and was the most important influence on sport in this period. In addition, social unrest demonstrated in the anti-Vietnam War movement, civil rights efforts, and the '60's women's movement created a climate which greatly affected sport, dance, and all forms of physical activity.

Television acquainted millions of people with unfamiliar sports and also showed more and more of the familiar games. The response was an increase in sport participation as well as an increase in the time television stations devoted to sport and sport-related themes. Television revenue financed professional sport and created a demand for sport, while at the same time, producers changed some aspects of sport to meet the requirements of television viewing and programming.

The civil rights movement included desegregating professional sport and efforts to correct injustices in amateur and school and college athletics. While the percentage of black players increased in baseball, football, and basketball, only in the latter were significant gains made in placing blacks in managerial positions.

The women's movement focused attention on sport and by 1976 a few professional sportswomen earned over one hundred thousand dollars in golf and tennis. In the schools and colleges, aided by federal legislation, girls and women competed on interschool and intercollegiate teams in a variety of sports. Universities initiated the serious study of sport as an institutionalized component of society which merited scholarly investigation.

Dance, too, reflected the increased interest of Americans in physical activity. Ballet, modern dance, dance in musicals, and jazz dance expanded. On the campuses, many dance programs moved from departments of physical education for women to departments of dance, the fine arts, or theater departments.

The three decades from 1945 to 1975 were generally affluent years which brought the "good life" within the reach of many Americans. With money to spend on non-essentials and time to pursue leisure time interests, people turned to sport and physical activities in greater and greater numbers. While professional and college sport programs set new attendance records, the average sport-minded families and persons forced expansion of parks, courts, diamonds, hiking trails, bicycle paths, and ski slopes. Sport and physical activity had, indeed, become pervasive forces in American society.

Questions for Discussion

1. Is the advent of television more or less important to sport today than the telegraph was a century ago?
2. Discuss the 19th and 20th century attitudes toward professionals and amateurs playing baseball.
3. Discuss the possible reasons for the increasing participation in sport in the 1970's.
4. To what degree has legislation affected the increase of women and minorities in all levels of sport? In what ways?
5. Compare the problems of intercollegiate athletics today with those cited in the 1929 Carnegie Foundation Report.
6. Some critics suggest that studying sport takes the "fun" out of it and others have called it the "toy department of life," unworthy of serious study. How would you answer these critics?
7. What is the most satisfying aesthetic experience you have had in dance, as a spectator or as a performer? What is the most satisfying sport experience you have had, as a spectator or as a performer? Analyze as clearly as possible why the experiences were satisfying. Are there any commonalities in the two experiences? Why or why not?

Suggestions for Further Reading

1. Berryman, Jack W. "From the Cradle to the Playing Field: America's Emphasis on Highly Organized Competitive Sports for Pre-adolescent Boys." *Journal of Sport History* 2, no. 2, (Fall, 1975): 112-131.
2. Gilbert, Bill, and Williamson, Nancy. "Sport is Unfair to Women." *Sports Illustrated* 38, no. 21 (May 28, 1973): 88-92, 94-98.
3. ———. "Are You Being Two-Faced?" *Sports Illustrated* 38, no. 22 (June 4, 1973): 44-48, 50, 53, 54.

4. ———. "Programmed to Be Losers." *Sports Illustrated* 38, no. 23 (June 11, 1973): 60-62, 65, 66, 68, 73.
5. Kraus, Richard. *History of the Dance in Art and Education.* Englewood Cliffs, N.J.: Prentice-Hall, Inc., 1969. Chapters 10, 11, 12, 13, 14.
6. Michener, James A. *Sports in America.* New York: Random House, 1976.
7. Olsen, Jack. *The Black Athlete: A Shameful Story.* New York: Time-Life Books, 1968.
8. Scott, Jack. "Sport and the Radical Ethic." *Quest* 19 (January, 1973): 71-77.
9. Wilson, Wayne. "Social Discontent and the Growth of Wilderness Sport in America: 1965-1974." *Quest* 27 (Winter, 1977): 54-60.

8 The Olympic Games, Ancient and Modern

The most influential organization in amateur sport today is probably the International Olympic Committee. The IOC is responsible for the conduct of the modern Olympic Games, the most prestigious competition for world-class athletes. Olympic competition affects almost every aspect of today's sport, from age-group AAU swimming to the promotion of field hockey for men. The modern Olympic Games, instituted in 1896, are a revival of an ancient festival that according to tradition began in 776 B.C.

In order to study the place of the Olympic Games in the history of sport we will examine both the ancient Olympic Games and the modern Olympic Games.

The Ancient Games

For over 1200 years the ancient games took place at Olympia, a large sanctuary on the Alpheus River in the northwest part of the Peloponnesus, the peninsula which forms the southern half of Greece. Other athletic competitions were held elsewhere in the Greek world. The Greek citizens appear to have been the first people who made sport and athletics an integral part of their daily lives. Evidence of their sport and physical activities is found in the myths that were handed down by word of mouth from generation to generation, in the literature of the period, and in the ruins and artifacts which have been discovered by archaeologists. To understand the influence of the ancient Greek Olympic Games on the modern Olympics we will study sport traditions found in poems by Homer; the use of athletics in two contrasting city-states, Sparta and Athens; the major games or festivals, the most important of which was the Olympic Games; and the changes that occurred in sport and athletics during the period of the festivals, from about 800 B.C. to 400 A.D.

Greece, 800 B.C. to 400 A.D.

Brilliant sunshine, a warm climate, rugged mountains, sparkling azure seas, and hundreds of islands dotting those seas—all these evoke some idea of Greece. The first Greeks are thought to have been wanderers from the north and east who settled in the sheltered valleys between the mountains. Others found their way to the islands and then to the mainland where they established settlements near the sea. Some continued east across the islands in the Aegean and founded colonies along the western shores of Asia Minor. Prior to the ninth century B.C. Greek, or Hellenic people as they were known, lived as far northeast as Troy, as far south as the islands of Thera, Rhodes, and Crete, and as far northwest as Elis.

In the early days the family or clan controlled Greek life. Clans claimed descent from a common male ancestor and were bound together with common religious rituals, burial practices, family ties, and military dependence. The beginnings of Greek sport and concepts of "an athlete" are attributed to rituals developed within the clans. Footraces besought the gods for good crops; games and contests honored the dead at funeral ceremonies; and both footraces and chariot races were used to establish the prowess of the clan's leader. Winners of the contests brought honor to their families through their victories and, slowly, the tradition of the elite, male athlete developed as men used sport to prove their *"arete,"* their total excellence— physical, mental, and moral. While winning wasn't everything, it *was* important. Hardy underscores the Greeks' emphasis ". . . on . . . success and achievement. A noble attempt did not prove nobility; success did. Greek society had no praise for the loser, regardless of how valiantly he struggled; success, not intention, made the man."[1]

These families with their strong ties, ritualistic customs, and traditions of success formed the aristocracy of the emerging city-states. For hundreds of years the city-states were frequently at war with one another and gradually formed leagues for their mutual protection. According to one legend, an effort to establish peace among the city-states resulted in the first Olympic Games. By 550 B.C. the four major athletic festivals as well as many minor ones had been initiated; games, gymnasiums, and stadiums had become part of daily life in Greece. In 490 B.C. the Persians invaded Greece, but, after a long war, were defeated. The Greeks, in turn, invaded and colonized parts of Asia Minor, southern Italy, and northern Egypt. They built their towns much like those in the homeland and lived much as they did in Greece, taking with them their love of athletics and their games. Indeed, gymnasiums have been found as far from mainland Greece as Jerusalem, Italy, and Egypt.

Among the Greek city-states Sparta and Athens engaged in a continuous rivalry ending in the Peloponnesian War in which Sparta defeated Athens.

---

1. Stephen H. Hardy, "Organized Sport and Community in Ancient Greece and Rome," M.S. thesis, University of Massachusetts, 1975, p. 17.

Frequent conflicts among other Greek city-states, as well as Sparta and Athens, further weakened Greece, until, by 190 B.C., she fell to the powerful Roman armies from the west. During the next two centuries difficulties within Greece and invasions from without brought to a halt Greek influence on civilization. However, year after year, at festival after festival, national and international interest in the games persisted. As the Christian influence increased, attempts were made to discontinue the Games. Finally, in 393 A.D. Theodosius I officially abolished the Olympic Games. Even after this edict, athletic festivals continued, but gradually diminished in importance until the Games faded out of existence.

Perhaps the wonder of our sport heritage from Greece is that sport was a part of the culture which has shaped much of our Western thought. Greek philosophers, mathematicians, poets, architects, sculptors, and playwrights have made major contributions to our world. We still admire the beauty of the Parthenon on the Athenian Acropolis, we still read the poetry of Homer and Sappho, we still study the philosophy of Plato and Aristotle, and we still watch the dramas of Aeschylus, Sophocles, Euripides, and Aristophanes. The choruses in those dramas, declaiming in unison their responses to the action and advancing and retreating in dignified movements, represent the beginnings of theatrical dance. In addition, our democratic form of government is patterned after Greek concepts of civil control. In a brief period of brilliance these people of Hellenic origin laid many of the foundations of Western civilization, including sport.

To the Greeks their gods were totally anthropomorphous beings, differing from men only in their extraordinary power and their freedom from death. From the top of Mount Olympus, where the deities lived, Zeus ruled the universe, Poseidon the sea, and Hades the underworld. Hera was the sister-wife of Zeus. Other major gods and goddesses included Apollo, Ares, Dionysius, Hephaestus, Hermes, Aphrodite, Artemis, and Demeter. There were also children of mortal women by Zeus or some other god. Rituals honoring the gods and asking for their help were performed at birth, marriage, death, opening sessions of government, athletic festivals, and many other functions. The Greeks bargained with the gods and goddesses in prayer, thanked them with sacrifices for special favors such as winning a contest, and blamed them for defeat. The Greeks also believed that the gods, jealous of their special prerogatives, condemned the sin of pride or *hubris* in men and women who forgot they were mortal.

Greek society was not a classless society. *Citizens,* the only class with voting privileges, conducted the affairs of the city-state. *Resident foreigners,* some of whom had been established in the city for years, were active in the business affairs of the city, but not the civic affairs. The third class in Greek society was the *slaves* and, even among the slaves, a hierarchy existed. It is estimated that half the slaves worked in the fields and industries while the other half were in domestic service. If the domestic slave was talented, his life was much like that of a family member, except for individual rights such as voting and participating openly in the affairs of the city.

Not only did men control the government and business of the city-state, but also they were the masters of the family. Home life was directed by the man and carried out by the woman. The woman's place, especially in Athens, was in the women's quarters of the Greek home. With the exception of attending the theater, she did not appear in the streets, engage in shopping, or transact other forms of business.

The woman's subordinate position explains, in part, the bisexuality of many Greek citizens. Upperclass Greek men frequently had a family and, at the same time, engaged in a sexual relationship with a youth from another upperclass family. Such relationships were accepted and expected. Ordinarily, an older man became the role-model for a young man, thus sponsoring him into the society of the adult Greek world. Several reasons have been proffered in explanation of this custom, one being that the gymnasium, which literally means "the place where men exercise naked," prized the male body and created an atmosphere in which homosexuality was fostered.

This brief sketch of Greek history and culture may serve as an introduction to the study of Greek sport and athletics.

The First Written Accounts of Athletics

Homer's epic poems, the *Iliad* and the *Odyssey,* contain the first descriptions of sport and organized athletics. Contemporary scholars assign the writing of the *Iliad* to the middle of the eighth century B.C. and the *Odyssey* to the end of that century. If this judgment is correct, the material in the *Iliad* would confirm those who believe that games were held prior to the Olympic Games and in places other than Olympia.

The *Iliad* describes a few weeks in the tenth year of the Trojan War, while the *Odyssey* recounts the return journey of Odysseus after the war. For centuries these two poems were memorized by Greek children and were the foundations of Greek education. The poems demonstrate the moral and ethical conduct valued by the ancient Greeks; Homer's heroes displayed that special brand of nobility and excellence called *"aretē."* In these two Greek classics, references to athletics, games, sport, and dance are interwoven, making it clear that these activities were part of daily Greek life in the epic period and that the language of sport was understood by the early Greeks.

In the *Iliad* there is a detailed description of games held to honor Patroclus, who was killed in battle. While memorial games are part of today's sport world, in the ancient days the games were held as part of the funeral ceremonies. The Trojan War started when Paris, a prince of Troy who was visiting Sparta, abducted Helen, the wife of King Menelaus. Menelaus' older brother, Agamemnon, King of Mycenae, led an army of a thousand ships from Greece to Troy to force her return. The siege of Troy proved difficult. The gods constantly intervened on both sides, and the war dragged on for ten years. In the tenth and final year, the period covered by the *Iliad,* Agamemnon quarreled with his best fighting man, Achilles, who withdrew from the fight, taking his men with him. The Trojans then gained the upper hand until Patroclus, Achilles' best friend, persuaded Achilles to let him return to the battle. Patroclus was killed and Achilles reentered the war and, with the help of the gods, turned back the Trojans. The funeral which Achilles conducted in honor of Patroclus involved building an enormous funeral pyre on which he placed the offering for the dead: honey, oil, horses, hunting dogs, and twelve young Trojans slain in reprisal for Patroclus. After the burning of the pyre, elaborate games were held in his honor.

These games are our introduction to the first literary account of athletics. Homer tells the story this way:

> Akhilleus held the troops upon the spot
> and seated them, forming a wide arena.
> Prizes out of the ships, caldrons and tripods,
> horses and mules and oxen he supplied,
> and softly belted girls, and hoary iron.
> First for charioteers he set the prizes:
> a girl adept at gentle handicraft
> to be taken by the winner, and a tripod
> holding twenty-six quarts, with handle-rings.
> For the runner-up he offered a six-year-old
> unbroken mare, big with a mule foal.
> For third prize a fine caldron of four gallons,
> never scorched, bright as on casting day,
> and for the fourth two measured bars of gold;
> for fifth, a new two-handled bowl.[2]

Throughout the description of the games, contemporary sport concepts appear. Achilles administered the games, selected the contestants, awarded the prizes, and settled disputes. In announcing the first race, the chariot race, Achilles withdrew his own horses in honor of Patroclus pointing out:

---

2. Homer, *The Iliad,* tr. by Robert Fitzgerald (New York: Anchor Press/Doubleday, 1975), pp. 543-544.

Now where they stand they droop their heads for him,
their manes brushing the ground, and grieve at heart.[3]

Five contestants entered the chariot race. Nestor's son, Antilochus, was one of the contestants and, not unlike a father of today advising his son at a sporting event, Nestor offered this advice:

these are slow horses, and they may turn in
a second-rate performance. The other teams
are faster. But the charioteers
know no more racing strategy than you do.
Work out a plan of action in your mind,
dear son, don't let the prize slip through your fingers.[4]

He concluded with careful instructions for rounding the turning-post:

As you drive near it,
hug it with cart and horses; you yourself
in the chariot basket lean a bit to the left
and at the same time lash your right-hand horse
and shout to him, and let his rein out. . . .

If on the turn you overtake and pass,
there's not a chance of someone catching you—[5]

The son did not win the race, and, indeed, came in second only as the result of such careless driving that he was accused of committing a foul. During the race the contestants alleged that the gods interfered resulting in disagreement over the awarding of the prizes. Achilles settled all arguments and announced the next event, boxing.

He invited any two men to enter the event. Huge and powerful Epeius entered and for a while it appeared as if there might not be another contestant, but finally Euryalos accepted the challenge. Epeius won the match and, after the final blow, "gallantly . . . gave him a hand and pulled him up."[6] The boxing was followed by the wrestling event in which Ajax and Odysseus wrestled until Achilles interfered, saying:

---

3. Homer, *The Iliad,* tr. by Robert Fitzgerald (New York: Anchor Press/Doubleday, 1975), p. 544.

4. Homer, *The Iliad,* tr. by Robert Fitzgerald (New York: Anchor Press/Doubleday, 1975), p. 545.

5. Homer, *The Iliad,* tr. by Robert Fitzgerald (New York: Anchor Press/Doubleday, 1975), p. 546.

6. Homer, *The Iliad,* tr. by Robert Fitzgerald (New York: Anchor Press/Doubleday, 1975), p. 557.

No more of this bone-cracking bout.
The victory goes to both. Take equal prizes.
Off with you, so the rest here can compete.[7]

The prizes for the next event, the footrace, included a bowl which had belonged to Patroclus and which Achilles gave as a prize in memory of his companion. Antilochus, Ajax, and Odysseus entered the race. Near the end of the race Ajax led, followed by Odysseus, who prayed to the goddess Athena to help *him* be the victor. His prayers were answered as Athena caused Ajax to slip and fall. When Ajax complained that the gods must have interfered, the crowd laughed. Other events at the funeral included a close combat fight in armor, finally pronounced a draw; a throwing contest similar to putting the shot; and an archery competition in which the target was a tethered, wild pigeon. The funeral games in honor of Patroclus ended with a spear throw. Homer completes the account of the games as the contestants and spectators left leaving Achilles alone with his grief:

The funeral games were over. Men dispersed
and turned their thoughts to supper in their quarters,
then to the boon of slumber. But Akhilleus
thought of his friend, and sleep that quiets all things
would not take hold of him. He tossed and turned
remembering with pain Patroklos' courage. . . .
With memory his eyes grew wet.[8]

The *Odyssey,* the tale of the journey of Odysseus from Troy back to his home, included a variety of adventures among which are many references to sport. After a banquet on the island of Phaeacia, games and contests were held in honor of Odysseus. After several contests, footraces, wrestling, discus, and boxing, among the Phaeacians, Odysseus was invited to compete, but declined. The Phaeacians taunted him, saying "As I see it . . . you never learned a sport, and have no skill in any of the contests of fighting men."[9] Odysseus answered the challenge by selecting a discus stone, heavier than those thrown by the Phaeacians, and tossing it further than any of his hosts. Throughout both the *Odyssey* and the *Iliad* Homer's descriptions of sport are detailed and vivid.

7. Homer, *The Iliad,* tr. by Robert Fitzgerald (New York: Anchor Press/Doubleday, 1975), p. 558.

8. Homer, *The Iliad,* tr. by Robert Fitzgerald (New York: Anchor Press/Doubleday, 1975), p. 567.

9. Homer, *The Odyssey,* tr. by Robert Fitzgerald (New York: Anchor Press/Doubleday, 1963), p. 129.

Only a few of Homer's more pertinent references to sport and athletics have been included here, but, from these, we can identify many sport traditions, customs, and behaviors with which we are familiar. Although we do not hold games as part of funeral ceremonies, we do commemorate individuals with annual sporting events. Just as now, spectators and contestants argued among themselves. A father advised his son on strategies for winning. In the games honoring Patroclus, Achilles was the organizer, the referee, and the umpire, indicating the need for officials to administer athletic events. Several situations emphasized fair play and sportsmanship. In the wrestling event the winner gave the loser a hand and pulled him up, and Achilles stopped the wrestling match before the contestants were badly hurt. Another example of sport behavior associated with sportsmanship is the ability to accept defeat. When Ajax complained about losing the footrace, the crowd laughed at him as if to tell him he should not complain. After the chariot race, Antilochus, the second-place winner, challenged the decision and Achilles ruled in his favor.

The athletes in Homer's classics displayed many of the sport behaviors we see today. Concepts of accepting decisions, fair play and good sportsmanship, and many others are illustrated in the funeral games for Patroclus. At the same time we also see some of the less desirable sport behaviors in Homer's time just as we do today. The athletes argued among themselves and the spectators gave opinions and behaved much the way our spectators behave today. These and many other passages from Homer demonstrate that our heritage of sport from Greece is over 2500 years old and consists of well-developed concepts and traditions.

Contrasting Views of Sport

Sparta and Athens were the two most important city-states in ancient Greece, less than two hundred miles apart but with vastly different governments, educational systems, and views of sport. Sparta reflected the use of sport and athletics by the government to further the purposes of the state. Her men sought to bring her glory both on the battlefield and in the stadium, while her women strived for perfect babies for the state. In Athens, while all citizens were expected to be loyal to the city and ready to fight, it was excellence of the individual man which was prized. Sport and athletics contributed to physical excellence, which was one aspect of *"aretē."*

These two major city-states, Sparta and Athens, spoke the same language, claimed the same heritage, worshipped the same gods, but although both took fierce pride in being Greek, were at opposite extremes in their political and cultural lives. Hale contrasts the two city-states:

Athens produced in statecraft a Solon, a Themistocles, a Pericles; in drama an Aeschylus, a Sophocles, a Euripides, an Aristophanes; in sculpture a Phidias, a Praxiteles; in architecture a Mnesicles, one of the builders of its new Acropolis; in history a Thucydides; in philosophy a Socrates, a Plato; whereas Sparta in its prime produced soldiers.[10]

Both city-states have contributed to our heritage in sport and athletics. Both Sparta and Athens provided education which emphasized body-building activities. Sparta is to be remembered as the first society which required a regimen of exercise for both boys and girls. In Athens moral and physical excellence, *"aretē,"* was the goal for the men. Its concepts of excellence and all-out performance are still prized in sport. Specialized facilities such as gymnasiums, stadiums, and other athletic facilities were very much a part of the life of the Greek citizens just as special athletic facilities are accepted and expected today.

Greek Athletic Festivals

For over twelve hundred years athletic festivals were an important part of Greek life, and they have left a significant legacy to modern sport. Archaeological findings at sites such as Olympia, Delphi, and Epidaurus reveal stadiums, starting devices, palaestras, statues bearing inscriptions about athletic contests, and lists of Olympic victors' names. During the period when the athletic festivals flourished and were at their height, the four major games were the Olympic, Pythian, Isthmian, and Nemean. They were Panhellenic in nature, meaning that contestants from all over Greece could compete. In the four-year cycle of an Olympiad, the Olympic Games and the Isthmian Games were held in the first year. The following year, the second year of the Olympiad, the Nemean Games were celebrated; in the third year the Pythian and Isthmian Games were held; and in the fourth, the Nemean Games.

While the Olympic Games were the most prestigious, next in importance were the Pythian Games which were held in Delphi, the sacred site of the oracle of Apollo and, according to Greek legend, the center of the world. Located northeast of Athens along the Gulf of Corinth, Delphi's mountainous setting accommodated a theater, temples, treasuries housing valuable displays from cities, and above the sanctuary, a stadium. One legend relates that the first Pythian Games celebrated Apollo's victory over the serpent Python, while another suggests that the Pythian competitions in music and literary works had been conducted for many centuries and that

---

10. William Harlan Hale, *Ancient Greece* (New York: American Heritage Press, 1970), pp. 103-104.

Summary of the Major Panhellenic Festivals

Festival	Site	Began	In Honor of	Prize	Year of Olympiad
Olympic	Olympia	776 B.C.	Zeus	Olive wreath	First
Pythian	Delphi	582 B.C.	Apollo	Laurel wreath	Third
Isthmian	Corinth	586 B.C.	Poseidon	Pine wreath	First and third
Nemean	Nemea	573 B.C.	Zeus	Celery wreath	Second and fourth

FIG. 8.1 Trophies won at Panathenaic and other games. The Metropolitan Museum of Art, Rogers Fund, 1959.

only later were the Games instituted. Originally reported to have been held every eight years, beginning in 582 B.C. the Pythian Games were staged on a four-year cycle in the third year of each Olympiad and in the same year as the Isthmian Games. The prizes awarded to the victors of the Pythian Games were wreaths of laurel.

The Isthmian Games honored Poseidon, the god of the sea, and celebrated not only athletic events, but also musical and literary competitions. The traditional prize wreaths were made of pine in recognition of the site of the Games, near Corinth in a pine grove sacred to Poseidon. The

Nemean Games, held in alternate years between the Olympic and Pythian Games, honored Zeus and awarded the victors wreaths of wild celery.

The Origin of the Olympic Games

Although the traditional date for the beginning of the Olympic Games is usually considered to be 776 B.C. the actual origins are lost in antiquity. Olympia, which was never a village or town, is a remote area about ten miles from the mouth of the Alpheus River in the district of Elis. The first temple at Olympia, dedicated to Hera, the wife of Zeus, was erected about the tenth or eleventh century B.C. The date lends credence to the tales of the worship of the Mother-goddess or Earth-Mother before the Greek gods came to live on Mount Olympus. Prior to 1000 B.C. there were, on occasion, athletic festivals at Olympia, first to honor the goddess Hera, and, later, the god Zeus. In the two centuries prior to 776 B.C., when the first records of the Games were kept, almost nothing is known about the games and the shrines at Olympia appear to have been neglected.

First-hand accounts of the early Olympic Games have never been discovered and, thus, our introduction to the Games is the choral poetry of Pindar, a fifth century B.C. poet, who composed odes or "hymns" celebrating victors in the festivals. Although Pindar does not describe the athletic events in detail, his odes impart a sense of the beauty of the ceremonies. The odes convey the importance of the victor and the glory accorded him both at the festival and in his home city-state. For Pindar, the Olympic Games were the most glorious of all:

> But, my heart, would you chant the glory of games,
> look never beyond the sun
> by day for any star shining brighter through the deserted air,
> nor any contest than Olympia greater to sing.[11]

In his second Olympic ode he attributed the origin of the Olympic Games to Heracles who "founded the Olympiad out of spoils of his warfare"; chose the olive tree ". . . the loveliest memorial of the games," from which to make wreaths for the victors (Olympia III);[12] and arranged sacrifices before and after the games. Pindar relates another legendary beginning in which Pelops won his bride in a chariot race and commemorated his victory with a shrine and games at Olympia. Later writers also mention Pelops and Heracles as founders of the games and Phlegon, writing in the second century A.D., recounts this interesting story. Three men, Lycurgus of Sparta,

---

11. *The Odes of Pindar,* tr. by Richmond Lattimore (Chicago: University of Chicago Press, 1947), Olympia I, p. 1.

12. *The Odes of Pindar,* tr. by Richmond Lattimore (Chicago: University of Chicago Press, 1947), Olympia II, p. 5, Olympia III, p. 9.

Iphitus of Elis, and Cleisthenes of Pisa, had the idea of holding games to promote political harmony among the city-states of Greece. They traveled to Delphi and consulted the oracle there. She directed them to declare a truce among the cities which would take part in the games. A messenger carried this edict throughout Greece. Some Peloponnesians who did not support the holding of the games " . . . were visited by disease and a blight on their crops which caused them distress."[13] The people sent their leaders back to Delphi where the priestess proclaimed that the disease and blight were the results of Zeus' anger because the people failed to celebrate the Olympic Games as promised. The citizens were not satisfied and consulted the oracle themselves. They were told:

> O inhabitants of Peloponnesus . . . go to the altar.
> Sacrifice and hearken to whatever the priests . . . enjoin.[14]

As a result of the ruling of the oracle, the priests of Elis administered the Games at Olympia. One other time the Delphic oracle was consulted about the Olympic Games. When asked whether or not wreaths should be placed on the victors, she affirmed the use of wreaths and directed that the wreaths be made from wild olive trees.

While Phlegon's version is but one of several concerning the beginning of the Olympic Games, it does account for some actual customs of the Games. A truce *was* declared during the year of the festival so that the competitors could travel to Olympia and participate in the games without fearing attack; the games *were* conducted by men from Elis; and the official prize awarded *was* the olive wreath. The Games were characterized by a religious quality, having been dedicated to Zeus and ordained by a sacred oracle from Delphi.

Conduct of the Games

During their first two centuries the Olympic Games were local in character. Most athletes were from Sparta or Athens and, traditionally, free-born citizens of Greek ancestry. The athletes, officials, and spectators were all men. The only woman permitted to watch was the priestess of Demeter, who presided over the Games from a seat of honor. Actually, authorities differ on this point. One account suggests that unmarried girls viewed the Games, while another reports that women who were in Olympia on the days of the events were thrown over the cliffs of nearby Mount Typaeum.

---

13. Rachel S. Robinson, *Sources for the History of Greek Athletics* (Cincinnati: published by the author, 1955), p. 41.

14. Rachel S. Robinson, *Sources for the History of Greek Athletics* (Cincinnati: published by the author, 1955), p. 42.

As the games became more important and the number of events increased, Olympia changed from a remote wooded glen where temples to Hera and Zeus stood and where occasional games were held in their honor to a crowded complex of temples, athletic facilities, buildings, and statues. Within the Altis, the name of the sacred area housing the temples, the largest and most important one was dedicated to Zeus and contained his statue, seven times life size, made by Phidias of gold and silver. Zeus' temple was surrounded by Hera's temple, other smaller ones, commemorative statues, and treasuries, which were small buildings erected by the city-states to hold offerings honoring their local victors. Outside the Altis were the athletic facilities, the stadium to the east and the hippodrome to the south. Beside the path leading to the stadium stood a number of Zanes or statues calling attention to athletes who violated the regulations of the games. The offending athletes were barred from future Games and paid a fine which was used to erect the Zanes, which served to remind the competitors of the shame and punishment they would receive if they broke any rules.

The stadium, a flat area for running, was enclosed by the Hill of Cronos and other embankments which accommodated some 40,000 spectators. The gymnasium and palaestra were west of the Altis. The gymnasium was typical of the period, a large area surrounded by two porticos which were used as practice tracks. The porticos were roofed to permit the athletes to practice in the shade. The palaestra or wrestling school was adjacent to the gymnasium; nearby baths completed the athletic complex.

A month before the Games, the athletes arrived to be tested, observed, and supervised by the Hellanodikai, the administrative committee of the

FIG. 8.2   Model of Olympia about 150 A.D. The Metropolitan Museum of Art, Dodge Fund, 1930.

Games. As the first day of the festival approached, more and more people arrived. Male members of the athlete's families, historians, philosophers, poets, painters, sculptors, and others interested in athletics came from near and far. Distinguished visitors were housed in the Leonidaion; but most citizens traveled with servants bearing tents, clothing, food, and utensils and created a temporary household for their stay at Olympia. The atmosphere was that of a fair; food, souvenirs, and amusements were peddled. Gardiner describes the occasion:

> Meanwhile, visitors of all classes and from every part were flocking to Olympia. The whole Greek world was represented, from Marseilles to the Black Sea, from Thrace to Africa. There were official embassies representing the various states, richly equipped; there were spectators from every part, men of every class. Men, I say: for the only people excluded from the festival were married women, and even if unmarried women were allowed to be present, few probably availed themselves of the right except those in the neighbourhood. Apart from this Olympia was open to all without distinction, to hardy peasants and fishermen of the Peloponnese and to nobles and tyrants from the rich states of Sicily or Italy. All had the same rights. There was no accommodation for them except such as they could provide or procure for themselves; there were no reserved seats at the games, indeed there were no seats at all. The plain outside the Altis was one great fair, full of tents and booths. There you might meet every one who wished to see or to be seen, to sell or to buy: politicians and soldiers, philosophers and men of letters, poets ready to write odes in honour of victors in the games, sculptors to provide them with statues, perhaps already made, horse-dealers from Elis, pedlars of votive offerings, charms, and amulets, peasants with their wine-skins and baskets of fruit and provisions, acrobats and conjurers, who were as dear to the Greek as to the modern crowd.[15]

The first day began with the chariot race and the horse races, followed by the footrace, the long jump, the discus, and the javelin. The pentathlon occupied the rest of the day. Another period of sacrifice took place on the morning of the third day and then came more athletic events until the fifth day. The final day consisted of feasting, rejoicing, and paying tributes promised to the gods. While other athletic festivals differed in detail, their general program and atmosphere was similar to that of the Olympic Games.

The Athletic Events

The program of events at athletic festivals changed relatively little during the 1200-year period of the ancient games but some changes did occur; events were added and dropped, but the program was more stable than today's sport programs. Footraces, jumping, discus, javelin throw, wres-

---

15. E. Norman Gardiner, *Athletics of the Ancient World* (Oxford: Clarendon Press, 1930), p. 224.

tling, boxing, and combinations of these events made up the contests in the festivals; in addition, there were chariot races and horse races. While these events seem familiar to us, there are a number of differences between the ancient and modern performances.

Although women did not compete in the Olympic Games, they did compete in other festivals. They wore a short garment with one shoulder bare and the skirt length just above the knees. Male athletes competed in the nude, perhaps to avoid any question of mistaken identity or, according to one legend, to avoid the disaster of one lead runner who lost the race when his garment fell around his ankles.

Footraces

At Olympia the men competed in four races: the stade, one length of the stadium; the diaulos or two lengths of the stadium; a race in armor, also two stades in length; and the dolichos, a long-distance race. While the dolichos could be any distance from seven to twenty-four stades, at Olympia it appears to have been twenty. Other festivals included a middle distance event of about 800 meters. The girls' course, about five-sixths the length of the stade, will be discussed under the topic, *Women in Athletic Festivals.*

The method of starting of the ancient footraces has never been satisfactorily explained. Archaeologists have uncovered what are assumed to be starting devices, but no first-hand accounts of their use have been found. At Olympia, Delphi, and Epidaurus stone sills with narrow, parallel grooves are embedded in the end of the stadiums. It is theorized that these are starting blocks on which the runners placed one foot on the back line and one foot on the front line, digging their toes in the grooves, starting in an upright position rather than the modern crouch. This idea is supported by figures on vases which depict racers with one foot in front of the other, knees slightly bent. A statue of a girl runner shows the back foot placed against a raised stone suggesting another method of starting.

Recent excavations at Isthmia have uncovered a more sophisticated system which permitted all runners a simultaneous start. The stone sill has no grooves, but at regular intervals there are sockets. Behind the starting sill is a pit and between the pit and the sill are brass staples. Harris explains:

Each runner had a starting gate like a railway signal. The moving arm was worked by a cord which ran from the short end of the arm through the staple and along the groove to the pit. All the cords were held by the starter standing in the pit, and when he released them, all the arms fell at the same time, thus ensuring a fair start.[16]

---

16. H.A. Harris, *Greek Athletes and Athletics* (London: Hutchinson, 1964), p. 68.

A careful examination of the illustrations of runners suggests that the style varied according to the distance of the race. Although we know something of the techniques used by the ancient runners, we know nothing of their times or records. The victors' lists indicate only the winners and thus we cannot compare the time of the early runners with modern runners.

The Jump

The Greeks did record the length of at least two jumps which far surpass any modern ones. Phayllus of Croton is reported to have jumped fifty-five feet and Chionis of Sparta fifty-two feet. One explanation of the superior jumps is that the Greeks actually performed a hop, skip, and jump. Gardiner, however, suggests that the records are fictitious:

> Herodotus, Aristophanes, Plutarch, and Pausanias all mention him [Phayllus] but know nothing of his fabulous jump. The epigram is said to have been inscribed on his statue at Delphi. But though the base of this statue has been found there is no trace on it of the epigram. Nor is there any evidence that the epigram was contemporary with the event. Indeed we cannot trace it further back than the second century A.D. But whatever its date there is no reason for taking it seriously. The sporting story is notorious: still more so is the sporting epigram; and this epigram is merely an alliterative jingle.[17]

In the ancient athletics jumpers carried weights or *halteres* in each hand, at least during part of the jump. Several *halteres* have been discovered and many appear on vases and other objects. Some resemble today's telephone receivers, some are similar to dumbbells, and still others have holes for the fingers. We do not know what the precise function of the *halteres* was, but it has been suggested that they might have been released at some point during the jump to provide more forward impetus. Philostratus, a third century A.D. writer, declared that the weights assured a firm landing.

Throwing the Discus

A number of reasons have been proffered for the many different shapes, sizes, and weights of the discus used in ancient times. One theory suggests that the antecedent of the discus throw was the stone throw used in battles and that the discus approximates a battle stone. It is generally assumed that the smaller and lighter instruments were used by boys. There appears to be more than one method of executing the throw. Perhaps the best-known sculpture of a discus thrower is that of Myron. Gardiner analyzes the sculpture:

---

17. E. Norman Gardiner, *Athletics of the Ancient World* (Oxford: Clarendon Press, 1930), pp. 152-153.

Myron has chosen to represent a moment between the backward swing and the forward swing where there is an apparent pause. . . . The thrower, raising the diskos level with his head in both hands, has swung it vigorously downwards and backwards in his right hand, at the same time turning his whole body and his head to the right. The right leg, which is advanced, is the pivot on which the whole body turns, the left foot and left arm merely helping to preserve the balance. We may note, too, the rope-like pull of the right arm. This turn of the body round a fixed point is the essence of the swing of the diskos. The force comes not from the arm, which serves only to connect the body and the weight, but from the lift of the thighs and the swing of the body.[18]

FIG. 8.3   Lead jumping weight. Courtesy Museum of Fine Arts, Boston, H.L. Pierce Fund.

Throwing the Javelin

There are numerous representations of the javelin throw showing at least one major difference between the ancient and modern event. To increase the distance of the throw, the ancient javelin thrower employed a leather thong bound to the center of the shaft and forming a loop through which one or two fingers could be inserted. It is believed that the thong imparted a spin which contributed to the steadiness of the flight and increased the distance of the throw.

---

18. E. Norman Gardiner, *Athletics of the Ancient World* (Oxford: Clarendon Press, 1930), pp. 160-161.

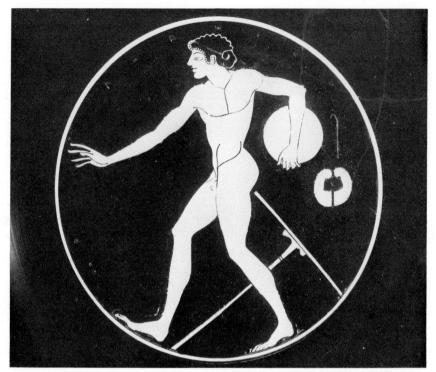

FIG. 8.4   Athlete with discus, early 5th century B.C. Courtesy Museum of Fine Arts, Boston, H.L. Pierce Fund.

Wrestling

The most popular Greek sport was wrestling, which took place in a specially prepared section of the stadium called a skamma. To protect the wrestlers in their falls, the area was dug up and covered with a layer of sand. Prior to competing, the wrestler oiled his body and dusted it lightly with sand. After wrestling and before bathing, the oil and sand were scraped off with a strigil, a small instrument designed for this purpose.

The match was scored on the best of three falls. Wrestling was a frequent subject in poetry and for vase paintings.

The Pentathlon

The pentathlon was introduced into the Olympic Games in 708 B.C. and combined the five events previously described: the footrace, jump, discus throw, javelin throw, and wrestling. The jump, discus throw, and javelin throw were performed only as part of the pentathlon. Scholars have debated two issues regarding this ancient event, the origins, and the method

FIG. 8.5   Athletes practicing. Courtesy Museum of Fine Arts, Boston, H.L. Pierce Fund.

of determining a winner. A legendary origin comes from Philostratus who relates that Jason created the pentathlon in order to name Peleus the best athlete among the Argonauts. Peleus was acclaimed victor after winning the wrestling, although he placed second in all the other events. According to Gardiner, "These five events were representative of the whole physical training of the Greeks, and the pentathlete was the typical product of that training. Inferior to the specialized athlete in his special events, he was superior to him in general development, in that harmonious union of strength and activity which produces perfect physical beauty . . ."[19]

Boxing

Although boxing was well known by Homer's time, it was not introduced at Olympia until 688 B.C. The Greek boxing "glove" was actually a strip of leather or thong about ten feet in length wound around the boxer's knuckles, hands, and up the forearms. Softer, padded thongs were worn for practice. Ancient boxing was not conducted in a ring, did not have rounds, and did not group fighters according to weight. The fight lasted until one man either was knocked out or admitted defeat.

---

19. E. Norman Gardiner, *Athletics of the Ancient World* (Oxford: Clarendon Press, 1930), p. 177.

Pancration

Philostratus described the pancration as the sport that is ". . . prized the highest even though it is composed of uncompleted wrestling and uncompleted boxing . . ."[20] Today we picture the contest as an "all-out" fight combining boxing and wrestling, permitting kicking, but prohibiting biting and gouging. The event was strictly regulated and, as in boxing, terminated when one opponent acknowledged defeat.

FIG. 8.6 Pancration, 550-500 B.C. The Metropolitan Museum of Art, Rogers Fund, 1905.

Horse Racing

Harris suggests that the Greek hippodromes were agricultural lands pressed into service as a race course after the crops were harvested.

Any flat stretch, as soon as the crops were taken off and the exposed soil baked by the summer sun, would afford adequate going for horses or chariots, provided it was not crossed by watercourses or irrigation channels. The only preparation needed to convert such a stretch for racing was the removal of any large stones and the provision of two turning-posts.[21]

20. Rachel S. Robinson, *Sources for the History of Greek Athletics* (Cincinnati: published by the author, 1955), p. 216.

21. H.A. Harris, *Sport in Greece and Rome* (Ithaca, N.Y.: Cornell University Press, 1972), p. 162.

Numerous athletic festivals throughout the Greek world included horse races. While the race-card varied, one program from Athens in the second century B.C. listed twenty-five events. In 680 B.C. four-horse chariot races were held at Olympia and, later, mule-cart races, jockey-ridden races, and races for colts added. The chariot race provided an opportunity for women to have some part in the Olympic Games. Although Cynisca of Sparta did not attend the Olympics or drive the chariot, her horses won the chariot race in 380 B.C.

FIG. 8.7   Athletes practicing, 5th century B.C. The Metropolitan Museum of Art, Fletcher Fund, 1927.

Training for the Festivals

The trainers and coaches were frequently former athletes, who, after their years of victories, taught others their knowledge and expertise. Numerous paintings on Greek vases provide ample evidence of training devices and methods. Apparently a long instrument was used to prod or correct the athletes. Not until the accounts of Galen and Philostratus in the early centuries of the Christian era is there much written evidence of athletic training. Nevertheless, scholars have developed a general theory of training based on the fragments that do exist. By the fifth century B.C. the informal athletic festivals of Homer's time had changed into organized meets with coaches and trainers. Young men spent much of their time practicing for the festivals and, if competing at Olympia, reported for special training a month before the Games. Lucian, a satirical writer of the second century A.D., imagines Solon, the Athenian law giver of the sixth century B.C., trying to explain the training of Greek athletes to Anacharsis, a bewildered visitor from Scythia. Solon tells Anacharsis that they have ". . . invented many forms of athletics and appointed teachers for each . . ." Each event had its purpose in training for all-round athletes from learning ". . . to fall safely and get up easily, to push, grip and twist . . ." to become ". . . accustomed to endure hardship and to meet blows . . . ," to run ". . . in deep sand, where it is not easy to plant one's foot solidly . . . ," and to jump obstacles ". . . carrying lead weights as large as they can grasp. . . ."[22] Gradually the emphasis on training to do well in every event changed to specializing in one event. By the fifth century B.C. special diets for boxers, wrestlers, and pancrationists were in vogue to increase their weight and strength.

By the second century A.D. when Greece was under Roman rule, there is more information on training. We know that the average Greek man still considered physical training and the gymnasium important. Galen traced the beginnings of the athletic events and made suggestions for suitable body types for each event. Thus, coaches and trainers of the period were well aware of the importance of diet, exercise, body types, and daily habits in the performance of athletic events. Lacking today's knowledge and sophisticated training devices, they utilized the information of the day and attempted to construct theories and practices that would improve performances.

Women in Athletic Festivals

Although they were barred from the Olympic Games, the women held their own festival at Olympia and, according to a few fragments of evidence, also participated in athletic events in other parts of Greece. The girls' games at Olympia honored Hera, the sister-wife of Zeus, and are thought to represent a very early matriarchal society. Older than many of the temples at Olympia is that of the great Earth Mother on the hill of Cronos within the Altis. Recent European scholars suggest that the footrace, the only event in the Heraean Games, represented an ancient fertility

---

22. Rachel S. Robinson, *Sources for the History of Greek Athletics* (Cincinnati: published by the author, 1955), pp. 69-71.

rite to give thanks for a good harvest. It is believed that such harvest races were formalized into the Heraean Games centuries before the Olympic Games. According to legend, one woman from each of the sixteen Elean city-states was sent to arrange a peace in a time of war. They settled the peace satisfactorily and were ordered to weave a gown for the statue of Hera every four years and to hold games in her honor. Pausanias describes the games:

> The games consist of footraces for maidens. These are not all of the same age. The first to run are the youngest; after them come the next in age, and the last to run are the oldest of the maidens. They run in the following way: Their hair hangs down, a tunic reaches to a little above the knee, and they bare the right shoulder as far as the breast. These too have the Olympic stadium reserved for their games, but the course of the stadium is shortened for them by about one-sixth of its length. To the winning maidens they give crowns of olive and a portion of the cow sacrificed to Hera. They may also dedicate statues with their names inscribed upon them . . . The games of the maidens too are traced back to ancient times. . . .[23]

When the patriarchal Hellenes arrived in Elis and discovered the Heraean festivals, they did not wish to offend the goddesses and thus founded their own separate games called Olympic Games. Because the girls' games honored Hera, the men honored Zeus with their games, and further copied the women by having only one event, the footrace. The men employed various traditions established by the girls' games and, to favor the goddesses, they invited the priestess of Demeter to watch the Olympic Games.

Other evidence for women competing in athletic festivals dates from the first century A.D. Inscriptions commemorate the daughters of Hermesianax, a citizen of both Athens and Delphi, who made the following dedication to Pythian Apollo:

> Tryphosa, who won at the Pythian games when they were directed by Antigonus and when they were directed by Cleomachidas, and at the next Isthmian games directed by Juventius Proclus, the one-lap race coming in first among the girls; Hedea, who won the chariot race in armor at the Isthmian games when they were directed by Cornelius Pulcher, and the one-lap race at the Nemean games directed by Antigonus and again at the Sicyonian games directed by Menoetas . . . ; and Dionysia, who won the one-lap race at the Isthmian games directed by Antigonus, and again at the Asclepieia in holy Epidaurus under the direction of Nicoteles.[24]

---

23. Rachel S. Robinson, *Sources for the History of Greek Athletics* (Cincinnati: published by the author, 1955), p. 109.

24. Rachel S. Robinson, *Sources for the History of Greek Athletics* (Cincinnati: published by the author, 1955), pp. 163-164.

Another inscription from Patras on the Gulf of Corinth reads, "I, Nicophilus, erected this statue of Parian marble to my beloved sister Nicegora, victor in the girls' race."[25] Even later in the third century A.D. a traveler described girls wrestling with boys, but one author suggests that this is not serious history but scandals of cafe society.

Changes in the Function of the Festivals

The purposes of the ancient athletic festivals changed gradually over the centuries. Originally, sport or athletic events honored the gods or heroes of a family and when contests between clans began, the victor brought honor to his clan. Later, winning a wreath at an athletic festival was a mark of social distinction. Robinson notes that the list of victors at Olympia reads ". . . like a page from the Social Register. It is to be expected that wealthy aristocrats and tyrants would be entering four-horse chariots in contests; but in these centuries future statesmen, generals, sons-in-law of wealthy tyrants and the like were also fighting hard pancratium matches of a far from gentle type of boxing and wrestling and were sprinting in the foot-races at Olympia during the stifling heat of August."[26] While the victor received only a wreath at the festival, he was treated like a hero and received other honors, such as having his statue erected at Olympia or having a poem dedicated to him, like the following Pindaric ode:

OLYMPIA 5

Accept, daughter of Ocean, in kindness of heart the blossoming
to delight of high deeds and Olympian garlands
for the mule car and the tireless feet, accept these gifts from Psaumis.

Increasing your city, Kamarina, that fosters its people,
he honored six double altars at the high festivals of the gods
with the sacrifice of oxen and with five-day games, races

for teams, mules, single horse. A winner, to you
he dedicated the delicate glory
and proclaimed his father Akron and the new-established dwelling.

He comes from the lovely precinct of Oinomaos and Pelops
and lifts again, Pallas, keeper of the city, your sacred wood,
your river Oanis with the lake near by,

and the stately channels whereby Hipparis waters the folk.
With speed he welds the high-groined forest of standing houses,
bringing back out of despair to the light this people, his citizens.

---

25. H.A. Harris, *Greek Athletes and Athletics* (London: Hutchinson, 1964), p. 181.
26. Rachel S. Robinson, *Sources for the History of Greek Athletics* (Cincinnati: published by the author, 1955), p. 58.

Always attendant on valor, work and substance struggle to win
the end veiled in danger;
but when men succeed, even their neighbors think them wise.

Savior Zeus, high in the clouds, at home on the Kronian hill,
with honor for the wide course of Alpheos and the sacred cave of Ida,
I come to you a suppliant, speaking above Lydian flutes.

I will ask that you glorify this city with fame
of good men; and you, Olympic champion, may you carry
your age in happiness to its end, with joy in Poseidon's horses,

your sons standing beside you, Psaumis. But if one water flowering wealth
in abundance of substance
and fair fame also, let him not seek to become God.[27]

As the city-states grew in importance, athletes represented their cities in the festivals rather than their families. The cities expressed their gratitude to victors by giving them food at public expense and presenting them with costly gifts. Gradually, men realized that they could gain personal profit from entering athletic contests and the athlete as a professional performer became an accepted part of the festivals. These men, frequently specializing in only one event, earned their living by traveling from festival to festival much as today's pros "play the circuit" in tennis or "play the tour" in golf. However, in ancient Greece, because these men were no longer from the socially elite, the professional athlete was looked down on by some aristocratic Greeks who considered professionalism undesirable. Isocrates reminds his listeners that his father:

disdained the gymnastic contests [at Olympia]; for he knew that some of the athletes were of low birth, inhabitants of petty states, and of mean education, but turned to the breeding of race-horses, which is possible only for those most blest by Fortune . . .[28]

By the first and second centuries A.D. professional athletes were organized into guilds much like today's unions. These organizations became powerful and could exact from notables such as Mark Antony promises of ". . . exemptions from military service, public duties, billeting of troops, a truce during the festival . . . , guarantee of personal safety, privilege of the purple . . ."[29]

---

27. *The Odes of Pindar,* tr. by Richmond Lattimore (Chicago: University of Chicago Press, 1947), pp. 13-14.

28 Rachel S. Robinson, *Sources for the History of Greek Athletics.* (Cincinnati: published by the author, 1955), p. 120.

29. Rachel S. Robinson, *Sources for the History of Greek Athletics* (Cincinnati: published by the author, 1955), p. 161.

The changes from religious athletic events honoring the gods to secular professional athletics entertaining multitudes took place over hundreds of years. Many scholars of the ancient festivals have considered the rise of professionalism to be the ruin of the Greek athletic festival; but today's concepts of professionalism and amateurism did not exist at that time. Authors of antiquity accepted the fact that there would be material benefits from Olympic victories. Finley and Pleket explain:

> If there was any change over the centuries, it was only the growth from the vanity of a small number of aristocratic champions to the more loudly proclaimed vanity of a far larger number of champions, many of whom, though by no means all, had been born among the lowest social classes in the later Greek world.
>   Their vanity . . . was accepted by society at large as a legitimate human quality. . . . If . . . they worked hard and lived moderately, they could count, after their retirement, on a life of affluence from "the fruits of their victories." Olympic wreaths and affluence remained part of one and the same complex to the very end of the thousand-year story.[30]

Decline of the Games

The athletic festivals and games declined slowly during the first centuries of the Christian era. During the second century A.D. the major festivals experienced a revival and many features were added for the comfort of the athletes and spectators. Eventually, however, the festivals and games came under the attack of Christian bishops and Roman rulers. The official banning of the Olympic Games is usually attributed to Emperor Theodosius I in 393 A.D. Early in the fifth century A.D. Theodosius II and Emperor Honorius of Rome ordered the destruction of all places dedicated to Greek gods. This ruling coupled with earthquakes the following century completed the destruction of Olympia. By 551 A.D. Olympia was in ruins and the festivals in the ancient sacred stadium were over.

The Modern Olympic Games

Background

The modern Olympic Games were initiated through the efforts of one man, Pierre de Frèdy, Baron de Coubertin. However, Coubertin was not the first to consider reenacting the ancient Olympic Games. From the time of the Renaissance and a rekindled interest in all things Greek, the idea of the Games appears in literary and educational works. For over two cen-

---

30. M.I. Finley and H.W. Pleket, *The Olympic Games: The First Thousand Years* (New York: The Viking Press, 1976), pp. 125-127.

turies, 1610 to 1860, the "Olympick Games" of England were conducted at Dover's Hill. Initiated by Captain Robert Dover, the games, also referred to as the Cotswold Games, lasted two days:

> . . . They were somewhat akin to a protest movement against the growing Puritanism in English life. The widely known games, conducted on Dover's property, consisted of wrestling, field hockey, fencing, jumping, and throwing the pole, hammer javelin.[31]

Also in the nineteenth century other games were held in England near Wenlock in Shropshire by Dr. W.P. Brookes. Coubertin attended these games on one of his visits to England and became friendly with Brookes. Also the Greeks themselves held modern games, called the National Greek Olympics, in 1859 and again in 1870.

> The opening ceremony was a combination of religious rites, the playing of an Olympic anthem and the swearing of an Olympic oath. Parallel to ancient traditions, the athletes were required to train together daily for three months prior to the Olympics. . . . The Games were also conducted in 1875 and 1889 and in each instance included athletic competitions, gymnastic exercises and shooting.[32]

Interest in the modern Olympic Games was further stimulated by archaeological developments in Greece. The first attempts to uncover Olympia began in 1829 by the French. Later the Germans, from 1875 to 1881, uncovered the remains of the temples of Hera and Zeus, the palaestra, gymnasium, the entrance to the stadium, and other buildings in the Altis. Again in 1937 the Germans led an expedition which unearthed items revealing the history of Olympia.

The early German excavations took place during Coubertin's boyhood and perhaps suggested to him the means to achieve his avowed purpose in life—improving mankind and promoting peace through a broad use of sport. Coubertin has been described as a visionary, a passionate patriot, a fervid Anglophile, and a man of action. Born on January 1, 1863, to Charles Louis Baron Frèdy de Coubertin and Agathe Gabrielle de Crisenoy, his childhood was shadowed by France's defeat in the Franco-Prussian War. As a boy he read *Tom Brown's School Days,* and the Rugby School's system of sports and games as well as Dr. Thomas Arnold, the Rugby head-

---

31. Horst Ueberhorst, "Return to Olympia and the Rebirth of the Games," in *The Modern Olympics,* ed. Peter J. Graham and Horst Ueberhorst (Cornwall, N.Y.: Leisure Press, 1976), p. 7.

32. Horst Ueberhorst, "Return to Olympia and the Rebirth of the Games," in *The Modern Olympics,* ed. Peter J. Graham and Horst Ueberhorst (Cornwall, N.Y.: Leisure Press, 1976), pp. 6-7.

master, became a guide for Coubertin's developing ideas. By the age of seventeen Coubertin had become aware of the need for reform in French education and started preparing himself to become involved in that reform. Studying at the Jesuit College of the rue de Madrid and taking further courses in law and political science, Coubertin visited England and became an even stronger proponent of English public school sport. He saw the revival of the ancient Olympic Games as "the logical consequence of the cosmopolitan tendencies of the period: a general awakening of a taste for athletics, inventions such as railroads and telegraphs; exhibitions, assemblies, and conferences [bringing] together people of similar backgrounds in science, literature, art and industry."[33]

Coubertin's first public proposal to establish the modern Olympic Games, made at the Unions des Sports Athlétiques at the Sorbonne in November, 1892, was not well received. He carefully planned his second attempt. He organized an International Congress of Paris for the Study and the Propagation of the Principles of Amateurism to be held at the Sorbonne in June, 1894, and sent invitations to sport associations all over the world. Not leaving anything to chance, Coubertin traveled to the United States and England in an effort to gain support for his plan. Coubertin organized the program together with the secretary of the Amateur Athletic Association of Great Britain, C. Herbert, and a Princeton University professor of history, William Sloane. During the week of meetings helpful suggestions on amateurism were made, other sport-related items were discussed, and slowly the idea of the revival of the Games developed. It was the last item on the agenda of the Congress:

> He must have known how to cast a spell over the seventy-nine delegates from twelve countries. There were poems, music and songs. And after every delegate had heard the hymn to Apollo, discovered at Delphi in 1893, set to music by Gabriel Fauré and sung by Jeanne Remacle from the Paris Opéra, the assembly, unanimously and by acclaim, decided to restore the Olympic Games.[34]

Organization

Coubertin was ready with detailed plans to implement the modern Games. They were organized as part of a wider Olympic Movement, or "Olympism" with these aims:

> [to] promote the development of those fine physical and moral qualities which are the basis of amateur sport and to bring together the athletes of the world in a

---

33. Mary H. Leigh, "The Evolution of Women's Participation in the Summer Olympic Games, 1900-1948," Ph.D. dissertation, The Ohio State University, 1974, p. 34.

34. Marie Thérèse Eyquem, "The Founder of the Modern Games," in *The Olympic Games,* ed. Michael Morris Killanin and John Rodda (New York: Macmillan, 1976), p. 139.

great quadrennial festival of sports thereby creating international respect and goodwill and thus helping to construct a better and more peaceful world.[35]

An analysis of the modern Olympic Games reveals Coubertin's understanding of both the ancient games and the world of his time. He selected certain timeless concepts from the ancient games and recast them into a complex structure in which a neutral, nonpolitical body, the International Olympic Committee, governed the Games. While the ancient Games were conducted by the men from Elis, Coubertin's governing body was to be a picked group of men from all over the world who then would proceed to select their own additional members. Coubertin believed that this system would create a body of administrators who could be influenced neither by national interests nor by sport organizations and, thus, would be impartial in any disputes concerning the Games. The original members were personally selected by Coubertin himself. He picked fourteen men, from Great Britain, France, Greece, Russia, Sweden, Bohemia, Hungary, Italy, Belgium, Argentina, New Zealand, and the United States of America. Members were originally appointed to the Committee for life, but, since 1965, retirement has been mandatory at 72. Counting Coubertin, the first IOC numbered fifteen men from twelve countries, and in 1974 the IOC consisted of seventy-eight men from sixty-two countries. Representing neither a country nor a sport, the members must be interested in promoting amateur sport, reside in a country which has a National Olympic Committee, speak both French and English, and be prepared to contribute an annual fee. While these qualifications have led the IOC to appoint members from many backgrounds, they also have contributed to the perception that the IOC is composed of a body of internationally elite men intensely interested in amateur sport but not necessarily familiar with contemporary sport. Coubertin considered these men to be stewards of the Olympic Movement and expected them to act as sport diplomats to their country and other countries in their part of the world. The self-perpetuating characteristic of the IOC has enabled it to consider problems and the development of the Olympic Movement theoretically without regard to world or national politics. The aims of the International Olympic Committee are stated as follows:

A. the regular celebration of the Games;
B. making the Games ever more worthy of their glorious history and of the high ideals which inspired their revival by Baron Pierre de Coubertin and his associates;

---

35. "Rules of the International Olympic Committee," in *The Olympic Games,* ed. Michael Morris Killanin and John Rodda (New York: Macmillan, 1976), p. 258.

C. encouraging the organization and development of amateur sport and sport competitions;
D. inspiring, and leading sport within the Olympic ideal, thereby promoting and strengthening friendship between sportsmen of all countries.[36]

The term Olympiad refers, as it did in ancient times, to the four-year period between the Games; however, in the modern Games it is not used in reference to the Olympic Winter Games, which were initiated in 1924. Coubertin believed firmly that, as opposed to the ancient Games being held only at Olympia, the modern Olympic Games should be celebrated in cities in various parts of the world. He considered this idea a further effort to remove the Games from national political influences. Thus, every four years the Games are awarded to a city, not a country, selected by the IOC.

The other responsibilities of the IOC include the overall conduct of the Games, financial arrangements, and the development of the Olympic Movement.

Seven men have been President of the IOC, perhaps the most influential position in amateur sport. From 1894-1896 Demetrius Vikelas served as president, followed by Baron Pierre de Coubertin from 1896 to 1925. During World War I the president was Baron Godefroy de Blonay. In 1925 Count Henri Baillet-Latour became president and served until 1942. Following World War II Sigfrid Edström held the position from 1946 to 1952, when Avery Brundage took over until 1972. Lord Killanin began his presidency in 1972.

Originally, it was anticipated that the IOC business would be conducted from the country celebrating the coming Games, but in 1915 Coubertin decided to move the IOC headquarters to Switzerland to protect its political neutrality and it has been in Switzerland since that time. Business is carried on at the Lausanne headquarters by a permanent staff, the Executive Board of the IOC, and by commissions which are appointed to deal with specific aspects of the program.

Athletes enter the Olympic Games through a dual route involving a National Olympic Committee (NOC), and an international sport federation. To be recognized by the IOC, National Olympic Committees must have at least five sport federations which are members of international sport federations affiliated with them. National Olympic Committees have the following responsibilities:

. . . the development and protection of the Olympic Movement and of amateur sport. They shall co-operate with the national amateur sport governing bodies

---

36. "Rules of the International Olympic Committee," in *The Olympic Games,* ed. Michael Morris Killanin and John Rodda (New York: Macmillan, 1976), p. 258.

(National Federations), affiliated to the International Federations recognized by the International Olympic Committee, in guarding and enforcing the eligibility rules. It is their duty, in co-operation with the National Federations, to organize and control the representatives of their country at the Olympic Games. They arrange to equip, transport and house these representatives.[37]

The Cycle of the Modern Olympic Games

Olympiad	Date	City	Winter Olympic Games
I	1896	Athens	
II	1900	Paris	
III	1904	St. Louis	
IV	1908	London	
V	1912	Stockholm	
VI	1916	not celebrated	
VII	1920	Antwerp	
VIII	1924	Paris	Chamonix, France
IX	1928	Amsterdam	St. Moritz
X	1932	Los Angeles	Lake Placid
XI	1936	Berlin	Garmisch-Partenkirchen
XII	1940	not celebrated	
XIII	1944	not celebrated	
XIV	1948	London	St. Moritz
XV	1952	Helsinki	Oslo
XVI	1956	Melbourne	Cortina d'Ampezzo, Italy
XVII	1960	Rome	Squaw Valley
XVIII	1964	Tokyo	Innsbruck, Austria
XIX	1968	Mexico City	Grenoble, France
XX	1972	Munich	Sapporo, Japan
XXI	1976	Montreal	Innsbruck
XXII	1980	Moscow	Lake Placid

37. "Rules of the International Olympic Committee," in *The Olympic Games,* ed. Michael Morris Killanin and John Rodda (New York: Macmillan, 1976), p. 260.

The NOC's are responsible for the development of the Olympic Movement in their countries. The committees are expected to be free from political ideology and influence. The IOC dictates that the membership of the NOC include IOC members who reside in the country and representatives of national federations who are members of their respective international federation; the IOC further suggests that delegates from a variety of sport bodies may serve on the committee. Professional athletes and coaches are excluded from membership, although exceptions are made. Beginning in 1965 the NOC's formed a General Assembly to examine issues of mutual concern.

Whereas the NOC's deal with the development of the Olympic Movement in their countries and are responsible for the athletes, the international sport federations retain the responsibility for the selection of events, the rules, and the conduct of events. For each sport the IOC must recognize one international sport federation which, in turn, recognizes one national federation in each country. The athletes must be members of the national federation which plans the competitive program for that sport. For example, a U.S. archer would join and compete in the National Archery Association, which is affiliated with the International Archery Federation. A track and field athlete would join the Amateur Athletic Union and compete in the AAU Track and Field Division, affiliated with the International Amateur Athletic Federation (IAAF), while a gymnast competes nationally through the United States Gymnastics Federation, an affiliate of the International Gymnastics Federation.

Thus, the organization of the Olympic Games may be visualized as follows:

The United States Olympic Committee (USOC) was incorporated by an Act of Congress in 1950 and has as its purpose:

Section 1. The objects and purposes of the corporation shall be:

(1) to arouse and maintain the interest of the people of the United States in, and to obtain their support of, creditable and sportsmanlike participation and

representation of the United States in all of the sports on the program of the Olympic Games and Pan American Games;

(2) to stimulate the interest of the people, particularly the youth, of the United States, in healthful, physical, moral and cultural education through sportsmanlike participation in competitions in accordance with amateur rules;

(3) to exercise exclusive jurisdiction, either directly or through its constituent members or committees, over all matters pertaining to the participation of the United States in the Olympic Games and in the Pan American Games, including the representation of the United States in such Games, and over the organization of the Olympic Games and the Pan American Games when celebrated in the United States; and in furtherance thereof to comply with and enforce all the rules and regulations of the International Olympic Committee;

(4) to select and obtain for the United States the most competent amateur representation possible in the competitions and events of the Olympic Games and of the Pan American Games;

(5) to maintain the highest ideals of amateurism and to promote general interest therein, particularly in connection with the Olympic Games and the Pan American Games;

(6) to instill and develop in the youth of America the qualities of courage, self-reliance, honesty, tolerance, and like virtues; and

(7) to promote and encourage the physical, moral, and cultural education of the youth of the United States to the end that their health, patriotism, character, and good citizenship may be fully developed.[38]

The United States Olympic Committee is made up of representatives of four classes of membership: Group A (national sports governing bodies), Group B (national multi-sport organizations), Group C (affiliated sports organizations), and Group D (state Olympic organizations). For each sport eligible to be included in the Games, the USOC recognizes one national amateur sport governing body, which has complete jurisdiction over the conduct of that sport in the United States and which is recognized by the appropriate international sport federation, which in turn has been recognized by the IOC.

National sport governing bodies, which comprise Group A, must be open to all athletes and must not discriminate on the basis of religion, age, sex, color, creed, or race. At least twenty percent of the membership of the governing board for the sport must be athletes or former athletes who have participated within the past ten years. The membership must be open to all appropriate athletes, coaches, trainers, and administrators. In Group B are multi-sport organizations, those which hold national championships in two or more sports eligible for the Games but who are not eligible for membership in Group A. Included in Group B are organizations such as the Amateur Athletic Union (AAU); Catholic Youth Organization (CYO); U.S.

---

38. *Constitution, By-Laws and General Rules* (New York: United States Olympic Committee, 1977), p. 1.

Armed Forces; and the American Alliance of Health, Physical Education, and Recreation. Group C includes national sports organizations which are not affiliated with the Games but which might be included in future Games. Group D consists of the Olympic organizations from each state. The responsibilities of the state organizations include promoting the United States Olympic Movement and raising funds for the conduct of Olympic programs.[39]

According to the IOC "Only citizens of a country or area in which a National Olympic Committee recognized by the IOC operates, are qualified to compete in the Olympic Games . . ." and "No discrimination in them [the Games] is allowed against any country or person on grounds of race, religion, or politics." It should be noted that the antidiscrimination clause of the IOC does not include "sex." There is in fact a special rule, Rule 32, concerning women's participation:

> Women are allowed to compete in Archery, Athletics, Basketball, Canoeing, Diving, Equestrian Sports, Fencing, Gymnastics, Handball, Hockey, Luge, Rowing, Shooting, Figure and Speed Skating, Skiing, Swimming, Volleyball and Yachting, according to the rules of the International Federation concerned.[40]

On the other hand, it should be further noted that the United States Olympic Committee does include "sex" in its antidiscrimination clause and, therefore, the United States women are fully a part of the United States Olympic Movement and Programs of the USOC.

Symbols, Rituals, and Ceremonies

The ancient Olympic Games originated as a religious, athletic festival to honor the Greek god Zeus. Symbols such as the laurel wreath for the prize, rituals such as the sacrifice before the Games, and other ceremonies were essential features of the ancient Games. Coubertin carefully designed symbols, rituals, and ceremonies as essential components of the modern Games, thus embodying "religious" qualities in the modern Games. His actual meaning of "religion" in reference to the Games is unclear:

> Coubertin . . . never precisely explained the sense in which he used the term "religion." In contrast to the genuine and traditional meaning of the concept . . . one could etymologically interpret "re-ligio" in a secularized manner. This

39. *Constitution, By-Laws and General Rules* (New York: United States Olympic Committee, 1977), pp. 3-5.
40. "Rules of the International Olympic Committee," in *The Olympic Games,* ed. Michael Morris Killanin and John Rodda (New York: Macmillan, 1976), pp. 258, 261.

interpretation would morally pertain to institutionalized rituals, rites and social ideologies not based on transcendent beings. Whereas the Games of antiquity certainly belong to the first category, Coubertin most likely had the second type in mind. Thus, the so-called religious significance of the Modern Games would radically differ from that of the ancient ones. Being a symbol of festive emotions, deep engagement, and human accomplishment at peak performance the Olympic Games incarnate the idea of actively achieved human excellence. . . . Rather than being magic and naturalistic, it is a historically developed myth of a sporting climax of life, and of sportsmanship institutionalized and symbolized by conventional social rules.[41]

Today the Games are characterized by symbols, rituals, and ceremonies which create, both for the spectators and for the athletes, some common emotional experiences, although they may vary in intensity from the thrill of watching the torch bearer arrive in the stadium to light the Olympic flame, to the victorious athlete's transcendent sensation when the ribbon with the gold medal is slipped over the head.

The Olympic hymn, officially adopted in 1958, was composed for the first modern Games in Athens by the Greek Spyros Samaras with words by Costis Palamas. The Olympic emblem, five interlaced rings, was adapted by Coubertin from an emblem at Delphi to symbolize the five continents of the world. The Olympic flag was designed with the rings in five different colors, yellow, black, green, blue and red, set against a field of white. These six colors encompass the colors in the flags of the participating nations. The flag was first flown in 1914 and incorporated into game ceremonies in 1920.

The Olympic motto, *Citius, Altius, Fortius* (Faster, Higher, Stronger) is ascribed to a Dominican monk, Father Henri Didon, who had influenced Coubertin. A second statement, "the most important thing in the Olympic Games is not to win, but to take part," now widely associated with the Olympic Games, appears to have been adopted by Coubertin after he heard it in a sermon.

Immediately following World War I in 1920, doves, signifying peace, became a part of the opening ceremony. The symbolic flame and the torch relay from Olympia were planned for 1928, but the relay did not take place, and was first used in the 1936 Berlin Olympics. The athletes' oath in the opening ceremony and the symbolic medal for victory are further examples of Coubertin's desire to emphasize the religious components of the Games.

From the beginning the head of state in the host country has opened the Games. Officially, the President of the IOC arrives with the head of state and "supervises" the ceremony. The athletes parade by nation, saluting or

41. Hans Lenk, "Toward a Social Philosophy of the Olympics . . .", in *The Modern Olympics,* ed. Peter J. Graham and Horst Ueberhorst (Cornwall, N.Y.: Leisure Press, 1976), p. 116.

acknowledging the President and head of state. Each delegation carries its country's flag, all of which are equal in size. The head of state recites the opening lines, "I declare open the Olympic Games of ___city___ celebrating the ___number___ Olympiad of the modern era." The Olympic hymn is played, the Olympic flag raised, the pigeons or doves released, and the Olympic flame lit by the final torch bearer from Olympia. A representative athlete of the country where the Games are held takes the oath on behalf of the athletes, and the host-city's national anthem is played. Then, the Games are officially underway. In recent years the host-city has staged a display which completes the opening ceremonies.

The victory ceremony is designed to honor the winning athlete with a symbolic prize. The first, second, and third place winners mount the podiums—the first place the middle one, the second to the right of the first place, and the third to the left. The president of the IOC or his representative slips a ribbon with the proper medal over the heads of the victors, and the flag of the winner's country is raised and the national anthem played.

The closing ceremony is altogether different from the opening ceremony and is meant to fulfill a different function from the opening ceremony. The athletes do not march by country, but instead walk together, eight to ten abreast, with the countries intermingled, thus signifying friendship through international sport. With the President of the IOC presiding, the Greek flag is raised on one of three flag poles. Next the flag of the host-city's country is raised and that national anthem played. Finally the flag of the country where the next Games will be celebrated is raised and that anthem played. The President of the IOC declares the Games ended, the trumpets sound, the Olympic flame is extinguished, the Olympic anthem played, the Olympic flag lowered, and the athletes march out.

Athens, 1896

Coubertin's original idea had been to hold the first modern Games in connection with the 1900 Paris World's Fair. However, Vikelas from Greece requested that the first modern Games be held in Athens in 1896. The 1894 Paris Congress approved Vikelas' proposal and preparations began immediately. Reconstructing the necessary facilities presented a severe financial strain on the Greek government, and Coubertin had to travel to Athens to lend his support to the Olympic idea and publicly acclaim the Greek origin of the Games. Finally, a commission of citizens, with Crown Prince Constantine as its Honorary President, undertook the organization and conduct of the Games.

The major difficulty was finding the money to reconstruct the ancient Panathenean Stadium so that it could be used. The Greek architect

Metaxes, also a member of the commission to organize the Games, designed the reconstruction, but the funds were difficult to obtain. Prince Constantine contacted a wealthy Alexandrian and Greek citizen, George Averoff, who made a gift of about one million drachmas for the stadium. The Greeks raised the other necessary funds in a variety of ways.

> The issue of the first stamps dedicated to the Olympic theme, brought in 400,000 drs. Much of the required money was provided by the distribution of commemorative medals and the sale of tickets.[42]

The first Games of the modern Olympics were simple but ceremonial. On Easter Sunday, March 24, 1896, King George of Greece opened the Games and the Olympic hymn was sung while the athletes stood in the center of the stadium. Many of the athletes travelled informally to Athens, not in teams as they do today. Most of the United States athletes were members of the Boston Athletic Club or students from Princeton University. From the beginning Coubertin had planned that the events in the modern Olympics would reflect contemporary sport. While the modern Games included more track and field athletic events than any other sport, thus reflecting the ancient Games, there were also events in sports such as cycling, shooting, and tennis.

Events in the 1896 Games[43]

Sport	Number of Events	Sport	Number of Events
Fencing	3	Shooting	5
Weight Lifting	2	Swimming	4
Athletics	12	Tennis	2
Cycling	6	Gymnastics	8
Wrestling	1		

The modern Olympic events brought some remarks from an American magazine:

> An ancient Greek, had he come to life again, would have missed some of the events of his old games. The pancration, with its brutalities, was happily lacking. Even boxing was omitted. He might have asked with some reason why the pen-

42. Otto Szymiczek, I ATHENS 1896, in *The Olympic Games,* ed. Michael Morris Killanin and John Rodda (New York: Macmillan, 1976), p. 27.

43. Erich Kamper, *Encyclopedia of the Olympic Games* (New York: McGraw-Hill, 1972), p. 299.

344   The Olympic Games

tathlon was not retained as a test of general athletic excellence. He would hardly have acquiesced in the substitution of the boat-races at Phaleron for the ancient chariot-races, and would doubtless have thought the pistol and rifle shooting a poor substitute for throwing the javelin. But of all the additions to his old list of games he would have found lawn-tennis and bicycling most removed from ancient athletics. Considering, however, not the shades of ancient Greeks, but the modern world, ought not the patrons of the contest to have persuaded Englishmen and Americans to add the sports games of football and baseball?[44]

There was one race specially designed for the occasion. In contrast to the ancient Games, which did not include a marathon race, Coubertin included a race to honor the Greek who ran almost twenty-five miles from Marathon to Athens in 490 B.C. to tell the Athenians that they had won the Battle of Marathon. The Americans had captured most of the events in athletics and the Germans in gymnastics; no Greek had won an event. To the delight of everyone, Spiridon Louis, a Greek shepherd, came in first in the marathon, followed by two other Greeks. A traveler described the scene as Louis finished the race:

It is impossible to describe the enthusiasm within the Stadium—nay, in the whole city of Athens—over the result of this the most important contest in the games during these ten days. The Stadium packed with over 50,000 people; the walls around it, the hills about, covered with a human crowd that from the distance looked like bees clustering over a comb; and this mass of humanity rising in one great shout of joy with the advent—the one runner who was first to cross the line within the Stadium, caught in the arms of the Crown-Prince, who led him before the King, embraced and kissed by those who could get near him; all this and much more sent a thrill through every heart which few could have experienced before with the same intensity. It might almost have been Philippides (sic) of old bringing to the anxious inhabitants of Athens the news of their glorious victory, the salvation of their country and home.[45]

From the beginning of the modern Games, nationalist feeling plagued the IOC over which countries would or would not compete. Even in 1894 Germany had not been invited to the Congress in Paris because the French Gymnastic Union had threatened to leave if it were invited. However, in 1895 Dr. W. Gebhardt from Germany became a member of the IOC and it appeared as if Germany would compete in Athens. Later the Germans announced that they would not compete, but through the continued efforts of the German Olympic Committee and Gebhardt, 19 Germans finally took part in the first modern Games.

---

44. Rufus B. Richardson, "The New Olympian Games," *Scribner's Magazine* 20, no. 3 (September, 1896): 269.

45. Charles Waldstein, "The Olympian Games at Athens," *Harper's Weekly* 40, no. 3 (September, 1896): 490.

Countries Represented by the 1896 Athletes[46]

Country	Number of Athletes	Country	Number of Athletes
Australia	1	Greece	230
Bulgaria	1	Great Britain	8
Chile	1	Austria	4
Denmark	4	Sweden	1
Germany	19	Switzerland	1
France	19	Hungary	8
U.S.A.	14		

Coubertin did not want women in the Olympics and no events were planned for women in 1896. However, there is a story that one woman, Melpomene, ran the marathon race in the Games at Athens. She had trained herself for the event and applied to enter the race but was refused. According to accounts, she ran alongside the male athletes and completed the race. Thus it appears that the women have participated in some fashion throughout the modern Olympic Games.

The first Games of the modern Olympics were clearly a Greek affair. In spite of the early difficulties the Greek people took great pride in the Games and also staged performances of two famous Greek dramas, *Medea* and *Antigone,* presented concerts, gave receptions, and created an atmosphere of festivity in the city. Coubertin remained in the background, with the satisfaction of seeing his dream of modern Olympic Games begin to come true.

The Period of Organization, 1900-1912

The modern Olympic Games were not firmly established until 1912. By that time, international sport federations were in existence, the techniques and performance of the sports had improved, the methods of measuring and judging had been developed, and the idea of international sport was generally accepted. The modern program was not as stable as the ancient games, and sports were added and dropped depending on the country and the available facilities.

For Coubertin, both the 1900 and 1904 Games were failures, probably due to the fact that they were held in conjunction with world fairs and had difficulties during the preparation period. Neither at Paris, the site of the 1900 Games, nor at St. Louis in 1904, were the events considered the serious sport competition which Coubertin had envisioned.

---

46. Erich Kamper, *Encyclopedia of the Olympic Games* (New York: McGraw-Hill, 1972), pp. 295-297.

The 1900 Games, planned for Paris, immediately had difficulties in organization. From 1897 to 1899, differences over the conduct of the Games, changes in personnel, and bickering took place, until Coubertin resigned from the Union of French Athletic Associations, in whose hands the organization had been placed. The Games reflected this background and were described as casual, held in various parts of the city, with many contestants not realizing the nature of the Olympic Games. The events occurred from May to October, in poor locations, on bumpy tracks and in muddy swimming water. In spite of the conditions and confusion, over 1300 men and eleven women participated. Tennis and golf, Olympic sports at that time, permitted women to compete, and thus from 1900 victors' records include women.

The Games in 1904 were held in connection with the St. Louis World's Fair, which celebrated the one hundredth anniversary of the Louisiana Purchase. It had been understood that the third Games of the modern era would be held in the United States. The first consideration was given to Buffalo, then Chicago, and finally St. Louis. Only twelve nations participated with most of the athletes from the United States. Again, the events were held during several weeks of the year and the issue arose as to which events of the many athletic and sport competitions held in St. Louis that summer were official. One report stated that "the International Olympic Committee expressed desires that all athletic competitions under the auspices of the Universal Exposition of 1904 bear the name, 'Olympic.' "[47]

Coubertin did not attend the 1904 Games and was even more disappointed than he had been in the Paris event when he learned of the "Anthropological Days" held in St. Louis in which the emphasis was placed on the origin of the competitors rather than on performance. The athletes were Patagonians, Filipinos, Ainus, Turks, native American Sioux Indians, and Syrians. The one highlight of the 1904 Olympics was the excellent athletic facilities used at Washington University.

For several reasons "interim" Games were held in Athens in 1906. Very few Europeans had competed in St. Louis and Coubertin did not want the idea of international sport to be forgotten. Both the Paris and St. Louis Games had dismayed Coubertin and he wished to reestablish the idea of serious sport competition in relation to the Olympic ideals. The 1906 Games were held without fanfare, and while not considered "official" they were successful. Even though they were not well attended, Coubertin believed they permitted the modern Games to continue in the direction he hoped to establish.

---

47. D.R. Francis, *The Universal Exposition of 1904* (St. Louis: Louisiana Purchase Exposition Co., 1913), p. 538.

The 1908 Games had been planned for Rome, but that city was unable to keep its commitment. British members of the IOC were approached about the possibility of holding the 1908 Games in London and agreed to do so. With years of sport tradition, an Amateur Athletic Association over three decades old, and the experience of conducting the Henley Royal Regatta, the London Games were the best example of modern international sport in the modern era. Experienced in conducting sports events, the British established rules for each event and distributed them in English, French, and German. In an effort to establish comparable status of the athletes, all competitors had to enter the Olympic Games as a member of a country's "team." Also, for the first time, an athletic complex of special sport facilities was built expressly for the Games. The stadium was used for athletics, fencing, gymnastics, swimming, and wrestling. The experience of the Henley Regatta served to improve the rowing events. Women entered three sports in 1908, tennis, archery, and figure skating, and also presented exhibitions in swimming, diving, and gymnastics, which were favorably received.

With the 1912 Games in Stockholm, Coubertin believed that the modern era of the Olympic Games would be successful. Twenty-eight countries sent 3,889 athletes. There were no ugly incidents between athletes or countries, and the events were held in a spirit of serious sport competition and international goodwill. By this time more sports had international federations and had several years experience with international rules. At least three countries, Germany, Sweden, and Great Britain, coached their teams especially for the Games. The United States also had developed its unique approach to athletics, ". . . inter-collegiate competition, professional coaching and sports scholarships . . ."[48]

Three sports were of special importance in the 1912 Olympics. One was swimming, in which women entered for the first time through the suggestion of the international federation. At the suggestion of Count Clarence von Rosen, the Master of the Horse to the King of Sweden, equestrian events had been approved for 1908 but they were unable to be conducted, and they were held for the first time in Stockholm.

A dream of Coubertin to identify the ideal all-round athlete was fulfilled in Stockholm when the modern pentathlon was initiated. It consisted of running, riding, swimming, fencing, and shooting. Coubertin explained the rationale:

> The thread combining all five events is that of the military messenger who is dispatched with vital orders for the front line: his horse is shot away from under

---

48. Tom McNab, "Athletics," in *The Olympic Games,* ed. Michael Morris Killanin and John Rodda (New York: Macmillan, 1976), p. 92.

him after clearing certain obstacles, he fights his way through with his sword which in turn breaks and he is forced to turn his revolver. Forcing his way to the river bank, he dives in to evade his captors and finally delivers the vital message on foot, like Pheidippides, the original runner in 490 B.C. from Marathon to Athens.[49]

The Period of Political Development, 1920-1936

The 1916 Games were not celebrated because of World War I, but the 1920 Games were held as soon as possible after the cessation of the conflict. The Games were awarded to Antwerp in recognition of the sacrifices which the Belgians had made during the World War. Perhaps the most important overall achievement of the period from 1920 to 1936 was that the Games became a major world event in their own right. The modern Olympic Movement demonstrated it could not be deterred by a world war which lasted longer than an Olympiad. The 1920 Games were modest, but by the 1924 Games in Paris there were forty-four nations which entered over 3,000 athletes.

The Games were international in character and victors emerged from a variety of nations. Uruguay was the Olympic champion in association football and athletes from Argentina won two gold medals, one of which was in swimming. A Japanese athlete won a gold in the triple jump, and both South Africa and Egypt had gold medalists. Three important developments occurred during this period. First, the women were admitted to athletic (track and field) events. Second, the Winter Games were initiated, and finally, the Games emerged as part of the international political arena.

The Fight for Women to Enter Athletic Events

Coubertin did not want women in the modern Olympic Games, and continued to resist efforts to include them officially. However, the result of an almost ten-year struggle ended with women officially in the athletic events of the Olympic Games. After World War I European women became interested in track and field or athletic competition and joined the newly formed Fédération Sportive Féminine Internationale (FSFI), which had been established by the French woman, Mme. Millait. International competitions in some fifteen events with distances as great as 1500 meters were held, and before the 1920 Games, Millait tried unsuccessfully to have women's athletic events added to the Olympic program. To demonstrate women's ability to engage in athletics, she organized and conducted the First Women's Olympic Games, held in 1922 and planned for the midpoint of each subsequent Olympiad.

---

49. James Coote, "Modern Pentathlon," in *The Olympic Games,* ed. Michael Morris Killanin and John Rodda (New York: Macmillan, 1976), pp. 117, 118.

The Women's Games were successful, even though the United States women physical educators objected to them. Preparations were underway for the second Women's Games when negotiations with the International Amateur Athletic Federation led to a plan to control women's athletics and to recommend an Olympic program of five events for women. Millait attempted to increase the number of events but was unsuccessful. The British women protested the meager program and refused to compete in the 1928 Games.

However, the five-event program was eventually accepted and, for the first time, women competed officially in the athletic events in the 1928 Games at Amsterdam. Even these few events were jeopardized when some of the contestants barely finished the 800-meter race. The FSFI proposed fifteen events for 1932, but the 800-meter race was deleted and a total of 6 events opened to women in 1932. However, the controversy continued throughout the deliberations on the possible harmful effects of athletics on women. Those opposed "threatened harm to future mothers" and "A 1921 newspaper reported that sport for women should not be severely competitive."[50]

The United States women physical educators objected to women in the Olympic Games, not so much on the grounds of health, but because of the cost and attention given to a few highly skilled athletes rather than instruction to a great many women. In 1928, and again in 1932, United States women physical education associations protested the women's participation to the IOC.

Millait continued to hold the Women's Olympic Games, changing the name to Women's World Games. From the beginning the Games were planned to honor a country as the winner and the first two Games honored Great Britain and the last two Germany. The Women's Games were held in Paris in 1922; Gothenburg, Sweden in 1926; Prague in 1930; and for the last time in London in 1934.

While the controversy over the entry of women into the Games ended in 1928, the problem was not completely resolved. The questions of the extent to which women could participate and their role in the sport-governing federations remained unsettled.

The Winter Games

Just as Coubertin was opposed to women in the Games, he also objected to the idea of Winter Games. He believed they would detract from the summer Games, but finally, convinced of the increased popularity of winter sports, he joined with the IOC in approving the Winter Games with certain

---

50. Betty Spears, "Women in the Olympics: An Unresolved Problem," in *The Modern Olympics,* ed. Peter J. Graham and Horst Ueberhorst (Cornwall, N.Y.: Leisure Press, 1976), p. 68.

stipulations. The name "Olympiad" is not used for the winter cycle, and while the country in which the summer Games are staged has the opportunity to offer the Games, if it is appropriate, the location of the Winter Games may be somewhat distant from the summer city. The Winter Games began with a modest program of five sports, ice hockey, figure skating for men and women, speed skating for men, four-man bob sled, Nordic cross-country skiing for men, and ski jumping. Sonja Henie was the child star of the first Winter Games.

The Politicizing of the Games

Although the VI Olympiad had to be cancelled because of World War I, the ability to celebrate the VII Games was an important factor in the post-war Olympic movement. The unpretentious 1920 Games were organized in a very short period of time, but their very celebration supported the ideals of the Olympic Movement. The later Olympiads of the period reemphasized the increasingly international nature of the Games. In Amsterdam at the 1928 Games forty-six nations entered 5470 athletes. Although the Los Angeles Games were smaller, the 105,000-seat stadium itself was the largest Olympic stadium yet built, representing the city's efforts to create a mammoth sport entertainment spectacular.

Throughout this period the Games became increasingly politicized. In the first few Games athletes from both large and small nations won gold medals. The prestige such a victory brought to a small nation became apparent and the athletes vied for victory to bring honor to themselves and to their country. Although Coubertin believed in honoring only individual winners, the addition of team sports made identification of winning countries a necessary part of the Olympics. Thus, more attention was paid to the country winning team events. Sports reporters and sportscasters devised an unofficial point system and the publicized "points" further identified countries rather than individuals. An additional factor introduced in Los Angeles was the civic pride displayed by the city as it produced a sport extravaganza for foreign visitors.

Added to this was the intensifying international political scene in which power over men's and women's opinions played a major role in the new totalitarian governments. Berlin had been awarded the 1936 Games in 1931, two years before Hitler came to power. Although Coubertin and the IOC placed the Olympic Games above political maneuvering and power plays, it was during this period that plans for the 1936 Games were formulated. By 1936 the Games had moved from the control of the German Olympic Organizing Committee to that of Hitler and the Nazi Party. Goodhue emphasizes the fact that "One cannot detach 1936 from the previous Olympic Games. It was not simply an aberration. The conditions that made

1936 possible were apparent in the development of the Games from 1900-1932.''[51]

Athletes and Performances

Amid the growing size and importance of the Olympic Games many men and women made their contributions to sport through their Olympic performances. Form improved, technical aids were invented and utilized, and sport organizations helped to regulate national and international competition.

In men's athletics the Finns were among the outstanding athletes. The famous Finn Paavo Nurmi suffered a defeat in his first Olympic event, but went ahead to win the 10,000-meter race. That was in 1920 and he continued to dominate the men's 1500- and 5000-meter races in 1924 and 1928. Although in the United States Charles Paddock was an exciting United States sprinter in the twenties, perhaps the most exciting track and field star in the 1932 Games was Mildred "Babe" Didrikson. Coming from Texas she qualified for the AAU championships in Chicago as a one-woman team and in Los Angeles took two gold medals and missed a third when she was disqualified for form in the running high jump.

In swimming, Duke Kahanamoku continued to excel in the various events and the child star Aileen Riggin won the gold in springboard diving. Kahanamoku and Weismuller were the famous United States swimmers of the period with Weismuller winning the 100-meter gold in 1924 and 1928 after Kahanamoku had won this event in 1912 and 1920. In 1932 Helene Madison and Eleanor Holm turned in outstanding performances while the Japanese men shattered records in several events.

Although Sonja Henie had placed last in the 1924 Winter Games as a child, in 1928, 1932, and 1936 she took gold medals. She was the first woman to win three consecutive gold medals in the Olympics. The 1928 Winter Games were held at St. Moritz and the 1932 Games at Lake Placid, where snow had to be trucked in from nearby Canada. The Winter Games attempted different organizations of the events, such as the unsuccessful massed starts in speed skating.

The Nazi Olympics, 1936

Within a year after the United States stock market crash in 1929, almost every major national economy was thrust into a world-wide Depression. Drastic measures were needed and within a few years Britain granted

---

51. Robert M. Goodhue, "The Development of Olympism, 1900-1932: Technical Success within a Threatening Political Reality," in *The Modern Olympics,* ed. Peter J. Graham and Horst Ueberhorst (Cornwall, N.Y.: Leisure Press, 1976), p. 30.

emergency powers to their national government, the United States operated under the New Deal, and in Germany the National Socialist Revolutionary Movement emerged. Mussolini was in power in Italy and in 1933 both Roosevelt and Hitler became heads of their governments. Many people in democratic countries, facing catastrophic government decisions themselves, viewed the Fascist and Nazi systems as experiments. As the web of control over the average citizen became evident in the new totalitarian states, and as the Nazi systematic extinction of Jews was announced and put into effect, many people from other countries were first dismayed and then horrified. Although these policies appeared to be in direct contradiction to the Olympic regulation forbidding discrimination on the grounds of race, politics, or religion, plans for the Games to be held in Berlin proceeded. However, some countries became concerned and indicated they might not participate in the 1936 Games. As early as 1933 the United States AAU passed a resolution against entering the Berlin Games unless Germany complied with the IOC policy of not discriminating on the basis of race or religion.

During the 1933 IOC meetings, the Committee was assured by the German IOC members that they would remain on the German Organizing Committee, thus maintaining the political neutrality of the Games. The German government also agreed that German Jews would not be "excluded from the German teams for the 11th Olympic Games."[52]

Brundage, President of the American Olympic Committee (AOC, former name of USOC), toured Germany in 1934 and decided that the German sport programs were in compliance with the letter and spirit of Olympism. Although the AOC had not yet accepted the invitation to participate in the 1936 Games, after Brundage's reassurance they voted to enter the Berlin Olympics. This did not stop the controversy over the entry of the United States athletes and in 1935 the situation was exacerbated when Hitler proclaimed further restrictions on German Jews. The movement against the Olympics gained strength from organizations such as the National Council of the Methodist Church and the American Federation of Labor; magazines such as *Commonweal;* and papers such as the New York *Times* and the New York *Daily News.* As late as 1935 the AAU remained in opposition to sending teams to Berlin. Those in favor of the United States entering the Games countered with arguments based on principles such as Coubertin's belief in the importance of holding the Games regularly, his creed of Olympism, and hopes of promoting international understanding.

The situation was finally resolved at the December, 1935 meeting of the AAU:

---

52. Arnd Kruger, "The 1936 Olympic Games—Berlin," in *The Modern Olympics,* ed. Peter J. Graham and Horst Ueberhorst (Cornwall, N.Y.: Leisure Press, 1976), p. 169.

Both sides gathered rhetorical ammunition for a great debate at the national convention of the Amateur Athletic Union which opened in New York in early December. The proponents of a boycott were armed with resolutions to that effect from regional associations of the A.A.U. The delegates met tensely, but the expected battle was never really joined. The executive committee of the A.A.U. met at the Hotel Commodore on Sunday, December 8, to listen to five hours of speeches for and against participation. The moguls of American amateur sport were hungry and tired when time for a vote came. The executives (who had weighted voting rights) defeated the proposed resolution against sending an American team by 2 1/2 votes. The narrow majority then succeeded in passing a motion in favor of participation, adding the specific rider that their affirmative action was not to be "construed to imply endorsement of the Nazi government."[53]

As a result of the action Mahoney, president of the AAU, resigned and Brundage was elected the AAU president. In his now dual role of president of both the AAU and the AOC, Brundage went ahead with plans for the Games.

The boycotts and furor over the Nazi regime resulted in the planning of the "Peoples Games" or "Workers' Games," for Barcelona, Spain, just prior to the Berlin Olympic Games. Athletic teams from many countries were in Spain to boycott the official 1936 Olympic Games and to protest the policies of Hitler, when on the eve of the Games the Spanish Civil War broke out.

In spite of the turmoil, the 1936 Berlin Olympic Games were celebrated in an elaborately staged sport spectacle during which athletes and visitors alike enjoyed the carefully planned German hospitality. As if to discredit Hitler's theory of Aryan superiority, the star of the Games was the black American, Jesse Owens. He won four gold medals in the 100-meter and 200-meter sprints, the broad jump, and the 400-meter relay. One of seven children, he grew up in Cleveland, Ohio, where one of his teachers suggested he try running to improve his health. He was soon found to be incredibly fast, and soon he was being trained for several track events. As a sophomore at Ohio State he broke four records in the 1935 Big Ten track and field championship meet.[54]

There was no question that the athletic events were well organized and that the athletic performances were the best the world had seen. The IOC gained more world-wide publicity than it had had in the past, but it also lost some of its credibility. Although the Games had more and more reflected the political atmosphere of the times, Germany moved the control of the games from the Organizing Committee to the German government while the

---

53. Richard D. Mandell, *The Nazi Olympics* (New York: Macmillan, 1971), p. 79.
54. John Durant, *Highlights of the Olympics* (New York: Hastings House, 1965), pp. 55-59.

IOC stood by. The 1936 Olympic Games thus became the instrument of the Nazi government, and although later Games would again be conducted by Organizing Committees, the Games themselves would never be the same.

Eight Successive Olympiads, 1948-1976

Demonstrating the importance of the Olympic movement as a world-wide phenomenon, the IOC awarded the 1940 Games to Tokyo. But neither the 1940 nor the 1944 Games were celebrated because of conflicts on three continents, culminating in World War II. It seemed that the world was seeking relief from the ravages of war, for as soon as possible after peace was declared the 1948 Olympics in London brought together almost 4500 athletes from 59 countries. The world character of the modern Games was emphasized by the fact that athletes from 42 countries competed in the final events of the sports. Still recovering from the war, London had to utilize many temporary and improvised facilities. With the exception of the closed circuit telecast in Berlin, this was the first time provision was made for televising the Games.

The London Games were the first in a series of eight successive Olympiads, the longest continuous series in the modern Olympic era. The U.S.S.R. was invited to enter the 1948 Games and, although they declined, they sent observers to London. Throughout this period, performances continued to improve due to better training, better health, better technical equipment, and a greater number of qualifying athletes from which to select Olympic contenders. Many of these factors were the results of what Coubertin had foreseen as part of the modern Olympic Movement.

The athletes in London varied from 17-year-old Bob Mathias from California to Holland's Fanny Blankers-Koen. After just three weeks' coaching young Mathias entered a regional decathlon meet, which he won. He then went on to the nationals where he earned a berth on the Olympic team and later won the gold medal in the decathlon. In contrast, Blankers-Koen had competed in the 1936 Games and twelve years later at almost thirty years of age, won four gold medals: the 80-meter hurdles, the 100- and 200-meter sprints, and member of the 4×100-meter relay. London saw the first appearance of Emil Zatopek, the Czechoslovakian runner, who competed again in 1952. Twenty-eight countries competed in the 1948 Winter Games at St. Moritz. Alpine skiing was introduced as a full-fledged event although there had been some competition in this area in 1936. The United States' Gretchen Fraser took first in the special slalom and Dick Button starred in the figure skating.

The Helsinki Games in 1952 were conducted with more dignified ceremony than the London ones but without the prewar pageantry of the 1936 Berlin Games. Almost all events reflected the increased attention given

FIG. 8.8   Seventeen-year-old Bob Mathias: 1948, 1952 Olympic Decathlon Champion. Wide World.

to sports in the Olympic countries after World War II. Russian athletes entered the Olympic Games in 1952 for the first time in forty years. They prepared very carefully for the Games, organizing a central sport authority which arranged mass competitions in schools and provided for the athletes selected to compete. The Russians began their practice of finding positions for adult athletes in which time was made available to prepare for and participate in international competitions.

Even though the next Games were held half-way around the world in Melbourne, Australia, athletes from 67 countries competed. The Games were celebrated in an atmosphere of world political unrest due to the 1956 unsuccessful Hungarian rebellion against the Soviet Union, and other international incidents. Although the fighting continued in Hungary, the Hungarians managed to send a team. The Netherlands and Spain, however, withdrew in protest of the conditions in Hungary; Egypt and Lebanon did not participate because of a Middle East crisis; and the People's Republic of China refused to compete because the Republic of China in Taiwan entered athletes in the Games.

Despite the dampening effect of international disputes the Games were considered successful. The Hungarian athletes who managed to reach Melbourne received a standing ovation as they marched into the stadium for the opening ceremonies. In the athletic events the United States men dominated the track events, taking the gold, silver, and bronze medals in four events. Young Wilma Rudolph earned her first Olympic medal, a bronze in the 4 × 100-meter relay. One of the outstanding women athletes was Australia's Betty Cuthbert, who won the 100- and 200-meter sprints. The Australian swimmers, working under innovative coaching techniques, won all the medals in swimming. Dawn Fraser won the 100-meter freestyle, a feat which she repeated in 1960 and 1964.

The most talked-about event was the USSR-Hungary water polo game, described as a replay in the swimming pool of the Hungarian rebellion. In marked contrast with the reality, Hungary won, 4-0. USSR athletes, on the whole, were well prepared for the Games and won five more gold medals than the United States, 37-32, and 24 additional medals, including silver and bronze. With the USSR and the USA recognized as major world powers, the press and many individuals interpolated political and ideological competitions into the rivalry in sport.

In 1960 at the Rome Games, the United States' long domination of men's track and field events ended when athletes from New Zealand, Poland, Germany, and Italy won gold medals. Of the ten women's track events, the USSR women took six, but the favorite woman athlete of the Rome Games was Wilma Rudolph, who won three gold medals. The United States swimmers reversed the Melbourne records and won eleven gold medals, breaking five world records. In boxing, Cassius Clay was awarded a gold medal in the light heavyweight division.

The Tokyo Games reflected the increasing size and complexity of staging modern sport competitions. Elaborate but functional facilities contributed to the excellent conduct of the Games and Japanese technology permitted live telecasts to 39 countries by way of a satellite. The increased coverage permitted millions who previously had read about the Games or listened to them on the radio to visually become part of the Olympic Games. The viewers saw many athletes from previous Games who repeated or bettered their performances, including Bikila, the Ethiopian marathon runner,

FIG. 8.9   Wilma Rudolph winning the 200-meter dash at the 1960 Olympic Games in Rome. Wide World.

swimmer Dawn Fraser, runner Snell from New Zealand, and gymnast Cáslavská from Czechoslovakia. South Africa by this time had been banned from the Olympics because of its *apartheid* policies.

FIG. 8.10   Bob Beamon at the 1968 Olympic Games. Wide World.

FIG. 8.11   Peggy Fleming, 1972 Olympic women's figure skating champion. Wide World.

When the 1968 Games were awarded to Mexico City apparently little thought was given to the effects of altitude on athletic performance. While a great deal of research and planning on how to train for the 1968 Games occurred, athletes from countries with high altitudes had advantages in the endurance events. Some athletes who did not live in high altitudes trained away from home to learn to accommodate to the thin air. Bob Beamon from the United States astounded everyone with his incredible jump of 29 ′ 2 1/2 ″. Among the innovations in Mexico City was the United States' Dick Fosbury's famous Fosbury Flop with which he edged out his teammate for a gold medal. The "Flop" was viewed with disbelief as Fosbury approached the high jump bar, leaped across the bar on his back and landed, also on his back. His championship jump set an Olympic record of 7 ′ 4 1/4 ″. Both the United States men and women set the pace in the swimming events and, in women's gymnastics, Cáslavská continued to dominate the events.

The United States athletes faced a controversy reflecting the relationship between the athlete and his country. In the midst of unrest over civil rights in the United States, a small group of black athletes threatened to boycott the Olympic Games to increase the awareness of the problems of the black athlete. The boycott did not occur, but after taking the gold and bronze medals in the 200-meter sprint, Tommie Smith and Juan Carlos stood on the winners' podiums and, as the national anthem was played, raised their fists in the black power salute. The shocked IOC debated on a suitable punishment and, at one point, it was rumored that the entire United States team might be removed from the Games. The final result was the suspension of Smith and Carlos by the USOC.

The Munich Games for 1972 were planned to be as perfect as possible in every respect. Each sport facility incorporated the latest technical developments, from advanced sweeping architecture to electronic measuring devices. Great care was taken with even the smallest details to create an atmosphere in which athletes could compete for the highest sport honors in the world. Almost 6,000 men and over 1,000 women entered events in 21 sports. The sports world turned its attention on Munich and watched the events on television, listened to the radio, or followed the events in the papers. Record after record fell as new Olympic champions mounted the podiums for the first time or repeated a victory from earlier Olympics. Mark Spitz from the United States achieved the seemingly impossible feat of winning seven gold medals in swimming. The women stars included gymnast Olga Korbut who endeared herself to the world and sparked a growing interest in women's gymnastics, the German sprinter Renate Stecher, and Mary Peters from Ireland, who won the pentathlon at the age of 32.

FIG. 8.12   Mark Spitz, winner of seven gold medals at the 1972 Olympic Games in Munich. Wide World.

In team sports the United States lost the basketball tournament for the first time in history in a controversial game with the USSR. Because of a mistaken signal during a final United States foul shot, which made the score 50-49 in their favor, the United States believed the game was over and that they had won, but the Russians thought they had signaled time out. After disputing the signal most of the night the officials announced a replay of the final three seconds of the game, during which the Russians scored a goal, officially winning the game, 51-50, and the basketball tournament.

Intruding into the schedule of the closely fought games and the many well-contested events was a 23-hour horror. The New York *Times* headline on September 6 told the story:

9 ISRAELIS ON OLYMPIC TEAM KILLED WITH 4 ARAB CAPTORS AS POLICE FIGHT BAND THAT DISRUPTED MUNICH GAMES

MUNICH, West Germany, Wednesday, Sept. 6—Eleven members of Israel's Olympic team and four Arab terrorists were killed yesterday in a 23-hour drama that began with an invasion of the Olympic Village by the Arabs. It ended in a shootout at a military airport some 15 miles away as the Arabs were preparing to fly to Cairo with their Israeli hostages.

The first two Israelis were killed early yesterday morning when Arab commandos, armed with automatic rifles, broke into the quarters of the Israeli team and seized nine others as hostages. The hostages were killed in the airport shootout between the Arabs and German policemen and soldiers.[55]

Never before had the tensions of the world ripped into the modern Olympic Games to this degree. The IOC, the athletes, and the world were stunned. After a debate as to whether or not to end the Games, the IOC decided to continue them, thus reaffirming its position that the Games transcend politically motivated violence:

The International Olympic Committee and the West German Olympic Committee will participate, together with the Olympic participants, in a memorial service for the victims tomorrow, Wednesday, at 10 o'clock in the Olympic Stadium. This service should make it clear the Olympic idea is stronger than terror and violence.[56]

The memorial service for the slain athletes was attended by 80,000; later that afternoon the Games went on.

The 1976 Winter Games also were held in Europe in Innsbruck where live television coverage made the Games a world-wide sport spectacular. England's John Curry and Dorothy Hamill of the United States, popular gold medalists in figure skating, both turned professional after the Games. The United States' Billy Koch's unexpected silver medal in the 30-kilometer Nordic ski race surprised everyone. Other outstanding performers included American speed skater Sheila Young.

After the tragedy in Munich, the Games of the XXI Olympiad, hosted by Montreal, Canada, were organized to provide maximum security. Heli-

---

55. David Binder, "9 Israelis on Olympic Team Killed," New York *Times,* 6 September 1972, p. 1.

56. Neil Amdur, "Games Suspended; Rites in Arena Set," New York *Times,* 6 September 1972, p. 18.

FIG. 8.13 Speed skater Sheila Young, gold medal winner in the 500-meter race at the 1976 Winter Olympic Games. Wide World.

copters hovered above the opening ceremonies over which England's Queen Elizabeth II presided. Watchful armed guards accompanied the athletes to and from the Olympic Village. Fortunately, no incidents occurred as the more than 7,000 athletes from 100 countries competed.

Nadia Comaneci, a 14-year-old Rumanian gymnast, astounded both the judges and the computer with scores of 10. By the end of her performances Comaneci had won three gold medals, a silver medal, and a bronze medal. Lasse Viren, the outstanding Finnish runner, again dominated the track and field events. In both 1972 and 1976 he took first place in the 5,000- and 10,000-meter race. The United States regained the gold medal in men's basketball, and in the first appearance of women's basketball in the Games, the United States women lost to Russia in the finals. Whereas the United States men swept the swimming events, it was the East German women who took the women's swimming events. While the Montreal Games themselves displayed world-class athletes in competition to prove their athletic prowess, the development of the Games, the near crises over completing the facilities, and the technology of world-wide communication coverage for the Olympic Games underscored many problems which the IOC would have to face in planning for the future of the Games.

The IOC and the Promotion of Amateur Sport

The IOC is charged with promoting amateur sport and the spirit of Olympism throughout the world. To accomplish this purpose the IOC grants patronage to selected regional games and an International Olympic Academy.

Regional Games

When the first request for sponsorship for games other than the Olympic Games was received, the IOC debated the issue and set a precedent by agreeing to sponsor the Far Eastern Games. Certain games were denied patronage because of government interference, while other games were planned but for a variety of reasons did not occur. Prior to the 1936 Olympics:

> . . . the proliferation of regional games was widespread. The I.O.C. was usually asked for its patronage, but not always. Games now held included the Balkan Games, the Colombian Games, the Central American Games, and several others. The situation was rapidly developing where several major "Games" meets were held each year.[57]

While regional games were disrupted by World War II, following the war, other games such as the Pan-American Games, the Mediterranean Games, and the Asian Games were introduced. These games occur in the third year of the Olympiad, follow the same general pattern of the Olympic Games, but do not always include the same program of sports.

Some games have created problems for the IOC. The Games of the New Emerging Forces (G.A.N.E.F.O.), initiated by the president of the Indonesian Republic, did not involve the international sport federations, and thus the conduct of the sports was difficult. Further, the invitations were issued through diplomatic channels, thus casting a political atmosphere on the contests. Leiper points out:

> The regional games appear to have achieved their original purpose of spreading interest in sport across the world, and of acting as a competitive preparation for Olympic athletes. The eventual intrusion of politics into these games was a reflection of conditions in many fields of endeavor involving international contacts.[58]

Additional Games have been spawned, not by region, but by educational institutions. Many Olympic athletes are students and through the efforts of the International Union of Students and a group of western European educators, the Federation Internationale du Sports Universitaire (FISU)

---

57. Jean M. Leiper, "The International Olympic Committee: The Pursuit of Olympism 1894-1970." Ph.D. dissertation, The University of Alberta, 1976, p. 245.

58. Jean M. Leiper, "The International Olympic Committee: The Pursuit of Olympism 1894-1970," Ph.D. dissertation, The University of Alberta, 1976, p. 249.

was established in 1948. The First World University Games were held in 1959 and have continued since that time.

The International Olympic Academy

One of Coubertin's ambitions was a permanent site where sport and the Olympic ideal could be discussed and studied by sport scholars from all over the world. Various suggestions were made, but it was not until 1949 that the IOC gave permission for an International Olympic Academy. The Academy, operated by the Hellenic Olympic Committee, is located in ancient Olympia, Greece, overlooking the ancient stadium. It opened in 1961 with 31 students from 24 countries. The Academy meets for two weeks each summer and is housed in a complex of classrooms, libraries, meeting rooms, and dormitories. The number of students is limited. Each student must be from a country with a recognized NOC. The Academy has grown to about 150 students and teachers from all over the world.

Summary

Many of today's athletic traditions and customs can be traced to ancient Greece. Homer's tales of the funeral games of Patroclus include sport customs and traditions which are part of today's sport. Our language utilizes many Greek words or their derivatives which relate to sport. The Greek word *athlos,* from which we have "athletics," embodies striving for excellence of body and mind, testing, and training. Gymnastics literally means exercising in the nude, but refers in general to physical exercise. Words such as gymnasium, stadium, discus, and pentathlon survive in our language from the ancient festivals.

Our most visible legacy of the ancient Olympic Games is today's modern Olympic Games, which were originally fashioned after many concepts from the sixth and fifth-century festivals when the Greek Games were at their height. When Coubertin revived the Games in 1896 it was his hope that the modern Games would represent the ancient concept of *arete* at its finest. The modern Olympic Games have grown from Coubertin's dream of an ideal international sport competition to be the greatest influence on amateur sport today. In spite of wars, crises, confrontations, and acts of terrorism, eighteen Olympic Games have been celebrated since 1896. Olympic teams represent millions of young people participating in sport organizations and competing in Olympic sports from childhood.

The modern Olympic Games have become a world arena which television brings into the homes of millions of people around the world. Each nation's athletes have been thrust into a role undreamed of by Coubertin. With the world's attention focused for days on summer and winter sport, the Games have suffered at the hands of politicians and terrorists. They carry more than the message of *aretē,* of amateur athletes striving and contesting for excellence; for many they carry a message of national prestige or status among the countries of the world. However, in spite of the many difficulties, the modern Olympic Games fulfill a unique function in today's world and, to a large extent, have achieved the goals of the Olympic Movement.

Questions for Discussion

1. Analyze the similarities and differences of the symbols, rituals, and ceremonies of the ancient and modern Games. Do the modern symbols, rituals, and ceremonies serve the same functions as the ancient symbols, rituals, and ceremonies?
2. Define professionalism in athletics. How did professionalism affect the ancient Games?
3. What evidence do we have that women entered ancient athletic festivals? How does their place in the ancient Games compare with their place in the modern Games?
4. Analyze Coubertin's contributions to and influences on the modern Games.
5. How have the modern Games contributed to the development of a world society? Which of these contributions do or do not relate to sport? Support your answers with at least three examples.
6. Should the Olympic Games continue? Support your position with a half page of carefully thought out reasons.

Suggestions for Further Reading

1. Finley, M.I., and Pleket, H.W. *The Olympic Games: The First Thousand Years.* New York: The Viking Press, 1976.
2. Graham, Peter J., and Ueberhorst, Horst, eds. *The Modern Olympics.* Cornwall, N.Y.: Leisure Press, 1976.
3. Killanin, Michael Morris, and Rodda, John, eds. *The Olympic Games.* New York: Macmillan, 1976.
4. Leigh, Mary. "Pierre de Coubertin: A Man of His Time." *Quest* 22 (Spring, 1974): 19-24.
5. Mandell, Richard D. *The Nazi Olympics.* New York: Macmillan, 1971.
6. Vendien, C. Lynn. "FISU (Federation Internationale du Sports Universitaire) and the World University Games." *Quest* 22 (Spring, 1974): 74-81.

Bibliography

A Course of Calisthenics for Young Ladies. Hartford, Conn.: H. and F.J. Huntington, 1831. No author given; generally presumed to be Catharine Beecher's work.

Adams, Henry. *The United States in 1800.* Ithaca, N.Y.: Great Seal Books, 1955.

Addams, Jane. *Spirit of Youth and the City Streets.* New York: Macmillan, 1909.

Albertson, Roxanne. "Sports and Games in New England Schools and Academies, 1780-1860." Paper presented at the North American Society for Sport History, Boston, Mass., April 16-19, 1975.

Allen, Nathan. *Physical Culture in Amherst College.* Lowell, Mass.: Stone and Huse, 1869.

"Americans: Splurging in Big Ways, Cutting Back in Small Ones." *U.S. News and World Report* 82 (April 25, 1977):26-27.

Anderson, William G. "The Early History of the American Association for Health, Physical Education and Recreation." *The Journal of Health and Physical Education* 12 (January, 1941):3-4, 61-62; (March, 1941):151-153, 200-201; April, 1941):244-245; (May, 1941):313-315, 340.

Armstrong, J. *A Discourse Uttered in Part at Annauskeeg Falls in the Fishing Season, 1739.* Boston: S. Kneeland and T. Green in Queen Street, 1743.

Associated Press Sports Staff. *A Century of Major American Sports.* Maplewood, N.J.: Hammond Inc., 1975.

Audubon, John James. "Kentucky Sports," from "Missouri River Journals (1843)," in *Audubon and His Journals,* Vol. II, ed. Maria R. Audubon. New York: Charles Scribner's Sons, 1897.

Aurther, Robert Alan. "Hanging Out." *Esquire* 84 (October, 1975):28, 54-58.

Ballintine, Harriet Isabel. *The History of Physical Training at Vassar College, 1865-1915.* Poughkeepsie, N.Y.: Lansing and Bros., 19 -?.

Bank, Theodore P. "Army Athletics." *Hygiea* 19 (November, 1941):876-880.

Barrows, Isabel C., ed. *Physical Training, A Full Report of the Papers and Discussion of the Conference Held in Boston in November, 1889.* Boston: George H. Ellis, 1890.

Beck, Robert Holmes. *A Social History of Education.* Englewood Cliffs, N.J.: Prentice-Hall, Inc., 1965.

Becker, Carl. *Everyman His Own Historian.* Chicago: Quadrangle Books, 1966.

Beecher, Catharine. *Letters to the People on Health and Happiness.* New York: Harper, 1855.

Benagh, Jim. *Incredible Olympic Feats.* New York: McGraw-Hill Book Co., 1976.

Bennett, Bruce L. "Christopher P. Linhart, M.D., Forgotten Physical Educator." *Research Quarterly* 35 (March, 1964):3-20.

———, ed. *The History of Physical Education and Sport.* Chicago: The Athletic Institute, 1972.

———. "The Making of Round Hill School." *Quest* 4 (April, 1965):53-64.

———. "Sports in the South Up to 1865." *Quest* 27 (Winter, 1977):4-18.

Bennett, Charles E. *Three Voyages of René Laudonnieré.* Gainesville: The University Presses of Florida, 1975.

Berenson, Senda. *Basket Ball for Women.* New York: American Sports Publishing Company, 1901.

———. "Editorial." *Basketball for Women.* New York: American Sports Publishing Company, 1903.

Berryman, Jack W. "The Animal in Sport: From Low Regard to Highest Esteem, 1778-1866." *Proceedings, 1973,* North American Society for Sport History, Columbus, Ohio (May, 1973):10-12.

———. "From the Cradle to the Playing Field: America's Emphasis on Highly Organized Competitive Sports for Pre-Adolescent Boys." *Journal of Sport History* 2, no. 2 (Fall, 1975):112-131.

Betts, John Rickards. *America's Sporting Heritage: 1850-1950.* Reading, Mass.: Addison-Wesley Publishing Company, 1974.

———. "Home Front, Battle Field, and Sport During the Civil War." *Research Quarterly* 42 (May, 1971):113-132.

———. "Organized Sport in Industrial America." Ph.D. dissertation, Columbia University, 1952.

———. "The Technological Revolution and the Rise of Sport, 1850-1900." *Mississippi Valley Historical Review* 40 (1953):231-256.

Blake, Sophia J. *A Visit to Some American Schools and Colleges.* London: Macmillan and Co., 1867.

Blount, Roy, Jr. "Losersville U.S.A." *Sports Illustrated* 46 (March 21, 1977):74-77, 81-82, 84-86.

Boone, Daniel. "The ADVENTURES of Col. Daniel Boon; containing a NARRATIVE of the WARS of Kentucke, 1798," in *The Discovery, Settlement and present state of Kentucke,* ed. John Filson. New York: Corinth Books, 1962.

Bowen, Wilbur P. "Seven Years of Progress in Preparing Teachers of Physical Education." *American Physical Education Review* 27 (February, 1922):64-65.

Bowes, F.P. *The Culture of Early Charleston.* Chapel Hill: The University of North Carolina Press, 1942.

Boy's and Girl's Book of Sports. Providence: George P. Daniels, 1839.

Bradford's History "Of Plymouth Plantation." Boston: Wright and Potter Printing Co., 1898.

Brailsford, Dennis. *Sport and Society, Elizabeth to Anne.* Toronto: University of Toronto Press, 1969.

Bridenbaugh, Carl. *Cities in the Wilderness.* New York: Ronald Press Co., 1938.

Brown, Joseph. "R. Tait McKenzie, In Tribute." *Journal of Health, Physical Education and Recreation* 38 (May, 1967):27.

Bulger, Margery A. "Ali Ali in Free . . . The Games Children Played in Colonial America." *Early American Life,* August, 1975, pp. 48-49, 82.

Bulletin (1920-1921). Mary Hemenway Alumnae Association, Department of Hygiene. Wellesley College, Wellesley, Mass.

Bulletin (March, 1927). Mary Hemenway Alumnae Association, Graduate Department of Hygiene and Physical Education. Wellesley College, Wellesley, Mass.

Carson, Jane. *Colonial Virginians at Play.* Charlottesville: University of Virginia Press, 1965.

Carver, Robin. *The Book of Sports.* Boston: Lilly, Wait, Colman, and Holden, 1834.

Cassidy, Rosalind. *New Directions in Physical Education for the Adolescent Girl in High School and College.* New York: A.S. Barnes and Co., 1938.

Chalk, Ocania. *Pioneers of Black Sport.* New York: Dodd, Mead and Co., 1975.

Cheska, Alyce. "Ball Game Participation of North American Indian Women." Paper presented at The Third Canadian Symposium on History of Sport and Physical Education, Dalhousie University, August, 1974.

Chujoy, Anatole, and Manchester, Phyllis W., eds. *Dance Encyclopedia.* New York: Simon and Schuster, 1967.

Cogswell, Joseph C., and Bancroft, George. *Prospectus of a School to Be Established at Round Hill, Northampton, Massachusetts.* Cambridge, Mass.: 1823.

Colby, Gertrude. *Natural Rhythms and Dances.* New York: A.S. Barnes & Company, 1922.

Cole, Arthur C. "Our Sporting Grandfathers." *Atlantic Monthly* 150 (July, 1932):88-96.

Collett, Glenna. "Golf We Women Play." *Saturday Evening Post* 200 (July 9, 1927):12-13.

Collier, John. *The Indians of the Americas.* New York: W.W. Norton, 1947.

Constitution, By-Laws and General Rules. New York: United States Olympic Committee, 1977.

Coulton, G.G. *The Medieval Scene.* Cambridge: Cambridge University Press, 1959.

Cozens, Frederick W., and Stumpf, Florence. *Sports in American Life.* Chicago: University of Chicago Press, 1953.

Cresswell, Nicholas. *The Journal of Nicholas Cresswell, 1774-1777.* New York: Lincoln MacVeagh, 1924.

Crowther, Samuel, and Ruhl, Arthur. *Rowing and Track Athletics.* New York: The Macmillan Co., 1905.

Culin, Stewart. *Games of the North American Indians.* New York: Dover, 1975.

Cummings, Parke. *American Tennis: The Story of a Game and Its People.* Boston: Little, Brown and Company, 1957.

Czarnowski, Lucile; Schurman, Nona; Imel, Carmen; and Murray, Ruth Lovell. "Four Dance Pioneers." *Journal of Health, Physical Education and Recreation* 41 (February, 1970):23-31.

Damon, S. Foster. *The History of Square-Dancing.* Worcester, Mass.: American Antiquarian Society, 1952.

Danoff, Eric. "The Struggle for Control of Amateur Track and Field in the United States—Part I." *The Canadian Journal of History of Sport and Physical Education* 6, no. 1 (May, 1975):43-85.

———. "The Struggle for Control of Amateur Track and Field in the United States—Part II." *The Canadian Journal of History of Sport and Physical Education* 6, no. 2 (December, 1975):1-43.

Danzig, Allison, and Brandwein, Peter, eds. *Sport's Golden Age.* New York: Harper, 1948.

Davidson, Basil. *The African Past.* London: Longmans, 1964.

Davidson, Judith. "Sport for Women in the Thirties." Unpublished paper, University of Massachusetts, 1977.

Davis, Thomas R. "Puritanism and Physical Education: The Shroud of Gloom

Lifted." *The Canadian Journal of History of Sport and Physical Education* 3, no. 2 (May, 1972):1-7.

Davis, William S. *Life on a Mediaeval Barony*. New York: Harper & Brothers, 1923.

De Borhegyi, Stephan F. "America's Ballgame." *Natural History* 69 (1960):48-59.

DeGroot, Dudley S. "A History of Physical Education in California (1848-1939)." Ph.D. dissertation, Stanford University, 1940.

Demarest, William H. *A History of Rutgers College*. New Brunswick: Rutgers College, 1924.

De Witt's Base-ball Guide for 1869, ed. Henry Chadwick. New York: Robert M. De Witt, Publisher, 1869.

De Witt's Base-ball Guide for 1875, ed. Henry Chadwick. New York: Robert M. De Witt, Publisher, 1875.

Division for Girls and Women's Sports. "Statement of Policies for Competition in Girls and Women's Sports." *Journal of Health, Physical Education and Recreation* 34 (September, 1963):31-33.

Driver, Harold E. *Indians of North America*. Chicago: University of Chicago Press, 1970.

Dulles, Foster Rhea. *America Learns to Play*. New York: D. Appleton-Century, 1940.

Durant, J. *Pictorial History of American Sports*. New York: A.S. Barnes and Co., 1952.

Durant, John, and Bettman, Otto. *Highlights of the Olympics*. New York: Hastings House, 1965.

Durant, John, and Rice, Edward. *Come Out Fighting*. New York: Duell, Sloan and Pearce, 1946.

Eastman, Mary F. *The Biography of Dio Lewis*. New York: Fowler & Wells, 1891.

Elyot, Sir Thomas. *The Boke Named the Governour,* Vol. II, ed. H.H.S. Croft. London: C. Kegan Paul & Co., 1880.

Emery, Lynne Fauley. *Black Dance in the United States from 1619 to 1970*. Palo Alto, Cal.: National Press Books, 1972.

Eyler, Marvin H. "Some Reflections on Objectivity and Selectivity in Historical Inquiry." *Journal of Sport History* 1, no. 1 (1974):63-76.

Fage, J.D. *An Introduction to the History of West Africa*. Cambridge: Cambridge University Press, 1955.

Federal Register 40, no. 108 (June 4, 1975):24141-24143.

Fidler, Merrie A. "The All-American Girls Baseball League, 1943-51." *Proceedings, 1975,* North American Society for Sport History, Boston, Mass. (April 16-19, 1975):35.

―――. "The Development and Decline of the All-American Girls Baseball League, 1943-54." M.S. thesis, University of Massachusetts, 1976.

Finley, M.I., and Pleket, H.W. *The Olympic Games: The First Thousand Years.* New York: The Viking Press, 1976.

Finley, Ruth E. *The Lady of Godey's: Sara Josepha Hale.* Philadelphia: J.B. Lippincott Co., 1931.

Fleming, Rhonda K. "A History of the Department of Physical Education at Winthrop College." M.S. thesis, University of North Carolina at Greensboro, 1973.

Flint, Timothy. *Recollections of the Last Ten Years,* ed. C. Hartley Grattan. New York: Alfred A. Knopf, 1932.

Forbes, Clarence A. *Greek Physical Education.* New York: The Century Co., 1929.

Forsythe, Lewis L. *Athletics in Michigan High Schools: The First Hundred Years.* New York: Prentice-Hall, Inc., 1950.

Francis, D.R. *The Universal Exposition of 1904.* St. Louis: Louisiana Purchase Exposition Co., 1913.

Franklin, Benjamin. *The Art of Swimming Rendered Easy, Dr. Franklin's Advice to Bathers.* Glassow: Printed for the book sellers, 184-?.

―――. *Benjamin Franklin on Education,* ed. John Hardin Best. New York: Bureau of Publications, Teachers College, 1962.

―――. *Proposals for the Education of Youth in Pennsylvania, 1749.* Ann Arbor: William L. Clements Library, 1927.

Fuess, Claude M. *Amherst.* Boston: Little, Brown, 1935.

Fullerton, H.S. "Baseball—the Business and the Sport." *American Review of Reviews* 63 (April, 1921):417-420.

Furnas, J.C. *The Americans: A Social History of the United States.* New York: G.P. Putnam's Sons, 1969.

Gallico, Paul. *The Golden People.* Garden City, N.Y.: Doubleday, 1964.

Gardiner, E. Norman. *Athletics of the Ancient World.* Oxford: Clarendon Press, 1930.

Garraty, John A., and Gay, Peter. *The Columbia History of the World.* New York: Harper & Row, 1972.

Georgetown College, 1814. Georgetown University Library.

Gerber, Ellen W. "The Ideas and Influences of McCloy, Nash, and Williams," in *The History of Physical Education and Sport,* ed. Bruce L. Bennett. Chicago: The Athletic Institute, 1972.

———. *Innovators and Institutions in Physical Education.* Philadelphia: Lea & Febiger, 1971.

Gerber, Ellen W.; Felshin, Jan; Berlin, Pearl; and Wyrick, Waneen. *The American Woman in Sport.* Reading, Mass.: Addison-Wesley Publishing Company, 1974.

———. "The Controlled Development of Collegiate Sport for Women, 1923-1936." *Journal of Sport History* 2, no. 1 (Spring, 1975):1-28.

Gilbert, Bill, and Williamson, Nancy. "Are You Being Two-Faced?" *Sports Illustrated* 38, no. 22 (June 4, 1973):44-48, 50, 53-54.

———. "Programmed to Be Losers." *Sports Illustrated* 38, no. 23 (June 11, 1973):60-62, 65-66, 68, 73.

———. "Sport Is Unfair to Women." *Sports Illustrated* 38, no. 21 (May 28, 1973):88-92, 94-98.

Goodsell, Willystine, ed. *Pioneers of Women's Education in the United States.* New York: McGraw-Hill Book Company, 1931.

Govett, L.A. *The King's Book of Sports.* London: Elliot Stock, 1890.

Graham, Peter J., and Ueberhorst, Horst, eds. *The Modern Olympics.* Cornwall, N.Y.: Leisure Press, 1976.

Grimsley, Will. *Golf: Its History, People and Events.* Englewood Cliffs, N.J.: Prentice-Hall, 1966.

———. *Tennis: Its History, People and Events.* Englewood Cliffs, N.J.: Prentice-Hall, 1971.

Gulick, Luther. *Physical Education by Muscular Exercise.* Philadelphia: P. Blakiston's Son & Company, 1904.

———. "Physical Education in the Y.M.C.A." *Proceedings,* American Association for the Advancement of Physical Education, 1891.

———. "What the American Young Men's Christian Associations Are Doing for the Physical Welfare of Young Men." *Annual Autumn Games.* Young Men's Christian Association of the City of New York, October 13, 1888.

Gutek, Gerald. *An Historical Introduction to American Education.* New York: Thomas Y. Crowell, 1970.

Hale, Creighton J. "What Research Says About Athletics for Pre-High School Age Children." *Journal of Health, Physical Education and Recreation* 30 (December, 1959):19-21, 23.

Hale, William Harlan. *Ancient Greece*. New York: American Heritage Press, 1970.

Haley, Alex. *Roots*. Garden City, N.Y.: Doubleday, 1976.

Hardy, Stephen H. "The Medieval Tournament: A Functional Sport of the Upper Class." *Journal of Sport History* 1, no. 2 (1974):91-105.

———. "Organized Sport and Community in Ancient Greece and Rome." M.S. thesis, University of Massachusetts, 1975.

Harper's Weekly 23 (September 13, 1879):73.

Harper's Weekly 29 (February 14, 1885):109.

Harris, H.A. *Greek Athletes and Athletics*. London: Hutchinson, 1964.

———. *Sport in Greece and Rome*. Ithaca, N.Y.: Cornell University Press, 1972.

Hart, Albert Bushnell. "Status of Athletic Sports in American Colleges." *Atlantic Monthly* 66 (July, 1890):63-71.

Hartwell, Edward M. *Physical Training in American Colleges and Universities*. Bureau of Education Circular of Information No. 5, 1885. Washington, D.C.: Government Printing Office, 1886.

Hazelton, Helen W. "The University of Minnesota Plan for Freshmen Work." *Bulletin* (September, 1927). Mary Hemenway Alumnae Association, Graduate Department of Hygiene and Physical Education. Wellesley College, Wellesley, Mass.

Henderson, Edwin B. *The Negro in Sports*. Washington, D.C.: Associated Publishers, 1949.

Henderson, Edwin B., and the Editors of Sport Magazine. *The Black Athlete— Emergence and Arrival*. New York: International Library of Negro History, 1968.

Henderson, Robert W. *Ball, Bat, and Bishop*. Reprint. Detroit: Gale Research Co., 1974.

———. *Early American Sport*. 2nd ed. New York: A.S. Barnes & Co., 1953.

Henry, William N. *History of the Olympic Games*. New York: G.P. Putnam's Sons, 1948.

Herskovits, Melville J. *The Myth of the Negro Past*. Boston: Beacon Press, 1958.

Higginson, Thomas Wentworth. "Gymnastics." *Atlantic Monthly* 7 (March, 1861):283-302.

Hill, Lucille Eaton. *Athletic and Out-Door Sports for Women*. New York: The Macmillan Co., 1903.

Hill, Phyllis J. "A Cultural History of Frontier Sport in Illinois, 1673-1820." Ph.D. dissertation, University of Illinois, 1966.

Hitchcock, Edward. *The Power of Christian Benevolence Illustrated in the Life and Labor of Mary Lyon.* Northampton, Mass.: Hopkins, Bridgman, and Company, 1852.

Hoepner, Barbara J., ed. *Women's Athletics: Coping with Controversy.* Washington, D.C.: American Alliance for Health, Physical Education, and Recreation, 1974.

Hole, Christina. *English Sports and Pastimes.* London: B.T. Batsford, 1949.

Hollander, Phyllis. *100 Greatest Women in Sports.* New York: Grosset & Dunlap, 1976.

Holliman, Jennie. *American Sports (1785-1835).* Durham, N.C.: The Seeman Press, 1931.

Holmes, Oliver Wendell. *The Autocrat of the Breakfast Table.* Boston: Houghton, Mifflin and Company, 1904.

Homer. *The Iliad,* tr. by Robert Fitzgerald. New York: Anchor Press/Doubleday, 1975.

———. *The Odyssey,* tr. by Robert Fitzgerald. New York: Anchor Press/Doubleday, 1963.

Honour, Hugh. *The European Vision of America.* Kent, Ohio: The Kent State University Press, 1975.

"Hooping It Up Big in the Cornbelt." *Time* 109 (March 28, 1977):85.

Hopkins, Charles Howard. *History of the Y.M.C.A. in North America.* New York: Association Press, 1951.

Hughes, S.F. *Letters and Recollections of John Murray Forbes.* Boston: Houghton Mifflin, 1899.

Huizanga, Johan. *Homo Ludens: A Study of the Play Element in Culture.* Boston: Beacon Press, 1955.

Isaacs, Neil D. *All the Moves: A History of College Basketball.* Philadelphia: J.B. Lippincott Company, 1975.

Jable, Thomas. "The English Puritans: Suppressors of Sport and Amusement?" *Canadian Journal of History of Sport and Physical Education* 7, no. 1 (May, 1976):33-40.

———. "Pennsylvania's Early Blue Laws: A Quaker Experiment in the Suppression of Sport and Amusements, 1682-1740." *Journal of Sport History* 1, no. 2 (November, 1974):107-121.

Jacobs, Edwin E. *A Study of the Physical Vigor of American Women.* Boston: Marshall Jones Company, 1920.

Jensen, Oliver. *The Revolt of American Women.* New York: Harcourt, Brace and Co., 1952.

Johnson, Elmer L. "A History of Physical Education in the YMCA." *69th Proceedings,* National College Physical Education Association for Men (December 28-31, 1966):20-21.

Johnson, Harold. *Who's Who in Major League Base Ball.* Chicago: Buxton Publishing Co., 1933.

Josephy, Alvin M., Jr., ed. *The American Heritage Book of Indians.* New York: McGraw-Hill Book Company, 1961.

Journals of the Continental Congress, Vol. I, 1774. Washington, D.C.: Government Printing Office, 1904.

Kamper, Erich. *Encyclopedia of the Olympic Games.* New York: McGraw-Hill Book Company, 1972.

Kaye, Ivan N. *Good Clean Violence: A History of College Football.* Philadelphia: J.B. Lippincott and Company, 1973.

Kelley, Robert F. *American Rowing: Its Background and Traditions.* New York: G.P. Putnam's Sons, 1932.

Kellor, Frances A. "Ethical Value of Sports for Women." *American Physical Education Review* 11 (September, 1906):160-171.

Kennard, June A. "Maryland Colonials at Play: Their Sports and Games." *Research Quarterly* 41 (1970):389-395.

Kenyon, Gerald, and Loy, John. "Toward a Sociology of Sport." *Journal of Health, Physical Education and Recreation* 36 (May, 1965):24-25, 68-69.

Kerman, Joseph. *The Beethoven Quartets.* New York: Alfred A. Knopf, 1967.

Killanin, Michael Morris, and Rodda, John, eds. *The Olympic Games.* New York: Macmillan, 1976.

Kirkpatrick, Curry. "There She Is: Ms. America." *Sports Illustrated* 39 (October 1, 1973):30-32, 37.

Kirstein, Lincoln. *The Book of the Dance.* New York: Garden City Publishing Company, 1942.

Knight, Madam. *The Journal of Madam Knight.* Edition of 1825. New York: Peter Smith, 1835.

Korsgaard, Robert. "The Formative Years of Sports Control and the Founding of the Amateur Athletic Union of the United States." *67th Proceedings,* National College Physical Education Association for Men (January 8-11, 1964):65-70.

———. "A History of the Amateur Athletic Union of the United States." Ph.D. dissertation, Columbia University, 1952.

Kozar, Andrew J. *R. Tait McKenzie*. Knoxville: The University of Tennessee Press, 1975.

Kozman, Hilda Clute. "Building the General Curriculum in Physical Education for College Women." Report of the Second Workshop for College Women Teachers, sponsored by the National Association for Physical Education of College Women, Estes Park, Colorado, June 18-27, 1947.

Kraus, Richard. *History of the Dance in Art and Education*. Englewood Cliffs, N.J.: Prentice-Hall, Inc., 1969.

Kroll, Walter P., and Lewis, Guy M. "America's First Sport Psychologist." *Quest* 13 (January, 1970):1-4.

———. "The First Academic Degree in Physical Education." *Journal of Health, Physical Education and Recreation* 40 (June, 1969):73-74.

———. *Perspectives in Physical Education*. New York: Academic Press, 1971.

Krout, John A. *Annals of American Sport,* Vol. XV of *Pageant of America*. New Haven: Yale University Press, 1929.

Lattimore, Richmond, and Grene, David. *The Complete Greek Tragedies*. New York: Modern Library, 1960.

Lawler, Lillian. *The Dance in Ancient Greece*. Middletown, Conn.: Wesleyan University Press, 1964.

———. "Terpsichore: The Story of the Dance in Ancient Greece." *Dance Perspectives* 13 (Winter, 1962):1-56.

Leacock, Eleanor Burke, and Lurie, Nancy Oestreich, eds. *North American Indians in Historical Perspective*. New York: Random House, 1971.

Lee, Mabel. "The Case for and Against Intercollegiate Athletics for Women and the Situation Since 1923." *Research Quarterly* 2 (May, 1931):93-127.

———. "Of Historical Interest." *Journal of Health, Physical Education, and Recreation* 39 (January, 1968):29-31.

———. *Memories of a Bloomer Girl*. Washington, D.C.: American Alliance for Health, Physical Education and Recreation, 1977.

Leigh, Mary. "The Evolution of Women's Participation in the Summer Olympic Games, 1900-1948." Ph.D. dissertation, The Ohio State University, 1974.

———. "Pierre de Coubertin: A Man of His Time." *Quest* 22 (Spring, 1974):19-24.

Leiper, Jean M. "The International Olympic Committee: The Pursuit of Olympism 1894-1970." Ph.D. dissertation, The University of Alberta, 1976.

Leonard, Fred E., and Affleck, George B. *A Guide to the History of Physical Education*. Philadelphia: Lea & Febiger, 1947.

Lewis, Dio. *The New Gymnastics for Men, Women and Children*. 8th ed. Boston: Ticknor and Fields, 1864.

Lewis, Guy M. "Adoption of the Sports Program, 1906-39: The Role of Accommodation in the Transformation of Physical Education." *Quest* 12 (May, 1969):34-46.

―――. "America's First Intercollegiate Sport: The Regattas from 1852 to 1875." *Research Quarterly* 38 (December, 1967):637-647.

―――. "1879: The Beginning of an Era in American Sport." *72nd Proceedings,* National College Physical Education Association for Men (January 8-11, 1969):136-145.

―――. "The Muscular Christianity Movement." *Journal of Health, Physical Education and Recreation* 37 (May, 1966):27-28.

―――. "Sport and the Making of American Higher Education: The Early Years, 1783-1875." *73rd Proceedings,* National College Physical Education Association for Men (December 27-30, 1970):208-213.

Lincoln, C. Eric. *The Negro Pilgrimage in America*. New York: Bantam Pathfinder, 1967.

Livermore, Mary A. *The Story of My Life*. Hartford, Conn.: A.D. Worthington, 1899.

Lockhart, Aileene S., and Spears, Betty. *Chronicle of American Physical Education, 1855-1930*. Dubuque, Iowa: Wm. C. Brown Company Publishers, 1972.

Lohse, Lola L. "One Hundred Years of Teaching Physical Education Instructors." *Journal of Health, Physical Education and Recreation* 37 (November-December, 1966):26-28.

Loy, John W., Jr. "The Nature of Sport: A Definitional Effort." *Quest* 10 (May, 1968):1-15.

Lucas, John A. "A Prelude to the Rise of Sport: Ante-bellum America, 1850-1860." *Quest* 11 (December, 1968):50-57.

Magriel, Paul, ed. *Chronicles of the American Dance*. New York: Henry Holt and Company, 1948.

Main, Jackson Turner. *The Social Structure of Revolutionary America*. Princeton, N.J.: Princeton University Press, 1965.

Manchester, Gertrude B. "Physical Education in the High School." *Bulletin* (1924-25). Mary Hemenway Alumnae Association, Graduate Department of Hygiene and Physical Education. Wellesley College, Wellesley, Mass.

Manchester, Herbert. *Four Centuries of Sport in America, 1490-1890*. New York: The Derrydale Press, 1931.

Mandell, Richard D. *The Nazi Olympics.* New York: The Macmillan Company, 1971.

Marks, Joseph E. *America Learns to Dance.* New York: Exposition Press, 1957.

Maynard, Olga. *The American Ballet.* Philadelphia: Macrae Smith Company, 1959.

McCracken, Harold. *George Catlin and the Old Frontier.* New York: Bonanza Books, 1959.

McGeehan, W.O. "Our Changing Sports Page." *Scribner's Magazine* 84, no. 1 (July, 1928):56-59.

McKelvey, Blake. *American Urbanization: A Comparative History.* Glenview, Ill.: Scott, Foresman and Company, 1973.

Menke, Frank G. *The Encyclopedia of Sports.* 5th ed. New York: A.S. Barnes and Company, 1975.

Metheny, Eleanor. *Movement and Meaning.* New York: McGraw-Hill Book Company, 1968.

Metzner, Henry. *History of the American Turners.* Rochester, N.Y.: National Council of the American Turners, 1974.

Michener, James A. *Sports in America.* New York: Random House, 1976.

Miller, Kenneth D. "Stearns, Hitchcock, and Amherst College." *Journal of Health, Physical Education and Recreation* 28 (May-June, 1957):29-30.

Mills, Paul R. "William Andrus Alcott, M.D. Pioneer Reformer in Physical Education, 1789-1859." *76th Proceedings,* National College Physical Education Association for Men (January 6-9, 1973):29-34.

Milnor, W. *Historical Memoir of the Schuylkill Fishing Company.* Philadelphia: Judah Dobson, 1830.

Mook, H. Telfer. "Training Day in New England." *New England Quarterly,* December, 1938, pp. 675-697.

Moolenjizer, Nicolaas J. "Our Legacy from the Middle Ages." *Quest* 11 (December, 1968):32-43.

Morison, Samuel Eliot. *The Oxford History of the American People.* New York: Oxford University Press, 1965.

Naismith, James. *Basketball, Its Origin and Development.* New York: Association Press, 1941.

National Section on Women's Athletics. "Desirable Practices in Athletics." Washington, D.C.: American Association for Health, Physical Education, and Recreation, 1949.

Nevins, Allan. *The Emergence of Modern America 1865-1878.* New York: The Macmillan Company, 1927.

Nevins, Allan, and Commager, Henry Steele. *A Pocket History of the United States.* New York: Washington Square Press, 1966.

Newcomer, Mabel. *A Century of Higher Education for American Women.* New York: Harper & Brothers, 1959.

"1976 Sports Participation Survey." Elgin, Ill.: National Federation of State High School Associations. Nov. 13, 1974.

Nye, R.B., and Morpurgo, J.E. *The Growth of the U.S.A.* Baltimore: Penguin Books, 1955.

Offenberg, R.S. "American College Football: Its Growth and Significance, 1869-1914." Paper presented at the North American Society for Sport History, Boston, Mass., April 16-19, 1975.

Olaudah, Equiano. *The Interesting Narrative of Olaudah Equiano, or Gustavus Vasa, the African* (2 vols., London, 1789), in *Africa Remembered,* ed. P. Curtin. Madison: The University of Wisconsin, 1967.

———. *The Life of Olaudah Equiano or Gustavus Vassa, the African,* Boston, 1837, in *The Negro in American History,* ed. M.J. Adler. Encyclopedia Britannica Educational Corporation, 1969.

Olsen, Jack. *The Black Athlete: A Shameful Story.* New York: Time-Life Books, 1968.

The Olympic Games. New York: United States Olympic Committee, 1970.

"One Hundred Years of Baseball." *Amherst Alumni News,* October, 1958, p. 4.

O'Neill, William L. *Everyone Was Brave.* Chicago: Quadrangle Books, 1971.

Orlick, Terry, and Botterill, Cal. *Every Kid Can Win.* Chicago: Nelson-Hall, 1975.

Owen, Janet. *Sports in Women's Colleges.* New York: New York *Herald-Tribune,* 1932.

Painter, Ruth E. "Tavern Amusements in Eighteenth Century America," in *The Leisure Class in America,* ed. Leon Stein. New York: Arno Press, 1975.

Painter, Sidney. *Mediaeval Society.* Ithaca, N.Y.: Cornell University Press, 1951.

Park, Roberta J. "History and Structure of the Department of Physical Education at the University of California with Special Reference to Women's Sports." Unpublished paper, University of California at Berkeley, 1976.

Parker, Garland G. *The Enrollment Explosion.* New York: School & Society Books, 1971.

Paxson, Frederic L. "The Rise of Sport." *Mississippi Valley Historical Review* 4 (1917):143-168.

Perham, Margery, and Simmons, J. *African Discovery.* London: Faber and Faber, 1957.

Peterson, Harold. *The Man Who Invented Baseball.* New York: Charles Scribner's Sons, 1973.

Peterson, James A., ed. *Intramural Administration: Theory and Practice.* Englewood Cliffs, N.J.: Prentice-Hall, Inc., 1976.

Peterson, Robert. *Only the Ball Was White.* Englewood Cliffs, N.J.: Prentice-Hall, Inc., 1970.

Phillips, Thomas. "A Journal of a Voyage to Africa and Barbadoes," in *A Collection of Voyages and Travels,* Vol. VI, ed. Churchill. London: 1732.

Pierce, Bessie Louise. *A History of Chicago,* Vol. I. New York: Alfred A. Knopf, 1937.

Pindar. *The Odes of Pindar,* tr. by Richmond Lattimore. Chicago: University of Chicago Press, 1947.

Potter, Robert E. *The Stream of American Education.* New York: American Book Company, 1967.

Professional Sports and the Law. Washington, D.C.: United States Government Printing Office, 1976.

Prospectus of the Vassar Female College. New York: Alford, 1865.

Rainwater, Clarence E. *The Play Movement in the United States.* Chicago: University of Chicago Press, 1922.

Records of the Court of Assistants of the Colony of Massachusetts Bay, 1630-1644, Vol. II. Boston: County of Suffolk, 1904.

Redmond, Gerald. *The Caledonian Games in Nineteenth-Century America.* Rutherford, N.J.: Fairleigh Dickinson University Press, 1971.

Richardson, Rufus B. "The New Olympian Games." *Scribner's Magazine* 20, no. 3 (September, 1896):267-286.

Richter, Frank C. *Richter's History and Records of Base Ball.* Philadelphia: Francis C. Richter, 1914.

Riess, Steven A. "The Baseball Magnate and Urban Politics in the Progressive Era: 1895-1920." *Journal of Sport History* 1, no. 1 (May, 1974):41-62.

Robinson, Rachel S. *Sources for the History of Greek Athletics.* Cincinnati: published by the author, 1955.

Rooney, John F., Jr. *A Geography of American Sport.* Reading, Mass.: Addison-Wesley Publishing Company, 1974.

Rosenberger, F.C., ed. *Virginia Reader.* New York: E.P. Dutton & Company, 1948.

Rowse, A.L. *The Use of History*. New York: Collier Books, 1963.

Sachs, Curt. *World History of the Dance*. New York: W.W. Norton and Company, Inc., 1937.

Sargent, Dudley Allen. "Athletics in Secondary Schools." *American Physical Education Review* 8 (June, 1903):57-69.

———. *An Autobiography,* ed. Ledyard W. Sargent. Philadelphia: Lea & Febiger, 1927.

———. "Interest in Sport and Physical Education as a Phase of Woman's Development." *Mind and Body* 22 (November, 1915):830-833.

———. "The Physical Development of Women." *Scribner's Magazine* 5, no. 2 (1889):172-185.

———. *Physical Education*. Boston: Ginn & Company, 1906.

Savage, Howard J. *American College Athletics*. New York: The Carnegie Foundation for the Advancement of Teaching, 1929.

Schlesinger, Arthur M. *The Rise of the City, 1878-1898*. New York: The Macmillan Company, 1933.

Schneider, Gretchen Adel. "Pigeon Wings and Polkas: The Dance of the California Miners." *Dance Perspectives* 39 (Winter, 1969):1-57.

Schollander, Don, and Savage, Duke. *Deep Water*. New York: Crown Publishers, Inc., 1971.

Schwarz, Marguerite. "The Athletic Federation of College Women." *Journal of Health and Physical Education* 7 (May, 1936):297, 345-346.

Scott, Gladys. "Competition for Women in American Colleges and Universities." *Research Quarterly* 16 (March, 1945):49-71.

Scott, Jack. "Sport and the Radical Ethic." *Quest* 19 (January, 1973):71-77.

Scott, Phebe, and Ulrich, Celeste. "Commission on Intercollegiate Sports for Women." *Journal of Health, Physical Education and Recreation* 37 (October, 1966):10, 76.

Sefton, Alice A. *The Women's Division, National Amateur Athletic Federation*. Stanford: Stanford University Press, 1941.

Seymour, Harold. *Baseball: The Early Years*. New York: Oxford University Press, 1959.

———. *Baseball: The Golden Years*. New York: Oxford University Press, 1971.

Shults, Frederick D. "Oberlin College: Molder of Four Great Men." *Quest* 11 (December, 1968):71-75.

Silvia, C.E. *Lifesaving and Water Safety Instruction.* New York: Association Press, 1960.

Singleton, Esther. *Social New York under the Georges, 1714-1776.* New York: D. Appleton, 1902.

Sklar, Kathryn Kish. *Catharine Beecher.* New Haven: Yale University Press, 1973.

Smelser, Marshall M. "The Babe on Balance." *The American Scholar* 44 (Spring, 1975):299-307.

Smith, Michael D. "Origins of Faculty Attitudes toward Intercollegiate Athletics." *Canadian Journal of History of Sport and Physical Education* 2, no. 2 (December, 1971):61-72.

Smith, Page. *Daughters of the Promised Land.* Boston: Little, Brown and Company, 1970.

Smith, Robert A. *A Social History of the Bicycle.* New York: American Heritage Press, 1972.

Snodgrass, Jeanne. "The Development of the American National Red Cross Aquatic Schools with Special Reference to Camp Kiwanis." M.S. thesis, Smith College, 1953.

Somers, Dale A. *The Rise of Sports in New Orleans, 1850-1900.* Baton Rouge: Louisiana State University Press, 1972.

Spalding, Albert G. *Base Ball, America's National Game.* New York: American Sports Publishing Company, 1911.

Spear, Ruth E. "A Study of the Needs and Provisions in Physical Education of Women Students in Selected Negro Colleges." M.S. thesis, Smith College, 1950.

Spears, Betty. "The Emergence of Women in Sport," in *Women's Athletics: Coping with Controversy,* ed. Barbara J. Hoepner. Washington, D.C.: American Association for Health, Physical Education and Recreation, 1974.

———. "Influences on Early Professional Physical Education Curriculums in the United States." *Proceedings,* The Second Canadian Symposium on the History of Sport and Physical Education, Windsor, Ontario (May 1-3, 1972):86-103.

Spicer, Edward H. *A Short History of the Indians of the United States.* New York: Van Nostrand Reinhold Co., 1969.

Staley, Seward C. "The Four Year Curriculum in Physical (Sports) Education." *Research Quarterly* 2 (March, 1931):76-90.

Starnes, Richard. "An Unprecedented Economic and Ethical Crisis Grips Big-Time Intercollegiate Sports." *The Chronicle of Higher Education* 24 September 1973, pp. 1, 6.

State of Michigan. Joint Legislative Study on Youth Sports Programs: *Agency Sponsored Sports, Phase I.* November, 1976.

Statistical Abstract of the United States, 1976. United States Department of Commerce, Bureau of the Census.

Stillman, Agnes C. "Senda Berenson Abbot: Her Life and Contributions to Smith College and to the Physical Education Profession." M.S. thesis, Smith College, 1971.

Stow, John. *A Survey of London.* Reprinted from 1603. Oxford: Clarendon Press, 1908.

Struna, Nancy, and Remley, Mary L. "Physical Education for Women at the University of Wisconsin, 1863-1913: A Half Century of Progress." *Canadian Journal of History of Sport and Physical Education* 4, no. 1 (1973):8-26.

———. "Sport and the Evolution of Massachusetts Bay Puritan Society, 1630-1730." M.A. thesis, University of Maryland, 1975.

Strutt, Joseph. *The Sports and Pastimes of the People of England.* London: William Tegg, 1867.

Swanson, Richard A. "The Acceptance and Influence of Play in American Protestantism." *Quest* 11 (December, 1968):58-70.

———. "American Protestantism and Play: 1865-1915." Ph.D. dissertation, The Ohio State University, 1967.

Swett, John. *Public Education in California.* New York: American Book Company, 1911.

Tappan, Lilian. Report to the President, 1877. Vassar College Archives, Poughkeepsie, New York.

Terry, Walter. "The Legacy of Isadora Duncan and Ruth St. Denis." *Dance Perspectives* 5 (Winter, 1960):1-60.

Theberge, Nancy. "Analysis of Women's Professional Golf." Ph.D. dissertation, University of Massachusetts, 1977.

Thompson, James G. "Ancient Greek Attitudes on Athletics." *Canadian Journal of History of Sport and Physical Education* 5, no. 2 (December, 1974):56-62.

Tilghman, T.F. "An Early Victorian College St. John's, 1830-1860." *Maryland Historical Society* 14, no. 4 (December, 1949):251-268.

Tunis, John R. "Changing Trends in Sport." *Harper's Monthly Magazine* 170 (December, 1934):75-86.

Twombly, Wells. *200 Years of Sport in America: A Pageant of a Nation at Play.* New York: McGraw-Hill Book Company, 1976.

U.S.A. 1776-1976, NCAA 1906-1976. Shawnee Mission, Kansas: National Collegiate Athletic Association, 1976.

United States Department of Health, Education, and Welfare. *HEW Fact Sheet.* June, 1975.

United States Office of Education. *Annual Report of the Federal Security Agency,* 1947.

United States Office of Education. *Biennial Survey of Education in the United States,* 1944-46.

Van Cleef, Joy. "Rural Felicity: Social Dance in 18th Century Connecticut." *Dance Perspectives* 65 (Spring, 1976):1-45.

Van Dalen, Deobold B., and Bennett, Bruce L. *A World History of Physical Education.* 2nd ed. Englewood Cliffs, N.J.: Prentice-Hall Inc., 1971.

Van Dyne, Larry. "College Sports Enforcement Squad." *The Chronicle of Higher Education* 7 March 1977, pp. 1, 14.

———. "The South's Black Colleges Lose a Football Monopoly." *The Chronicle of Higher Education* 15 November 1976, pp. 1, 8.

Vassar, Matthew. "Communications." June 25, 1867. Vassar College Archives, Poughkeepsie, New York.

Vaughan, Linda. "A Century of Rowing at Wellesley, 1875-1975." Paper presented at the North American Society for Sport History, Boston, Mass., April 16-19, 1975.

Vendien, Lynn C. "FISU (Federation Internationale du Sports Universitaire) and the World University Games." *Quest* 22 (Spring, 1974):74-81.

Voight, David Q. *American Baseball,* Vol. I. Norman: University of Oklahoma Press, 1966.

———. *American Baseball,* Vol. II. Norman: University of Oklahoma Press, 1970.

———. "Reflections on Diamonds: American Baseball and American Culture." *Journal of Sport History* 1, no. 1 (May, 1974):3-25.

Wagner, Peter. "Puritan Attitudes Towards Physical Recreation in 17th Century New England." *Journal of Sport History* 3, no. 2 (Summer, 1976):139-151.

Waldstein, Charles. "The Olympian Games at Athens." *Harper's Weekly* 40, no. 3 (September, 1896):490.

Wallace, William N. *The Macmillan Book of Boating.* New York: Crown Publishers, Inc., 1973.

Walters, M.L. "The Physical Education Society of the Y.M.C.A.'s of North America." *Journal of Health and Physical Education* 17 (May, 1947):311-312, 357-358.

Walton, Izaak. *The Compleat Angler.* New York: The Heritage Press, 1938.

Wayman, Agnes R. *Education Through Physical Education.* Philadelphia: Lea & Febiger, 1934.

―――. "Women's Athletics—All Uses—No Abuses." *American Physical Education Review* 29 (November, 1924):517.

Weaver, Robert B. *Amusements and Sports in American Life.* Chicago: University of Chicago Press, 1939.

Webb, Bernice Larson. *The Basketball Man: James Naismith.* Lawrence: The University Press of Kansas, 1973.

Webb, Walter Prescott. *The Great Frontier.* Austin: University of Texas Press, 1964.

Webster, F.A.M. *Athletics of Today for Women.* New York: Frederick Warne and Co., Ltd., 1930.

Wecter, Dixon. *The Saga of American Society: A Record of Social Aspiration, 1607-1937.* New York: Charles Scribner's Sons, 1937.

Wedgwood, C.V. *The Sense of the Past.* New York: Collier Books, 1960.

Welch. J. Edmund. "George J. Fisher: Leader of Youth." *Journal of Health, Physical Education, and Recreation* 39 (May, 1968):37.

―――. "The Origin, Development, and Effect of YMCA Junior Leaders Schools on Physical Education in the United States and Canada." *71st Proceedings,* National College Physical Education Association for Men (January 10-13, 1968):172-179.

Westermeier, Clifford P. "Seventy-five Years of Rodeo in Colorado." *Colorado Magazine* 28 (January, 1951):13-27; (April, 1951):127-145; (July, 1951):219-231.

Weston, Arthur. *The Making of American Physical Education.* New York: Appleton-Century-Crofts, 1962.

Whited, Clark V. "Sport Science, The Modern Disciplinary Concept of Physical Education." *73rd Proceedings,* National College Physical Education Association for Men (December 27-30, 1970):223-230.

Williams, John. "William Ellery Channing's Philosophy of Physical Education and Recreation." *Quest* 4 (April, 1965):49-52.

Willis, Joseph D., and Wettan, Richard G. "Social Stratification in New York City Athletic Clubs, 1865-1915." *Journal of Sport History* 3, no. 1 (Spring, 1976):45-63.

Wilson, Elizabeth. *Fifty Years of Association Work Among Young Women, 1866-1916.* New York: National Board of the Young Women's Christian Associations, 1916.

Wilson, Kenneth L., and Brondfield, Jerry. *The Big Ten.* Englewood Cliffs, N.J.: Prentice-Hall, Inc., 1967.

Wilson, S.S. "Bicycle Technology." *Scientific American* 228 (March, 1973):81-91.

Wilson, Wayne. "Social Discontent and the Growth of Wilderness Sport in America: 1965-1974." *Quest* 27 (Winter, 1977):54-60.

Wind, Herbert Warren, ed. *The Realm of Sport.* New York: Simon and Schuster, 1966.

Winks, Robin W. *The Historian as Detective.* New York: Harper & Row, 1968.

Winship, George B. "Physical Culture." *Massachusetts Teacher* 13 (April, 1860):132.

Wood, Thomas Denison. *Ninth Yearbook of the National Society for the Study of Education.* Chicago: University of Chicago Press, 1910.

Woodmason, Charles. *The Carolina Backcountry on the Eve of the Revolution,* ed. R.J. Hooker. Chapel Hill: University of North Carolina Press, 1953.

Woods, John. "Two Years' Residence in the Settlement on the English Prairie, in the Illinois Country, United States," in *Early Western Travels,* 1748-1846, Vol. X, ed. R.G. Thwaites. Cleveland: The Arthur H. Clark Company, 1904.

Woody, Thomas. *Life and Education in Early Societies.* New York: Macmillan, 1949.

Wright, Louis B. *The Cultural Life of the American Colonies.* New York: Harper & Row, 1957.

Wynne, Shirley. "From Ballet to Ballroom: Dance in the Revolutionary Era." *Dance Scope* 10, no. 1 (Fall/Winter, 1975/1976):65-73.

Yee, Min S. *The Sports Book.* New York: Bantam Books, 1976.

YMCA Training School Catalogue, 1890-91. Springfield, Mass.

Yoder, Paton. *Taverns and Travelers.* Bloomington: Indiana University Press, 1969.

Young, Alexander J., Jr. "The Rejuvenation of Major League Baseball in the Twenties." *Canadian Journal of History of Sport and Physical Education* 3, no. 2 (May, 1972):8-25.

———. "Sam Langford, 'The Boston Tarbaby.' " *Proceedings,* The Second Canadian Symposium on the History of Sport and Physical Education, Windsor, Ontario (May 1-3, 1972):45-67.

Zaharias, Babe Didrikson. *This Life I've Led.* New York: A.S. Barnes & Co., 1955.

Zeigler, Earle F., ed. *A History of Physical Education and Sport in the United States and Canada.* Champaign, Ill.: Stipes Publishing Company, 1975.

Zuckerman, Jerome; Stull, G. Allan; and Eyler, Marvin H. "The Black Athlete in Post-Bellum 19th Century." *The Physical Educator* 29 (October, 1972):142-146.

Index